Gender and Foreign Policy in the Clinton Administration

Gender and Foreign Policy in the Clinton Administration

Karen Garner

FIRSTFORUMPRESS

A DIVISION OF LYNNE RIENNER PUBLISHERS, INC. • BOULDER & LONDON

Published in the United States of America in 2013 by
FirstForumPress
A division of Lynne Rienner Publishers, Inc.
1800 30th Street, Boulder, Colorado 80301
www.firstforumpress.com
www.rienner.com

and in the United Kingdom by
FirstForumPress
A division of Lynne Rienner Publishers, Inc.
3 Henrietta Street, Covent Garden, London WC2E 8LU

Library of Congress Cataloging-in-Publication Data
A Cataloging-in-Publication record for this book
is available from the Library of Congress.
ISBN: 978-1-935049-60-9

British Cataloguing in Publication Data
A Cataloguing in Publication record for this book
is available from the British Library.

This book was produced from digital files prepared by the author
using the FirstForumComposer.

Printed and bound in the United States of America

The paper used in this publication meets the requirements
of the American National Standard for Permanence of
Paper for Printed Library Materials Z39.48-1992.

5 4 3 2 1

For Emily and Megan, who cheer me on and make me proud,
and for Charles A., my sweetheart

Contents

Acknowledgments

First and foremost, I want to thank the women who gave their time for interviews conducted between 2006 and 2010. These women shared their memories and experiences of working for feminist transformational change—from positions both inside and outside the Clinton Administration—with regard to the U.S. foreign policies that affected global women. My sincere thanks go to Anita Botti, Charlotte Bunch, Mayra Buvinic, Ellen Chesler, Arvonne Fraser, Sarah Gauger, Kathleen Hendrix, Gracia Hillman, Susan Crais Hovanec, Suzanne Kindervatter, Sarah Kovner, Tamara Kreinin, Laura Liswood, Theresa Loar, Ruth Mandel, Ellen Marshall, Alice Miller, Karen Mulhauser, Alyse Nelson, Regan Ralph, Donna Shalala, Wendy Sherman, Linda Tarr-Whelan, Marie Wilson, and Melanne Verveer.

I also owe many intellectual debts. To Leila Rupp, whose book *Worlds of Women: The Making of an International Women's Movement* provided a model and inspiration for writing the history of international women's organizations. To Mary Meyer and Elisabeth Prügl and the scholars whose work is included in their edited study *Gender Politics in Global Governance,* who introduced me to the many ways that ideas about gender infuse the operations of global forums. To Mrinhalini Sinha, Donna Guy, Angela Woollacott, and the scholars whose work is included in their collection *Feminisms and Internationalism,* who presented a variety of global feminist perspectives regarding the changes necessary to raise the status and serve the needs of different populations of global women. To Cynthia Enloe, whose many pathbreaking works of scholarship and whose engaging self-reflections included in *The Curious Feminist* opened my eyes to the influence of gender discourse on the theory and practice of U.S. foreign relations. To Georgia Duerst-Lahti and Lee Ann Banaszak, whose scholarly works revealed important contributions made by women who have worked in U.S. federal government offices and who interjected feminist values into a wide range of government policies and programs. These scholars' intellectual powers inspire me every time I read their words; of course, any misunderstandings of their ideas and feminist analyses are my own.

I owe a debt of gratitude to readers of earlier drafts of this manuscript. Many thanks go out to my daughter Emily Garner, my mentor

Stephen G. Rabe, scholars at various academic conferences where I presented my work over the past few years, and anonymous readers at the *Journal of Women's History* and at Lynne Rienner Publishers's FirstForumPress. These readers' comments and critiques helped me define my ideas and arguments and deepened my analysis of the sources considered here.

I owe particular thanks to Jessica Gribble, editor at Lynne Rienner Publishers, for her enthusiastic interest in this manuscript throughout the review and revision process.

I also want to express sincere thanks for the multiple letters of recommendation for funding and time that my dean, Dr. Gerald Lorentz, has written for me. I truly appreciate his moral support.

In addition, the Office of Academic Affairs at SUNY Empire State College provided much-appreciated financial support for research trips and sabbatical leave. The Schlesinger Library at the Radcliffe Institute for Advanced Study at Harvard University, the Sallie Bingham Center for Women's History and Culture at Duke University, and the United University Professionals Union at the State University of New York also provided additional research grants for travel to archival collections. I am very grateful for this institutional support, which enabled my development as a scholar and teacher.

1

Feminist Foreign Policy in the Clinton Administration

> America's credo should ring clearly: A democracy without the full participation of women is a contradiction in terms. To reach its full potential, it must include all of its citizens. Clearly, whether we succeed in strengthening democratic values around the world is of special consequence to women, who in our country and elsewhere are still striving to attain, and even define their rightful place in government, the economy, and civil society, and to claim their rightful share of personal, political, economic and civic power.
>
> ~Hillary Rodham Clinton, March 12, 1997[1]

The William Jefferson Clinton Administration (1993 to 2001) broke many barriers to challenge global women's unequal status vis-à-vis men and to incorporate women's gendered needs into United States' foreign policy making and foreign aid programs. More so than in previous U.S. presidential administrations that had been in power since the 1970s when a second wave of American feminist activism moved women's rights and women's empowerment onto national social and political agendas, the Clinton Administration interjected feminist aims "into the mainstream of American foreign policy." As President Clinton asserted, "We cannot advance our ideals and interests unless we focus more attention on the fundamental human rights and basic needs of women and girls."[2]

President Clinton's words provide just one example of how officials at the highest levels of leadership in the White House, cabinet agencies, State Department, and U.S. Agency for International Development (USAID) raised the level of feminist rhetoric to unprecedented prominence in their foreign policy addresses. More importantly, the administration enacted institutional changes at the State Department and

USAID that empowered global women. That is, these institutional changes enabled women's more equitable access to social, political and legal power and to economic resources that allowed them to make independent decisions about their own lives.[3]

During the Clinton Administration's tenure the State Department and USAID increased the descriptive, or numerical, representation of women in foreign policy making roles. Madeleine K. Albright was the most visible woman within the administration's foreign policy ranks; she served as ambassador to the United Nations from 1993 to 1997 and as the nation's first female secretary of state from 1997 to 2001. Additionally, President Clinton appointed Alexis Herman, Hazel O'Leary, Janet Reno and Donna Shalala to lead cabinet agencies and increased the number and influence of women who occupied high-level positions and made day-to-day governing decisions that had both national and international scope and impact during his two terms in office.[4]

Feminists internationally have long argued that a true democracy does not exist if the female half of its adult population does not participate equally in the public realm.[5] If that premise is accepted, then, with more women holding key leadership positions within the Clinton Administration, the federal government became more democratic and more representative of the entire U.S. population during the Clinton presidency. While the presence of even a critical mass of women holding policy making positions does not guarantee that the nature of government will change to represent the substantive interests of women as women,[6] or that women occupying policy making positions in government can be singled out as the direct cause of any specific policy change,[7] this study also asserts that the substantive representation of women's interests in U.S. foreign policy making also expanded during Clinton's presidency.

The liberal feminist women that President Clinton appointed increased federal government attention to gender equity in policy and programs generally. They worked from within the state and sought to break down the U.S. government's patriarchal institutional structures in order to meet women's needs and to address women's interests. The women who served in foreign policy making posts consulted with U.S. feminist movement activists and organizations. They sought to incorporate feminist aims to expand women's legal, political, social and economic rights and to ameliorate women's unequal status through the nation's foreign policies and foreign aid allocations, especially as those policies and aid affected populations of global women. This study adopts "global women," an imperfect term, to refer to women living in countries that U.S. foreign policy initiatives targeted, that is, countries that were engaged in international wars or civil wars or that were developing countries that received foreign aid.

To be sure, the meaning of feminism and what constitutes feminist policy are contested concepts. Indeed, by the 1980s many scholars and activists began referring to "feminisms" in the plural. This strategic term acknowledged fundamental theoretical disagreements regarding the sources and remedies for various women's oppression.[8] It also facilitated political collaborations among those who could agree, in the most basic sense, "that 'feminist' indicates a challenge to patriarchy and 'contests political, social and other power arrangements of domination and subordination on the basis of gender.'"[9] The feminists who worked inside the Clinton Administration represented a "liberal feminist" orientation. They employed mainstreaming strategies to integrate "new [feminist] frameworks, agendas, findings and strategies into mainstream policies, programs and projects."[10] Although in some instances these feminist insiders may have been advocating for radical changes to the status quo, they did not represent a "radical feminist" perspective. This study employs the terms liberal feminist and radical feminist as historian Julie Ajinkya defined them in the context of the U.S. women's movement. According to these definitions radical feminists rejected any collaboration with the U.S. government or other state systems that they believed perpetuated patriarchy, racism, classism, nativism and heterosexism.[11]

Although this study focuses on liberal feminists who worked from positions inside the state, and their feminist collaborators who occupied positions in movements and organizations outside the state, radical feminist and other critiques of the Clinton-era foreign policies that affected global women are not minimized or neglected here. While U.S. government actions that occurred during the 1990s are very recent history, and historic consequences are certainly still unfolding, this study attempts to evaluate whether the Clinton Administration's foreign policies had a feminist or progressive outcome as the liberal feminist foreign policy makers intended, whether the rights of various populations of global women were expanded and whether their needs were met. This study pays attention to who defined feminist goals, which cohorts of women were advantaged and which were disadvantaged, which global gender issues were recognized as problems that warranted U.S. government attention and action and which issues were ignored.

Linking Foreign Policy to Feminist Goals during the Clinton Administration

This study focuses on the years of Bill Clinton's presidency, when a post-Cold War moment focused U.S. government foreign policy goals on promoting democratization and expanding market economies globally.[12] These changes were connected to global historical transformations as the world experienced the end of the Cold War era (1945 to 1989). As the Cold War ended, the ideological, political, military and economic conflicts between Western democracies led by the United States and Eastern socialist bloc states led by the Soviet Union no longer dominated all intergovernmental relations. Beginning in the 1980s, U.S. government leaders grappled with new international challenges that grew out of specific historical developments. The Soviet Union and the Warsaw Pact alliance in Eastern Europe both broke apart. It was unclear who controlled and managed the former Soviet Union's nuclear and conventional weapons arsenal. The North Atlantic Treaty Organization expanded its military alliance membership as other regional military alliances were reconfigured. Without a viable socialist economic model to provide competition, transnational corporations, financial institutions and Western governments supported the global expansion of a neoliberal capitalist economic system. Governments worldwide reduced national trade barriers and restrictions on private investment, weakened public sector protections for workers and cut social spending. At the same time, many newly independent nations, freed from a Cold War era East/West international relations system and "superpower" domination, established "democratic" and pluralistic political systems in which political rivals competed in ostensibly free elections. Some of these "free" elections put undemocratic and oppressive governments into power. Several unstable regions of the world erupted in ethnically-driven conflicts. Bitter internecine conflicts and genocidal warfare triggered humanitarian crises that threatened human security in the Caribbean, Southeastern Europe and East Africa.

A new international system defined by divisions between the global "haves" and "have nots," that is, the developed and wealthy nations of the global North and the underdeveloped and indebted nations of the global South, exposed the threats and benefits of all these transformations. In reaction to the new international order, the expansion of progressive global social movements that promoted human rights, environmental protections and women's rights to counterbalance various inequities that neoliberal economic policies caused also distinguished the end of the Cold War era, as did the rise of reactionary and politicized fundamentalist

Christian and Islamic movements that also opposed economic globalization and secular "modernization" models that emanated from the global North.[13]

As the Clinton Administration took office in 1993, it defined what it believed was necessary to achieve its foreign policy goals and to promote U.S. national security. Recognizing that the international arena had changed considerably since the bi-polar Cold War era, the administration focused its attention on global threats and challenges that jeopardized international security and by extension threatened U.S. national security. These threats and challenges included North/South competition for economic resources, international wars, civil conflicts, terrorism and other violent acts that displaced populations and abused human rights, preservation and protection of the environment and burgeoning global population growth. To deal with the new post-Cold War global conditions, the Clinton Administration State Department created a new bureau: the Office of Global Affairs led by Undersecretary of State Timothy Wirth.[14]

As attention to global issues redirected U.S. State Department activities, another historical development was underway simultaneously. A rising number of global organizations working outside formal government institutions—the nongovernmental organizations or NGOs who viewed themselves as representatives of "civil society"[15]—were engaged in global politics at the United Nations and in other global governance forums. During the 1990s, NGOs provided structure and defined leadership for a variety of global social movements across the political spectrum whose members shared a conscious group identity and a cause or a goal to challenge some aspect of the status quo "politics as usual." In general, NGOs enabled and mobilized the global social movements, collected funding and other resources and made demands on governments and intergovernmental institutions on behalf of movement members.[16] The NGOs that worked on behalf of the global human rights movement, global environmental movement and the global feminist movement also emphasized their linked and common goals.

In the 1990s, global feminist NGO activism that coalesced around a series of United Nations conferences that marked the end of the Cold War era is often cited as the driving force that elevated gender consciousness among governments worldwide and stimulated the creation of a variety of national women's policy offices to address social, political and economic inequalities between women and men, as well as an array of women's human rights issues.[17] In terms of global gender policy making, the most significant of the 1990s UN conferences were the 1992 Conference on Environment and Development (UNCED), the 1993

Human Rights Conference (HRC), the 1994 International Conference on Population and Development (ICPD), the 1995 World Summit on Social Development (WSSD), the 1995 Fourth World Conference on Women and the 2000 Special Session of the UN General Assembly called to address "Women 2000: Gender Equality, Development and Peace for the 21st Century," or, as it was better known, the "Beijing + 5" conference. Global feminist NGOs actively lobbied U.S. government delegations to these UN conferences to incorporate their perspectives and used these forums to influence U.S. foreign policies that had a specific gendered impact on global women throughout the decade. Global feminist NGOs often invoked "women" as an untapped human resource whose productive and reconstructive potential was far from realized. They also identified "women" as key players in addressing global problems because of women's supposed peace-loving and nurturing natures and their attention to building civil societies.[18] Over time, the Clinton Administration accepted the feminists' assertions and came to believe that achieving U.S. national and global security goals required enlisting "the full participation of women in the political and economic lives of their countries."[19]

The Center for Global Women's Leadership, Equality Now, Human Rights Watch Women's Rights Division, the International Women's Health Coalition, the International Women's Tribune Centre and the Women's Environment and Development Organization, to name a few influential NGOs whose activism is highlighted in this study, focused the Clinton Administration's attention on global gender policies to assert and defend women's economic, educational, environmental, human, political and reproductive rights. These organizations represented global constituencies and realized they could not look to individual national governments to achieve global reforms; nonetheless, they were based in the United States and American feminists figured prominently among their leadership.[20] Although these feminist organizations worked through global arenas such as UN conferences and forums, they also collaborated productively with liberal feminists positioned inside the Clinton Administration, most visibly with First Lady Hillary Rodham Clinton and Secretary of State Madeleine Albright but also with many others whose efforts are examined in the chapters ahead.

Together, liberal feminist insiders and NGO outsiders convinced President Clinton and sympathetic U.S. government officials that making progress toward achieving global feminist goals was possible and desirable. They made strategic linkages that persuaded the White House, State Department and USAID to incorporate women's human rights and gender equality goals into foreign policies and programs promoting U.S. national and global security interests. In order to redirect and utilize state power to incorporate global women's needs and interests, and to address the global problems of violence against women and women's universally unequal political and economic status, these "feminist issues" were connected to post-Cold War U.S. security goals: to promote the growth of democratic governments and civil societies and to develop the global capitalist economy as the Cold War ended. Consequently, because feminist insiders and outsiders made these strategic connections, U.S. government foreign policy and foreign aid officers began to address global women's rights and women's empowerment in their rhetoric, policies and programs to a much greater degree than they had in the past.

Clinton Administration Global Gender Policy: A Synopsis

In substantial ways, the Clinton Administration transformed its foreign policy and foreign aid rhetoric and programs based on feminist women's rights and women's empowerment prescriptions. Beginning in January 1993 when the administration took office, President Clinton reversed U.S. policy that the Ronald Reagan Administration established at the 1984 UN World Conference on Population. With an executive order, Clinton lifted restrictions that prohibited some family planning organizations from receiving U.S. government funding because of abortion-related activities.[21] At the UN Human Rights Conference held in June 1993, the United States delegation supported several policies promoted by U.S. and global feminist women's human rights advocates and signed the UN Declaration on the Elimination of Violence Against Women. In the aftermath of the HRC, Assistant Secretary of State for Human Rights and Humanitarian Affairs John Shattuck announced to Congress: "The Clinton Administration regards promoting the cause of women's rights as a key element of our overall human rights policy." [22] U.S. embassies abroad were instructed to include accounting of the state of women's human rights and to note any abuses of women's human rights that had occurred in their annual country reports.[23] Also following the HRC, feminist activists lobbied the U.S. Congress and the Clinton State Department to add appropriations for "women's human rights protection" to the Fiscal Year 1994 foreign aid bill.[24] The adoption of these provisions led to a significant institutional change at the State Department: the creation of the Office of International Women's Issues (OIWI) in 1994. These emphases on women's human rights, and on human rights generally, during the conflict-ridden decade of the 1990s also led to the Clinton Administration's support for punishing perpetrators of rape during genocidal wars that took place in the Balkans and in Africa and at International War Crimes Tribunals established in 1995 and 1996.

In November 1993, the administration announced that USAID would refocus its efforts on "enhancing 'sustainable development' and 'promoting peace' rather than supporting individual nations" as it had during the Cold War and would include nongovernmental organizations in USAID policy making and program planning processes.[25] The U.S. delegation to the 1994 UN International Conference on Population and Development exhibited strong leadership endorsing women's health and reproductive rights outlined in the conference document,[26] earning the praise of feminists who joined in the conference preparations and served on the U.S. delegation[27] as well as the U.S. Religious Right's and the Vatican's condemnation.[28] At the 1995 UN World Summit on Social Development, First Lady Hillary Rodham Clinton announced the U.S. government's support for microcredit initiatives that funded many small businesses started by poor women in developing nations[29] and new foreign aid resources dedicated to education programs for women and girls in developing nations.[30] Vice President Al Gore also announced the USAID's "New Partnerships Initiative," whereby 40 percent of the U.S. annual foreign aid allocation of $10 billion would be distributed through NGOs with the goals to empower NGOs and small business people and increase democracy in countries at the local levels, with special considerations for directing aid to women.[31]

Prompted and assisted by feminist activists and NGOs, the State Department and the U.S. delegation to the 1995 UN Fourth World Conference on Women also continued to express strong support for women's human rights and for reproductive rights that had been incorporated into the HRC and ICPD conference documents, but that were under attack from fundamentalist religious organizations and predominantly Catholic and Muslim nations. [32] Hillary Clinton delivered a famous address to world governments and NGO delegates at the Beijing conference in which she popularized the feminist slogan that "human rights are women's rights, and women's rights are human rights."[33] Her speech and repetition of this slogan by feminists working inside and outside government transformed government policy language, and women's human rights issues gained more prominence in the United States and throughout the UN system. Feminist NGOs strongly supported the Australian government's resolution that the Beijing conference be a "Conference of Commitments" that identified concrete government actions and established monitoring mechanisms to address women's rights and empowerment issues,[34] and the Clinton Administration took this charge seriously. The administration identified seven commitments at the Beijing conference to promote working women's economic issues and work and family life balance among U.S. employers, to expand awareness regarding the problem of violence against women, to lobby the U.S. Senate to ratify the Convention to Eliminate all forms of Discrimination Against Women (CEDAW), to promote microenterprise funding abroad and women-owned businesses domestically as avenues to women's economic security, to promote women's health programs and research at home and abroad through USAID and to promote global women's democratic political participation and legal rights and to fund education programs for women and girls through USAID.[35] In order to carry through on its Commitments to Women the administration created the President's Interagency Council on Women (PICW) in August 1995, made up of high-level administration leaders who promoted various government initiatives in their cabinet agencies in consultation with feminist NGOs.[36] Secretary of Health and Human Services Donna Shalala served as the PICW's first chair from 1995 to 1996; Secretary of State Madeleine Albright chaired the PICW from 1997 to 2000; First Lady Hillary Clinton served as PICW honorary chair from 1995 to 2000.[37]

J. Brian Atwood, the Clinton-appointed administrator of the US Agency for International Development, also directed new resources to the Women in Development office (WID) established in 1974 at USAID and initiated the practice of "gender mainstreaming" in USAID operations in 1996.[38] That is, USAID made "women's concerns integral to the design, implementation, monitoring and evaluation of policies and programs" in order to promote gender equality.[39] Following the takeover of Afghanistan by the Islamist Taliban regime in 1996, the U.S. government advocated non-recognition of the Taliban government among the international community to protest, in part, the Taliban's repression of Afghan women. Theresa Loar, who directed the State Department Office of International Women's Issues and who also directed the PICW, played a significant role in forwarding information on the Taliban's policy toward women from U.S. feminist organizations to Secretary of State Warren Christopher in 1996 and to Secretary of State Madeleine Albright after her appointment in January 1997.[40] With Secretary Albright's Senate confirmation, "advancing the status of women" became an even more pronounced U.S. foreign policy theme that further affected the Clinton Administration's global gender policy decisions.[41] Administration rhetoric focusing on women's empowerment also intensified. As Secretary Albright announced in honor of International Women's Day in March 1997 and repeated often, "Let me begin this morning with one very simple statement. Advancing the status of women is not only a moral imperative; it is being actively integrated into the foreign policy of the United States. It is our mission. It is the right thing to do, and, frankly, it is the smart thing to do."[42]

In July 1997, the Office of International Women's Issues coordinated with the Office of the First Lady at the White House, the U.S. Embassy in Austria and USAID to establish the "Vital Voices: Women in Democracy" conference. An original conference program facilitating networks of U.S. and Western and Eastern European women leaders took place in Vienna and became a model for subsequent Vital Voices conferences held in Northern Ireland, Uruguay, Iceland, Trinidad, Turkey and Nigeria from 1998 through 2000. In the State Department's institutional history, the Vital Voices initiative was recognized as one of the "most innovative" of the Clinton Administration's efforts to promote women's leadership and democratic participation worldwide.[43]

The Office of International Women's Issues also led interagency efforts to establish the U.S. government's anti-trafficking "prevention, protection, and prosecution" policy and programs that were announced in President Clinton's March 1998 Directive on Steps to Combat Violence Against Women and Trafficking in Women and Girls.[44] The OIWI coordinated efforts of the State Department bureaus of International Narcotics and Law Enforcement, Consular Affairs, Democracy, Human Rights and Labor, Diplomatic Security and Population, Refugees and Migration, along with the Department of Justice. These offices collaborated with the U.S. Congress to draft the Trafficking Victims Protection Act of 2000 and to propose a Protocol to Prevent, Suppress and Punish Trafficking in Persons, Especially Women and Children as a supplement to the United Nations Convention against Transnational Organized Crime that the UN Millennium Assembly adopted in November 2000.[45]

At the Special Session of the UN General Assembly, "Women 2000: Gender Equality, Development and Peace for the 21st Century," held in New York City in June 2000, U.S. delegation co-chairs Madeleine Albright and Donna Shalala signaled the Clinton Administration's continuing commitments to global women by signing UN documents condemning global violence against women, encouraging participation of women in peace building and conflict resolution efforts, advancing women's status and role in civil society and combating the global HIV/AIDS epidemic and recognizing its gendered impact on women's health.[46] Secretary Albright addressed the UN Special Session and focused on the "fairness" of government support for women's equality. Secretary Shalala recounted the significant increases in U.S. government funding for women's health research, women's reproductive health initiatives that included global family planning programs and global efforts to combat HIV/AIDS since the 1995 UN Fourth World Conference on Women.[47] In a popular address where she was interrupted repeatedly by applause, Hillary Clinton asserted continued administration support for microcredit initiatives and other measures to promote women's equality at a symposium arranged by the UN Development Fund for Women (UNIFEM).[48]

Methodology

In order to make the historical argument that the Clinton presidency marked a watershed era in terms of its demonstrated awareness of global women's disadvantaged status, recognition of liberal feminist prescriptions to address global women's immediate and strategic needs and incorporation of those feminist prescriptions into U.S. foreign policy and foreign aid program design and outcome goals, this study begins with a survey of how American women have historically sought to influence U.S. foreign policy and an examination of the extent to which liberal feminist ideas have shaped U.S. foreign policy since the 1970s. Due to some early feminist interventions, the State Department, USAID and the executive branch of federal government began to pay attention to global women in regard to U.S. foreign policy in the 1970s, 1980s and early 1990s, during the Richard Nixon, Gerald Ford, Jimmy Carter, Ronald Reagan and George Herbert Walker Bush Administrations. Analysis of these earlier presidential administrations provides historical context and locates the origins of specific global gender policies adopted by the Clinton Administration, which is the main focus of this study.

This contemporary history traces the origins of social and political concerns in the pre-formative stages of policy making and identifies the state and non-state actors, specific historical circumstances and particular feminist frames that led to global gender policy decisions and shaped policy implementation and outcomes. This policy tracing process adapted from the discipline of political science[49] is achieved through archival research into the manuscript collections of feminist organizations, the records of the National Commission for the Observance of International Women's Year and the personal papers of feminist activists. A variety of digitized and published primary sources including contemporary publications by feminist activists and their organizations that analyzed public policy and public policy documents and statements produced by government officials, the State Department, USAID, cabinet agencies and the White House, also provide rich source materials to trace the origins and evolution of global gender policy rhetoric and program development and implementation.

Finally, this study draws on semi-structured informational interviews with government officials and feminist activists who worked with the

Clinton Administration in the 1990s. Appendix A includes a list of interview subjects and their relationships to the Clinton Administration and the general topics covered in phone or face-to-face interviews. Following an initial interview conducted with Theresa Loar, a career foreign service officer, director of the President's Interagency Council on Women and the second appointed senior coordinator for the Office of International Women's Issues, interview subjects identified and referred others. Subjects discussed freely their specific roles in global gender policy making and identified and analyzed what they each believed were key events or developments affecting global women's rights and status during the decade of the 1990s. Interviewees provided valuable information regarding perceptions of policy makers and activists who sought to influence Clinton Administration global gender policy. The information was recorded, transcribed and then used as the basis for further research into the documentary record to corroborate interviewees' perceptions or as entry points for new lines of inquiry.

These varied archival sources, the contemporary published record, government documents and scholarly analyses, as well as points of information and the more impressionistic perspectives culled from one-to-one interviews, all analyzed in relation to one another, allow for a more holistic understanding of the emergence, evolution and outcomes of U.S. global gender policy during the 1990s. Clinton Administration policy can then be judged in terms of its feminist impact and legacy. Moreover, the global feminist movement's record of gaining government acceptance for their definitions of global women's needs, and the strategies that feminist NGOs adopted to persuade government officials to implement the movement's prescriptions for global women's empowerment and advancement, can also be evaluated.

Historiography

Until the late twentieth century, the perception that women's direct involvement in U.S. foreign policy offices or indirect influence on U.S. foreign policy making had been marginal prevailed among scholars and the general public.[50] Beginning in the 1980s, political scientists and historians who contributed to the growing academic field of women's studies challenged those views. Feminist international relations scholars and historians began to study the impact of ideas about masculinity and femininity on U.S. foreign policy and intergovernmental relations.[51] Also beginning in the 1980s, various historical recovery projects asserted American women's long-running interests in the nation's foreign policy and international relations and illuminated their roles as "lobbyists, critics and insiders," as one historian, Edward Crapol, categorized women's modes of engagement.[52] Most often, women's interest in foreign relations and attempts to influence government foreign policy makers were wielded from positions outside government, and numerous histories have documented the influence of women who worked with the peace movement,[53] or with national and international organizations[54] or as individuals advocating for or against particular U.S. foreign policies.[55] A few histories have also documented the lives and contributions of the relatively few women who held leadership positions in the State Department or who influenced foreign policy making from other positions inside government. Prior to the 1990s, exceptional women such as Eleanor Roosevelt,[56] Jeane Kirkpatrick[57] and Bella Abzug[58] stand out among the cohort of American women with recognized foreign policy credentials, although numerous other women with international experience and influence worked from lower-profile locations within the U.S. government, as well.[59]

Although this study's focus on the influence of feminist ideas and the implementation of global feminist organizations' agendas for women's advancement through U.S. government foreign policy making offices in the 1990s is new, it builds on the work of political scientists such as Georgia Duerst-Lahti and Lee Ann Banaszak. These scholars traced interactions between feminist activists who worked outside the state and feminist women who held positions inside U.S. government and highlighted their joint influence on public policy that addressed feminist issues such as equal employment, educational equity and women in development and in establishing women's policy agencies that furthered women's movement goals, beginning in the 1960s and continuing into the 1990s.[60] Duerst-Lahti and Banaszak both assert that feminist women working from positions within government furthered the progress of the U.S. feminist movement and its women's equality goals. Various politics and policy scholars sometimes refer to feminist insiders who practiced a form of "state feminism," that is, "the advocacy of women's movement demands inside the state,"[61] as "femocrats."[62] As Duerst-Lahti, Banaszak and others have argued, feminist insiders provided critical assistance to the U.S. feminist movement. Insiders mobilized support for the feminist movement among the general population and provided legitimacy for movement goals. They gave movement activists access to government information and directed public funding to movement causes.[63]

To be sure, the positive contributions that U.S. femocrats have made to the feminist movement have been limited. Feminist insiders have had to defer to broader government policy agendas that could overlap in some situational contexts with the women's movement agenda. Nonetheless, these agendas differed from one another. Moreover, Banaszak makes the important points that the feminists who most often worked within government structures were elite, white, educated women who faced fewer obstacles blocking their entry into the halls of power than other groups of women and therefore, "the part of the women's movement that intersects the state is not representative of the whole movement" in terms of its demographic composition.[64] Nor were feminist insiders representative of the range of feminist theoretical locations, as "most were drawn from the many variants of liberal feminism."[65] Nonetheless, while some feminist theorists and activists question the fundamental concept of "state feminism" and whether the state can ever be employed to achieve feminist ends[66] because government institutions are inherently "gender-biased," that is, "either patriarchal or driven by organizational masculinism,"[67] this study, like the works of Duerst-Lahti and Banaszak, asserts that feminist insiders have the potential to undermine patriarchal ideology and relationships within state structures and to further feminist aims. Moreover, this study also agrees with political scientists who argue that the state cannot be understood as a "monolithic patriarchal entity oppressing women,"[68] and that more research on specific government actions and their impact on women's status is needed to assess whether those government policies and programs further or act against women's interests and progress toward equality.[69] This study contributes to that project and provides historical documentation to analyze insider-outsider collaborations during the 1990s in order to assess the degree of progress made incorporating feminist movement aims into U.S. global gender policy.

Learning from Recent History

There is a re-energized focus on global women's rights and women's empowerment receiving widespread media attention in the United States and internationally. For example, a popular book, *Half the Sky: Turning Oppression into Opportunity for Women Worldwide,* by Nicholas Kristof and Sheryl WuDunn, published in October 2009, argued persuasively that empowering women in developing countries through education and employment and incorporating those women into public life to achieve gender equality is "the paramount moral challenge" of the twenty-first century.[70] In July 2010, the United Nations General Assembly established a new office, "UN Women," with the goal of promoting global gender equality and women's empowerment more effectively by merging the work of four former UN offices devoted to women's social and political advancement, academic research on women, advising the UN Secretariat on women's issues and the UN Development Fund for Women. Michelle Bachelet, former president of Chile, leads the new office to accelerate progress towards achieving gender justice. In October 2011, the Nobel Peace Prize Committee awarded three women, Tawakkol Karman of Yemen and Ellen Sirleaf Johnson and Lyemah Gbowee of Liberia, with the prestigious international honor, commending the women's pro-peace and human rights' activism and signaling support for global women's empowerment. The prize citation read: "We cannot achieve democracy and lasting peace in the world unless women obtain the same opportunities as men to influence developments at all levels of society."[71]

While this recent attention to women's rights and women's empowerment is presented as a new phenomenon,[72] the Clinton Administration's institutional transformations had already shifted U.S. foreign policy makers' focus onto these global gender issues. Therefore, it seems critically important to understand the historical lessons that can be drawn from the Clinton Administration's attempts to revise U.S. foreign policy to incorporate the rights and needs of women, as various global gender policy initiatives originating in the 1990s have been revived and strengthened by some of the key gender policy makers of the 1990s who are now back in power. The former first lady, Hillary Clinton, led the State Department as secretary of state for the Barak Obama Administration's first term in office (from 2009 to 2013). Hillary Clinton's former White House chief of staff, Melanne Verveer, directs the State Department Office of International Women's Issues, which the Obama Administration has re-named the Office of Global Women's Issues, at the elevated rank of U.S. ambassador. In addition to various U.S. foreign policy statements of support for women's rights and women's empowerment issued in President Obama's first term,[73] as he began his second term in January 2013 the president issued a "Memorandum on Promoting Gender Equality and Empowering Women and Girls Globally" that recognized that "countries are more peaceful and prosperous when women are accorded full and equal rights and opportunity. When those rights and opportunities are denied, countries lag behind."[74]

These recent developments beg the question: has the Obama Administration's global gender policy incorporated lessons from the Clinton Administration's successes and its failures? This pressing question is certainly significant, and current policy initiatives should be analyzed in the context of the historical record. Moreover, global feminist movement activists can also assess and apply the historic lessons of working with and through U.S. government offices, as they did in the 1990s, to further feminist aims in the world today. This study begins the assessment of the Clinton Administration's global gender policy making in order to open a critical feminist conversation focused on activist strategies that might be employed to impact public policy making and government operations in ways that promote feminist interests.

---

[1]Remarks by First Lady Hillary Rodham Clinton, International Women's Day, Dean Acheson Auditorium, The State Department, March 12, 1997.

[2]"Human Rights Day Event, Remarks by the President," December 10, 1996, The President's Interagency Council on Women Archives.

[3]Mayoux, "Gender Equity, Equality and Women's Empowerment."

[4]"1999 Update: America's Commitment: Federal Programs Benefiting Women and New Initiatives as Follow Up to the UN Fourth World Conference on Women." According to the Clinton Administration's self-reporting in 1999: "The Clinton Administration has appointed more women to senior positions in the Cabinet and Administration than any other U.S. President, expanding the number of Presidential judicial nominees and nominating the second woman to serve on the nation's highest court. As of April 1999, under the Clinton Administration women held 27 percent of the top positions requiring Senate confirmation, 34 percent of the presidential appointments to boards and commissions, 40 percent of non-career senior executive service positions, and 57 percent of schedule C or policy and supporting positions."

[5]Lovenduski, *Feminizing Politics*, p. 22. Arguments for women's equal representation in democratic states can be based on "justice," that is, because it is fair to all members of society to be represented; or on "pragmatism," because women's essential "difference" from men in regard to their world views and their gendered ways of operating in the world provides a value-added component to the governing policies and process and it makes sense to incorporate women's value.

[6]McBride and Mazur, *The Politics of State Feminism*, pp. 165-6.

[7]Lovenduski, *Feminizing Politics*, p. 179.

[8]Miller, "Feminisms and Transnationalism," in *Feminisms and Internationalism*, p. 225. "'Feminisms' ... is intended to deny the claim of feminism by any one group of feminists and to signify the multiplicity of ways in which those who share a feminist critique may come together to address issues. 'Feminisms' acknowledged that specific historical and cultural experiences will differently construct understandings of gender at different times and places. 'Feminisms' is meant to create a discursive space in a fraught arena. It is quintessentially historical, resisting homogenization, generalization, nostalgia."

[9]Beckwith, "Mapping Strategic Engagements," p. 314.

[10]'Mainstreaming' defined by Antrobus, *The Global Women's Movement,* p. 122.

[11]Ajinkya, "Intersecting Oppressions: Rethinking Women's Movements in the United States," in *Women's Movements in the Global Era,* pp. 420-1 and 425.

[12]Christopher, "Budget Priorities for Shaping a New Foreign Policy."

[13]Cohen and Rai, eds., *Global Social Movements*, pp. 7-10.

[14]History of the Department of State during the Clinton Presidency.

[15]Ottaway and Carothers, "Toward Civil Society Realism," in Ottaway and Carothers, eds. *Funding Virtue*, p. 294.

[16]On the distinctions between social movements and nongovernmental organizations, see Stienstra, "Of Roots, Leave, and Trees: Gender, Social Movements and Global Governance" in Mayer and Prügl, eds. *Gender Politics in Global Governance*, pp. 263-4.

[17]Scholars note the significant impact of feminist activism at the United Nations conferences of the 1990s in shaping national government responses to feminist aims. For example: Antrobus, *The Global Women's Movement*; Martha Alter Chen, "Engendering World Conferences: the International Women's Movement and the UN," in *NGOs, the UN, and Global Governance*; Jane Connors, "NGOs and the Human Rights of Women at the United Nations," in *'The Conscience of the World,' the Influence of Non-governmental Organizations in the UN System*; Friedman, "Gendering the Agenda"; Meyer and Prügl, eds. *Gender Politics in Global Governance*; Moghadam, *Globalizing Women*; Jan Jindy Pettman, "Global Politics and Transnational Feminisms" in *Feminist Politics, Activism & Vision*.

[18]Douglas, "Eastern European, US Women Meet," 17; Tolchin, "Women as Policy Makers"; USAID, "The Participation Forum, Topic: Participation and Gender," November 17, 1994, KT, box 7.

[19]History of the Department of State during the Clinton Presidency.

[20]Stienstra, "Making Global Connections among Women, 1970-99," in Cohen and Rai, eds. *Global Social Movements,* p. 80.

[21]William Jefferson Clinton, "Family Planning Grants."

[22]Shattuck, "Violations of Women's Human Rights."

[23]Ibid.

[24] Foreign Relations Authorization Act, 1994, Section 137 "Women's Human Rights Protection."

[25]Goshko and Lippman, "Foreign Aid Shift by Clinton."

[26]Wirth, "U.S. Statement on Population and Development."

[27]"US Gears Up for UN Conferences," *WEDO News & Views*; Higer, "International Women's Activism and the Cairo Conference" in Meyer and Prügl, eds. *Gender Politics in Global Governance,* 137.

[28]Danguilan, *Women in Brackets*, pp. 85-94.

[29]Hillary Rodham Clinton, "Remarks at special event to the World Summit for Social Development."

[30]Hillary Rodham Clinton, "Announcement of U.S. Initiative to Expand Girls' and Women's Education in the Developing World."

[31]Gore, "Remarks at UN World Summit for Social Development," and "Fact Sheet: The New Partnerships Initiative--Strengthening Grass-roots Political and Economic Institutions."

[32]"The UN Fourth World Conference on Women: Action for Equality, Development and Peace," *On the Road to Beijing* (April 1994), IWTC, Acc. #95S-69, box 11. The Women's Bureau, U.S. Department of Labor and the U.S. Department of State convened 10 official preparatory meetings across the nation with nongovernmental organizations, and the government produced a national report on the status of U.S. women based on information from government agencies and NGOs. See also: Sharon Kotok, Global Conference Secretariat, U.S. Department of State, "Development of the Platform for Action," *On the Road to Beijing* (October 1994), CWGL, IV World Conference on Women, Beijing, China 1995, box 1; Gracia Hillman, Senior Coordinator OIWI, "Report on Donor's Meeting The Ford Foundation/ Women and Philanthropy, on UN Fourth

World Conference on Women," February 15, 1995, KT, box 7; Friedman, "Gendering the Agenda," p. 324.

[33]Hillary Rodham Clinton, "Remarks to the United Nations Fourth World Conference in Women."

[34]Bella Abzug, "Moving to the door of the 21st Century," *The Earth Times* (March 31-April 4, 1995), KT, box 6.

[35]"Follow-up on U.S. Commitments Made at the UN Fourth World Conference on Women, September 4-15, 1995," The President's Interagency Council on Women Archives.

[36]Ibid.

[37]"The President's Interagency Council on Women," Women's Health.Gov, A Project of the U.S. Department of Health and Human Services.

[38]"USAID initiatives relating to Women and Gender 1990s: Statement by J. Brian Atwood, Administrator for US Agency for International Development, Gender Plan of Action."

[39]Mayoux, "Gender Equity, Equality and Women's Empowerment."

[40]Loar, The Association for Diplomatic Studies and Training Foreign Affairs Oral History Project.

[41]Albright, "Advancing the Status of Women in the 21st Century"; Gedda, "Albright Champions Women's Rights"; Lippman, *Madeleine Albright and the New American Diplomacy,* pp. 285-90, 299-310.

[42]Albright and Clinton, "Remarks at special program in honor of International Women's Day."

[43]History of the Department of State during the Clinton Presidency.

[44]President William J. Clinton, "Memorandum on Steps to Combat Violence Against Women and Trafficking in Women and Girls," March 11, 1998, The President's Interagency Council on Women Archives.

[45]History of the Department of State during the Clinton Presidency.

[46]"Highlights from Women 2000: Beijing Plus Five June 2000 UN Meeting, June 5-9, 2000."

[47]Shalala, "Building a Women's Health Agenda that is Woman-Centered."

[48]Singh, "Hillary Clinton Issues Call."

[49]Mazur, *Theorizing Feminist Policy*, p. 33.

[50]For example, Joan Hoff Wilson wrote in 1987: "Most simply stated, women have played and continue to play, insignificant roles in determining U.S. diplomacy because they were (and are) not present in top policy-making circles." Hoff Wilson, "Conclusion: Of Mice and Men" in Crapol, ed. *Women and Foreign Policy*, p. 174.

[51]For example, Enloe, *Bananas, Beaches, and Bases*; Enloe, *The Morning After: Sexual Politics at the End of the Cold War*; Hoganson, *Fighting For Manhood*; Peterson, *Gendered States*; Zalewski and Parpart, *The Man Question in International Relations*.

[52]Crapol, ed. *Women and Foreign Policy*.

[53]For example, Alonso, *Peace as a Woman's Issue*; Lynch, *Beyond Appeasement*; Swerdlow, *Women Strike for Peace*; Wilson, "Peace is a Woman's Job: Jeanette Rankin's Foreign Policy."

[54]For example, Fraser, *The UN Decade for Women*; Garner, *Shaping a Global Women's Agenda*; Laville, *Cold War Women*; Rupp, *Worlds of Women*; Snyder, "The Influence of Transnational Peace Groups on US Foreign Policy Decision-Makers During the 1930s."

[55]For example, Garner, *Precious Fire*; Holzer and Holzer, *Aid and Comfort: Jane Fonda in North Vietnam*; MacKinnon and MacKinnon, *Agnes Smedley*; Strong, *I Change Worlds*; Van Vorhis, *Carrie Chapman Catt*.

[56]Black, *Courage in a Dangerous World*; Glendon, *A World Made New: Eleanor Roosevelt and the Universal Declaration of Human Rights*; Lash, *Eleanor: The Years Alone*.

[57]Harrison, Jeane Kirkpatrick, Diplomat; Krasno, Interview with Jeane Kirkpatrick; Judith Ewell, "Barely in the Inner Circle: Jeane Kirkpatrick," in Crapol, ed. *Women and Foreign Policy*.

[58]Levine and Thom, *Bella Abzug*.

[59]For example, Calkin, *Women in the Department of State*; Crapol, ed. *Women and Foreign Policy*; Glen and Sarkees, *Women in Foreign Policy: The Insiders*; Jeffreys-Jones, *Changing Differences: Women and the Shaping of American Foreign Policy*.

[60]Duerst-Lahti, "The Government's Role in Building the Women's Movement; Banaszak, *The Women's Movement Inside and Outside the State*.

[61]Lovenduski, *State Feminism and Political Representation*, p. 4.

[62]Hernes, *Welfare State and Woman Power*; Mazur, *Theorizing Feminist Policy*, p. 27-8.

[63]Duerst-Lahti , "The Government's Role in Building the Women's Movement, pp. 250, 253, 255; McBride and Mazur, *The Politics of State Feminism,* pp. 28-9.

[64]Banaszak, p. 4.

[65]Ibid., p. 15.

[66]Mazur, *Theorizing Feminist Policy,* 8. "For many feminist theorists, the state is highly problematic given that they see it as a product of systems of power based on male dominance or 'patriarchy.' From the assumption of the patriarchal nature of the state, whereby state actions, structures and actors seek to perpetuate the systems of gender domination that keep women in their inferior positions in the public and private spheres, many feminist analysts dismiss or are highly critical of the state as an arena for positive social change."

[67]Joni Lovenduski quoted in MacBride and Mazur, *The Politics of State Feminism*, p. 218.

[68]Mazur, *Theorizing Feminist Policy,* p. 9.

[69]McBride and Mazur, *The Politics of State Feminism*, pp. 7-8.

[70]Kristof and WuDunn, *Half the Sky*, p. xvii.

[71]Kasinof and Worth, "Among 3 Women Awarded Nobel Prize, a Nod to the Arab Spring."

[72]See themed issue, "Saving the World's Women," *New York Times Magazine*.

[73]See for example: Solis, "Remarks at International Women's Day Luncheon"; Obama, "Speech, Cairo University, June 4, 2009." The Obama Administration once again publicly asserts "women's empowerment" is a "central pillar" of U.S. foreign policy. In a speech President Obama delivered in Cairo, Egypt in 2009 to address contentious issues that divided the West and the "Muslim world," "women's rights" was specifically named. In his speech, the President publicly committed U.S. support for global women's and girls' education and economic rights and opportunities.

[74]Hillary Rodham Clinton, "Presidential Memorandum on Promoting Gender Equality and Empowering Women and Girls Globally."

2

A Brief History of Gender in U.S. Foreign Policy

This study begins with a brief history of American women's interventions into U.S. foreign policy making and an account of the government foreign policy offices and programs that have had a gendered focus on global women, especially those established as the second wave of the U.S. feminist movement crested. From the 1970s onward, liberal feminist women working inside government foreign policy offices have collaborated with feminist movement activists working in nongovernmental organizations (NGOs) to shape U.S. global gender policy. Even in these formative years, insider-outsider feminist collaborations were fruitful. They led to the founding of the Women in Development (WID) office at the U.S. Agency for International Development (USAID) in 1974 that directed some economic resources to address global women's needs and into gender policy research. Insider-outsider feminist collaborations also influenced the State Department's preparations for the United Nations-sponsored International Women's Year Conference in 1975, the related U.S. National Women's Conference in 1977 and the UN Decade for Women conferences held in 1980 and 1985; all these conferences raised gender consciousness among U.S. government officials. Yet these early collaborations also exposed the limits of feminist influence on U.S. foreign policy and the extent of feminist benefits to global women during the Nixon, Ford, Carter and Reagan Administrations as the following pages reveal. These limits became especially obvious as the Reagan Administration increasingly employed neoliberal economic policies, prompted congressional lawmakers to cut funding for social programs and financial support for intergovernmental bodies and incorporated some of the Christian Right's conservative anti-feminist social agenda into U.S. global gender policy.

American Women and U.S. Government Policy Making: The Pre-History

Until the second half of the twentieth century the ranks of United States government policy makers were nearly all male; consequently, U.S. government policy, domestic and foreign, has historically reflected patriarchal values and institutionalized male privilege. From the 1840s when the first wave of the U.S. feminist movement for women's equal rights and full participation in the U.S. democracy was launched, until 1920 when American women formally gained full citizenship with the right to vote guaranteed by the 19th Amendment to the U.S. Constitution, women's engagement in government policy making was confined to exerting informal influence, which had some significant impact. Many domestic social reform campaigns that resulted in changes in law and governing policy, especially during the Progressive era (1890 to 1920), were informed by women's needs and interests, even though feminist outcomes were only partially achieved.[1] From the late nineteenth century era of imperial expansion through the world wars of the twentieth century, American women's peace advocacy was by far the most common feminist intervention into U.S. foreign policy making.[2] In the 1920s and 1930s, American and Western European women joined forces to form international organizations. Together they interjected their self-defined feminist values promoting peace and disarmament at League of Nations conferences and in global publicity and petition campaigns in response to the increasingly hostile international climate.[3] These feminist interventions, however, rarely achieved women's goals of settling conflicts through negotiated agreements or preventing the outbreak of war.

American women also played leading roles in the twelve Western organizations that founded the Liaison Committee of Women's International Organizations in 1925.[4] Liaison Committee members used their powers of persuasion to shape public opinion and to influence U.S. foreign policy throughout the interwar years. In addition to peace advocacy, these women's NGOs hoped to influence U.S. government, as well as other national governments that had joined the League of Nations,[5] to enact universal voting rights for women, include women in government-appointed posts at the League, address the problem of global trafficking in women and children and other international migration issues, outlaw prostitution, protect women's nationality rights when they married men from other nations, promote universal education for girls and boys worldwide, enact global health standards and practices, establish laws that guaranteed women equal remuneration with men for equal work, embark on a global inquiry into the status of women and more.[6]

When the League of Nations failed to deter outrageous attacks on humanity unleashed by Nazi Germany and its fascist allies in Italy and Japan, World War II raged from 1939 to 1945.[7] During World War II, many American women who had previously advocated for peace revised their positions, joined in support of the anti-fascist Allied Powers' war efforts and performed crucial duties on the home and battle fronts. Although they had opposed the formal outbreak of war, many American women's organizations joined the United Service Organizations (USO) and worked closely with the Department of Defense to support the U.S. armed forces. Some American women joined the ranks of the military and served in the newly formed the Women's Army Core (WACs), the Women Accepted for Voluntary Service in the Navy (WAVES), the Marine Corps Women's Reserve (MCWR), the Women's Coast Guard Reserve (SPARs) and the Women's Airforce Service Pilots (WASPs). Out of necessity, because men could not perform all the increased war work, the U.S. government incorporated women into its military institutions and Washington policy making bureaus. The U.S. government did not intend to transform gender relations or to promote feminist gains toward women's equality through these wartime adjustments although these changes inevitably occurred.[8]

A new intergovernmental body, the United Nations Organization (UN), formed as World War II ended to replace the defunct League of Nations. The U.S. government played a leading role at the UN in defining the postwar international order with its WWII Western allies. However, the revival of the Soviet Union challenged the Western allies' vision of a world capitalist market economy, free trade and liberal democratic governments established through electoral political systems—all policed by the threat of the West's nuclear weapons. Beginning in 1945, the Soviet Union opposed the Western nations' world vision, established a sphere of friendly socialist states on its borders in Eastern Europe and set out to break the West's nuclear power monopoly. The resulting East-West bi-polar global system became institutionalized within United Nations forums and agencies and a Cold War prevailed for the next forty-five years, from 1945 to 1989. Western-led women's international organizations adjusted to the Cold War world order and American and Western European women engaged in their own rivalry for the hearts and minds of global women with Soviet-inspired socialist women's international organizations who formed the Women's International Democratic Federation. The East-West women's rivalry also permeated

UN forums, especially the newly-formed UN Commission on the Status of Women.[9]

During the Cold War, American women continued to lead many of the women's international organizations that participated at the UN through the newly-negotiated "consultative status" that the Economic and Social Council (ECOSOC) and the UN Specialized Agencies awarded to carefully screened NGOs.[10] Women's NGOs with formal consultative status gained access to U.S. State Department policy makers. A very few American women also entered the ranks of the State Department foreign service.[11] American military and civilian women were also involved in post-World War II reconstruction efforts in Germany and Japan. They served as Women's Affairs officers who worked with the Supreme Command of Allied Powers in Occupied Japan and with the Office of the Military Government of the United States in Occupied Germany.[12] Other American women were appointed as U.S. delegates to the UN Commission on the Status of Women[13] or they worked in the Women's Affairs office of the United States Information Agency (USIA) that was created in 1953.[14] Women also played a role in the U.S. Agency for International Development that was created in 1961; a few women were hired as development officers and American women's NGOs were tapped to develop overseas NGO networks, to design women's programming in Latin America, Africa and Asia and to host training seminars for global women in New York and Washington DC.[15]

American women who took charge of women's programming in U.S. foreign policy agencies usually played minor and peripheral roles with little access to funding and limited influence in determining U.S. foreign policy during the first two decades of the Cold War, from 1945 to 1965. As historian Helen Laville has explained, the most influential American women's NGOs and the few women who held government positions during these decades for the most part "embrace[d] the cold war imperatives of their government."[16] The women who engaged with U.S. government foreign policy makers were, in many instances, Cold War liberals. Cold War liberals, intellectuals and activists alike, were skeptical or "realistic" liberals who were driven by anti-communist convictions. As liberals they continued to believe in the power of democratic governments to promote social progress. However, their world views were also shaped by the extreme violations of human rights they had witnessed at mid-century, as perpetrated by the fascist powers during World War II and by the Soviet Union as it was led by Joseph Stalin from 1928 to 1953. They were determined that Western democracies would police the post-World War II international system to prevent the spread of socialist totalitarianism that was equated with fascist totalitarianism. Female Cold

War liberals did not challenge the prevalent anti-Soviet U.S. foreign policy; in fact, many were convinced that American women had an important role to play as public opinion-makers and propagandists promoting American democratic values and networking with women in developing and newly-independent nations that might succumb to the Soviet Union's socialist message.

The Committee of Correspondence was one American women's organization that adhered to the Cold War liberal foreign policy agenda. During the years of the committee's operations, from 1952 to 1969, it disseminated "positive propaganda" about U.S. social and technological advances worldwide through its publications. The committee defended U.S. foreign policies including the waging of anti-communist war in Vietnam. Committee members hosted international seminars for women's organizations in conjunction with the meetings of the UN Commission on the Status of Women and they provided democratic leadership training for women in Africa, Asia and Latin America, all in collaboration with U.S. government Women's Affairs officers and with funding from the USIA, USAID and the Central Intelligence Agency.[17]

During the 1960s, other independent American women's NGOs challenged U.S. foreign policy makers. Women Strike for Peace (WSP), founded in 1961, protested U.S. Cold War policy to test nuclear weapons in the atmosphere, the nuclear arms race with the Soviet Union and the U.S. war in Vietnam.[18] As an organization that opposed the U.S. government's Cold War orientation, WSP never gained access to "the policy-making inner circle or to the 'network' of establishment women."[19] Nonetheless, WSP members established cultural legitimacy by emphasizing that their objections to building nuclear weapons for war sprang from their concerns as mothers for the health and safety of their children. Using familiar gender stereotypes allowed the WSP representatives to face down their male critics at House Un-American Activities Committee hearings in 1962, where they were accused of aiding the Soviet Union by opposing U.S. nuclear policy. They gained the sympathy of the press and general public and, partly due to their activism, the U.S. government signed a nuclear test ban treaty with the Soviet Union in 1963.[20] However, one of the WSP's unapologetically feminist members, Bella Abzug, believed women should make their case against U.S. Cold War policy on behalf of themselves, as human beings and women, rather than couched in a socially-acceptable plea for their children. During the 1960s, Abzug, then a lawyer in the private sector, came to believe that feminist women were needed within the ranks of government in order to challenge the entrenched patriarchy and to further feminist- and humanist-inspired policy agendas.[21]

Feminists and Government Policy Making, 1960s-1970s

A growing second wave of the American feminist movement that focused on eliminating gender-based discrimination energized and mobilized many American women during the 1960s and 1970s. Second wave feminists challenged a variety of government policies and social practices that discriminated against women. Historian Julie Ajinkya has explained that a major point of contention among second wave feminists was the disagreement over whether the state could, or should, be viewed and used as an ally in the quest for gender equality or whether the state by its fundamentally patriarchal nature would always oppose and undercut feminist political and social agendas. As Ajinkya described the line of division, U.S. liberal feminists believed the state could be reformed and that women should work from within the power structure to achieve equality; U.S. radical feminists disagreed and rejected collaboration with the state due to its inevitable cooptation of feminist goals.[22] Radical feminist critiques notwithstanding, liberal feminists who worked within the U.S. government offices and liberal feminists working from positions outside state structures collaborated to enact government reforms. During the 1960s and 1970s, these liberal feminists could point to significant discursive and legislative victories that benefitted American women.

Liberal feminist women began to influence U.S. policy making during the 1960s. Feminists working inside federal government offices and their feminist counterparts in nongovernmental organizations together persuaded President John F. Kennedy to establish the President's Commission on the Status of Women through an executive order in 1961. Kennedy's executive order laid the groundwork for state-level governments to follow suit. Once the federal and state commissions were established, their mandates prompted government research into women's status in regard to employment, education, Social Security and other domestic policy. A report based on research that detailed American women's inferior status in all these realms was published in 1965. Feminist women working in federal government agencies distributed over 200,000 copies of the report nationwide.[23]

Soon after the President's Commission on the Status of Women was founded, additional executive orders created the Interdepartmental Committee on the Status of Women, made up of government officials representing the cabinet agencies, and the Citizen's Advisory Council on the Status of Women (CAC), a presidentially-appointed committee that liaised with women's NGOs and monitored the federal government's response to formal gender discrimination.[24] The CAC reported annually to the president and recommended actions that feminist NGOs endorsed, including the repeal of laws criminalizing abortion and passage of an Equal Rights Amendment to the U.S. Constitution in 1970. The CAC also funneled feminist policy recommendations to the various presidential cabinet agencies through the Interdepartmental Committee on the Status of Women.[25] Esther Peterson, who headed the Women's Bureau in the Department of Labor, Marguerite Rawalt, a lawyer for the Internal Revenue Service, Mary Eastwood, a Department of Justice attorney, Virginia Allan at the State Department and Catherine East at the Department of Labor were among the liberal feminist government insiders who played influential roles at this time.

Catherine East served as executive secretary to both the Interdepartmental Committee and the Citizen's Advisory Council throughout the 1960s and into the 1970s. In an oral history interview conducted in 1987, East explained that she had a long history of working for the federal government that began in the 1940s. That gave her some employment security and legitimacy that allowed her to use the committee and advisory council to feminist advantage. East asserted: "I had the background and access to resources in the government. I had contacts in all the agencies and in Personnel. I knew where to get information, I knew who to call and I knew how to get speakers for Council meetings."[26]

East also understood that independent NGOs could exert pressure on government policy makers to promote feminist goals that demanded women's legal equality. As a government employee, East could not freely apply this pressure.[27] In 1966, Catherine East and Mary Eastwood persuaded Betty Friedan, who had just published *The Feminine Mystique,* to form the National Organization for Women (NOW) and to use NOW to successfully press the Equal Employment Opportunity Commission (EEOC) to enforce laws against sex discrimination required by Title VII of the Civil Rights Act of 1964.[28] Far beyond this specific action targeting the EEOC, Catherine East continued to promote a broad liberal feminist agenda throughout the 1970s from her federal government posts.[29] Many of her government insider and NGO outsider allies recognized the important role East played in nurturing the American feminist movement during its earliest phases. In a tribute paid to East in 1993, Gene Boyer recalled:

> Perhaps her most important function during those years was to let us know the insider's view of the political climate in Washington. It was Catherine who whispered in our ears when the time was ripe for action and when we were barking up the wrong tree... or the wrong congressman! ...Catherine's help during those fruitful years of feminist activism was invaluable. From it grew the miracles of affirmative

action, equal credit opportunity, and the principles of education equity.[30]

In regard to foreign policy, the State Department, United States Information Agency and U.S. Agency for International Development only selectively recognized the value of addressing global women's issues or including American women among the ranks of foreign policy makers before the 1970s. Moreover, American women could not insert feminist values into U.S. foreign policy or take up a global feminist policy agenda until they established themselves in the foreign service bureaus and raised their own consciousness in regard to the needs and interests of women beyond their national borders. These two developments occurred in the 1970s as the foreign service offices hired and promoted a growing number of professional women into diplomatic posts, as voters elected a few feminist women with international interests to national Congress and as the United Nations convened the International Women's Year Conference in Mexico City in 1975 and established the UN Decade for Women that ran from 1976 to 1985.

Feminist Women Enter the U.S. Foreign Service

Up to the 1970s, beyond the clerical staff, the leadership and diplomatic ranks of the State Department, USIA and USAID were nearly all-male; in 1969, women constituted only 4.8 percent of all foreign service officers.[31] Moreover, these few women were not promoted at the same rates as men and married women were not eligible to serve in the overseas embassy diplomatic corps. At the same time, U.S. embassies abroad welcomed married men and expected male diplomats' wives to perform numerous unpaid hostess duties and other public services for the U.S. government in foreign countries. In order to challenge these various discriminatory policies, female employees working for foreign service agencies formed the Women's Action Organization (WAO) in 1970. Mildred Marcy, a USIA Women's Affairs officer since 1961, and Barbara Good, a career foreign service officer since 1952, helped to found the WAO and steered the organization into fruitful negotiations with the State Department's senior management in order to reform the foreign service bureaus from within.

As a consequence of WAO advocacy, the State Department lifted the ban on married women's diplomatic service overseas in 1971. President Richard Nixon and Secretary of State Henry Kissinger made some public pronouncements supporting women's contributions to foreign policy making, and Nixon directed the foreign service agencies to draft action plans to recruit more women into their professional ranks. Women's representation on foreign service promotion boards also increased, and the WAO received a Presidential Management Improvement Award in 1972.[32] The State Department started celebrating a "Women's Week" annually in 1974 that coincided with August 26 Women's Equality Day and hosted events highlighting the history of women in foreign affairs.[33] As a result of these changes, women made some slow gains increasing the numbers of female foreign service officers hired throughout the 1970s.[34]

When President James Earl (Jimmy) Carter took office in 1977 his administration appointed a few liberal feminist women to elevated leadership ranks at the State Department. Most notably, Patricia Derian filled the post of assistant secretary of state for Human Rights and Humanitarian Affairs from 1977 to 1981, and Patsy Mink, former congresswoman from Hawaii, served as assistant secretary of state for Oceans and International Environmental and Scientific Affairs from 1977 to 1978.[35] With increased descriptive representation of feminist women in the nation's foreign affairs offices these women were poised to make a substantive difference in U.S. foreign policy making, as well.

Mildred Marcy proposed one of the most significant substantive changes that originated from a female foreign service officer during the 1970s, one that had long-term feminist impact on distribution of U.S. foreign aid. Marcy seized an opportunity to channel some economic aid to global women as the fundamental orientation of U.S. foreign aid to Third World countries began to shift in the 1970s. In the 1950s and 1960s, foreign economic aid had generally funded capital-intensive, large-scale infrastructure projects to spur economic development. In the 1970s, foreign aid began to fund more health care, education and population planning programs in order to address the needs of the "poorest of the poor."[36]

Marcy became aware of the needs of global women who often occupied the ranks of the "poorest of the poor" through feminist policy advocates such as Irene Tinker, co-founder in 1974 of the Wellesley Center for Research on Women, and Ester Boserup, author of the path-breaking study *Women's Role in Economic Development,* published in 1970. In a 1991 oral history interview Marcy recalled her own intellectual epiphany and the course of action it inspired:

> Women are always at the bottom of the economic scale. There ought to be something in [foreign aid] legislation that directs the AID mission directors to look at the role that women are playing in their countries to see whether or not the humanitarian assistance is going to where it ought to go. So I sat down at the typewriter and drafted a two or three line

> amendment to the foreign assistance legislation that year—'section 116: integrating women into national economies; sections 102-107 should be administered so as to give particular attention to those programs and projects and activities which tend to integrate women into the national economies of foreign countries thus improving their status and assisting the total developmental effort.'[37]

Mildred Marcy's husband Carl Marcy, the Senate Foreign Relations Committee chief of staff, knew that Republican Senator Charles Percy was considering a run for president. He funneled the amendment to Percy, who attached it to the Senate version of the foreign aid bill with hopes of securing the "women's vote." Although Senate passed the "Percy Amendment," it almost disappeared in the House version of the appropriations bill. With defeat imminent, Mildred Marcy and Deputy Assistant Secretary of State for Public Affairs Virginia Allan alerted their feminist networks among national women's organizations. These NGOs flooded congressional offices with letters of support for the Percy Amendment. This pressure from their female constituents swayed congressmen's votes.[38]

Feminist government insiders and NGO outsiders rallied congressional support and the Percy Amendment became law. This led to the establishment of the Women in Development office at USAID in 1974 to carry out the law's provisions. The WID office started operations on a very small scale with an annual budget of $300,000. Later in the decade, from 1977 to 1981, after the Carter Administration appointed liberal feminist Arvonne Fraser to direct WID, the office's scope expanded. By 1980, the annual WID budget had increased to $10 million.[39]

2.1 Arvonne Fraser, director of USAID Women in Development Office, 1977-1980, with Hapsita N'Guariera, director for adult literacy, government of Chad, 1978. Courtesy of Arvonne Fraser.

Arvonne Fraser, former president of the Women's Equity Action League, maximized the feminist impact on WID office operations. She hired Elsa M. Chaney, a scholar of women and development in Latin America who had public policy experience, as her deputy, and she enlisted feminist NGOs in WID's work. Under Fraser's leadership, WID commissioned its own studies and collected data on global women and development projects from the women's NGOs who ran WID grant-funded programs. Fraser realized that WID could fund grants of up to $10,000 without further USAID bureaucratic approvals so she spent government money in modest amounts to support projects that would have a widespread feminist impact. The new data that WID collected justified further funding. The increased attention to improving women's status in developing countries consequently became a more-commonly practiced U.S. foreign aid strategy.[40] The feminist foundations that Mildred Marcy laid down through the Percy Amendment, and that Arvonne Fraser expanded with her creative administrative vision as director of the Women in Development office during its formative years, were built on by subsequent feminist government officers in the 1990s, when the Clinton Administration took office.

Feminist Women Enter U.S. Congress

Few elected congresswomen could consistently advocate for feminist policies during their terms in office because they were elected as members of political parties with broad, non-feminist legislative agendas. Congresswomen were elected to represent all their constituents' interests within specific historic and social contexts.[41] Nonetheless, in general, the women who served in U.S. Congress during the 1960s and 1970s represented a "new guard" that was more educated, more professional and more "feminist" than the first generations of female national office holders. According to a congressional history, "More explicitly than their predecessors, the women elected between 1955 and 1976 legislated regarding issues that affected women's lives. Their feminism—their belief in the social, political, and economic equality of the sexes–shaped their agendas." Among the congresswomen who vocally supported feminist positions, Bella Abzug, Yvonne Burke, Shirley Chisholm, Martha Griffiths, Margaret Heckler, Elizabeth Holtzman, Patsy Mink and Patricia Schroeder stand out.[42]

Bella Abzug in particular understood the power structure in Washington and was willing to use the political system to further feminist goals. In collaboration with National Organization for Women leaders Betty Friedan and Gloria Steinem and with her colleague Congresswoman

Shirley Chisholm, Abzug determined that an organization of female government insiders could promote women's political participation generally and would leverage elected women's gendered impact on policy making. In consequence, Abzug and Chisholm organized the National Women's Political Caucus (NWPC) in 1971.[43] Abzug also served as a chief strategist for the Democratic Women's Committee that pushed for gender equity in party appointments and party-backed candidates for elected office. As New York's congresswoman from 1970 to 1976 she sponsored bills to support women's equitable access to credit, extension of Social Security to cover women homemakers who did not work for wages outside the home, women's access to contraceptives and abortion rights, as well as civil rights for gays and lesbians.[44]

In regard to foreign affairs, Abzug was a vocal critic of Cold War anti-communism and militarism in all its manifestations. She was an avowed internationalist who believed that the United Nations was the best forum to work out global conflicts peacefully. She also believed that strategic use of economic assistance rather than military aid was the best way for the U.S. government to encourage the spread of democracy worldwide.[45] From the time that Women Strike for Peace was founded and Bella Abzug joined the organization in 1961, she never stopped denouncing the U.S. stockpile of nuclear weapons and global nuclear arms proliferation. Moreover, Abzug was an early critic of the U.S. anti-communist war in Southeast Asia. On the first day of her first congressional session she introduced a resolution calling for U.S. military withdrawal from Vietnam.[46] Bella Abzug was also a strong supporter of the United States' participation in International Women's Year (IWY) and she served as one of four congressional advisers to the U.S. delegation to the IWY Conference in Mexico City held in June 1975. (See Appendix B) Following the IWY Conference Abzug sponsored a bill in the House of Representatives calling for a National Women's Conference to recognize women's contributions to U.S. democracy and to raise awareness about the issues important to American women and the discriminations that American women still faced.[47]

Bella Abzug's important role in organizing the National Women's Conference and her efforts to implement the prescriptions for gender equity that conference called for will be discussed ahead. But regardless of where Abzug focused her unwavering feminist moral compass, on U.S. domestic or foreign policy, she was able to see the connections between local, national and international politics and along various axes of oppression. In a biography of Abzug based on interviews conducted with her friends and political cohorts, Faye Wattleton, then-president of Planned Parenthood, identified Abzug's shrewd political instincts that

Abzug used throughout her lifetime of public service and advocacy for the underdog:

> It sounds like a cliché, but Bella could walk into a room and know that room within minutes, if not seconds. She could know who in that room to avoid, who in that room she needed to get to, and what was the lay of the land. She had the rare capacity to integrate a landscape—not unlike the way Henry Kissinger can see the world in its broadest terms. … She could see all of these movements and how they made sense in relationship to each other and apart from each other. … Bella had the capacity to see how the peace movement was intricately tied to the women's movement, and how the environment movement would never go anyplace if you didn't do something about women, and how the political process could be used for all of that.[48]

The United Nations International Women's Year: Globalizing the American Feminist Movement

One of the common criticisms leveled at white, middle-class and educated liberal American feminists during the decade of the 1970s, whether the criticism came from global feminists or from American working-class women or women of color, is that those privileged feminists were myopic and focused on narrowly-defined gender discrimination and on U.S. domestic policy issues. White, middle-class liberal feminists were often accused of exhibiting a kind of chauvinism when defining so-called "universal" feminist issues during the United Nations-sponsored International Women's Year and at the IWY Conference held in Mexico City in 1975.

Global feminists challenged American liberal feminists' privileged place and "loudest voice" at the IWY Conference and at the NGO tribune that met in Mexico City parallel to the official UN conference. One such incident involved Betty Friedan who represented the U.S. National Organization for Women and who raised contentious issues at the Mexico City meetings. Friedan demanded that the UN conference, a gathering of UN member governments' official delegations, be opened to all nongovernmental organization representatives, as well. She also demanded that the IWY Conference treaty, the World Plan of Action that had been devised through circumscribed and arcane government negotiations during several years' preparatory meetings, be reopened to include NGOs' input in Mexico City. Friedan did not comprehend the UN intergovernmental process. Nor did she understand that the World Plan of Action treaty was in fact "soft law" that relied on sovereign national governments to follow through on their conference pledges and to enact specific laws, policies and practices to prohibit gender discrimination and improve women's status. Nonetheless, Friedan's demands drew more criticism from global feminists than from UN member governments at the Mexico City meetings where feminists accused Friedan of claiming to speak for global women without consulting them about the interests that were most relevant to their lives, a practice they labeled "typically American."[49]

The NGO tribune chair, Mildred Persinger, a white, middle-class American liberal feminist, also drew fire from global feminists for organizing structured panel sessions at the NGO tribune that prevented open discussion of "Third World" women's issues.[50] Native American women, who believed that the official U.S. government delegation to the UN conference and the NGO tribune organizers had both ignored their concerns, voiced one harsh critique. They asserted that "No discussion of important subjects such as racism, imperialism, and colonialism were scheduled anywhere. ... Many of the U.S. women such as the National Organization of Women members were concerned only with so-called 'women's problems': abortion, rape, women's right to vote, job equality and so on. Their position was that talk of politics gets in the way of women's communication. The reply from many of the Third World women was that 'they were compelled to talk about the realities of the lives of their people before any discussion of special women's problems could take place.'"[51]

These global women's criticisms had significant consequences. For one, they raised the consciousness of American liberal feminists who attended the international gathering. Mildred Persinger, for example, appreciated the variety of issues activists raised at the widely diverse IWY meetings and she identified the valuable messages that global women delivered to white, middle-class American liberal feminists, who, she claimed:

> heard the women of the world say that justice is indivisible; that ... gaps between rich and poor, literate and illiterate, over-fed and starving, do not discriminate on the basis of sex. When some said, 'We demand access to professional education,' others said, 'we have no schools.' When some said 'we demand equal participation in the political process,' others said 'our brothers and sisters are in prison because they tried it.'...They said to each other: 'Women must work for justice within their countries as well as justice among countries.'...[52]

Feminists Shape U.S. Government Participation in the International Women's Year

American liberal feminists working inside and outside government had been involved in planning for International Women's Year for several years. These women had participated in UN IWY Conference preparatory meetings at which governments advised by NGOs drafted the World Plan of Action. The World Plan that governments in Mexico City ultimately approved was weakened by watered-down language and its soft law status.[53] Nonetheless, the World Plan articulated feminist goals for global women's advancement. The World Plan instigated some institutional changes at the UN and launched the UN Decade for Women (1976 to 1985).[54] In Mexico City, Betty Friedan had asserted that "women" had been shut out of official UN IWY activities, but that was not completely true. From 1973 onward, American liberal feminists had not only joined United Nations' IWY committees, they also helped to define U.S. government participation in International Women's Year in significant ways.

Soon after the UN General Assembly resolved in December 1972 to designate 1975 as International Women's Year, in January 1973, the U.S. government established the U.S. Center for IWY with a $36,000 grant from the State Department. Kathryn Wallace at the Department of Labor Women's Bureau and Virginia Allan at the State Department pushed for the establishment of the center. Former foreign service officer Ruth Bacon directed the center's operations. Although it was not a U.S. government agency and operated "outside the governmental chain of command and [was] policy free," the center was based in the nation's capital and it publicized and coordinated U.S. government and NGO activities related to the IWY commemorations.[55]

From its inception the U.S. Center for IWY became a primary mechanism for American women's NGOs, especially those liberal feminist organizations that had been actively campaigning for an Equal Rights Amendment (ERA) to the U.S. Constitution, to exert influence on the U.S. government and its global gender policy. At center meetings feminist NGO outsiders pushed their liberal feminist counterparts working inside government offices to take concrete actions in support of IWY goals.[56] Mildred Marcy's intervention dedicating specific funds to women's development needs added to the Fiscal Year 1974 foreign aid bill was one result.[57] In late 1974 Senators Charles Percy and Stuart Symington also pressed the State Department to act after they were contacted by the "women's movement" that "wishes the Federal Government to establish some tangible evidence of the importance we attach to International Women's Year." Consequently, the State Department and USIA each assigned two staff members (Mildred Marcy among them) to organize federal government participation and solicit cabinet agency contributions in the amount of $500,000 to support UN IWY activities.[58] Inspired by requests coming out of the U.S. Center for IWY, Deputy Secretary of State Robert Ingersoll urged President Gerald Ford to establish a National Commission on the Observance of International Women's Year (NCOIWY).[59] President Ford did so with Executive Order 11832 issued on January 9, 1975, wherein Ford also took the opportunity to announce his administration's support for the ERA.[60]

With the establishment of the NCOIWY, Mildred Marcy was appointed executive director for the commission secretariat from 1975 to 1977 and coordinator for the U.S. delegation to the 1975 IWY Mexico City conference. In these positions Marcy relied heavily on input from liberal feminist NGOs to define the National Commission's activities and to advise the U.S. conference delegation.[61] Aided by her deputy director Catherine East, Marcy conducted research for the NCOIWY and the conference delegation in consultation with NGOs. She established a Government Liaison Advisory Committee that met at the U.S. Center for IWY where NGOs provided advice on a range of gender policy positions to the National Commission and to the U.S. delegation to the IWY Conference.[62]

The NCOIWY operated with a mandate to investigate American women's status and advise the president with specific recommendations for overcoming political, legal, social and economic discriminations against women in a formal report to be filed by mid-1976.[63] A bipartisan body, the NCOIWY was made up of thirty-five presidential appointees and four representatives selected from among the ranks of elected congressmen and senators. Yet at its first meeting the National Commission demonstrated a prevailing liberal feminist orientation "by unanimously adopting a strongly worded resolution favoring the ratification of the Equal Rights Amendment … chosen as the top priority issue of the Commission." The commission's presiding officer, Jill Ruckelshaus, a Republican, along with Republican Congresswoman Margaret Heckler and actor Alan Alda, co-chaired the commission's committee on ERA ratification.[64] The commission also formed internal committees to focus on topics such as women and the media, women and political power, childcare for working mothers, issues important to women of color, enforcement of anti-discrimination laws, U.S. ratification of International Labor Organization conventions affecting working women and the need for a women's policy office at the federal government level. The commission solicited input from feminist women's

NGOs on all these issues[65] and sometimes invited NGO representatives to serve on NCOIWY committees.[66] Out of this committee work that was grounded in research conducted by NGOs and the U.S. Center for IWY, and through the experience of national participation at the IWY Conference, the commission formulated a 400-page, 115-point program with recommendations for improving the status of American women and submitted its final report, "To Form a More Perfect Union … Justice for American Women," to President Ford on July 1, 1976.[67]

Although the U.S. Center for IWY, the National Commission, and the U.S. delegation to the IWY Conference were all separate entities, they worked together and shared some important members along with a liberal feminist orientation. Former Republican Party National Committee vice chair and head of the U.S. delegation to the UN Commission on the Status of Women Pat Hutar also headed the U.S. delegation to the IWY Conference and chaired the NCOIWY committee on international affairs; Jill Ruckelshaus chaired the NCOIWY and served on the IWY Conference delegation; Gilda Gjurich served on the NCOIWY and advised the conference delegation; Ruth Bacon directed the U.S. Center for IWY and advised the conference delegation; and Margaret Heckler and Bella Abzug served as congressional representatives to both the NCOIWY and the IWY Conference delegation. (See Appendices B and C)

During the IWY Conference preparatory process liberal feminist NGOs' input influenced the selection of U.S. delegation members, and their expertise on gender policy issues was incorporated into U.S. position papers. In part, this was due to Mildred Marcy's and Catherine East's staff leadership roles; they both believed strongly that involving NGOs affirmed the U.S. democratic process and that the liberal feminist NGOs they consulted with expressed the will of the majority of American women.[68] A few NGO women also served as official U.S. delegation members in Mexico City.

Liberal feminist ideas also inspired U.S. government actions at the IWY Conference in Mexico City. Senator Charles Percy who represented the Senate Republicans on the U.S. delegation bolstered his reputation as an advocate for incorporating "women" into global development initiatives. He chaired a panel on women and development at the NGO tribune. In his post-conference report to the congressional Government Operations Committee, Senator Percy noted with pride that IWY Conference had adopted thirty-five resolutions that were incorporated into the World Plan, and that the United States' delegation had authored or co-sponsored seven of those resolutions. Those seven resolutions expressed positions American liberal feminists had long supported. The resolutions called for integrating women into UN development agencies and programs on an equal basis with men, affirmed the right of all individuals, male and female, to a basic education, directed the UN secretariat and UN specialized agencies to hire and to promote more women, called on all UN member nations to include more women in world conference delegations, urged all civic and nongovernmental organizations to promote the status of women and their families in programs and services, established the Institute for Training and Research for the Advancement of Women (INSTRAW), urged member governments to fund INSTRAW with their voluntary contributions and affirmed the 1974 World Population Conference Plan of Action's support for family planning education and resources as these were linked to international socioeconomic development goals and global population plans.[69]

Following the Mexico City conference liberal feminists continued to influence U.S. government policy makers. Feminist NGO representatives met with U.S. State Department officials, including U.S. Ambassador to the UN Barbara White, Deputy Secretary of State Robert Ingersoll and NCOIWY chair Jill Ruckelshaus, to develop plans to carry out IWY World Plan of Action goals for women's advancement within the specific U.S. national context.[70] Based on feminist NGO suggestions the State Department and Jill Ruckelshaus convened an Interagency Task Force meeting with representatives from all the cabinet agencies to determine how well federal programs served the needs of American women. These gender impact assessments, a new initiative within U.S. government agencies, were intended to expose and eliminate institutional gender discrimination in order to advance women's equality.[71] Moreover, the National Commission's final report to President Ford included several recommendations related to U.S. foreign policy making made by feminist NGOs: to establish a new position at the State Department to focus on women's affairs, to consult with women's organizations when forming U.S. positions at international conferences and to increase the number of women serving in foreign posts and on international conference delegations.[72]

In June 1976 the State Department followed through on NGO recommendations established a new office for International Women's Programs within the Bureau of International Organization Affairs that was headed by Shirley Hendsch. Hendsch had also been involved in writing position papers for the U.S. IWY Conference delegation.[73] The office for International Women's Programs was mandated to oversee "measures of an international nature that are of primary concern to women and for the advancement of women, particularly in areas of equality and women's full integration in the total development effort."[74] This office satisfied some of the needs that NGO's had identified for an on-going, national-level bureau to keep the government focused on women's issues throughout the UN Decade for Women as the U.S. Center for IWY was dissolved in December 1975.[75] While these U.S. government initiatives certainly did not incorporate all the NGOs' ideas or the participation of all feminist women's organizations, they strove to address a wide array of feminist issues just as they strove to answer their anti-feminist critics.[76]

Critiques of Liberal Feminism from the Political Right

In addition to the global feminist critiques regarding U.S. participation at the IWY Conference discussed above, the neo-conservative right wing of the Republican Party and New Religious Right anti-feminist evangelicals also objected to the year-long work of the National Commission on the Observance of International Women's Year and to U.S. participation in the UN-sponsored IWY Conference. Neo-conservative Republicans and the Religious Right shared core ideological beliefs in economic libertarianism or "free enterprise," social conservatism and militant anti-communism. In the 1970s, neo-conservatives criticized U.S. participation in United Nations' forums generally because developing nations, such as the Group of 77, used those forums to challenge U.S. capitalist economic policy and its "imperialist" foreign relations. The Group of 77 developing nations, non-aligned with the Western capitalist democracies in regard to Cold War geopolitics, together devised multilateral trade and aid policy proposals they called the New International Economic Order (NIEO). As the NIEO gained a global platform at the UN, neo-conservative business and political leaders denounced its "anti-American" orientation.[77] Neo-conservatives objected to showing any tacit U.S. acceptance of the legitimacy of NIEO positions. Their concerns prevented First Lady Betty Ford from attending the IWY Conference in Mexico City to the dismay of liberal feminists inside and outside U.S. government who also recognized that Betty Ford's presence would have signaled support for International Women's Year from the highest level of the Ford Administration.[78]

Moreover, critics of Israel, the United States' strongest ally in the Middle East, also used UN IWY Conference meetings to denounce Israel's Palestinian occupation policy, to charge that Zionism was an expression of racism and to disrespect Lea Rabin, wife of the Israeli Prime Minister, when she spoke at a conference session. These controversial anti-Israeli and anti-Semitic protests disrupted conference meetings and their gist was incorporated into a second document formulated at the IWY

Conference, the Declaration of Mexico, signed by eighty-nine nations. The U.S. government and neo-conservative politicians considered the declaration to be an attack on U.S. foreign policy, facilitated by the United Nations and its global summits.[79]

The work of the National Commission and U.S. delegation throughout International Women's Year also provoked cultural conservatives who identified with the New Religious Right that played an active role in American politics in the 1970s and 1980s. The Religious Right objected to spending any government funds or supporting any government entities that advanced a liberal feminist agenda, which they identified as an affront to traditional family values and social relations grounded in their fundamentalist religious beliefs. Adding fuel to the Religious Right's belief that a battle between the forces of good and evil was underway were: the Supreme Court's 1973 decision in *Roe v. Wade* that most state and federal laws banning or restricting abortions were unconstitutional, the Watergate scandal that exposed President Richard Nixon's lies to the American people, permissive laws that had allowed for expanded distribution of pornography, an increasingly vocal gay rights movement, the rising national divorce rate and the feminist campaign for passage of the Equal Rights Amendment. Anti-feminist evangelicals targeted the NCOIWY, the U.S. IWY Conference delegation, the State Department and USAID for criticisms because they worked with liberal feminist organizations that advocated for the ERA, and because U.S. population policy expressed in United Nations forums and U.S. dollars distributed through UN agencies supported global family planning initiatives, which they opposed. These objections were raised during International Women's Year and they intensified when Bella Abzug and fourteen other congresswomen introduced a bill to fund a National Women's Conference, initially proposed for 1976, during the United States' Bicentennial.[80] The National Women's Conference, discussed ahead, took place in November 1977.

Anti-Feminist Objections to the ERA

The Equal Rights Amendment to the U.S. Constitution, first proposed in 1923, asserted that "equality of rights under the law shall not be denied or abridged by the United States, or by any state, on account of sex."[81] After interest in adopting the ERA revived among liberal feminist women who were inspired by civil rights activism of the 1960s,[82] in 1972 Congress approved the ERA and sent it to the states for ratification. After twenty-two states immediately ratified the ERA, the anti-feminist Religious Right organized quickly and successfully forestalled ERA ratification by the required thirty-eight states that would make women's equality the law of the land.

In some instances, objections were based on fears that federal government funds would aid politicians who supported the ERA and would penalize those politicians who opposed ERA.[83] Confronting these anti-ERA critics, the National Commission's presiding officer Jill Ruckelshaus defended the NCOIWY's pro-ERA position. In 1975 Ruckelshaus asserted that support for the ERA was well within the U.S. political mainstream:

> All presidential advisory groups on the status of women since 1969 have endorsed the ERA. The National Association of Commissions on Women, made up of state and local government commissions, appointed by governors, mayors, and legislative bodies, have also endorsed the Amendment as have both major political parties. Practically all the voluntary organizations with a tradition of concern and action to improve the status of women have endorsed the Amendment.
>
> The Congress, after extensive and thorough hearings in both the Senate and the House of Representatives, passed the ERA by overwhelming votes in both houses.
>
> As to the Commission's role, it is anticipated that the Commission will strive to educate the public. We believe that too many citizens are uninformed or misinformed as to the intent of the Congress in passing the Amendment and the importance of that intent to the courts in interpreting it....[84]

Much of the misinformation that Ruckelshaus referred to came from anti-feminist groups such as the Eagle Forum/STOP ERA that Phyllis Schlafly mobilized and that objected to the social consequences of the ERA. Anti-feminists predicted that the Equal Rights Amendment would de-sex American men and women. They believed the ERA would force married women and mothers into the paid workforce, would force women into military service and into combat roles and would promote civil rights for homosexuals. Most significantly, anti-ERA forces asserted that such an amendment would be used to constitutionally protect abortion rights for women that fundamentalist religious groups abhorred and hoped to overturn in the legal system and in the court of public opinion.[85] Again, NCOIWY chair Jill Ruckelshaus tried to counter the anti-ERA forces' fears:

> The Equal Rights Amendment consists of nothing more than twenty-six words saying that women shouldn't be denied equal rights because of their sex. It doesn't say that all bathrooms have to be shared—though may I say that the unisex nature of toilets on airplanes and trains and buses doesn't seem to have resulted in a general lowering of this nation's moral fiber. It doesn't say that the American family, as we know it, should be destroyed—I, as a mother of five, couldn't go for that. Really, I think the only serious threat of the Amendment is that it might put a damper on the pedestal business.[86]

Women associated with the Catholic Church also tried to explain that there was no legal basis to connect the ERA with legalized abortion:

> Abortion laws are not necessary to relieve women of the 'unequal' burden of bearing an unwanted child for the same reason: Pregnancy is unique to women; men can't bear any children; thus, the question of equal treatment of the sexes is not relevant....
>
> Persons concerned with the protection of fetal life can and do support the Equal Rights Amendment with integrity and enthusiasm. Reverence for life does indeed include reverence for equality.[87]

Nonetheless, in spite of the seemingly widespread support for the ERA in the mid-1970s, anti-ERA campaigns succeeded in preventing states' ratification and frustrated liberal feminists working inside and outside government for the next several decades.

Conservative Critiques of Global Family Planning Initiatives

The U.S. government's support for funding family planning educational materials and for distributing contraceptives to slow down global population growth had been defined at the 1974 UN World Population and World Food Conferences. This population policy had become part of the U.S. global development aid strategy and, insofar as it targeted women, it was incorporated into U.S. platform proposals at the IWY Conference:

> Family Planning [is] a strategy for raising women's status and increasing their participation in public life. ... Almost all women need family planning. They need it to safeguard their family's health, improve their minds, acquire marketable skills, increase their confidence in themselves and their collective potential.

> The widespread availability of family planning services, information, and above all, education, should be a basic objective of any strategy for raising women's status and increasing their participation in public fields.[88]

In spite of their well-defined rationale, government officials recognized that anti-feminist activists were hyper-sensitive to any expressions of support or tacit endorsement of the ERA, or for any government funding dedicated to global family planning programs, because religious conservatives believed those programs were linked to support for legalized abortion. These two hot-button issues, the ERA and funding for family planning, had the potential to hijack all government efforts to advance the status of women domestically and internationally. They almost derailed the National Women's Conference that was organized to define a U.S. national agenda to achieve women's equality and that was linked to the IWY World Plan of Action's global feminist goals.[89]

The National Women's Conference

In tandem with the work of the National Commission for the Observance of International Women's Year in 1975, Congresswoman Bella Abzug introduced a bill to Congress to fund a National Women's Conference and to extend the life of the National Commission beyond July 1976 so that it could organize the National Conference.[90] Abzug initially requested $10 million to fund fifty state and six territorial conferences that would develop a platform for women's advancement, to be adopted at a culminating National Conference. Her proposals united the opposition forces, neo-conservatives and the Religious Right, who used the opportunity to denounce liberal feminism and to oppose the ERA and the U.S. government's support for global family planning programs.[91] After much debate and assertions by Abzug and other congressional supporters that a National Women's Conference would provide "opportunity for women of all kinds to come, women of all backgrounds, … women of lower-income levels, women of every racial, religious, and ethnic group and representing every point of view," Congress whittled the funding appropriation down to $5 million and passed the resolution calling for a National Women's Conference into law.[92] Congress also extended the life of the National Commission to March 31, 1978, in order to organize the National Conference, set to take place in November 1977.[93]

Although ninety-two American women's NGOs had already formed the Women's Action Alliance and had begun organizing an independent meeting to define a national women's agenda to achieve women's equality,[94] following passage of Public Law 94-167 the NCOIWY stepped into the organizational leadership role and invited representatives of these and other women's NGOs to meet in Washington to discuss participation and plan for the various state and national conferences.[95]

Throughout the 1976 presidential election cycle, anti-feminists criticized the National Commission and accused its members of engaging in illegal lobbying activities by advocating for passage of the ERA and by voicing support for legalized abortion as defined by the Supreme Court in 1973. Nonetheless, Mildred Marcy and others who understood the National Commission's importance persuaded the incoming Democratic President Jimmy Carter to continue the Commission's work. Even though she left her post as executive director of the NCOIWY secretariat soon after the Carter Administration took office in January 1977, Marcy argued vigorously that no other government office filled the roles of the "chameleon"-like Commission. The Commission performed a wide array of "advisory, supervisory, operational and regulatory functions" that related to "to the unfinished business on behalf of human and women's rights."[96] President Carter, an evangelical born-again Christian who also led the liberal Democratic Party that supported passage of the ERA, subsequently appointed outspoken feminist Bella Abzug, who was no longer a member of Congress, to chair the National Commission.[97] Additionally, President Carter appointed former first lady Betty Ford, civil rights leader Coretta Scott King and Native American activist LaDonna Harris to the reconstituted and enlarged Commission.[98] (See Appendix C)

Although President Carter's appointments guaranteed the Commission's work would continue with some high-level liberal feminist political support, the appointments elicited an extreme anti-feminist reaction once again. One irate citizen wrote to President Carter in May 1977, "In June, the Kentucky IWY Coordinating Committee plan to have a conference in Lexington. The workshops will be used to propagate ERA, child care centers, gay rights, abortion and disarmament. Both the national and state IWY committees are unbalanced. The philosophies they promote are unchristian as well as un-American. This is a gross misuse and mismanagement of tax money. What do you intend to do about it?"[99] These views were echoed and championed by neo-conservative politicians in Washington such as Republican Senator Jesse Helms who spoke out in Senate chambers: "The IWY program to date appears to be a distortion of the intent and purpose of Federal statutes authorizing and funding IWY, and perhaps may even represent a violation of Federal law. At any rate, the IWY program represents a violation of the rights of women who believe in the positive and moral values of womanhood."[100] In September 1977 Senator Helms launched a congressional investigation into the National Commission's alleged misuse of federal funding.[101]

To be sure, liberal feminist women working inside and outside government, affiliated with both the Republican and Democratic political parties, predominated among the National Women's Conference organizers. However, by the National Commission's deliberate design there was also great diversity of "race, ethnicity, class, sexuality and other identities," as well as significant representation of a range of political views from the radical feminist left to the extreme anti-feminist right among the delegates who attended the state conferences and the National Conference held in Houston, Texas.[102] The National Commission that operated under Bella Abzug's strong leadership countered charges of liberal feminist bias with their own charges of racism exhibited by some of the cultural and political conservatives that dominated a few state-wide conferences.[103] Using its powers to appoint delegates at-large, the Commission promoted inclusivity and balance among the 2000 official state delegates who attended the National Women's Conference along with 18,000 Americans who attended the conference in unofficial capacities.[104] A "Pro-Plan Caucus" comprised of pro-ERA delegates to the conference, supported by the Commission but organized independently, kept delegates in Houston focused on the task of approving by majority vote the National Plan of Action for Women that anti-ERA, anti-abortion and anti-gay rights activists who also attended the conference tried, but failed, to defeat.[105]

International Issues at the National Women's Conference

Although the main conference agenda and media spotlights focused on U.S. national women's issues and domestic political debates, the National Commission invited global women to the National Women's Conference as well. Mildred Persinger chaired the Commission's international committee. Building on convictions that she developed when organizing the IWY NGO tribune in Mexico City, Persinger believed that American women could learn a great deal about global women's needs through diverse conference forums. She created opportunities for global women to exchange visions and strategies to promote gender equality in Houston. Her committee invited women from over twenty countries, and over eighty global women attended. The State Department provided travel grants for thirty-nine of these women. Of course, the U.S. government funded women from USAID-recipient countries who were reformers, not revolutionaries. These global women were government officials, educators and social workers; they were not radical activists who would vocally denounce U.S. foreign policy. Nonetheless, other global women who were funded by foreign associations or by their home governments, such as women from South Africa and Libya, criticized the U.S. liberal feminist women's emancipation model and brought their own competing feminist perspectives to the Houston conference forums.[106]

Prior to the opening of the National Conference, Arvonne Fraser, director of the USAID/WID office, organized a seminar on women and development for these international guests.[107] The international committee also hosted a conference session to promote women's participation in foreign policy making at which Margaret Mead highlighted the importance of women's input to formulating women-friendly global population and development policies.[108] The National Plan of Action that emerged from the conference deliberations included an "International Plank" that called on the U.S. government to increase women's influence in foreign policy making, to support the work of the UN Commission on the Status of Women and the UN Decade for Women activities and to increase its support for development programs, international human rights treaties and conventions, peace and disarmament and international education, as they all affected women.[109]

The National Advisory Committee on Women

Following the Houston conference, feminist women working in the Carter Administration conferred with National Commission members in order to develop strategies to implement the National Plan of Action for Women after the Commission was dissolved on March 31, 1978.[110] The wide ranging National Plan called for legal and social action to address key issues that perpetuated American women's unequal status. These included widespread violence against women, economic discrimination against women, under-researched and under-funded programs focused on women's health issues, advancing civil rights for women of color and lesbians, unequal educational opportunities for women and girls and political under-representation of women.[111]

Following the suggestions of liberal feminists working inside his administration, in April 1978 President Carter established a presidential National Advisory Committee on Women (NACW) with Executive Order 12050.[112] The NACW was directed to advise the White House "on a regular basis" regarding "initiatives needed to promote full equality for American women" addressed in the National Plan of Action through March 1, 1980. Executive Order 12050 also established an Interdepartmental Task Force of cabinet agency representatives who were responsible for eliminating government policies and practices that discriminated against women within their agencies' purview and for consulting regularly with the NACW.[113] In June 1978, the president appointed Bella Abzug and Carmen Delgado Votaw as co-chairs of the NACW to provide leadership for forty presidentially-appointed Committee members.[114] Additionally, a continuing committee of liberal feminist NGO activists who had worked with the National Commission to organize the National Women's Conference in Houston provided nongovernmental advice and support to the official NACW, with Bella Abzug's strong support and encouragement.[115]

Under Abzug's leadership the NACW pushed for federal government action on a broad range of domestic policy issues that affected women's status. These included women's job rights, economic rights, and educational equality, protecting women's legal rights to abortion and promoting passage of the ERA. However, when Abzug and NACW members publicly criticized the Carter Administration's anti-inflation policies that disproportionately penalized Americans living on low-incomes, many of them women and their families, President Carter fired Abzug from the co-chair position.[116] This incident provided an illuminating lesson regarding the limits to freedom of expression for all feminists who sought to work within the state system. As the consummate government insider and pragmatist Catherine East explained:

> Well, Bella Abzug was a fool and should have known better. An advisory group like that, the kind I worked for, you make your impact by providing information and recommendations to the groups that can lobby, the women's organizations. You can't criticize the president or cabinet officers. We never did that at the Citizen's Advisory Council. We made recommendations that would have required changes in their policies. We never attacked the president or the secretary of labor, or anyone else who was responsible for those policies. Never did it privately or publicly. When you're appointed by the president, and Bella was, and the others, you can't go around attacking him. She asked to be fired.[117]

Following Abzug's firing, the Carter Administration's previously friendly relations with liberal feminists cooled considerably. Reacting to President Carter's "unceremonious sacking" of Bella Abzug, NACW co-chair Carmen Votaw and twenty-three of its members resigned from the Advisory Committee.[118] In May 1979 President Carter appointed Lynda Johnson Robb as the new chair of the NACW. However, in the view of Abzug and her supporters, the Committee became "more of a President's committee representing the President's view to the public. ... Before, it was a committee of women leaders, who represented the views of their constituents to the administration."[119]

Liberal feminists were deeply disappointed with the Carter Administration because it had seemed to promise support liberal feminist initiatives both at home and abroad.[120] For example, President Carter prided himself on bringing human rights' and women's rights' considerations into the conduct of U.S. foreign policy. Carter publicly denounced South Africa's apartheid policy, and his secretary of state, Cyrus Vance, had initiated a practice of including specific reports on women's legal status and women's participation in government and society in the annual Human Rights Country Reports that U.S. embassies abroad were required to file, with the intent to collect data on women's rights globally.[121]

Nonetheless, radical feminists such as Andrea Dworkin held no illusions that President Carter had ever seriously considered women's human rights when formulating government policy. Dworkin penned a scathing critique of liberal President Carter's hypocrisy after his state visit to Saudi Arabia in January 1978. The press covering the trip noted that Saudi Arabia "enchanted" President Carter. Dworkin noted, "I remember that Mrs. Carter used the back door. I remember that the use of contraceptives in Saudi Arabia is a capital crime. I remember that in Saudi Arabia, women are a despised and imprisoned caste, denied all civil rights, sold into marriage, imprisoned as sexual and domestic servants in harems. I remember that in Saudi Arabia women are forced to breed babies, who had better be boys, until they die." President Carter made "impassioned statements on the importance of human rights elsewhere," yet in the United States, Dworkin asserted that women's human rights were compromised on a daily basis. American women were not guaranteed equal rights in the constitution. Domestic violence against women had reached epidemic proportions. Congress had attached the "Hyde Amendment" to the 1976 Health and Human Services appropriations bill that banned federal government funding of abortions for American women on welfare, even when pregnancy threatened their lives. Dworkin asked key questions of the Carter Administration that feminists would continue to ask of the subsequent Reagan, Bush and Clinton Administrations, as well: "Do women matter or not? Is there a single standard of human rights that includes women or not?"[122]

The Mid-Decade Conference on Women

In spite of strained relations with the Carter Administration, liberal feminists on the Continuing Committee of NGOs that had helped to plan the National Women's Conference in Houston kept their focus on the upcoming UN Decade for Women conference to be held in Copenhagen in 1980. The NGO Continuing Committee lobbied the State Department to include feminist women on the official U.S. conference delegation and to consult with NGOs when drafting U.S. gender policy positions.[123] By mid-1979, the State Department had established a conference delegation secretariat and dedicated $200,000 in conference funding, doubling the amount the government had allocated to the IWY Conference delegation.[124] However, global politics challenged U.S. foreign policy, shook-up the ranks of the State Department leadership and negatively affected U.S. participation at the Copenhagen women's conference.

U.S. Middle Eastern policy faced several challenges in 1979, including ongoing disputes with Palestinians who denounced U.S. support for Israel and new confrontations with militant Islamists in Iran. Although the Carter Administration asserted that human rights were a U.S. foreign policy priority, a longtime regional ally, Mohammad Reza Shah Pahlavi who was brought to power through a CIA-sponsored coup, had governed Iran under strict authoritarian rule since 1953. The Shah had imprisoned, tortured and executed his political rivals on the communist-affiliated left wing and on the fundamentalist Islamic right wing throughout the decades of the 1950s, 1960s and 1970s. By January 1979, widespread opposition to the Shah turned into revolution that forced the Shah and his family to flee the country. The Shah's successor, the Islamist cleric Ayatollah Khomeini, established the Islamic Republic of Iran in April. Over fierce Iranian objections, President Carter allowed the exiled Shah to enter the United States for medical treatment in October 1979. Following an anti-American outcry, radical Islamist students stormed the U.S. Embassy in Teheran, took fifty-two Americans hostage and held them captive until Carter left office in January 1981.

The long hostage crisis exposed deep divisions within the Carter Administration regarding the U.S. government's response. Secretary of State Cyrus Vance opposed a military operation to recapture the embassy and free the hostages. Nonetheless, Operation Eagle Claw was launched over Vance's objections in April 1980. The operation failed completely when several of the rescue helicopters were damaged in a sandstorm, the mission was aborted and two of the retreating helicopters crashed into a U.S. transport aircraft. Vance resigned his post and President Carter appointed Senator Edmund Muskie as secretary of state.

The UN women's conference, held July 1980, took place amidst this political debacle in the Middle East. At the same time, the Group of 77 non-aligned nations launched renewed attacks on Western capitalist trade and aid policies. Expecting that attacks on U.S. foreign policies on all these fronts would dominate intergovernmental debates at the UN women's conference, Congress pressured Secretary Muskie to instruct the U.S. conference delegation to oppose any "politicized resolutions" and to keep focused on "women's issues," that is, on inequalities between men and women within individual countries, and not on global inequalities.[125] Although the U.S. delegation that included liberal feminist NGO representatives may have tried to comply with congressional advice, the UN women's conference debates focused on contentious geopolitical conflicts of the day.[126]

In part, the UN mid-decade women's conference's focus on geopolitics can be ascribed to its general secretary, Lucille Mair, who was in charge of organizing the UN conference secretariat and drafting the conference documents in consultation with world governments and international NGOs. Mair was from Jamaica, a developing nation that had struggled with the burdens of high international debts and severe poverty, all legacies of its former colonial status. Mair could not ignore global inequalities and the "violence" that Western economic prescriptions for development had inflicted on men and women in Third World nations. She encouraged widespread participation among UN member governments as well as from the Palestinian Liberation Organization (PLO), the anti-apartheid African National Congress (ANC) and the Pan-African Congress. Developing nations and these various opposition movements all criticized the Western-dominated international order in UN conference preparatory meetings and at the mid-decade conference and in NGO forums.[127]

As the women's conference convened in Copenhagen, controversies erupted when Egyptian First Lady Jehan Sadat rose to speak at the general assembly of government delegates. Egypt had recognized Israel's right to exist, and delegates from many Arab nations, the Soviet Union, Eastern European socialist states and the ANC walked out of the assembly in protest as a sign of solidarity with the PLO. Moreover, the official mid-decade conference document, the Copenhagen Program of Action, formally recognized the PLO as a legitimate representative government of the Palestinian occupied territories and defined Zionism as racism. As a result of the inclusion of these controversial clauses, the United States, Israel and several Western allies refused to sign the conference Program of Action.[128]

As these controversies unfurled, USAID and its Women in Development office were making some efforts to address the needs of global women living in Third World nations. USAID spent nearly $100,000 to bring women from developing countries to the Copenhagen conference and to the parallel NGO forum.[129] Although the U.S.

government refused to sign the conference Program of Action, WID director Arvonne Fraser strongly supported the program planks that called for global women's formal and informal economic participation and access to education and other resources that empowered women.[130] Fraser had worked closely with the Development Assistance Committee (DAC) of the European Organization for Economic Cooperation of aid-donor nations during the mid-decade conference preparatory meetings, and she asserted that the DAC/WID coalition had "inserted language in almost every section of the Program of Action":

> that explained, amplified, or instructed governments about the goals of the women in development movement. We also inserted language about the importance of women's organizations in assisting development efforts. In various paragraphs it was stated that NGOs could aid governments by investigating the problems of different groups of women, by promoting attitudinal change and public acceptance of family planning, and by explaining government policies as well as international standards and UN programs for improving women's situation. Inserting this and much more language into the document couldn't have been done without our DAC/WID network.[131]

Moreover in December 1980, President Jimmy Carter signed the landmark UN Convention on the Elimination of All Forms of Discrimination Against Women (CEDAW) that was presented to world governments at the UN mid-decade women's conference. The fact that President Carter signed the international women's rights treaty was important to feminists worldwide—even though the U.S. Senate has never ratified it. The United States' failure to ratify CEDAW will be discussed further in upcoming chapters focused on global gender policy developments during the Clinton Administration's tenure in office.

American Feminists and the Reagan Administration

Democratic Party President Jimmy Carter left office in January 1981 with a mixed record of support for feminist issues. However, feminists considered the election of Carter's successor, Republican Ronald Reagan, as the beginning of a decidedly "anti-feminist" era in U.S. politics.[132] Feminist influence on government policy dropped precipitously as the President's National Advisory Committee on Women, the Interdepartmental Task Force of Cabinet Agency representatives and the long-running Citizen's Advisory Council on Women all dissolved when the executive orders that established them expired in December 1980.

Liberal feminist Arvonne Fraser, a political appointee, was replaced at USAID/WID when Reagan took office in 1981.

Ronald Reagan swept into office as the result of a successful campaign run by the neo-conservative/ New Religious Right coalition that maintained its political dominance throughout the 1980s. Throughout the "decade of destiny," Religious Right Christian fundamentalist evangelists pressed their congregations to take their moral values with them to the voting booths.[133] Religious Right leaders promoted neo-conservative Republican Party politicians like Ronald Reagan who opposed abortion rights, gay rights, the teaching of sex education in schools and liberal laws regarding divorce and pornography, and who supported large military budgets to maintain America's strength in what they believed to be a threatening world system. Throughout his two terms in office, from 1981 to 1989, President Reagan consistently expressed verbal support for the Religious Right's moralistic "pro-family" social reform agenda and he acted on the economic and foreign policy agendas that his neo-conservative supporters advocated.

Liberal and radical feminists alike denounced the Reagan Administration's economic attacks on "feminist interests." These critics linked the increasing "feminization of poverty" to the administration's neoliberal economic policies that privatized previously state-run services and cut social spending while increasing military spending.[134] The Continuing Committee of NGOs that had participated in the National Women's Conference issued a "Statement of Concern" in 1982 cataloging the social programs that had already been decimated. They decried national budget cuts that the Reagan Administration called on Congress to enact: "nearly $1 billion cut in Aid to Families with Dependent Children, $2 billion cut in Medicaid funding, $3.8 billion cut in job training funds, closing of child care centers serving low income women, two-thirds of the units of subsidized housing (cut 33 percent and rents raised) are women-headed families, 69 percent of food stamp recipients (cut $2.4 billion) are women, and practically all of the clients of family planning services (cut 25 percent) are women. ..." And the list went on. The feminist NGOs charged that, "Rather than a reduction in military spending and foreign military sales called for in our resolution, we witness the most exorbitant military budget in our nation's history. Rather than taking the lead in urging all nuclear powers to start phasing out their nuclear arsenals, the U.S. is escalating weapons development and deployment in unprecedented degree."[135]

During the 1980s the pro-ERA campaign also suffered serious setbacks when state ratifications stalled and the Republican Party, shifting to the right ideologically, removed support for the ERA from its national party platform.[136] American and global feminists alike condemned the World Bank's and the International Monetary Fund's structural adjustment policies that the Reagan Administration promoted throughout the decade. These global funders forced developing nations that received Western economic aid and loans to reduce foreign trade barriers, lift government restrictions on private investment and cut social spending—all policies that enriched a few government leaders but kept the majority of Third World populations living in poverty.[137]

The global rise in religious fundamentalism, paralleling the rise of the Christian fundamentalist New Religious Right in the United States, also eroded women's reproductive rights worldwide during the 1980s. The Religious Right's influence was revealed when the Reagan Administration's delegation to the 1984 UN-sponsored World Conference on Population held in Mexico City introduced the United States' new global population policy, that was characterized as the "global gag rule" by its critics. This Reagan Administration policy reversed previous U.S. population policy established in the 1970s and restricted the dissemination of information regarding family planning (i.e. condoms or other contraceptives) or information about abortion services by any foreign agency that accepted U.S. economic aid. The Reagan Administration USAID also cut off aid to all NGOs and foreign government agencies that performed abortion services, even if USAID funds were not used for these purposes.

All these anti-feminist developments taking place during the 1980s threatened global populations of women. At the same time, there were growing numbers of "educated, employed, mobile and politically conscious women around the world."[138] Consequently, new global feminist coalitions formed that included U.S. women's NGOs and global women's NGOs located in developing countries. These coalitions linked women living in the global North with women living in the global South and energized feminist activism surrounding the final UN Decade for Women conference held in Nairobi, Kenya in 1985.[139]

A new "reproductive rights" movement, for example, coalesced in the mid-1980s and brought together feminist activists from the global North and South, along with women's health activists, to devise new "feminist principles of reproductive rights." These principles emphasized expanding the customarily-narrow government policy debates about family planning or "birth limitation" to address "women's health" more holistically. Feminist reproductive rights advocates called for women's universal access to legal and safe abortion services, women's rights "to lead self-determined sexual lives, free of the fear of pregnancy, cultural stigma, or disease" and "neutral" government population policies, whereby women were able to make the decisions about their fertility, rather than allowing governments to promote "pro-natalist" or "anti-natalist" policy agendas.[140] Global feminist coalitions, such as the feminist reproductive rights movement, provided progressive activist space for American women whose status in the United States seemed to be eroding during the 1980s.

Global Feminist Coalitions Emerge at the Nairobi Conference

Government delegations at the last UN Decade for Women conference held in 1985, including the U.S. delegation led by Ronald Reagan's daughter Maureen (who also led the U.S. delegation to the UN Commission on the Status of Women at the time), adopted by consensus the women's conference treaty: the "Forward Looking Strategies for the Advancement of Women to the Year 2000" (FLS). The FLS recognized the need for the "empowerment of women through participation in decision making in all areas" in order to progress toward gender equality.[141] As at previous UN conferences, geopolitical conflicts of the day permeated the government debates and NGO forum activities in Nairobi, but the goal to move forward on global feminist issues prevailed among the women in attendance.[142] A "critical mass" of the record numbers of 14,000 women who attended the NGO forum had decided "that they could be feminists and still disagree on certain issues" according to Arvonne Fraser who represented a new-formed NGO, the International Women's Rights Action Watch, in Nairobi .[143]

As the UN Decade for Women ended, the global feminist movement had entered "a new stage in our understandings about the struggle for social transformation," according to Nilufer Cagatay, Caren Gowan and Aida Santiago, who assessed the meaning of the Nairobi NGO forum and the outcomes of the UN Decade for Women. These scholars asserted that "Women have only recently begun to identify and discuss ways to tackle the problems that are the product of complex historical processes," and to devise ways to achieve a "fundamental restructuring of the economic and social order, one that does not reproduce the hierarchies under which we presently live." In order to achieve that goal, women needed *"to develop more concrete and powerful strategies at the local, regional, and global levels; to strengthen our links and networks to be supportive of each other's struggles; and to be in positions to ensure that the implementation of our visions have a longer lasting impact."*[144] [Emphasis added]

Women and U.S. Foreign Policy Making in the 1980s

American liberal feminists interpreted this prescription to mean that more feminist women were needed in positions of power within U.S. government, especially in those offices that devised and implemented foreign policy. In 1982, Reagan's feminist critics noted that in regard to appointed positions, the administration's record was particularly poor in terms of representation for women: "The only bright spot in the administration's record in respect to women has been the appointment of Sandra Day O'Connor to the Supreme Court. ... Only 44 of the [administration's] 398 top level appointments have gone to women. There are no women cabinet officers."[145]

Jeane Kirkpatrick, appointed as U.S. ambassador to the United Nations from 1981 to 1985, was the most visible female member of the Reagan foreign policy making team, but she was not a feminist.[146] According to Judith Ewell who compiled a biographical profile of Kirkpatrick, "Neither Kirkpatrick nor her critics would claim that she brought a uniquely female perspective to U.S. foreign policy." Nor did she transform Reagan's neo-conservative and adamantly anti-communist foreign policy because she agreed with its premises and supported it with "aggressive rhetoric." Moreover, Jeane Kirkpatrick did not "pull much weight within the Cabinet or National Security Council in day-to-day decision-making on specific issues." Because she was "not one of the boys" and was abrasive rather than diplomatic in her personal style, she never established influence among foreign government representatives in the United Nations, in formal or informal meetings.[147] As historian Joan Hoff Wilson summed up the feminist lesson to be learned from Kirkpatrick's example, "In the final analysis ... until there is a generation of women foreign policy formulators who are feminists, the diplomacy of the United States will not fundamentally change."[148]

Bella Abzug concurred. She believed that feminist women brought different perspectives to all policy issues, raised women's issues as policy priorities and acted differently from men who held elected office or served as government appointees.[149] Research conducted by political scientists in the 1980s regarding gender and political behavior in state legislatures confirmed Abzug's convictions.[150] In May 1987 Abzug had formed the Women's Foreign Policy Council (WFPC). She also compiled the Council's directory that included biographies of 275 American women with foreign policy experience in order to substantiate her claims that many American women had the requisite credentials to contribute to foreign policy making and that the all-male foreign policy making establishment was failing the nation. Indeed, as Congress investigated the

Iran-Contra affair following the discovery that the Reagan Administration had covertly aided anti-communist paramilitary squads in Nicaragua with funds from illegal arms sales to the Islamist regime in Iran, Abzug called attention to the fact that women were not involved in the scandal, other than the secretary to National Security Council staffer and Marine Corps Colonel Oliver North, Fawn Hall, "who shredded and regretted and finally told." Abzug noted, "There isn't even one woman from Congress or the Senate sitting in on this hearing—and this is 1987."[151]

By November 1987, on the tenth anniversary of the National Women's Conference, Bella Abzug, members of the National Women's Conference Continuing Committee and the Women's Foreign Policy Council hosted informal hearings in Washington DC. They invited members of the House Committee on Foreign Affairs to listen to "women leaders who are experts in their respective fields," who shared their views on "the United Nations, arms control and disarmament, economic and family planning needs, and human rights." Their goal: to draw attention to "the almost total absence of women from any governmental role in formulating and conducting our foreign policy. ... We know there are only 2 women in the U.S. Senate and only 23 in the House of Representatives. Within the State Department, where knowledgeable women abound in the middle ranks, as of 1986, white females made up only 3.6 percent of senior level foreign service officers and career candidates."[152]

Abzug had formed the Women's Foreign Policy Council to address the lack of women involved in foreign policy making, which she identified as a major problem. In Abzug's view, women added different values and perspectives to global relationships. Maryland Senator Barbara Mikulski who served on the Senate Foreign Operations Subcommittee proved Abzug's point when she recounted her struggles to allocate $219,000 to fund UNIFEM, the UN Development Fund for Women. Senator Mikulski recalled "The [Reagan] administration came in and didn't ask for one nickel, and I had to arm twist, I had to badger, and I had to speak up to get a lousy $219,000 for UNIFEM--$219,000 and they said they couldn't afford it in our UN funding. I show you that because in the whole big picture, what was $219,000? But for UNIFEM, that was life and death."[153] In this instance, as in other efforts to support the UN Population Fund or UNICEF, women's presence made a difference in defining foreign aid priorities.

Abzug coordinated a Women's Foreign Policy Council campaign that challenged the Reagan Administration's conduct of international relations and the unprecedented increase in U.S. military spending. Throughout the 1980s, U.S. foreign aid budgets had focused on increased military spending rather than on economic development, and the Defense Department budget nearly doubled between 1981 and 1984. Congress revived the MX missile and B-1 Bomber weapons programs that the Carter Administration had cancelled. Congress also funded other nuclear weapons programs as well as the Reagan Administration's Strategic Defense Initiative, estimated to cost trillions of dollars, to build space stations to defend against nuclear missiles launched by the Soviet Union. Thomas Ferguson and Joel Rogers, authors of *Right Turn: The Decline of the Democrats and the Future of American Politics,* documented the social spending cuts that Congress also enacted as a consequence of adopting the Reagan Administration's military spending priorities:

> Overall, by [Fiscal Year] 1985 the various Reagan budget cuts in social programs reduced social spending by about 10 percent, below the levels projected under prior policy (roughly half of what the administration initially sought); aggregate cuts on the nonmilitary side of the budget totaled about $175 billion over 1982-85. Especially given the emphasis on cuts in low-income programs (which, while accounting for only 10 percent of the budget, sustained one-third of all spending cuts during Reagan's first term), their impact was profoundly regressive. Approximately half the benefit reductions achieved during the administration's first three years fell on households with annual incomes of less than $10,000; approximately 70 percent fell on households making less than $20,000. Households with incomes in excess of $80,000 carried only 1 percent of the burden. …
>
> By the end of Reagan's first term, U.S. income distribution was more unequal than at any time since 1947, the year the Census Bureau first began collecting data on the subject. … On any reasonable measure … poverty increased dramatically.[154]

Despite the significant hardships that Americans who struggled to keep above the poverty line experienced, the Reagan Administration's emphasis on military spending increased pressure on the Soviet Union's leadership to negotiate their way out of global commitments to Cold War allies, and to formalize treaties with the U.S. government to limit and eventually ban Intermediate-Range Nuclear Forces missiles. Mikhail Gorbachev, selected as the Soviet Communist Party General Secretary in 1985, engaged in domestic reforms to revitalize the failing Soviet economy, a restructuring policy known as *perestroika*. He encouraged more openness, or *glasnost*, between the communist party and the Soviet people who were allowed more personal freedoms than any time in their previous history. Additionally, Gorbachev established a policy of international engagement with the United States and the Western democracies based on "New Thinking." In 1988, Soviet troops withdrew from their long-running military operations that propped up an unpopular socialist government in Afghanistan and Gorbachev announced that the Soviet Union would no longer sustain socialist party regimes in Eastern European states. Changes in Soviet foreign policy opened the way for popular uprisings that swept through Eastern Europe in 1989, and those uprisings marked the end of the Cold War world order.

Bella Abzug wrote to her supporters among the Women's Foreign Policy Council as the Reagan presidency ended, "The American counterpart of '*perestroika*' should call for a restructuring of our foreign policy process to include the views, needs, and participation of women and other groups to redefine present concepts of national security, human rights, and development."[155] As it had in Europe, the end of the Cold War opened new possibilities for democratic transformations in U.S. foreign policy and American feminists put forward their proposals for such changes. These feminist proposals had some minimal effects on U.S. foreign policy making during the George Herbert Walker Bush Administration, in office from 1989 to 1993, as chapter three explains.

---

[1]For example, Bordin, Frances Willard: A Biography; Giddings, Ida, A Sword among Lions; Knight, Citizen: Jane Addams and the Struggle for Democracy.

[2]Goldstein, *War and Gender*. Although there has never been a single "feminist theory of war," as Joshua Goldstein has explained, women's peace advocacy is one expression of "difference feminism" that recognizes essentially different masculine (aggressive and prone to violence) and feminine (nurturing and prone to peacemaking) value systems. Conversely, 'liberal feminism,' as Goldstein explains it, historically asserted that women and men are equal in all abilities, including the ability to make war, and that the gendering of war as a male preserve merely reflects and perpetuates male discrimination against women.

[3]Lynch, *Beyond Appeasement*; Reardon, *Women and Peace*; Barbara J. Steinson, "The Mother Half of Humanity: American Women in Peace and Preparedness Movements in World War I," in Berkin and Lovett, eds. *Women, War and Revolution*, pp. 259-84; Garner, *Shaping a Global Women's Agenda*, introduction and chapter 1; Miller, "'Geneva: The Key to Equality'."

[4]The "Joint Standing Committee of Women's International Organizations" was founded in 1925 and renamed the "Liaison Committee of Women's International Organizations" in 1931. Its founding member organizations included: the International Council of Women, the International Women's Suffrage Alliance, the World Young Women's Christian Association, the Women's International League for Peace and Freedom, the International Federation of University Women, the World Union of Women for International Concord, the World's Young Women's Christian Temperance Union, St. Joan's Social and Political Alliance, the International Federation of Women Magistrates

and Members of the Legal Profession, the International Federation of Business and Professional Women, the International Cooperative Women's Guild, and the American National Committee on the Cause and Cure of War.

[5]Kuehl and Dunne, *Keeping the Covenant*. Even though the U.S. government never joined the League of Nations as many American women's organizations had hoped it would, the United States participated in the League's international policymaking, weighing in on such issues as disarmament negotiations and when to enact sanctions and condemn states for violations of national sovereignty and human rights, the formulation of international social policy such as efforts to end trafficking in drugs and human beings, and international labor policy.

[6]Garner, *Shaping a Global Women's Agenda,* Part I; Miller, "'Geneva: The Key to Equality'."

[7]For many reasons, the League of Nations was a weak and fatally flawed global governance body. See: Bendinger, *No Time for Angels*; Noel-Baker, *The First World Disarmament Conference 1932-33*; Walters, *A History of the League of Nations*.

[8]Rupp, *Mobilizing Women for War*.

[9]Garner, *Shaping a Global Women's Agenda,* pp. 111-12, 168. Laville, *Cold War Women.*

[10]Peter Willetts, "Consultative Status for NGOs at the United Nations," in *'The Conscience of the World'*, pp. 37-40.

[11]Good, The Association for Diplomatic Studies and Training Foreign Affairs Oral History Project.

[12]Ruth Frances Woodsmall Papers; High Commissioner for Germany, Women's Affairs Branch Records; Garner, *Shaping a Global Women's Agenda,* pp. 158-78; Laville, *Cold War Women*, pp. 68-95; Gordon, *The Only Woman in the Room*.

[13]Dorothy Kenyon Papers; Weigand and Horowitz, "Dorothy Kenyon."

[14]Marcy, The Association for Diplomatic Studies and Training Foreign Affairs Oral History Project. The USIA oversaw various cultural programs and propaganda outlets such as the Voice of America, U.S. libraries abroad, and the U.S. Information Service. See: "Overview" and "History", United States Information Agency. "Propaganda Cold War," *Encyclopedia of the New America Nation*.

[15]Committee of Correspondence Records, box 4; Marcy, The Association for Diplomatic Studies and Training Foreign Affairs Oral History Project.

[16]Laville, *Cold War Women*, pp. 197-204.

[17]Committee of Correspondence Records, boxes 1 and 4; Laville, *Cold War Women,* 171-96. The Central Intelligence Agency covertly funded the Committee of Correspondence, and when that CIA connection was exposed in 1967, it destroyed the Committee's credibility as a nongovernmental organization, leading to its dissolution in 1969.

[18]"Historical Background," Women Strike for Peace Records.

[19]Jeffreys-Jones, *Changing Differences,* p. 134.

[20]Swerdlow, *Women Strike for Peace,* pp. 86-87; 93-95; 234-35.

[21]Jeffreys-Jones, *Changing Differences,* pp. 135-37.

[22]Ajinkya, "Intersecting Oppressions: Rethinking Women's Movements in the United States," in *Women's Movements in the Global Era,* pp. 420-21.

[23]Duerst-Lahti, "The Government's Role in Building the Women's Movement," p. 256.

[24]Banaszak, *The Women's Movement Inside and Outside the State*, p. 94.

[25]Catherine East, Coordinator Policies and Plans National Commission on the Observance of International Women's Year to F. Ray Marshall, Secretary of Labor, January 28, 1977, Catherine East Papers, (hereafter CE), box 18.

[26]Cally S. Zann, "Catherine East: Gatekeeper of the Women's Movement" (MA Thesis, University of Maryland), May 18, 1987, CE, box 1.

[27]Ibid. and Duerst-Lahti, "The Government's Role in Building the Women's Movement," p. 259.

[28]Banaszak, *The Women's Movement Inside and Outside the State*, 94-98; Duerst-Lahti, "The Government's Role in Building the Women's Movement," pp. 264-65.

[29]Catherine S. East, March 26, 1982, Women in the Federal Government Oral History Project.

[30]"Three Catherines: Veteran Feminists of American Reunion—A Tribute to Catherine East by Gene Boyer," May 26, 1993, Betty Friedan Papers, box 42.

[31]Good, The Association for Diplomatic Studies and Training Foreign Affairs Oral History Project.

[32]Announcement by Secretary of State Henry A. Kissinger, August 14, 1975, National Commission on the Observance of the International Women's Year Records (hereafter NCOIWY), box. 58; Banaszak, *The Women's Movement Inside and Outside the State*, pp. 110-12; Calkin, *Women in the Department of State,* pp. 132-150.

[33]State Department Newsletter: "Looking Back to 1974 and Looking Ahead to 1975", c. December 1974, NCOIWY, box 59.

[34]Plank 15: International Affairs, *The Spirit of Houston: The First National Women's Conference.* In 1977: "… in the State Department as a whole (including both civil service posts at home and Foreign Service posts abroad), only 4.3 percent of senior level and 15.1 percent of mid-level positions are held by women."

[35]Calkin, *Women in the Department of State,* p. 227.

[36]Marcy, The Association for Diplomatic Studies and Training Foreign Affairs Oral History Project.

[37]Ibid.

[38]Ibid.

[39]Arvonne S. Fraser, "Seizing Opportunities: USAID, WID, and CEDAW," in Fraser and Tinker, eds., *Developing Power*, pp. 168-69; Banaszak, *The Women's Movement Inside and Outside the State*, pp. 156-59.

[40]Arvonne S. Fraser, "Seizing Opportunities: USAID, WID, and CEDAW," in Fraser and Tinker, eds., *Developing Power*, pp. 168-69.

[41]Paxton and Hughes, *Women, Politics, and Power*, pp. 194-96.

[42]"Women in Congress: A Changing of the Guard, Traditionalist, Feminists, and the New Face of Women in Congress, 1955-1976."

[43]Press Release, Bella Abzug for Congress, 20th Congressional District, "Abzug Reasserts Commitment to Women's Rights", August 18, 1986, Robin Morgan Papers, (hereafter RM), box S18.

[44]Cook, "Bella Abzug, 1920-1998."

[45]Jeffreys-Jones, *Changing Differences*, pp. 137-47.

[46]"Women in Congress: Bella Savitsky Abzug."

[47]"Providing for a National Women's Conference," *Congressional Record—House*, December 10, 1975, p. H 12195, NCOIWY, box 62.

[48]Levine and Thom, How One Tough Broad from the Bronx, pp. 230-31.

[49]Garner, *Shaping a Global Women's Agenda*, pp. 229-30.

[50]Here, the term 'Third World women' refers to non-white, non-Western women generally living in under-developed countries or to non-white women living in developed countries where they experienced racial discrimination and economic disadvantages.

[51]"Native American Women Denied a Voice at International Women's Year Conference," *AKWESASNE Notes* (early autumn, 1975): 33, IWTC, box 3.

[52]Persinger, "On Stage at Last."

[53]Zinsser, "From Mexico to Copenhagen to Nairobi," pp. 143, 148-49.

[54]Fraser, *The UN Decade for Women.*

[55]State Department Newsletter: "Looking Back to 1974 and Looking Ahead to 1975", c. December 1974, NCOIWY, box 59; *The Year that Became a Decade*, U.S. Center for International Women's Year, December 1975, NCOIWY, box 61.

[56]Hosken, "Win News Editorial: First Issue January 1975."

[57]Marcy, The Association for Diplomatic Studies and Training Foreign Affairs Oral History Project.

[58]William B. Buffum, IO, Carol C. Laise, PA, Department of State, to the Deputy Secretary of State Robert Ingersoll, Subject "Federal Responsibility for International Women's Year," December 13, 1974, NCOIWY, box 62.

[59]Memorandum for the President from Robert B. Ingersoll, Deputy Secretary of State, Subject: "National Observance of International Women's Year," December 18, 1974, NCOIWY, box 62.

[60]"Women in 1974" [Publication of] Citizen's Advisory Council on the Status of Women, Washington DC, Transmitted to the President, May 1975, Mildred Robbins Leet Papers (hereafter MRL), box 3.

[61]Telegram sent to President Gerald Ford by women's NGOs, April 18, 1975, NCOIWY, box 62. These NGOs included (among others): Women's Action Alliance, American Association of University Women, American Federation of State and Municipal Employees Committee on Sex Discrimination, Association of American Colleges Project on the Status and Education of Women, Association of Junior Leagues, Catalyst, Center for the American Woman and Politics, Center for Women Policy Studies, Federation of Organizations of Professional Women, Task Force on IWY Girl Scouts of the USA, League of Women Voters, Ms. Magazine, National Association of Commissions on Women, National Board of the YWCA, National Committee on Household Employment, National Conference of Puerto Rican Women, National Council of Jewish Women, National Council of Negro Women, National Federation of Business and Professional Women's Clubs, National Organization for Women, National Resource Center on Women Offenders, National Women's Political Caucus, United Auto Workers International Workers and Women's Department, Women's Action Alliance, and Women's Equity Action League.

[62]Government Liaison Advisory Committee Meeting Minutes, January 30, 1975; March 19, 1975; May 8, 1975, NCOIWY, box 61; Department of State Memo No. 54 "Mildred Marcy Appointed Coordinator for International Women's Year," February 11, 1975, and State Department Memo No. 190, "International Women's Year Staff Appointments Announced by IWY Coordinator Mildred Marcy," April 10, 1975, CE box 18.

[63]Memo: Mildred Marcy to Ruth Abram, Subject: "Meeting on October 20, 1975 between Ruth Abram, Four Members of the Working Committee of the

National Women's Agenda, and Pam Curtis and Mildred Marcy of the IWY Secretariat," CE, box 22.

[64] Department of State Press Release, "Equal Rights Amendment Adopted as Top Priority of International Women's Year Commission", April 16, 1975, NCOIWY, box 62.

[65]Government Liaison Advisory Committee Meeting Minutes, May 8, 1975, NCOIWY, box 61.

[66]Jill Ruckelshaus, Presiding Officer NCOIWY to Committee Chairs, August 12, 1975, NCOIWY, box 62.

[67]Press Release, Office of Public Information, IWY Commission, Department of State, July 1, 1976, NCOIWY, box 66.

[68]Marcy, The Association for Diplomatic Studies and Training Foreign Affairs Oral History Project.

[69]Senator Charles H. Percy, "Report to the Committee on Government Operations, United States Senate," September 8, 1975, NCOIWY, box 66.

[70]Meeting Minutes: National Commission on the Observance of IWY, August 29, 1975 and Maxine Hitchcock, IWY Secretariat, to Mildred Marcy, IWY Secretariat, September 12, 1975, NCOIWY, box 66; "Transcript of a press briefing by ambassador Barbara M. White, United States Representative for Special Political Affairs at the United Nations Headquarters on the results of the International Women's Year conference in Mexico City," USUN Press Briefing 79, July 14, 1975, and "Eyewitness Report from Mexico City," Jacki Ratner to Ambassador Barbara White, July 23, 1975, Barbara M. White Papers, box 1.

[71]"Report on IWY Interdepartmental Task Force," Maxine Hitchcock, IWY Secretariat, to Mildred Marcy, IWY Secretariat, September 12, 1975; Jill Ruckelshaus, Presiding Officer NCOIWY to President Ford, December 18, 1975; "International Women's Year Activities, The United States of America," May 26, 1976, NCOIWY, box 66; Marcy, The Association for Diplomatic Studies and Training Foreign Affairs Oral History Project.

[72]Isabelle Shelton, "Women Ask for Foreign Policy Role," *The Washington Star* (January 7, 1976), CE, box 22; Final Report "To Form a More Perfect Union... Justice for American Women," Letter of Transmittal from Jill Ruckelshaus, Presiding Officer, to The President, July 1, 1976, p. 97, NCOIWY, box 52.

[73]Marcy, The Association for Diplomatic Studies and Training Foreign Affairs Oral History Project.

[74]Press Release, Department of State, "New Directorate Established for International Women's Programs," June 23, 1976, NCOIWY, box 66.

[75]Ruth Bacon, "Essentials for a Central National Clearinghouse for IWY," October 17, 1975, NCOIWY, box 61.

[76]Ruth Abram to Mildred Marcy, Memorandum on October 20 Meeting, October 31, 1975, and National Women's Agenda Project Women's Organizations to President Gerald Ford, November 11, 1975, CE, box 22. For example, Mildred Marcy and Pam Curtis of the IWY Secretariat met with representatives of the "National Women's Agenda," an organization of NGOs that included disparate groups including: the Association of Women Business Owners; Church Women United; Girls Clubs of America; Leadership Conference of Women Religious; Lesbian Feminist Liberation; National Conference of Puerto Rican Women; National Committee on Household Employment; National Council of Negro Women; National Gay Task Force; National Women's Political

Caucus; UAW Community Action Program; WEAL; YWCA; and Women's Action Alliance, who sought a meeting with President Gerald Ford and hoped to organize a national women's conference led by NGOs, rather than by US government officials.

[77]Sneyd, "New International Economic Order."

[78]Ghodsee, "Revisiting the United Nations Decade for Women," p. 5.

[79]Virginia R. Allan, Margaret E. Galey, and Mildred E. Persinger, "World Conference of the International Women's Year," in *Women, Politics and the United Nations*, pp. 35-9.

[80]Meeting Minutes, National Commission on the Observance of IWY, August 29, 1975, NCOIWY, box 66.

[81]"The Equal Rights Amendment."

[82]The National Organization for Women and ERAmerica, a coalition of 80 other liberal feminist organizations, led pro-ERA activism in the 1970s and 1980s.

[83]Mary L Gant, Missouri State Senate to Secretary of State Henry Kissinger, June 11, 1975, CE, box 22.

[84]Jill Ruckelshaus to Stuart Symington, U.S. Senate, September 3, 1975, CE, box 22.

[85]Roberta W. Francis, "The History behind the Equal Rights Amendment," at "The Equal Rights Amendment."

[86]Speech by Jill Ruckelshaus, National Press Club, Washington DC, "Is the Press Asleep at the Switch?" September 12, 1975, NCOIWY, box 66.

[87]Elizabeth Alexander and Maureen Fiedler, "The Equal Rights Amendment and Abortion: Separate and Distinct" *America* Published by the Jesuits of the United States and Canada, April 12, 1980, CE, box 22.

[88]Briefing Book for U.S. Delegation to [IWY] Conference in Mexico City, "Population, the Status of Women, and the Role of Women in Development", Agenda Items 9, 10, and 11, June 11, 1975, CE, box 22.

[89]"Senate Votes $5 Million for National Women's Conferences," *Women Today* VI, no. 11 (May 24, 1976), NCOIWY, box 59.

[90]Meeting Minutes, August 29, 1975, NCOIWY, box 66.

[91]"House OKs Parleys on Women," *Washington Star* (December 11, 1975), NCOIWY, box 62.

[92]"Providing for a National Women's Conference" *Congressional Record—House*, December 10, 1975, p. H 12195, NCOIWY, box 62.

[93]"'Stop Talking, Start Changing' That's Bias-Fighter's Goal."

[94]*Women's Agenda* 1, no. 1 (February 1976) published by Women's Action Alliance; "The U.S. National Women's Agenda: A Background Paper," c. July 1976, CE, box 22.

[95]"Public Affairs Implications for the Department of State of PL 94-167", May 27, 1976; Maxine Hitchcock, IWY Secretariat, to Mildred Marcy, IWY Secretariat, "Subject: Summary of Discussions on Women's Conferences by NGOs at National Commission Meeting, April 1, 1976" June 22, 1976, NCOIWY, box 66; State Department Press Release PR-23A, December 1976, CE, box 18.

[96]"US Commission on Women Resumes Fight for ERA," *Des Moines Tribune* (September 8, 1976), NCOIWY, box 66; Department of State Briefing Paper [for Carter Transition Team], Mildred Marcy, "National Commission on

the Observance of [IWY] and its Secretariat Staff (D/IWY), c. January 1, 1977, NCOIWY, box 74.

[97]Press Release, Office of the White House Press Secretary, March 28, 1977, NCOIWY, box 61.

[98]State Department Press Release, "Carter Names International Women's Year Commission," March 1977, CE, box 18.

[99]Marlene Peck to President Carter, May 26, 1977, CE, box 18.

[100]Senator Jesse Helms, "Who Really Represents the Views of the Majority of American Women?" *Congressional Record* (Senate), July 21, 1977, p. S 12500, NCOIWY, box 74.

[101]News Release from Senator Jesse Helms, September 7, 1977, CE, box 19.

[102]Bella Abzug Presiding Officer IWY Commission to All State Coordinating Committee Chairs, August 4, 1977, CE, box 18; Ajinkya, "Intersecting Oppressions: Rethinking Women's Movements in the United States," in *Women's Movements in the Global Era,* 428-29. See also NCOIWY, box 64 (entire).

[103]Press Release 103, September 1977, NCOIWY, box 74. According this press release issued by the National Commission, at the Mississippi state conference, "a state whose population is 36.8 percent black, ... will be represented in Houston by an all-white delegation, five of whom are men, whose election is alleged by local authorities to be the result of Klan-like activities."

[104]Dublin, Sklar and Henderson, "How Did the National Women's Conference in Houston in 1977 Shape a Feminist Agenda for the Future?"

[105]Lynne Gallagher Stitt, "Unity in Houston: They Said it couldn't be done," AAUW Journal (January 1978), CE, box 20.

[106]Elizabeth Sullivan "Houston and the Third World" *The Interdependent* [undated newspaper clipping c. November 1977], MRL, box 3.

[107]Summary of Commission Meeting, August 11-12, 1977, International Affairs Committee Report, NCOIWY, box 74; Mildred Persinger, Chair, IWTC to Arvonne Fraser, Women in Development Office, USAID, 27 October 1977, IWTC, Acc. # 91S-88, box 1.

[108]Persinger, "Personal Narrative."

[109]Plank 15: International Affairs, *The Spirit of Houston: The First National Women's Conference,* pp. 63-66.

[110]Lee Novick to Bella Abzug, "Meeting with Administration Women," January 25, 1978, NCOIWY, box 74. Liberal Feminists working in the Carter Administration included Midge Costanza in the White House Public Liaison Office, Barbara Babcock and Pat Wald at the Justice Department, Pat Cloherty at the Small Business Administration, Arvonne Fraser at USAID, Alexis Herman at the Labor Department, Eleanor Norton at the Equal Employment Opportunity Commission, Donna Shalala at Housing and Urban Development, and Sarah Weddington at the U.S. Department of Agriculture.

[111]Dublin, Sklar, and Henderson, "How did the National Women's Conference in Houston Shape a Feminist Agenda for the Future?"

[112]Memorandum for the President from Midge Costanza, Stu Eisenstat, Bob Lipshutz, "Executive Order Re Advisory National Committee for Women," March 24, 1978, CE, box 19.

[113]Executive Order 12050, "Establishing a National Advisory Committee for Women," April 4, 1978, *Federal Register* 43, no. 67, April 6, 1978, CE, box 19.

[114]Office of the White House Press Secretary, Press Release Announcing Membership of the National Advisory Committee on Women, June 20, 1978, CE, box 19.

[115]Continuing Committee of the Conference, Minutes of July 8, 1978 Meeting, CE, box 18.

[116]Letter from National Advisory Committee for Women to President Carter, November 21, 1978, CE, box 20; "What She Deserved," *Richmond Times-Dispatch* (January 22, 1979) and Office of the White House Press Secretary, Press Release, May 9, 1979, CE, box 19; Levine and Thom, *How One Tough Broad from the Bronx,* 207-25; National Advisory Committee for Women, Press Release, January 13, 1979, RM, box S17.

[117]Cally S. Zann, "Catherine East: Gatekeeper of the Women's Movement," CE, box 1.

[118]"Women's Committee Still Fights Aftermath of Abzug Dismissal," *Washington Star*, March 18, 1979, CE, box 18.

[119]"Lynda Bird Robb and the debate over Feminism," *Washington Star,* May 15, 1979, CE, box 19.

[120]Sarah Weddington, "The Record of Jimmy Carter on Women's Issues," October 1979, CE, box 18, explained the administration's record of support for liberal feminist initiatives.

[121]Hosken, "Toward a Definition of Women's Human Rights," pp. 7-8. See: PL 94-161, US Foreign Assistance Act of 1961, as amended, Human Rights and Development Assistance, Section 116, Section 310 Part 1 of the International Development and Food Assistance Act of 1975. In 1975, Congress had directed the State Department to report on the state of human rights in countries that received U.S. foreign aid, and to withhold aid from those countries that violated international human rights' conventions, and the Carter Administration expanded this little-publicized practice to incorporate specific reporting on the condition of women's rights.

[122]Dworkin, "A Feminist Looks at Saudi Arabia, 1978."

[123]The Continuing Committee of the National Women's Conference to Charles William Maynes, Assistant Secretary for International Organizational Affairs, U.S. State Department, Re: Mid-Decade Conference for Women, September 27, 1979, CE, box 18.

[124]Weddington, "The Record of Jimmy Carter on Women's Issues.".

[125]Ghodsee, "Revisiting the United Nations Decade for Women." p. 4.

[126]Continuing Committee of the National Women's Conference, Co-Chairs Anne Turpeau and Sarah Harder to Vivian Derryck, Director, U.S. Secretariat for the World Conference, April 15, 1980, CE, box 18.

[127]Garner, *Shaping a Global Women's Agenda,* 251-52; Peggy Antrobus, "A Caribbean Journey: Defending Feminist Politics," in Fraser and Tinker, eds., *Developing Power,* p. 139.

[128]Garner, *Shaping a Global Women's Agenda*, p. 260; Tinker, "A Feminist View of Copenhagen," p. 534.

[129]Mildred Persinger, Chair, IWTC, to Fran Hosken, WIN, September 22, 1980, IWTC, Acc. # 91S-88, box 1.

[130]Jane S. Jaquette "Crossing the Line: From Academia to the WID Office at USAID," in Fraser and Tinker, eds., *Developing Power*, pp. 197-98.

[131]Arvonne S. Fraser, "Seizing Opportunities: USAID, WID, CEDAW," in Fraser and Tinker, eds., *Developing Power*, p. 171.

[132]Cally S. Zann, "Catherine East: Gatekeeper of the Women's Movement," CE, box 1; The Continuing Committee of the National Women's Conference, to the Communication Network from Sarah Harder and Anne Turpeau [Co Chairs], November 7, 1980, CE, box 18; Good, The Association for Diplomatic Studies and Training Foreign Affairs Oral History Project, Banaszak, *The Women's Movement Inside and Outside the State*,162, citing Sylvia Bashevikin, *Women on the Defensive: Living Through Conservative Times* (Chicago: University of Chicago Press, 1998).

[133]The Reverend Jerry Falwell designated the 1980s the "decade of destiny" in his popular treatise *Listen America!* The following evangelists with popular television ministries participated in national politics throughout the 1980s: Jerry Falwell, Pat Robertson, James Robison, W.A. Criswell, Robert Schuller, Oral Roberts, Jim and Tammy Faye Bakker, and Jimmy Swaggart, among others.

[134]Jeffreys-Jones, *Changing Differences,* p. 154.

[135]"Statement of Concern" National Women's Conference Committee, c. February 1982, Charlotte Bunch Papers (hereafter CB), box 2.

[136]"Notes for Presentation by Mary Crisp [former Co-Chair of the Republican National Committee], IWY Continuing Committee Meeting," February 15, 1981, CE, box 18; Francis, "The History behind the Equal Rights Amendment."

[137]*Markers on the Way: The DAWN Debates on Alternative Development, DAWN's Platform for the Fourth World Conference on Women,* September 1995, IWTC, Acc. #00S-8, box 8.

[138]Moghadam, *Globalizing Women*, pp. 85-88. See also: Jan Jindy Pettman, "Global Politics and Transnational Feminisms" in Ricciutelli, Miles, and McFadden, eds., *Feminist Politics, Activism & Vision*, p. 50.

[139]Here, 'global North' refers to the so-called First World countries with industrialized or post-industrial economies that controlled a disproportionately large share of the world's wealth and provided development aid to disadvantaged nations.

[140]Rosalind P. Petchesky and Jennifer A. Weiner, "Global Feminist Perspectives on Reproductive Rights and Reproductive Health: A Report on the Special Sessions Held at the Fourth International Interdisciplinary Congress on Women", Hunter College, NYC, 3-7 June 1990, CWGL.

[141]Laura Reanda, "The Commission on the Status of Women," in Philip Alston ed., *The United Nations and Human Rights*, p. 298.

[142]Leticia Ramos Shahani, "The UN, Women and Development: The World Conferences on Women" in Fraser and Tinker, eds., *Developing Power,* p. 34.

[143]Fraser, *The UN Decade for Women,* pp. 206 and 210.

[144]Cagatay, Gowen, and Santiago, "The Nairobi Women's Conference," pp. 409-10.

[145]"Statement of Concern," February 1982, CB, box 2.

[146]Jeffreys-Jones, *Changing Differences,* p. 190. Kirkpatrick believed that some right-wing authoritarian regimes were worthy of American support; she defended the whites-only regime in South Africa; and she was a member of the Committee on the Present Danger, a lobby for a stronger national defense.

[147]Judith Ewell, "Barely in the Inner Circle: Jeane Kirkpatrick," in Crapol ed., *Women and American Foreign Policy*, pp. 153-67.

[148]Ibid. Joan Hoff Wilson, "Conclusion: Of Mice and Men," p. 186.

[149]Opening Remarks by Bella Abzug, Informal Congressional Hearing on Women's Perspectives on US Foreign Policy, Nov. 19, 1987, in "Women's Perspectives on U.S. Foreign Policy," Report of A Women's Foreign Policy Council Congressional Hearing, at National Women's Conference, Washington DC, November 19, 1987, to the Committee on Foreign Affairs, US House of Representatives, KT, box 7.

[150]Paxton and Hughes, *Women, Politics and Power,* pp. 192-93, citing research conducted by Beth Reingold and published in *Legislative Studies Quarterly* in 1992, and Sue Thomas in *The Journal of Politics* in 1991.

[151]"The Iran-Contra Hearings: Abzug Bemoans Lack of Women."

[152]"Women's Perspectives on U.S. Foreign Policy," KT, box 7.

[153] Ibid.

[154]Ferguson and Rogers, *Right Turn, The Decline of the Democrats*, pp. 129-130.

[155]Bella Abzug and Mim Kelber, Coordinators, Women's Foreign Policy Council, Announcement of publication and call for coordinated action among groups interested in promoting women's involvement in foreign policymaking, c. May 1988, IWTC, Acc. # 91S-88, box 7.

3

Promoting Global Democracy and Women's Political Power

The end of the Cold War era transformed the bi-polar East-West power structure that had defined international politics since 1945. Cold War allegiances to the global superpowers of the Soviet Union and the United States and deference to their colossal nuclear weapons arsenals broke down among developing nations. New threats to human security emerged. Ever-increasing social and economic inequalities caused violent upheavals in societies around the world. In part, these inequalities resulted from the expansion of a world capitalist market economy driven by neoliberal economic policies that favored the already-wealthy nations and transnational corporate power holders and narrowly restricted the path to development for the majority of the world's population. In some regions of the world, genocidal warfare erupted and destroyed the social and moral order.[1]

These world events reconfigured the global balance of power. The United Nations Organization, formerly split along East-West lines, became a forum for burgeoning new global social movements represented by nongovernmental organizations, as well as for national government members, to respond to world crises. Global social movements grew exponentially during the post-Cold War decade of the 1990s.[2] "Progressive" global social movements promoted peace, workers rights', human rights, environmental protections and women's rights and opposed neoliberal economic policies. "Reactionary" fundamentalist religious movements opposed various consequences of secular modernity. All these movements, and the NGOs that mobilized supporters and represented them, transformed the United Nations' global governance agenda even as they barely affected intergovernmental agreements in regard to military security or global economic policy.[3]

In the United States the end of the Cold War did not bring about immediate changes in the national government. The Republican Party neo-conservative/Religious Right political coalition maintained control over the White House and continued to influence foreign and domestic policy making. Ronald Reagan's vice president throughout the 1980s, George Herbert Walker Bush, was elected president and served from 1989 through 1992. During President Bush's term in office, feminist influence on U.S. policy was limited as it had been during the Reagan era. The global feminist movement, however, gained momentum and wielded substantial influence at the United Nations. American feminists participated actively in UN global policy making forums during these post-Cold War transition years.

American feminists played an important role in the international campaign for women's human rights after 1989. The Center for Women's Global Leadership at Rutgers University, along with other feminist NGOs and female victims of ethnic violence in the Balkans and of gendered violence elsewhere, focused world leaders' attention on previously unacknowledged attacks on women's bodies that violated their human rights. Consequently, the women's human rights campaign began to gain traction at the UN and gained some attention within the legislative branch of the U.S. government.

Also during these early post-Cold War years, American feminists founded the Women's Environment and Development Organization. WEDO enlarged and strengthened role of NGOs generally and women's NGOs in particular at the 1992 UN Conference on the Environment and Development (UNCED) that was held in Rio de Janeiro, Brazil. Although American feminists' influence on the environmental and global gender policies that the Bush Administration supported at UNCED remained negligible, their organizational skills and strategic vision mobilized networks of women's and environmental NGOs at the global meetings in Rio. As a result, American feminists contributed significantly to the rising influence of the global feminist movement within global governance bodies. Moreover, throughout the Bush Administration's tenure in office American feminists were laying the groundwork to expand their role within the American political system when the Democratic Party regained the White House following the 1992 presidential election.

Post-Cold War U.S. Foreign Policy

The George H. W. Bush Administration witnessed the official end of the Cold War era although in January 1989, as President Bush took office, uncertainty reigned and "it was still too early to say that the Cold War was 'really' over."[4] As widespread popular opposition to the Cold War status quo mounted in the Soviet Union in the mid-1980s, the Soviet head of state Mikhail Gorbachev had initiated reforms that responded to fundamental weaknesses in the Soviet Union's socialist economy. Responding to demands for domestic economic relief Gorbachev had recognized that the Soviet Union could not maintain a global military presence in order to sustain communist party governments in its client states. Gorbachev initiated arms reduction agreements with the West and withdrew Soviet troops from a long and unpopular war in Afghanistan. He allowed the Warsaw Pact alliance in Eastern Europe to deteriorate and witnessed the subsequent collapse of communist party rule in Poland, Hungary, East Germany and Czechoslovakia: "by Christmas Day [1989] virtually every Communist state in East Europe had announced plans for free elections by the spring of 1990."[5]

In August 1991 communist party hard-liners in Moscow attempted to turn back the tide that Mikhail Gorbachev had set in motion and launched an anti-reform coup. However, president of the Russian Republic Boris Yeltsin rallied hundreds of thousands of supporters to defend the reform government. When the Red Army refused to suppress the popular demonstrations with force the reactionary coup collapsed. Soon afterward the communist party lost its monopoly control over governing power in the Soviet Union as well. One by one the Soviet Republics claimed their independence and formed a new confederation, the "Commonwealth of Independent States," to replace the party-led Soviet Union.

The speed and scope of all these developments rocked what had for decades appeared to be a static world order. By 1991 the dissolution of the Soviet Union forced the Bush Administration to redefine U.S. national security goals. During the Cold War, U.S. national security depended upon curtailing the Soviet Union's military, political, economic and ideological influence around the world. With the Soviet threat diminished, promoting the growth of democratic governments and civil societies and expanding the world capitalist economy became priority national security interests.[6] Consequently, the rhetoric and substance of U.S. foreign policy was transformed. In general, the U.S. government reenergized the proactive nature of its democracy promotion programs, redefined its long-term foreign aid distributions to Cold War allies as more temporary "assistance" and redirected the lion's share of assistance funds towards its former enemies: the countries of the former Communist Bloc.

During the Bush Administration's tenure in office, U.S. foreign policy supported the "transition" of these Communist Bloc states from communist party-led centralized governments to pluralistic systems where political rivals competed in popular elections and from socialist command economies into the global capitalist market economy. A "transition paradigm" quickly became a "universalist prescription" that guided the Bush Administration State Department and USAID thinking. As former USAID official Thomas Carothers explained the post-Cold War U.S. government stance:

> [I]n the first half of the 1990s … numerous policy makers and aid practitioners reflexively labeled any former authoritarian country that was attempting some political liberalization as a 'transitional country.' Transitional countries were perceived as being on a path towards establishing clearly defined democratic institutions and free market economies. They were being described and evaluated on the basis of the degree of progress made along these lines. The assumption was that all it took was the desire to abandon communist legacies and to embrace new democratic and capitalist ideals. The paradigm postulated a so-called 'snowballing' effect amongst democratizing countries, as a result of which countries could not help but democratize following the examples set by others.[7]

However, the democratic transitions that occurred during the Bush Administration's tenure did not necessarily bring about the expected or desired results such as "economic prosperity," "social justice," and "civil society groups that hold values of pluralism, tolerance, and gender equality."[8] All these laudable transition outcomes generally eluded the New Independent States (NIS) that U.S. policy makers targeted. In part this was due to flaws in the design of USAID programs and distribution of foreign aid monies.

As the Cold War ended, USAID and other Western aid programs distributed benefits unevenly among different segments of global populations. Bush Administration era U.S. foreign aid flowed primarily through the Support for East European Democracy (SEED) Act (1989), and Freedom for Russia and the Emerging Eurasian Democracies and Open Markets (FREEDOM) Support Act (FSA) (1992).[9] The Bush Administration also cultivated U.S. private sector investors that supported the privatization of the centrally-directed economies of the former Communist Bloc.[10] Other areas of the world that were no longer strategically important as they had been during the Cold War era experienced deep cuts in U.S. (and former Soviet Union) foreign aid.[11] Consequently, as UN General Secretary Boutros Boutros-Ghali explained, these regions that lost foreign aid monies "[sank] into economic underdevelopment, or [foundered] in political disorder."[12]

The Latin American region proved to be the one major exception to this generalized global pattern. In Latin America during the 1970s and

1980s, democratic transitions had proceeded throughout the region, albeit not without brutal, bloody battles, widespread torture and other human rights abuses. These transitions occurred even as long-term Cold War era U.S. military interventions and covert operations—including those in El Salvador, Nicaragua, and Panama that occurred during the Reagan Administration's tenure when George Bush served as vice president—had suppressed popular revolutionary movements and propped up authoritarian military regimes. Nonetheless, in spite of U.S. anti-democratic interventions In Latin America, native revolutionary movements—not U.S. foreign aid policy—had sparked democratic transitions. Popular revolutions had forced military dictators to give up their monopolies on ruling power and in some instances installed more representative governments.

The Impact of Democratic Transitions on Global Women

In Latin America, the democratic transitions of the 1970s and 1980s led to more political opportunities for women in the 1990s. Again, these results were not due to targeted USAID policies but were consequences of revolutionary victories over dictatorial military regimes and were testament to Latin American women's creative participation in the radical movements. During the 1970s and 1980s as revolutionaries overthrew authoritarian governments throughout the Latin American region, Latin American women used predominant cultural stereotypes that idealized wives and mothers (*marianismo*) to join the revolutionary movements. Women made the argument that they were compelled to fight against the repressive regimes that had destroyed their families. As the revolutionaries succeeded in overthrowing autocratic rulers popular votes installed more democratic governments. Latin American women, whose revolutionary participation had politicized them, defied cultural gender stereotypes again and entered the political arena. During the 1990s in many of the new democratic states in the region Latin American women fought for and achieved the passage of laws that imposed gender quotas on all political parties,[13] a measure that was adamantly opposed in the U.S. political system. As a consequence of the new national gender quota laws, women's political representation increased in many Latin American governments.[14]

In Eastern Europe and in the former Soviet Union women lost ground in terms of numerical representation in their governments during the early years of the post-Cold War democratic transitions. Throughout the Cold War era communist ideology had decreed women's equality in the public sphere. Consequently, women served in Eastern European and Soviet

Union communist party governments at higher rates of representation than in any other region of the world (although Scandinavian countries matched levels of representation in the Communist Bloc states by the 1980s). However, these numbers did not signal women's political power or social equality. Many women who served in Cold War era communist party governments had been included as "tokens" and their presence served merely to substantiate communist propaganda that gender equality existed. Moreover, many women and many men who served in communist state legislatures acted as "rubber stamps" for the real decision making bodies in their countries, the communist party central committees.[15] Nonetheless, the numbers of Eastern European and Russian women participating in governing bodies did decline in the post-Cold War years. As many political studies now document, "[d]uring the 1990s, women's political representation in the former communist countries plummeted, often dropping from levels around 30% to less than 10%, and sometimes less than 5%."[16]

Bush Administration USAID reports made these same observations in 1991, noting East European and Soviet women's lack of real political power before the fall of communist party governments: "Women were figureheads without a voice. Women in the legislatures were often farmers or workers, loyal Party members selected to serve as support for the claim that women had achieved equality, rather than because they were ranking Party Leaders." USAID reports also documented pervasive cultural gender stereotypes throughout Eastern Europe and Russia that defined post-Cold War politics as "man's business." USAID analysts expressed hopes that even though women's representation in post-communist governments was numerically smaller, "current representation may be a more accurate reflection of women's political role than the artificially high level maintained in the past" and that "the new women now in office are true politicians, willing to speak up and carry an effective vote; they are no longer appointed figureheads."[17] Yet the few women who served in post-communist governments still faced "the prevalence of antifeminist attitudes" that limited "the abilities of women to successfully organize and the ability of female politicians to represent women's interests."[18] In general, men ran the new "democratic" governments that Bush Administration foreign policies and foreign aid supported, and those governments adopted the administration's neoliberal economic development strategies that incorporated their nations into the world capitalist market economy.

Neoliberal Economic Development Strategies Impact Global Women

Beginning during the Carter Administration and accelerating during the Reagan and Bush Administrations the United States and its Western European allies began transforming the global capitalist market economy based on neoliberal philosophy. Neoliberalism promoted balanced government budgets rather than deficit financing, strict credit practices that reduced the amount of money in circulation and curbed social welfare spending, reductions in trade union protections and, as a result, reductions in public and private sector labor costs. Throughout the 1980s the United States and Great Britain adopted these neoliberal "austerity" policies domestically, and the World Bank and the International Monetary Fund imposed these policies on Second and Third World governments that accepted loans and aid money from First World donors. Neoliberal austerity policies especially impacted women who, because of their reproductive roles, were generally more dependent on government social welfare spending than men. The negative consequences of these neoliberal economic policies—shrinking government bureaucracies, reduction in public sector jobs and social services (especially health care and child care), competition for scarce private sector jobs and breakdowns in "law and order" in developing nations—all disadvantaged women more than men as well.[19]

Neoliberal austerity policies resulted in the phenomenon that has been termed "the feminization of poverty," that is, "the growing female share of the population living under the poverty line." The feminization of poverty proceeded even as, simultaneously, the global capitalist workforce employed more women as "cheap labor" than at any time previously in world history. Women worldwide more often than men worked for wages as "part-time," "temporary" or "casual" labor, which allowed global capitalist employers to minimize labor costs and maximize profits. These changes also inspired economists to coin the phrase "the feminization of labor" to describe the transformation of the global labor market in the decades since the 1980s that included reductions in the number of full-time salaried positions with pensions, health and other employment benefits attached to them.[20] As these changes in the global capitalist workforce took place, women continued to serve as the primary (and unpaid) household laborers and care givers for children and the elderly within their families.

In the former Communist Bloc states where the transition from centralized command economies into the global capitalist market economy caused similar developments, the Bush Administration USAID held its own biased view that past communist party-led governments had "forced" women to work and the emerging democratic states would give women the "choice" to work: "Women were thrust into the workforce by the [socialist] political system, rather than forging their own place gradually, by their own choice, as women in the U.S. and Western Europe have done." Regardless of their enforced participation in the workforce during the Cold War era, according to the USAID analysts, women in socialist states had not fared well in job markets, rarely rising to the top positions in the professions. Moreover, women in socialist countries also bore the burdens of childcare and housework. During the post-Cold War transition women in Eastern Europe might choose *not* to work outside the home—at least until they were forced back into the paid work force out of economic necessity. However, "as new opportunities develop … women's sense of disillusionment with the work environment may well change. In the new economic and political context women will gain the right to choose where, when and how they will participate in the newly emerging Eastern European economies; these are choices that were unavailable to them under socialism."[21]

In spite of the Bush Administration's misconceptions in regard to working women's "choice" to work or not, the expanding global capitalist market economy negatively impacted women in all regions of the world who became the "shock absorbers of neoliberal economic policies," in one way or another. [22] At the same time, in the 1980s and 1990s a concurrent global rise in religious fundamentalism that was also responding to the expansion of the global capitalist economy and to the social and political "fallout" associated with modernization added to pressures on global women. Fundamentalist religions worldwide sought to impose strict controls on women's public and private behavior in order "to recuperate traditional norms and codes, including patriarchal laws and [exclusive] family roles for women."[23] Global feminist reactions to all these pressures in the 1990s, according to sociologist Valentine Moghadam, "led to a convergence of feminist perspectives across the globe: for many First World feminists, economic issues and development policy became increasingly important, and for many Third World feminists, increased attention was now directed to women's legal status, autonomy, and rights."[24] According to feminist activist and economist Peggy Antrobus, the world events of the 1980s and 1990s ensured that "women's organizing took place in the context of two contradictory trends: on the one hand, … an increasingly confident global women's movement succeeded to a large extent in advancing policy frameworks in the area of women's rights. At the same time, neo-liberalism and a rising tide of religious fundamentalism worked against these advances."[25]

As many scholars and activists have argued, the expansion of the global capitalist market economy in the neoliberal framework of the 1980s and 1990s disproportionately penalized already-disadvantaged poor women[26] and "the gender as well as class biases of structural adjustment were clear."[27] In the United States, the impact of neoliberal economic policies that the Reagan and Bush Administrations adhered to forced deep cuts in congressional appropriations for USAID. These cuts especially impacted the Women in Development office whose annual operations and programming budget was cut in half during the 1980s.[28] The WID office budget was not restored to its 1980 level of $10 million until the Clinton Administration took office in 1993.[29]

In order to coordinate aid programs with neoliberal economic philosophy, Reagan-Bush era WID programs had focused on "efficiency." WID-funded programs were designed "to ensure that women's [productive] labor is harnessed for national development goals. ... Women [were] seen primarily in terms of their capacity to replace the declining family and social resources brought on by government spending cuts, recessions, and the effects of structural readjustment" in Third World nations.[30] In 1989 a USAID report argued that "gender is an essential and critical variable in the 'development equation'" because women's productive activities contributed to the food supply, to the large informal sector of the economy in developing nations and to the service, farming and manufacturing-for-export labor forces. Moreover, funding women's education "[could] lead to lower fertility, better family health, reduced infant and child mortality, higher formal labor force participation, and greater economic growth."[31] Following the logic of efficiency, USAID funders tended to see women as "investments" rather than as "full human beings."[32] To the extent that global women and girls were seen as investments, educating them and meeting their basic needs made good economic sense. Therefore, the Bush Administration funded a new "Girls and Women's Education Project,"[33] as well as other projects that allowed women to contribute to national development and to simultaneously fulfill their traditional roles. The new projects gave global women access to credit, public services, health care, etc.

The Bush Administration increasingly relied on nongovernmental organizations to design development projects and deliver USAID and WID monies, as the previous Carter and Reagan Administrations had done as well.[34] The U.S. government believed that NGOs, those based in the West and their counterparts in aid-recipient countries, represented "civil society." As such, NGOs were necessary components of democratic societies. Moreover, funding NGOs could be cost effective. NGOs had developed indispensable delivery mechanisms for social services that liberal and socialist governments no longer provided due to national and foreign aid budget cuts. During the Bush Administration liberal feminist NGOs such as the International Center for Research on Women (ICRW) and the NGOs that were members of the Association for Women in Development (AWID) in many cases designed and implemented USAID Women in Development projects.[35] For example, in 1989 USAID funded an ICRW study on the gender impact of agricultural policy reforms in developing countries to determine how reforms affected women's productivity and earnings. USAID also co-sponsored ICRW research on maternal nutrition and health care in developing countries. The ICRW's goal in working with the U.S. government was "to create an environment where 'women in development' ... concerns become 'development' concerns,"[36] although progress toward this gender mainstreaming goal was minimal during the Bush Administration's tenure.

The USAID and Western liberal feminist NGOs may have understood the positive benefits of these trends but Kateryna Pishchikova, who studied post-Cold War USAID policies in the Ukraine, has documented numerous unrecognized drawbacks to the ever-increasing reliance on NGOs to design and deliver foreign aid and development assistance in the 1980s and 1990s. Western-based NGOs, including the American liberal feminist NGOs that created a role for themselves in USAID/WID offices as well as "an opportunity to expand their activities to the 'global scale'," also participated in creating an "assistance discourse" that recognized certain key terms and familiar concepts, and did not recognize unfamiliar others. For example, if aid recipients and NGOs incorporated "gender analyses" into their reports and proposals, or if they designed discrete "projects" that produced "quantifiable results within a short-term framework," USAID and Western donors were more likely to recognize their utility and fund them.[37]

These developments were consequences of reduced USAID budgets but they were also consequences of the U.S. government's and Western NGO's ethnocentricity, as the following anecdote that Pishchikova related illustrates. Pishchikova visited the home of the head of a Ukrainian NGO in Kiev and found a fax machine and a computer that a donor agency supplied. She asserted that the donor agency would have recognized this equipment as "technical assistance" that "promot[ed] democracy in the Ukraine." To the donors, funding these items would have "made sense" as an appropriate expenditure of aid money regardless of any further actions.[38] These types of foreign aid expenditures socialized non-Western organizations and activists into the "assistance industry" so that they learned the "rules of operations for NGOs" and developed a "businesslike professionalism."[39] Moreover, Pishchikova has argued that, in general, the USAID's post-Cold War Women in Development programs did not address the fundamental inequalities embedded in the global capitalist market economic system. Instead, they "targeted" women as "underprivileged and marginalized" members within the system and sought to address only women's underprivileged status vis-à-vis men through various "microcredit, trainings, and educational programs."[40]

Liberal feminists working through U.S.-based NGOs, such as Elise Fiber Smith who worked for Winrock International in Russia and the Ukraine during 1992 and 1993, came to very different conclusions than those Kateryna Pishchikova has identified, regarding the benefits of Western NGOs' participation in various WID projects. Fiber Smith recounted her experiences:

> In 1992 Winrock began a second major initiative called the Global Women's Leadership program when development assistance was extended to Eastern Europe at the end of the Cold War. During the transition era from Soviet domination, women had been particularly negatively affected. … My job in the program was to assess the changing situation of women and the newly emerging independent women's organizations and identify possibilities for collaboration with U.S. organizations.
>
> Russian and Ukrainian women wanted a consortium of equals through peer to peer relationships with U.S. women's groups to obtain information and training in leadership, law, advocacy, and fund-raising. They also wanted access to credit and to entrepreneurial training so they could start small businesses. They did not want charity but rather increased capacity to manage their own organizations using their own strategies. They never had an independent women's movement but were highly educated compared to women in many other countries. Yet like women everywhere, they suffered from serious discrimination in their patriarchal societies. We set up a consortium involving women's groups in the former Soviet Union and U.S. women's groups advocating at USAID and before Congress to provide more resources to support the emerging women's movement in these countries. The consortium gave women's groups in the former Soviet states more visibility, voice, and power and helped in soliciting more resources for the emerging women's movements Returning to the United States, I advocated that women's participation was critical to the development of more democratic societies, free market economies, and most importantly, the long term stability of the two countries.[41]

The stark contrasts between Elise Fiber Smith's and Kateryna Pishchikova's perspectives illuminate some of the disconnects among global feminist women, including those Russian and Ukrainian women that Fiber Smith encountered versus the women Pishchikova interviewed. Operating from a privileged position inside the United States, Fiber Smith believed that it was possible for women to improve their lives within the structure of the existing global capitalist market system; from a less-advantaged position, Pishchikova was skeptical.

Nonetheless, some groups of women in Eastern Europe and the former Soviet Union embraced the aid that Western governments and Western NGOs provided. Kristen Ghodsee has argued that a mood of Western capitalist "triumphalism" ruled at the end of the Cold War—among Western governments, among Western liberal feminist organizations and activists and among some global women who organized NGOs in the former Communist Bloc states. In these cases, "new Western-funded NGOs were staffed by women willing to accept that capitalism was the most efficient way to organize an economy. They focused on giving women access to the new system by promoting female entrepreneurship and teaching women how to be social and economic 'risk takers'." Ghodsee has argued that since the 1990s and into the 2000s fewer global women have challenged the world capitalist market power structure that privileged certain male elites above everyone else. Moreover, recent efforts to mainstream gender into all governing institutions at the national and international levels have not questioned the legitimacy of those institutions as sharply as they should have done.[42] These critiques are considered in the chapters ahead that focus on Clinton Administration's foreign aid policy that in many ways continued to be based on the foundations that USAID and its Women in Development programs and American liberal feminist NGOs established during the George H. W. Bush Administration.

Threats to Human Security and Women's Human Rights Activism

The new world order generated new threats to human security that the Bush Administration did not anticipate and, in some cases, did not respond to in a decisive way. A global redefinition of "human security" that was emerging in the post-Cold War global governance arenas put less emphasis on the military strength and defense capabilities of states and more emphasis on "the rights and well-being of people."[43] However, the Bush Administration may have been slower to focus on intrastate human security issues because a more "traditional" military conflict erupted between states in the Persian Gulf that captured the administration's attention.[44]

In August 1990 Iraq invaded Kuwait in order to control Kuwait's oil resources and, possibly, to establish a staging ground for further advances into Saudi Arabia. President Bush immediately mobilized U.S. air, ground and naval forces in the Persian Gulf region and persuaded twenty-seven other coalition partner-governments at the United Nations to do the same.[45] When trade blockades and other economic sanctions that the UN imposed failed to force Iraq's withdrawal by the pre-determined deadline, January 15, 1991, President Bush launched U.S. air strikes targeting Iraq on January 16. Following the destruction of Iraq's communications networks, U.S. ground troops invaded Iraq in mid-February and crippled the Iraqi Army. By February 27 President Bush declared "victory" in the "liberation" of Kuwait.[46] Iraq was forced to retreat from Kuwait and to pay all costs of war.[47] Following the conclusion of combat, in April 1991 the Bush Administration also persuaded the UN Security Council to pass Resolution 688 demanding that Iraq's leader, Saddam Hussein, end his regime's "repression" of those among the Iraqi people who opposed his regime, especially the Kurds in the North and the Shi'a Muslims in the South. The U.S. air force began armed surveillance flights over Iraqi territory to ensure Hussein's compliance.[48]

At the same time as the Persian Gulf War was underway, in Eastern Europe, Yugoslavia was breaking apart into the separate ethnically-defined states of Slovenia, Croatia, Bosnia-Herzegovina, Montenegro, Macedonia and Serbia. Serbian leader Slobodan Milosevic exploited ethnic hatreds and called for targeted violence and murder on a mass scale of the large population of Muslims living in the region in order to create a "Greater Serbia" by carving territory out of multi-ethnic Bosnia-Herzegovina.[49] Serbian-instigated "ethnic cleansing" operations defined a "new" form of genocidal civil war that threatened global human security and violated universal human rights, but the Bush Administration did not recognize it as such. As Secretary of State James Baker famously argued against calls for U.S. intervention, "We don't have a dog in that fight."[50]

Until mid-1991 the Bush Administration had supported the reunification of Yugoslavia. However, as the regional conflict continued and escalated, in October 1991 the administration changed its policy and called for a ceasefire and diplomatic negotiations between the newly-created states.[51] In April 1992, the U.S. government formally recognized the independence of Bosnia-Herzegovina, Croatia and Slovenia and lifted economic sanctions while maintaining an arms embargo on the region.[52] After that point the Bush Administration tried to "defuse and contain" what it defined as a "blood feud" that "[grew] out of age-old animosities."[53]

In addition to the genocidal massacres of Muslim men that over time came to be recognized as "crimes against humanity" by the world community,[54] the violent attacks on Bosnian Muslims included a weapon of war—rape—that was gendered and directed at women's bodies but was also "intended to humiliate, shame, degrade and terrify an entire population."[55] The rapes of an estimated 20,000 Muslim women in Bosnia by Serbian soldiers were reported at the United Nations and publicized by the mainstream world press and the global feminist media as full-fledged war broke out in 1992.[56] Media coverage garnered widespread sympathy for women that allowed feminists in the former Yugoslavia to raise global consciousness regarding escalating violence toward women, even if that media coverage did not lead to feminist responses:

> For the first time, rape in war found its place on the international agenda and in legal and human rights discourses; it was a crucial moment for feminists to try to make critical interventions into these discourses and to struggle for a feminist reconceptualization of violence against women. ... But soon the media coverage became sensationalist. Graphic depictions of atrocities appeared in the media, exploiting the topic without caring about possible adverse consequences ... showing women on television without protecting their identities and asking them to talk about their horrible experiences.[57]

Nor did the media coverage elicit much more than sympathy from the Bush Administration. As historian William H. Meyer explained:

> Warren Strobel argues convincingly that it was during the summer and fall of 1992, when the war was still fresh and Gutman and others had just exposed the Serbian concentration camps, that the U.S. government faced the greatest pressure to intervene. Administration officials admit that the reports forced the government to respond, but because Bush was dead set on nonintervention, the responses were aimed less at actual events and more at the political problems created by the stories and pictures. Public denunciations of the Serb camps and violence were made and even some minor policy initiatives were pursued to make it appear that the administration was responding appropriately. Bush's call for access to and closure of the camps and increased international humanitarian access to victims in August seems to fit this description. In the end though, Bush did not change his Bosnia policy, even in the face of such intense media-driven public pressure.[58]

The administration was fully informed of the atrocities committed against men and women in Bosnia and made regular reports on these "war crimes" to the United Nations that included testimony about widespread rapes of women.[59] The administration also sent Cyrus Vance as its emissary to the London International Conference on the former Yugoslavia in fall 1992. Although the London conference tried, it failed to negotiate an end to the humanitarian crisis.[60] As George H. W. Bush prepared to leave office in January 1993, he struggled to justify his administration's tentative response to "Serbian aggression":

> Sometimes the decision not to use force—to stay our hand—I can tell you, it's just as difficult as the decision to send our soldiers into battle. The former Yugoslavia—well, it's been such a situation. There are, we all know, important humanitarian and strategic interests at stake there. But up to now, it's not been clear that the application of limited amounts of force by the United States and its traditional friends and allies would have had the desired effect given the nature and complexity of that situation. Our assessment of the situation in the former Yugoslavia could well change if and as the situation changes. The stakes could grow; the conflict could threaten to spread. Indeed, we are constantly reassessing our options and are actively consulting with others about steps that might be taken to contain the fighting, protect the humanitarian effort, and deny Serbia the fruits of aggression.[61]

Did President Bush's confusion signify a failure to imagine a new understanding of human security? At the time, feminists such as Betty Reardon recognized fundamental differences between male and female perceptions of the world. Reardon was convinced that male world leaders were not ready to meet the post-Cold War future:

> Current policy makers do not seem to be able to envision a truly different world, one that is authentically secure, peaceful, and humane. In "The New World Order," they seem to see a future very much the same as the present, with minor adjustments in power arrangements still held in place by force or the threat of force to be applied with the sanction of the United Nations. They seldom grasp the possibilities for alternatives to arms and violence in extreme conflict situations. Women know the world can be very different, and they can and do envision alternative futures in which the peoples of the world can live together so as to enhance the quality of life for all. Women have conceptualized a peaceful world, not as one without conflict, but one without violence. Women's visions of the future involve the achievement of authentic, comprehensive global security.[62]

American Feminists Respond to Global Violence Against Women

As ethnic and gender war raged through Bosnia, feminist activists such as those based at Amnesty International and at the Center for Women's Global Leadership (CWGL) at Rutgers University, also focused government attention on widespread violent acts against women that were framed as violations of "women's human rights." These included domestic violence, trafficking in women, female genital mutilation and other forms of institutionalized, state-led violence against women such as wartime rape. In making their case for a new rights-based understanding of violence against women these activists asserted that historically advocates for "human rights" and advocates for "women's rights" had worked separately, along different tracks within UN agencies and in separate nongovernmental organizations. Feminist activists argued that both men and women were jailed, tortured, subjected to degrading punishments and executed based on their beliefs or origins. These abuses were recognized by the human rights advocates. Yet women, they argued, were also subject to rape, sexual assault and sexual humiliation in defiance of national and international laws and these sex-based crimes, too, were violations of women's human rights and should be so recognized.[63]

Other feminist groups such as the Women's Rights Division of Human Rights Watch that formed in 1990, Equality Now, a consortium of human rights activists and organizations founded in New York in 1992, and established feminist NGOs such as the International Women's Tribune Centre, the World YWCA and many more, all adopted the arguments that violence against women violated existing international human rights treaties.[64] In June 1991, Charlotte Bunch, founding director of the Center for Women's Global Leadership, convened a meeting of global feminists, "twenty-two women policy makers, public officials, activists and scholars," two years in advance of the UN World Conference on Human Rights that was planned to take place in June 1993, to devise strategies to get discussions of violence against women and women's human rights onto the world conference agenda.[65]

As a result of these meetings, on November 25, 1991 women's NGOs launched a global campaign. The "16 Days of Activism against Gender Violence" was conceived of as "a global umbrella for local activities that promote public awareness about gender-based violence as a human rights concern." The "16 Days" campaign became an annual event. In the campaign's founding year, 1991, participating NGOs also launched a global petition appealing to the nations that would be attending the 1993

World Conference on Human Rights to "comprehensively address women's human rights at every level of its proceedings" and to recognize "gender violence, a universal phenomenon which takes many forms across culture, race, and class ... as a violation of human rights requiring immediate action."[66] The first 75,000 signatures on the global petition were presented to the UN Human Rights Center in New York in March 1992. Campaign leaders testified before U.S. Congress and the UN General Assembly and appealed to the U.S. State Department and to the Secretary General of the World Conference on Human Rights.[67]

Social movement theory can be used to explain the rapid rise of the "women's human rights" movement. The United Nations conferences and forums held since the UN Decade for Women provided the "political opportunity structure" for the emergence of a new social movement. The networks of like-minded feminist organizations that formed through personal connections made at these UN forums and sustained by new global communications technology provided the "mobilizing structure" for the movement. Activists such as Charlotte Bunch and her colleagues in feminist NGOs provided rhetorical "frames" to explain that "women's rights were human rights." They also provided the women's human rights movement's "repertoires," such as testimonies, petition campaigns, personal appeals and demonstrations that set "the patterns of strategic participation that movement participants follow."[68]

The women's human rights movement in its earliest stages was made up of mostly middle-class and highly educated women whose organizations were often based in the United States and were funded by foundations based in the global North. As such, they were not descriptively representative of the world's women. Nonetheless, as Valentine Moghadam has pointed out, the status of the movement's elite actors could be used to global feminist advantage: "given that an important objective of these feminist networks is to challenge the ideas, attitudes, policies, and decisions of large sophisticated organizations—including international financial institutions and state agencies—the presence of highly educated women advocates of alternative economics and of women's rights is necessary and effective."[69] The women's human rights movement gained global visibility during the Bush Administration but its impact on U.S. foreign policy did not become significant until the Clinton Administration took office, as upcoming chapters explain.

Feminist Links to the Global Environmental Movement

By the early 1990s a widespread sense that the world was in crisis prevailed. The end of the Cold War and demise of the super powers' global policing unleashed arms trading on a grand scale, spawned massive military spending and led to the outbreak of violent conflicts in all regions of the world. In 1992 it was estimated that "world military spending equaled the combined income of 49 percent of the world's population."[70] Government, World Bank and International Monetary Fund policies diverted funds from social spending and elevated business interests over those of the general populace. Fallout from these policies sparked labor crises as workers lost jobs or were underemployed. Expanding global populations, rising global poverty rates and widespread social disintegration all triggered what were perceived as development and environmental crises. In response, the United Nations sponsored a series of global conferences to deal with the global crises of the post-Cold War world.[71]

Among the first of these global summits, the United Nations Conference on the Environment and Development, held in Rio de Janeiro, Brazil in June 1992 was organized to devise a "sustainable development" plan for the planet and to secure financial commitments from governments and private corporations and investors in order to realize the plan. Sustainable development included measures to protect bio-diversity and fast-disappearing forests, measures to reduce human consumption of natural resources and to reduce human causes of global warming (i.e. the burning of fossil fuels that emitted carbon dioxide and trapped heat in the atmosphere), all secured through legal measures that would go into effect immediately and continue into the long-term future.

At UNCED preparatory meetings held in March 1992, conference General Secretary Maurice Strong sought increased public and private sector contributions to established United Nations' environment and development funds, increased green technology transfers from developed to developing countries and debt reduction for developing countries. He also voiced his strong support for the "important work" that environmental NGOs performed in raising global consciousness regarding the precarious state of the world's ecological systems.[72] Reflecting world governments' recognition of NGOs' critical contributions to global governance, by the 1990s United Nations' standards for accrediting NGOs were relaxed; in addition to accrediting NGOs with international scope and membership, regional and even "grassroots" or community-based NGOs were granted UN "consultative status."[73] Consequently, for the first time at a UN world conference, more than 1400 accredited NGOs attended UNCED and they could enter the government conference negotiation rooms in addition to observing the conference from the galleries or informally lobbying government delegates in the conference hall corridors.[74]

The Bush Administration supported the inclusion of the private business sector in global environmental policy deliberations at UNCED as it consistently promoted "free-market" solutions as the most efficient approach to tackling world problems.[75] But the administration resisted Maurice Strong's other proposals and generally identified "over population" as the root cause of environmental crisis rather than "over consumption" of the world's resources by developed countries.[76] The administration also balked at setting targets and establishing timetables for reductions in greenhouse gas emissions, rejected the premise that Western First World governments should take independent actions or assume sole financial responsibility to address environmental degradation unless developing nations took similar actions. The Administration also opposed uncompensated technology transfers to the underdeveloped world.[77] Finally, the Bush Administration refused to accept Principle 3 of the Rio Declaration that added the "right to development" to the list of internationally-recognized and protected human rights without adding the following reservation: "The United States understands and accepts the thrust of Principle 3 to be that economic development goals and objectives must be pursued in such a way that the development and environmental needs of present and future generations are taken into account. The United States cannot agree to, and would disassociate itself from, any interpretation of Principle 3 that accepts a 'right to development' or otherwise goes beyond that understanding."[78]

These disputes all strained the Bush Administration's relationships with developing nations and with environmental activists and NGOs as they disagreed on fundamental causes and solutions to global environmental challenges. Further adding to the tensions, President Bush delayed his decision to attend the UN conference where he would be among 116 heads of state in attendance, until days before UNCED opened in Rio on June 3. Young activists from around the globe held raucous protests outside the United Nations headquarters in New York City at the March UNCED preparatory meetings. Protesters condemned the Bush Administration for blocking progress on measures to limit consumption among the developed nations, or to slow down global warming, deforestation, or militarization or to address the many violations of the rights of indigenous peoples that they had identified.[79]

Additionally, women were not included in great numbers in the Bush Administration's UNCED delegation. When it became evident early on in the preparatory process that women and their particular gendered environmental concerns would not be well-represented at UNCED, former Congresswoman Bella Abzug and feminist activist and journalist Mim Kelber took action. Abzug and Kelber formed a new NGO, the

Women's Environment and Development Organization in 1990, in order to participate in the various UNCED preparatory meetings hosted by the UN secretariat where global governance agreements including the "Rio Declaration" of principles regarding sustainable development, and the "Agenda 21" action plan to implement environmental protection standards into the 21st century were hammered out. Acting through WEDO, Bella Abzug was a key player in organizing the first World Women's Congress for a Healthy Planet in November 1991. At the congress, global delegates formulated an alternative "women's agenda" that identified and emphasized the gendered impacts of global environmental decline.[80] Abzug also led women's NGOs in an effective Women's Caucus that interjected important elements of the women's agenda into the Rio Declaration and into Agenda 21.[81]

Bella Abzug had long been a vocal feminist proponent of peace and women's involvement in U.S. foreign policy making. In the 1990s, she linked her feminist activism to the global environmental movement. At that time, environmental activists, alarmed at the accelerating pace of environmental degradation and shrinking bio-diversity, had recognized that protecting the environment could only succeed if they countered the capitalist growth-for-profit economic development model with an "earth-friendly" sustainable economic growth model. Abzug recognized fundamental connections between protecting the planet from an array of hazardous and man-made threats and "empowering women," that is, enabling women to play an equitable role with men in determining global development strategies that would sustain and nurture life on earth. Sustainable development was also intrinsically linked to global population policies, which were linked to the feminist reproductive rights movement.

Certainly, there was no single "women's" or "feminist" position on these complex, layered policy issues, but WEDO and an array of other feminist NGOs such as Development Alternatives with Women for a New Era (DAWN) founded in 1984, Women in Development Europe (WIDE) formed in 1985, and the International Women's Health Coalition (IWHC) established in 1984, understood that global governance and state policies on the environment, development, population, human rights and human security all intersected through women's bodies. Reflecting the liberal feminist biases of its leaders Bella Abzug and Mim Kelber, WEDO advocated working from within the United Nations system to reform intergovernmental and state policies by mobilizing extensive global feminist networks that pressured UN agencies and governments to meet women's needs and address women's interests.[82]

In November 1991 WEDO convened a meeting of 1500 feminist activists from over eighty countries in Miami, Florida to ensure that women would play a significant political role at UNCED in Rio in 1992.[83] The UN Environmental Program sponsored the Women's Congress for a Healthy Planet and funded attendance for two hundred global women who had designed successful environmental protection and sustainable development projects in their home communities so that they could share their experiences in Miami. Together, the activists devised their own global development plan, the "Women's Action Agenda 21," in order to introduce women's innovations and the foundational concept of "gender equality" as a necessary component of sustainable development into global policy making at the upcoming UN conference.[84]

Although Abzug was not a member of the official U.S. delegation to UNCED she entered the spotlight at the conference preparatory meetings in New York in March 1992 where she spoke on behalf of populations that the government meetings seemed to ignore or actively suppressed: women, children and indigenous peoples.[85] Subsequently, she became a "senior adviser" to UNCED Secretary General Maurice Strong.[86] Though many found her "abrasive and de-stabilizing,"[87] Abzug's interventions in particular led Norway's delegation to add several amendments regarding necessary consultations with women's NGOs so that their particular gendered expertise on population and sustainable development issues was incorporated into the draft version, and eventually into the final version, of the government conference treaty, Agenda 21.[88] Abzug organized women's NGOs into a caucus at the preparatory meetings and at the UN conference that kept those NGOs well-informed about the evolving treaty language, so they could effectively lobby their governments in support of feminist positions.[89] Bella Abzug also stood out among the 20,000 environmental activists representing 9000 NGOs at the Global Forum that was held in Rio de Janeiro parallel to the UNCED governmental meetings.[90] There, she helped to organize "Planeta Femea," the women's tent at the Rio NGO Global Forum, as well as caucus sessions for women's NGOs.[91]

Some feminist activists have criticized these interventions at UNCED and at subsequent UN conferences held during the 1990s. As WEDO and other feminist NGOs actively sought to enlarge their role at the UN conferences, organizations such as the Committee on Women, Population and the Environment (CWPE), a coalition of feminist activists who came out of the environmental and women's health fields, rejected collaborations with UN agencies or with governments because they believed that those male-led institutions perpetuated global inequalities through their military and neoliberal structural adjustment policies.

CWPE also opposed any state-imposed policies to limit population growth although they supported women's "right" to safe and voluntary birth control and abortion.[92] NGOs such as CWPE recognized dangers in alliances between some environmentalists and feminists, because some environmentalists identified "over-population" as one cause of environmental degradation and seemingly "blamed" women and high fertility rates for global population pressures. Feminist NGOs like CWPE were loath to accept any state-sanctioned form of "family planning" because they identified "economic systems that exploit and misuse nature and people" as the overwhelming cause of the global environmental crisis.[93] Historian Deborah Stienstra has offered the following explanation of the dilemmas that feminists faced throughout the 1990s when deciding whether to employ insider strategies and to work through UN forums to achieve social change:

> Some would argue that these [global conferences] are examples of states co-opting NGOs for their own purposes. … Yet what we have here is more complex. Indeed, the states, through the institution of the United Nations, enabled NGOs to have greater participation than they have had in the past. For many NGOs, this greater participation was equated with more "power" or influence in the process. Not only did they provide significant contributions to the development of the text [of global treaties], thus assisting many states that did not have sufficient resources to do the type of analysis required, but also they came to have a stake in the outcome of the conferences and in the implementation of commitments.[94]

Feminist NGOs' experiences at UNCED demonstrated that in some cases governments were willing to work together with NGOs to establish global norms that mediated some of the most harmful polluting practices of global corporations, and in efforts to diminish global inequalities based on sexist, classist, racist, heterosexist and other dominant power structures. Nonetheless, in the 1990s governments also increasingly worked in tandem with transnational capital and global financial institutions. During the decade it became apparent that "[t]he system of global governance [was] recreated around one comprehensive norm, the liberalization and globalization of economies. In many ways, this norm [came] to replace the 'first principle' or comprehensive norm of military security that guided the international community during the Cold War."[95]

Feminists Look Ahead to a New Administration

The 1992 presidential contest between the Republican Party candidate, President George H.W. Bush, and the Democratic Party candidate, Arkansas Governor Bill Clinton, seemed to present a real choice to liberal feminist women in the United States. The Democratic Party supported women's rights to control their reproductive lives and progressive positions on other social issues; the Republican Party embraced the views of its Religious Right membership, voiced support for "traditional family values," and opposed abortion rights and civil rights for homosexuals.[96] Moreover, in 1991, Republican President George Bush had nominated Clarence Thomas to replace retiring Supreme Court Justice Thurgood Marshall. That nomination touched off a national debate on the pervasiveness of sexual harassment that American working women faced when Thomas's former employee, Anita Hill, came forward to accuse Thomas of bringing inappropriately sexual language and behavior into the workplace. Although the debate exposed a real problem, the U.S. Senate, comprised of ninety-eight men and two women, voted fifty-two to forty-eight to confirm Thomas, with the majority of votes made along partisan lines, most Republicans in favor and most Democrats opposed to confirmation.

For many feminists, the Clarence Thomas confirmation hearings highlighted widespread male ignorance regarding the scope and seriousness of the problem of sexual harassment, as well as American women's general lack of political power. Consequently, feminists mobilized a significant increase in the number of women who voted in 1992, the majority of whom voted for Democratic Party candidates, revealing a measurable "gender gap" among voters. Voters elected twenty-four women candidates to the House of Representatives, five women to the Senate, and Democrats Bill Clinton as president and Tennessee Senator Al Gore as vice president in November 1992, in an election year thereafter heralded at the "Year of the Woman" in U.S. politics.[97]

Bill Clinton and Al Gore were "two white Southern males" and yet "in the [Democratic Party] platform and their speeches, this same team articulated values and policy positions that only twenty years ago were viewed as radical (abortion) or even unthinkable (gay rights), and did so as though they really believed them." [98] In 1992, many liberal feminists believed that:

> The Democratic Party is pluralistic, with multiple power centers which compete for membership support in order to make demands on, as well

> as determine the leaders. When challenged by the social movements of the sixties, it followed its usual strategy of co-opting them into the Democratic coalition—changing the nature of the coalition in the process. These groups in turn were sufficiently well organized and committed to claim hegemony over those issues that were their primary concern. Feminists in particular, though not in isolation, put the "personal" on the political agenda and convinced the Democrats that government had a responsibility for righting the wrongs of private life and balancing the burdens of an inequitable social structure.[99]

With a total of six women serving in the Senate and forty-seven women seated in the House of Representatives, women were represented inside the national legislature in larger numbers than ever before in U.S. history. Liberal feminists expected to exert greater influence on domestic and foreign policy making as the Clinton Administration entered the White House in January 1993.[100]

---

[1]Karns and Mingst, *International Organizations,* pp. 129-30.

[2]Boutros Boutros-Ghali, "Foreward," in Weiss and Gordenker, *NGOs, the UN, and Global Governance*, pp. 7-8; Cohen and Rai, eds., *Global Social Movements,* pp. 7-10; "Development at the Crossroads: Women in the Center, " Alt-WID Resource Center Bulletin, no. 41, August 1995, CWGL, box 5. [Alt-WID was an ad hoc group of women from different development organizations in the USA.]

[3]Jutta Jochim, "Shaping the Human Rights Agenda: The Case of Violence Against Women," and Deborah Stienstra, "Of Roots, Leaves, and Trees: Gender, Social Movements and Global Governance" in Meyer and Prügl, eds., *Gender Politics in Global Governance*, pp. 151 and 270.

[4]Hartmann and Wendzel, *America's Foreign Policy in a Changing World,* p. 315.

[5] Ibid., p. 356.

[6]Baker, "U.S. Foreign Policy Priorities and Fiscal Year 1991 Budget Request."

[7]Pishchikova, Promoting Democracy in Postcommunist Ukraine, p. 40.

[8]Moghadam, *Globalizing Women*, 42-3; See also: Marina Ottaway and Thomas Carothers, "Toward Civil Society Realism" in Ottaway and Carothers, eds. *Funding Virtue*, pp. 293-6.

[9]Pishchikova, Promoting Democracy in Postcommunist Ukraine, pp. 78-9. "According to the cumulative figures for the fiscal years 1992-2009 released by the U.S. Department of State, the U.S. government spent a total of about 30 billion dollars on assistance programs to the twelve countries of the former Soviet Union." See also: Baker, "Efforts to Aid New Independent States at 'Defining Moment in History'"; Baker, "Securing a Democratic Peace."

[10]Armitage, "Achieving National Consensus on the FREEDOM Support Act." See also: Eagleburger, "A Democratic Partnership for the Post Cold War Era."

[11]"Development at the Crossroads: Women in the Center": "With the demise of the former Soviet Union in 1989 many of the political and economic relations

that had dictated the development policy since World War II changed. There was no longer a strategic reason for the West to court and coerce client states in the South. Countries that formerly commanded a geopolitical commitment—such as Somalia, which was critical to U.S. access to the Indian Ocean and the Red Sea—were no longer important. Former clients of the Soviet Union, such as Angola, whose people had been held hostage in a civil war between the Soviet-backed government and rebel forces funded by the United States, were left to carry on their civil war. In the 'new world order' each country would have to compete on its own merits."

[12]Boutros Boutros-Ghali, "Forward" in Weiss and Gordenker, eds. *NGOs, the UN, and Global Governance*, p. 10.

[13]Pande and Ford, "Gender Quotas and Female Leadership: A Review," p. 32. See Table 2: Political quotas. Latin American countries with voluntary political party gender quotas and with legislated gender quotas identified.

[14]Paxton and Hughes, *Women, Politics and Power*, pp. 233-5.

[15]Ibid., p. 225.

[16]Ibid., p. 224, citing Richard E. Matland and Kathleen A. Montgomery, eds. *Women's Access to Political Power in Post-Communist Europe* (Oxford, UK: Oxford University Press, 2003) and Steven Saxonberg, "Women in East European Parliaments," *Journal of Democracy* 11 (2000): 145-58.

[17]"Women in the Newly Emerging Democracies of Eastern Europe, Phase I."

[18]Paxton and Hughes, *Women, Politics and Power,* pp. 226-7.

[19]Hirschmann, "Democracy and Gender: A Practical Guide to USAID Programs."

[20]Moghadam, *Globalizing Women*, pp. 6-7.

[21]"Women in the Newly Emerging Democracies of Eastern Europe, Phase I," pp. i-ii.

[22]Moghadam, *Globalizing Women*, p. 39.

[23]Ibid. p. 7.

[24]Ibid. p. 8.

[25]Antrobus, *The Global Women's Movement*, 99-100. See also: *Markers on the Way: The DAWN Debates on Alternative Development, DAWN's Platform for the Fourth World Conference on Women,* September 1995, IWTC, Acc. #00S-8, box 8.

[26]Anne Sisson Runyan, "Women in the Neoliberal 'Frame'" and Deborah Stienstra, "Of Roots, Leaves, and Trees" in Meyer and Prügl, eds., *Gender Politics in Global Governance*, pp. 210 and 269; Jan Jindy Pettman, "Global Politics and Transnational Feminisms" in Ricciutelli, Miles, and McFadden, eds., *Feminist Politics, Activism & Vision*, pp. 55-6.

[27]Moghadam, *Globalizing Women*, p. 39.

[28]In Fiscal Year 1989, the Women in Development Office (WID) had a budget of $5 million. "AID Program for Integration of Women in Development: Strategies for Access to PPC/WID Assistance."

[29]Rea, The Association for Diplomatic Studies and Training Foreign Affairs Oral History Project.

[30]"Development at the Crossroads: Women at the Center." See also: Pettman, "Global Politics and Transnational Feminisms," in Ricciutelli, Miles, and McFadden, eds., *Feminist Politics, Activism & Vision*, p. 56.

[31]Blumberg, "Making the Case for the Gender Variable: Women and the Wealth and Well-Being of Nations."

[32]Meredith Tax leveled these critiques at World Bank and USAID development programs, focusing on the period from 1985 to 1995. Meredith Tax, *The Power of the Word: Culture, Censorship and Voice* (Women's World Organization for Rights, Literature and Development, 1995), IWTC, Acc. #00S-8, box 2. See also: Rea, The Association for Diplomatic Studies and Training Foreign Affairs Oral History Project. Samuel Rea recalled that the Bush Administration USAID was strongly influenced by a World Bank report and its conclusion written by the Bank's Chief Economist Lawrence Summers that argued "educating girls quite likely yields a higher rate of return than any other investment available in the developing world."

[33]Rea, The Association for Diplomatic Studies and Training Foreign Affairs Oral History Project.

[34]"Interaction Meeting with AID Asia/Near East Bureau, January 30, 1989 on AID/ANE Bureau Initiatives for Implementation of New WID Legislation," Statement by Mildred Robbins Leet, Co-Chair person Interaction Subcommittee WID, MRL, box 3.

[35]"AID Program for Integration of Women in Development: Strategies for Access to PPC/WID Assistance."

[36]International Center for Research on Women, Director's Statement, Annual Report, 1989.

[37]Pishchikova, *Promoting Democracy in Postcommunist Ukraine*, pp. 44-51, 116-18.

[38]Ibid. p. 4.

[39]Ibid. p. 125-6.

[40]Ibid. pp. 98, 107-8.

[41]Elise Fiber Smith, "Women Empowering Women in NGOs," in Fraser and Tinker, eds. *Developing Power,* pp. 257-9. "Winrock International, a nonprofit organization, is a heritage of the philanthropy of Winthrop Rockefeller and other Rockefeller family members. It works worldwide to help the poor and disadvantaged by increasing economic opportunity, sustaining natural resources, and protecting the environment."

[42]Ghodsee, "Revisiting the United Nations Decade for Women," pp. 9-10: "The critique of capitalism has been almost entirely evicted from the global feminist movement as it is currently configured, with Western governments now proposing to "mainstream gender" into the very institutions that the Soviet women and their allies were trying to tear down. Rather than questioning the nature of the system within which both women and men must compete for increasingly 'scarce' resources because wealth has been concentrated in the hands of a few, criminal elites, many (though admittedly not all) Western feminist organizations content themselves with lobbying for equal opportunity and anti-discrimination laws that are almost impossible to enforce."

[43]Jochim, "Shaping the Human Rights Agenda," in Meyer and Prügl, eds., *Gender Politics in Global Governance*, p. 151.

[44]The Persian Gulf War, a 'traditional' state-to-state conflict was also 'non-traditional' in that it was fought with sophisticated military technology that precluded a great deal of ground force battles. And, the U.S. volunteer military included a larger proportion of female soldiers than previous wars that precipitated a national debate regarding appropriate roles for women in the

military. See: Lowry, *The Gulf War Chronicles: A Military History of the First War with Iraq* and Skaine, *Women at War.*

[45]"Gulf Crisis Update."

[46]Bush, "Kuwait is Liberated."

[47]Hartmann and Wendzel, *America's Foreign Policy in a Changing World,* pp. 11-16.

[48]Bush, "No-Fly Zone in Southern Iraq"; Meyer, Security, Economics, and Morality in American Foreign Policy, p. 101.

[49]Hunt, "Muslim Women in the Bosnia Crucible."

[50]Meyer, *Security, Economics and Morality in American Foreign Policy,* pp. 137-8.

[51]Johnson, "U.S. Efforts to Promote a Peaceful Settlement in Yugoslavia."

[52]Baker, "Securing a Democratic Peace."

[53]Bush, "Containing the Crisis in Bosnia and the Former Yugoslavia." See also: Kornblum, "Continued Aggression in Bosnia-Herzegovina"; Shattuck, *Freedom on Fire: Human Rights Wars and America's Response,* p. 119.

[54]Amanpour, "Newseum War Stories: Christianne Amanpour"; Copelon, "Rape and Gender Violence: From Impunity to Accountability in International Law."

[55]Douglas, "What About Bosnia?," p. 10.

[56]"Bosnia: 20,000 Women Raped," p. 5; See also: "An International Appeal: Word Out of Bosnia," p. 2; "Taking Our Lives Into Our Own Hands," Special 50th Issue *The Tribune* (1993), International Women's Tribune Centre Records, IWTC, Acc. # 93S-60, box 2.

[57]Batinic, "Feminism, Nationalism, and War: The 'Yugoslav Case' in Feminist Texts," pp. 8-9.

[58]Meyer, *Security, Economics, and Morality in American Foreign Policy,* p. 336, n. 76. Meyer cites Warren P. Strobel, *Late-Breaking Foreign Policy, The News Media's Influence on Peace Operations* (Washington DC: United States Institute for Peace, 1997), p. 153.

[59]"First U.S. Report on War Crimes in the Former Yugoslavia"; "Third U.S. Report on War Crimes in the Former Yugoslavia."

[60]"Fifth Report on War Crimes in the Former Yugoslavia"; Eagleburger, "The Need to Respond to War Crimes in the Former Yugoslavia."

[61]Bush, "America's Role in the World."

[62]Reardon, *Women and Peace: Feminist Visions of Global Security*, p. 35.

[63]"Prepared Statement of Amnesty International USA, Hearings on Human Rights Abuses Against Women before the Subcommittee on Human Rights and International Organizations, Committee on Foreign Relations, House of Representatives," March 1, 1990, CWGL, box 5.

[64]See for example: *Equality Now 1992-1993 Annual Report.*

[65]"Violence Against Women: Confronting Invisible Barriers to Development" *The Tribune* (June 1991), IWTC, Acc. # 93S-60, box 2.

[66]Charlotte Bunch, "International Networking for Women's Human Rights," in Edwards and Gaventa, eds. *Global Citizen Action,* chapter 16.

[67]"Women's Human Rights, Vienna," *The Tribune* (June 1993), IWTC, Acc. # 93S-60, box 2; Dorothy Thomas, Director Women's Rights Project, Human Rights Watch, to Ambassador Richard Schifter, Assistant Secretary for Human Rights and Humanitarian Affairs, U.S. Department of State, March 13, 1992, Sisterhood Is Global Institute Records, 1963-2005, Duke University (hereafter

SIGI), box CONF 11; Charlotte Bunch, "After Twenty Years We Have Global Recognition" in Lee and Clauson-Wicker, eds., *Voice of Women: Moving Forward with Dignity and Wholeness*, pp. 18-19; Bunch and Frost, "Women's Human Rights: An Introduction," in *International Encyclopedia of Women: Global Women's Issues and Knowledge*. See also: Pettman, "Global Politics and Transnational Feminisms," p. 52 and Brooke A. Ackerly, "Women Human Rights Activists as Political Theorists," pp. 302-3, in Ricciutelli, Miles, and McFadden, eds., *Feminist Politics, Activism & Vision*; Antrobus, *The Global Women's Movement,* pp. 91-3 and 118-19.

[68]Friedman, "Gendering the Agenda," pp. 314-15.

[69]Moghadam, *Globalizing Women*, p. 101.

[70]"Development at the Crossroads: Women at the Center."

[71]Pettman, "Global Politics and Transnational Feminisms," in Ricciutelli, Miles, and McFadden, eds., *Feminist Politics, Activism & Vision*, p. 51.

[72]"Strong Delivers Keynote Address to Plenary, Emphasizes Agenda 21 and Financial Resources."

[73]Preston, "The 1992 Rio Summit and Beyond."

[74]Jochim, "Shaping the Human Rights Agenda," in Meyer and Prügl, eds., *Gender Politics in Global Governance*, p. 151.

[75]"Prep Com Highlights."

[76]Meyer, *Security, Economics and Morality in American Foreign Policy,* p. 283.

[77]Bohlen, "US Prepares for UN Conference on Environment and Development"; Bush, "America's Commitment to the Global Environment"; Fletcher, "Earth Summit Summary: The United Nations Conference on Environment and Development."

[78]Young, "U.S. Delegation Press Briefings."

[79]"Save Earth Summit" [video].

[80]"WEDO, Bella Abzug, 1920-1998." See also: Moghadam, *Globalizing Women*, p. 98; United Nations Environmental Program. Champions of the Earth. "2006 Laureate: Women's Environment & Development Organization."

[81]See for example: Rio Declaration Principle 20: "Women have a vital role in environmental management and development. Their full participation is therefore essential to achieve sustainable development." See also: Stienstra, "Of Roots, Leave, and Trees" in Meyer and Prügl, eds., *Gender Politics in Global Governance*, p. 267; Jack Freeman, "I remember Beijing ... also Rio, Vienna, Copenhagen, Cairo, Istanbul, and much, much more," *The Earth Times* 9, no. 7 (June 5, 2000), Kristen Timothy Papers (hereafter KT), box 9.

[82]Amy J. Higer, "International Women's Activism and the Cairo Conference" in Meyer and Prügl, eds., *Gender Politics in Global Governance*, pp. 130-1.

[83]Cook, "Bella Abzug, 1920-1998."

[84]WEDO Network Profile, IWTC, Acc. #00S-8, box 7; Irene Tinker, "Nongovernmental Organizations: An Alternative Power Base for Women?" in Meyer and Prügl, eds., *Gender Politics in Global Governance*, p. 99.

[85]"PrepCom Highlights."

[86]"About Bella Abzug," (circulated by WEDO during Abzug's campaign for Representative of New York's 8th Congressional District), September 15, 1992, Robin Morgan Papers (hereafter RM), box S18.

[87]Robin Chandler Duke to Robert McNamara, head of World Bank, April 7, 1992, Robin Chandler Duke Papers (hereafter RCD), Accessions 1998-0350 and 1998-0372, box 1.

[88]"A Summary of the Proceedings at the Fourth Session of the UNCED Preparatory Committee."

[89]Anne S. Walker, "The International Women's Tribune Center: Expanding the Struggle for Women's Rights at the UN," in Fraser and Tinker, eds. *Developing Power*, p. 96. See also: Levine and Thom, *Bella Abzug*, pp. 263-6.

[90]Fletcher, "Earth Summit Summary."

[91]Friedman, "Gendering the Agenda," p. 320.

[92]Amy J. Higer, "International Women's Activism" in Meyer and Prügl, eds., *Gender Politics in Global Governance*, p. 130; Committee on Women, Population and the Environment, http://cwpe.org .

[93]Jessica Matthews, "Politically Correct Environmentalists," *Washington Post* (April 12, 1992), RCD, Accessions 1998-0350 and 1998-0372, box 1.

[94]Stienstra, "Of Roots, Leaves, and Trees" in Meyer and Prügl, eds., *Gender Politics in Global Governance*, p. 268.

[95]Ibid. p. 269.

[96]Freeman, "Feminism vs. Family Values."

[97]Malcolm, "The Year of the Women Voter," and Rosenzweig, "An Outline of the Anita Hill-Clarence Thomas Controversy."

[98]Freeman, "Feminism vs. Family Values."

[99]Ibid.

[100]Douglas, "Good Election News for a change, if you aren't a lesbian in Colorado," p. 1.

4

Recognizing Women's Rights

During the Reagan and Bush Republican Administrations (1981 to 1993) American liberal feminist organizations with an international scope of operations had made progress in getting some of the issues that were important to global women onto intergovernmental agendas in United Nations forums. Also due to liberal feminist influence, U.S. development aid discourse and aid distribution to the former Communist Bloc countries and to the developing Third World had begun to change in ways that acknowledged global women's needs. The Reagan/Bush Administrations, however, had not been receptive to liberal feminist advocacy regarding women's human rights or reproductive rights.

When the Clinton Administration entered the White House in 1993 liberal feminists were expecting great changes in their relationship with the federal government and new opportunities to advocate for global women's rights. In many ways their expectations were fulfilled. When the Clinton Administration took office, new post-Cold War global issues came to the forefront of foreign policy making. Both the State Department and USAID underwent significant reorganization. Liberal feminists were again represented among the highest ranks of the administration and First Lady Hillary Clinton began to raise the visibility of "women's issues" in national and international settings. A series of world crises including wars in Bosnia, Somalia and Rwanda had exposed escalating violence and crimes against all humanity and especially against women.

This chapter explains how the Clinton Administration responded to women's rights issues that liberal feminist government insiders and feminist activists working outside government raised in United States' and United Nations' forums during the administration's first two years in office. During these years, the United Nations sponsored two conferences that were especially significant in terms of defining the rights and raising the status of global women: the 1993 UN World Conference on Human

Rights (HRC) and the 1994 UN International Population and Development Conference (ICPD). In part due to the influence of U.S.-based feminist NGOs, in more explicit ways than at previous UN-sponsored global gatherings, the 1993 UN HRC applied human rights language to guarantee women's rights; in signing the HRC treaty governments agreed that women's rights are human rights and are universal, indivisible and inalienable. Within the United States these UN agreements led to further government actions. Following the HRC and in response to demands by American feminist NGOs and their congressional allies the Clinton Administration State Department created two new departmental offices: the UN conference secretariat and the Office of International Women's Issues (OIWI). Liberal feminist activists and feminists working inside the Clinton Administration collaborated to shape the missions and work of these two offices that both focused government attention on global women's needs and status. Together feminist insiders and outsiders prepared U.S. platforms that incorporated liberal feminist positions for the 1994 ICPD (and for UN conferences held in 1995, discussed ahead in chapter five). Also due in part to the influence of American feminist activists and in part to the influence of the Clinton Administration delegation, the 1994 ICPD adopted a treaty that included feminist positions supporting global women's reproductive health and rights.

The Clinton Administration and Its "New" Approach to Global Issues

When the Clinton Administration entered office in January 1993 the global gender policy making climate was transformed. On January 23 President Clinton reversed the Reagan/Bush Administration's policy that had prevented all USAID monies from supporting global family planning projects and agencies.[1] New leadership in the White House led to bureaucratic reorganization at the State Department and the creation of a new Office of Global Affairs headed by Undersecretary of State and feminist ally Timothy Wirth.[2] President Clinton appointed liberal feminist Arvonne Fraser as ambassador to head the 1993 U.S. delegation to the UN Commission on the Status of Women and to serve on the U.S. delegation to the UN World Conference on Human Rights. All these developments signaled new directions in global gender policy.

To be sure, the Clinton Administration faced ongoing global challenges and a state of international affairs that had emerged during the previous decade. Its overall foreign policy priorities did not differ dramatically from those of the Bush Administration. The Clinton

Administration generally adopted the Bush Administration's post-Cold War U.S. national security goals: to promote the growth of democratic governments and civil societies and to develop the global capitalist economy.[3] Nonetheless, Clinton Administration Secretary of State Warren Christopher, who had worked for Democratic administrations since the Kennedy era, recognized "the multi-dimensionality and complexity of 'security,' stressing those economic and global interests like trade and the environment were just as important to American diplomacy as military security." According to a State Department history of the Clinton presidency, Secretary Christopher "aimed to transform the State Department, both conceptually and bureaucratically, to deal with the new array of global challenges. He called for actively supporting democracy and human rights everywhere; a mantra of his tenure as Secretary was 'open markets and open societies.'"[4] In an inaugural address to the State Department diplomatic corps President Clinton defined the "three pillars" on which U.S. foreign policy would be based: economic growth and security, use of military might when necessary to defend U.S. security interests and international peace and democracy promotion. President Clinton pledged: "Whenever possible we will support those who share our values, because it is in the interests of America and the world at large for us to do so. History has borne out these enduring truths: Democracies do not wage war against one another; they make better partners in trade and diplomacy; and, despite their inherent problems, they offer the best guarantee for the protection of human rights."[5]

Lofty rhetoric flowed from the new administration expressing high hopes for a new, more peaceful and humane world order. At the same time violent conflicts in Bosnia, Somalia, Haiti and Rwanda that had begun in 1991 and 1992 were raging. In Bosnia, in spite of the well-publicized atrocities that Bosnian Serbs committed against Bosnian Muslims and that fell under the rubric of the Serb's genocidal "ethnic cleansing" policy including massacres of Muslim men, torture and mass rape of Muslim women, the Bush Administration had determined "that there was no reason strong enough to justify an armed intervention."[6] President Bush had deferred leadership in Bosnian cease-fire negotiations to European powers. After entering the White House, from 1993 to 1995 the Clinton Administration slowly assumed leadership of peace negotiations while it aided UN forces in airlifting food and supplies to besieged Bosnians and in establishing "safe havens" for Muslims in Bosnian cities that were nonetheless violated by Serb troops.[7] Only after a brutal massacre of over 8000 Muslims in Srebrenica in July 1995 and continued shelling of civilians in Sarajevo in August provoked international outcry, did the

Clinton Administration finally dispatch the U.S. air force to lead NATO forces in bombing Serbian targets.[8] At that time, dating from the beginning of the Bosnian conflict in 1991, "250,000 people [had] died and an estimated 20,000 rapes" had occurred.[9] The August 1995 NATO intervention forced the warring parties to engage in U.S.-led peace negotiations in Dayton, Ohio. Negotiations produced a peace accord in November.[10] Following through on the delayed leadership that it had displayed in Dayton, the Clinton Administration contributed 20,000 American troops to a continuing 60,000-strong NATO peacekeeping ground force that was deployed to prevent resumption of the civil war and genocide.[11] Although her conclusion has been disputed by others,[12] CNN reporter Christiane Amanpour has argued that, in the end, the media transformed the U.S. and Western European governments' response to the war because the media told the story of the war "objectively," but not "neutrally," and they named what was happening in Bosnia "genocide." Amanpour credits the media for forcing the global power holders in NATO, including a reluctant President Clinton, to intervene in the Balkans with firepower. The NATO military campaign finally persuaded the Serbs to end the slaughter of Bosnian Muslims.[13]

In regard to the ongoing conflict in Somalia, in one of his final acts in office in December 1992 President George H. W. Bush had sent U.S. troops to join a United Nations Relief Mission to deliver food aid to the Somali people, as the war and drought had combined to create a humanitarian crisis of mass proportions.[14] Under the Clinton Administration's directions the combined U.S./UN forces expanded the humanitarian relief mission in March 1993, and thereafter sought to disarm warring Somali clans, repatriate refugees and restore a functioning government. These actions led to a bloody firefight with one of the reigning Somali warlords, Mohammed Farah Aidid, and the loss of eighteen U.S. soldiers and over 200 Somalis in an unsuccessful attempt to defeat Aidid in October 1993. President Clinton quickly changed course and proceeded to withdraw all U.S. troops from Somalia over the next six months.[15] The Clinton Administration learned an early lesson from its experience in Somalia that placed limits on subsequent U.S. forays abroad: "humanitarian intervention would not be pursued if it posed too great a risk to military personnel." In other words, realism trumped idealism in Clinton's foreign policy.[16]

In a conflict that was closer to home, a September 1991 military coup had overthrown the duly elected president of Haiti, Jean-Bertrand Aristide, who fled to the United States where he lived in exile as he mustered U.S. political support.[17] Waves of impoverished and desperate refugees who fled the country followed Aristide and sought asylum in the

United States from the repressive Haitian military rulers. The large numbers of Haitian exiles entering South Florida had created a "refugee problem" for President Bush[18] and for President Clinton who followed him in office. Clinton continued President Bush's unpopular refugee repatriation policy until political pressures from the Congressional Black Caucus and the mounting humanitarian crisis in Haiti forced a policy change. In September 1994, three years after the brutal military regime seized power in Haiti, the Clinton Administration led a multinational coalition that threatened to launch military operations to overturn the coup and restore Aristide to power.[19] The credible threat of military intervention persuaded military leaders to back down, and Aristide returned to Haiti to govern in September 1994.[20] A U.S. humanitarian mission carried out by the military provided temporary assistance to facilitate President Aristide's return to power, but according to Assistant Secretary of State John Shattuck, "As soon as the multinational force was on the ground, Congress began sniping at its mandate. Having previously forced the President to set a date for its withdrawal within six months, congressional appropriators now sharply limited the 'nation-building' capacity of the U.S. part of the multinational force."[21]

At the same time, genocidal war that had erupted in Rwanda also challenged Clinton Administration foreign policy makers.[22] Extremists among the Rwandan Hutu peoples flouted global human rights treaties and global standards of morality. They viciously attacked the Tutsi peoples with the intent of eradicating the entire Rwandan Tutsi population between April and July 1994. Violent conflicts over land and political loyalties dating back to the colonial era had marred relations between the majority Hutus and minority Tutsis since the 1960s, but the massacre of over 800,000 Tutsis in the three-month period in 1994 led to withdrawal of a U.S.-supported UN humanitarian aid mission. Finally, after weeks of media pressure on the Clinton Administration to take some action to end the "mass exterminations" that according to United Nations investigators clearly violated the international Convention on the Prevention and Punishment of the Crime of Genocide, the administration sent 3000 troops to assist NGO Humanitarian Relief Operations in Rwanda on July 23, 1994.[23] Even then, the administration acted only after the genocidal massacres had ended; it "took *no* action to stop the genocide while it was occurring. The United States also prevented *other* members of the Security Council from acting to stop the genocide. And [the July 1994 humanitarian relief support mission, Operation Support Hope (OSH), authorized by President Clinton] had no mandate to carry out any security functions." According to international relations scholar William H. Meyer's analysis, "enthusiasm for the limited benefits of OSH must be tempered with disgust for the lack of earlier, more forceful intervention during the three months of unparalleled slaughter."[24]

During the Clinton Administration's first two years in office as these foreign policy crises engaged the U.S. military and diplomatic corps the administration also focused on the Middle Eastern peace process, building on foundations that the Bush Administration had laid down. After the Persian Gulf War ended the Bush Administration had organized a multilateral Middle East peace conference in Madrid, Spain in October 1991 that brought Israel and the PLO together with representatives of Middle Eastern and European governments and the UN Secretariat. The conference sparked forward movement.

President Clinton took on a more active leadership role than President Bush had in promoting the Middle East peace process when he entered office. His administration facilitated bilateral talks between the Israelis and Palestinians held in Oslo, Norway.[25] The Oslo peace talks resulted in a peace treaty signed at Camp David in September 1993. The Camp David Accords and the peace process that continued for several years afterward represented the most progressive agreements regarding control of land and governing authority between the Israelis and Palestinian leadership to date. Moreover, the peace process that the Clinton Administration fostered also "broke the logjam between Israel and the larger Arab world." Tragically, the assassination of Israeli Prime Minister Yitzhak Rabin in November 1995 and the subsequent devolution of Israeli-Palestinian relations led all parties to retreat from the accords after 1996. The Middle East peace process never got back on track before or after President Clinton left office in January 2001.[26]

Finally, during the Clinton Administration's first two years in office and throughout the 1990s, the U.S. government, Western governments, the World Bank, the International Monetary Fund and other international lenders continued to promote neoliberal capitalist development policies, breaking down barriers to globalization of the world's economy and applying structural adjustment programs in debt-ridden developing countries. Globalization of the capitalist marketplace and labor force had caused temporary downturns in the U.S. economy and job market losses in the early 1990s. With 7.7 percent of American workers unemployed and economic growth stagnant, voters had turned against incumbent President Bush in 1992 and elected Bill Clinton.[27]

Following Clinton's election, ongoing reductions in state-sponsored social welfare spending in the U.S. federal budget, as well as structural adjustment programs enforced throughout the global South, continued to place the most crushing economic burdens on the world's poor—overwhelmingly women and children. Domestically, the Clinton

Administration's economic policy sought to ameliorate this burden by promoting economic growth with "investments in public infrastructure, research and [education and job] training activities" to aid the "working poor."[28] This state of economic affairs provoked push back from progressive social forces including many liberal activists and voters based in the United States who were increasingly concerned about the rising costs of health care and the increasing numbers of Americans, including children, who were impoverished and had no health care insurance. In part, this public pressure was responsible for the Clinton Administration's major domestic policy initiative throughout 1993 and 1994: reform of the U.S. health care system to lower costs and establish universal health care.

President Clinton appointed First Lady Hillary Rodham Clinton to lead a national health care reform task force to develop policy proposals, but the task force ultimately failed in its mission.[29] While there were many reasons for the failures of health care system reform, Republican Party politicians mounted steady attacks on the administration's progressive and not-so-progressive policy proposals and on all other policy fronts: domestic social and health policy, economic policy and foreign policy. Indeed, the 1990s were an era when, according to one contemporary political analyst, "the prospects of there actually being bipartisan coalitions [in support of any policy proposals or new legislation] range from faint to nonexistent."[30]

Feminist Influence on Global Gender Policy

In the midst of the contentious political climate and facing these various foreign and domestic policy crises, U.S. and global feminists exerted progressive influence on U.S. global gender policy. As the Clinton State Department directed attention to global issues, feminist activists and female and male policy makers alike often invoked "women" as untapped human resources whose productive potential was far from realized. It was assumed that women would serve as a kind of remediating factor in addressing global problems because of their supposed peace-loving and nurturing natures and their attention to building communities.[31]

A February 1993 policy study conducted for the Clinton Administration USAID Office of Women in Development cataloged the benefits of "constructively integrating gender" into democracy promotion programs. Analyzing democratic and capitalist market transitions in Eastern Europe and the former Soviet Union, this study recognized that women often "suffered" more than men as they lost state-sponsored welfare assistance. Nonetheless, the report argued that "women are central to economic progress: as entrepreneurs, professionals, and managers in the formal sector; traders and craftspeople in the informal sector; full-time, part-time, piece or home workers in the industrial or the service sectors; agricultural producers and farm laborers; and as major consumers of goods and services. Equally important to the economy are their vital roles in social reproduction and human resource development." If U.S. government-sponsored programs sought to instill democratic values in transition states, they should be concerned with women's exclusion from governments in those countries as well. U.S. democracy promotion initiatives, "in whichever of [their] many forms, will be more effective and more equitable the more [they] open up opportunities to women as well as to other social categories." Moreover, the report recognized that "In particular circumstances, the inclusion of women may bring a specific advantage to the [democracy promotion] process. … [I]n seeking creative solutions to particular problems such as chronic corruption, a culture of violence, or inter-ethnic conflict, one may consider the possibility of turning to women to end deadlocks and promote positive and peaceful momentum."[32] To fully benefit from women's contributions governments needed to address formal and informal discriminations against women that caused women's unequal status worldwide, and to take steps to achieve "women's empowerment" by promoting women's equitable access to educational, economic and family planning resources that would allow them to direct their own lives.[33]

When the Clinton Administration took office feminist activists were already fully engaged with the human rights crisis in Bosnia. From mid-1992 and into the spring of 1993, as they organized for the June 1993 UN World Conference on Human Rights, the feminist media and feminist activists were reporting that tens of thousands of Muslim women had been raped in a way that was "calculated and intentional policy in the service of genocide."[34] In spring 1993, Equality Now was one of many networks of feminist and human rights NGOs that condemned the barbarity in Bosnia as they sought to mobilize the Clinton Administration and the international community to intervene to end the mass slaughter and systematic rape. The U.S.-based consortium of international NGOs had sent its own feminist "mission" to the Balkan war zones and these women came back to New York to testify before United Nations assemblies and at U.S. congressional hearings to explain the gendered nature of the wartime human rights violations.[35] Former U.S. Congresswoman Bella Abzug also spoke at International Hearings on Violations of Women's Human Rights hosted by women's international NGOs at the United Nations Church Center. Abzug challenged commonly held beliefs that defined violence against women as a "private" matter because it often occurred in the domestic sphere where perpetrators of rape and violence acted without fear of government intervention. According to Abzug, mass rapes of women in Bosnia had destroyed "[false] distinctions between private and public human rights violations."[36]

As these feminists knew, rape was "an effective weapon of war." Historically wartime rape of women was considered a victorious soldier's "right" and an expression of "naturally" violent masculinity. In ways that were particularly relevant in the ethnically-driven conflict in Bosnia, systematic wartime rape was also used to destroy a culture. Men used the act of rape to demonstrate their "triumph" over male adversaries who failed to protect their women.[37] Feminists sought to expose these historic and dangerous ideas and to make their case that these wartime practices in fact violated "women's human rights," a concept that had to be explicitly defined in 1993 as: "rights to which women are entitled simply by being human … related to one's dignity; they are universal, inalienable, indivisible, interconnected and interdependent; governments are obligated to enforce such rights in a way that promoted equality and nondiscrimination."[38]

Responding to wartime conditions in Bosnia documented by State Department on-the-ground observers,[39] in April 1993 the Clinton Administration announced that it was funneling "$6.75 million to assist victims of violence, rape, and torture in the former Yugoslavia through programs funded by the Bureau for Refugee Programs and the U.S. Agency for International Development" and an additional $1.5 million in aid, to be distributed through the International Red Cross "in support of its social welfare program for victims of abuse, rape, and torture among the refugees and displaced persons in Croatia and Slovenia."[40] This aid demonstrated the administration's impulse to protect victimized women, but at that time there was no corresponding assertion of the principle of women's human rights.

Western NGOs and human rights activists recognized that continued global media attention focused on the insidious nature of rape as a weapon of genocidal war could be used to develop a deeper understanding and wider acceptance among governments of the need to protect women's human rights—even though it could also produce some negative and anti-feminist consequences. On the one hand, the media focused on "systematic" rapes that were a part of the combatants' genocidal war policy. But feminists also argued that "every individual rape" was a crime against humanity, as well. Human rights activist and legal scholar Rhonda Copelon wrote in 1995 as Bosnian War Crimes Tribunals were being established, "Bosnian-Muslim women are being persecuted based on multiple elemental aspects of identity: gender and ethnicity and religion.

But the effect on women of rape apart from genocide may be no less life-shattering, given the enormity of the assault on a woman's integrity and personality and the unacceptability of a raped woman to the patriarchal community and, as a result, to herself."[41]

Moreover, media attention often exploited the victimized women. When "journalists flocked to Bosnia asking to interview 'raped women' and some foreign humanitarian groups set up offices and treatment facilities for 'raped women'," Bosnian women were publicly exposed. Some women felt shamed and many felt angry and used for purposes they did not choose. Many rape victims had ongoing mental health issues and international aid donors only slowly recognized their needs and gradually modified aid programs, as local women's organizations emerged in the post-war reconstruction period and articulated their needs and advocated for themselves.[42] Alice Miller, who worked with Amnesty International in the 1990s during the Bosnian War recalled that "'yes, the media *was* helpful' and 'no, the media *was not* helpful', in the sense that you had to take what they had done in order to make good law and policy and then unpack it quite a bit." As she elaborated on the situation:

> What some of the reporters were doing … was walking up to women and shoving microphones in their face and saying 'are you a rape victim?' Which was a really deeply offensive practice that quite a number of women's rights groups that I worked with in the later years from Bosnia, from Croatia were really critical of the way in which people kept running around and looking for rape victims, but didn't ask the people who had been kidnapped, whose husbands had been killed, and whose houses had been destroyed. … We needed the media to validate the claim [that rape was being used as a weapon of genocidal war], but the media over-stated it in some cases, and mis-characterized it and contributed to the kind of further isolation of women as *only* rape victims and not as members of their community who also lost brothers and husbands, who were looking for their sisters who had fled, and who needed houses and land.[43]

Sensitivity to women's local situations gradually emerged but in the immediacy of the crisis the media, and sometimes Western feminists and human rights activists as well, took actions that inadvertently exploited global women. Western and global feminist NGOs nonetheless continued to wage what was ultimately a successful campaign that transformed political discourse and institutional policy regarding women's human rights, in regard to the U.S. government and to the United Nations. In retrospect, feminists could argue that "Bosnia was a turning point in international recognition of protection of women in conflict and in attempts by governments and aid workers to solve the [wartime and post-war] problems of women and girls."[44] The Bosnian war became a turning point because of effective feminist interventions at the June 1993 World Conference on Human Rights.[45] After the conference in the United States feminist NGOs and activists kept up political pressure on the State Department and on USAID to follow through on HRC treaty agreements.

Feminist Interventions at the World Conference on Human Rights

Beginning in 1991 Charlotte Bunch and her colleagues at the Center for Women's Global Leadership (CWGL) at Rutgers University mobilized feminist NGOs to support a grassroots political campaign intended to shape the agenda and outcome of the United Nations HRC. They articulated specific goals to gain UN member governments' recognition and support for "women's human rights" and to include those understandings in the conference treaty negotiated at the upcoming human rights conference.[46] As chapter three has explained, in November 1991 the CWGL launched a global petition drive that "call[ed] upon the 1993 United Nations World Conference on Human Rights to comprehensively address women's human rights at every level of the proceedings. We demand that gender violence, a universal phenomenon which takes many forms across culture, race and class, be recognized as a violation of human rights requiring immediate action." This petition ultimately reached 124 countries and gathered a half million signatures.

The CWGL and its feminist NGO partners also organized and publicized global consciousness-raising actions, protests and demonstrations that took place in 1991 and 1992, between November 25 (International Day against Violence against Women) and December 10 (International Human Rights Day) that was designated as the "16 Days of Activism against Gender Violence."[47] Through these efforts the Center for Women's Global Leadership, as well as the International Women's Tribune Centre, the International Women's Rights Action Watch and the International Women's Network, identified by political scientist Jutta Jochim as "among the most important organizations in this effort," successfully moved violence against women onto the United Nations' human rights agenda. Joachim has argued that "in the case of gender violence, international women's organizations derived their influence primarily from the dynamic interaction of two factors: the political opportunity structure in which international women's organizations were embedded and the institutional and ideational resources that these organizations mobilized over time."[48] Alice Miller explained further that it was not just the crisis women faced in Bosnia but the array of concurrent human rights crises around the world that propelled gender violence against women onto the UN HRC agenda. Attention to human rights generally had an "exploding power" in the 1990s, "a force that women's rights proponents sought to harness," and the issue of violence against women provided for the "mainstreaming of feminism."[49]

"Mainstreaming" feminist issues or "integrating gender" into government policy considerations or into existing institutions is considered a controversial social change strategy among some feminist activists because it did not always yield progressive results. According to critics such as Sonia Alvarez and Catherine Eschle, "mainstreaming *gender* considerations" could take the focus off programs and resources that specifically targeted "women." Jacqui True has also noted that mainstreaming gender considerations sometimes created a space for elite women, the so-called "gender experts," to have a role in policy making, "without opening the political space or changing the material conditions for women at the grassroots."[50] Nonetheless, mainstreaming was one strategy that feminists who intervened at UN conferences or who engaged with Clinton Administration policy makers during the 1990s carefully considered and utilized. Charlotte Bunch defined mainstreaming and its potential for promoting social progress in 1993:

> Mainstreaming is an interactive process in which we are adding women to the agenda and thus forcing it to be transformed. For me, that is what transformational politics is all about. … I think this is what we are now doing with human rights. We are saying that the world community not only must integrate women but also transform how human rights are understood. In other words, we cannot integrate what women see as human rights issues into the existing human rights framework without changing the framework.[51]

4.1 Charlotte Bunch at the Tribunal on Violations of Women's Human Rights, World Conference on Human Rights NGO Forum, Vienna, Austria, June 1993. Courtesy of the Center for Women's Global Leadership.

In Vienna in June 1993, Charlotte Bunch and others convened a "Global Tribunal on Violations of Women's Human Rights" that took place at the NGO forum held just prior to the opening of the UN government conference. At the tribunal, thirty-three women from twenty-four countries gave emotional and powerful testimony documenting widespread instances of domestic violence, female genital mutilation, torture, terrorism and war crimes specifically directed at women. Their testimonies allowed marginalized women to have their rarely-heard, specific and local perspectives included and legitimized in a global UN forum where universalist and elitist government discourse is the norm.[52] A panel of international judges who connected these abuses to violations of existing international human rights treaties presided over the tribunal and elite government delegates attended the tribunal. Alice Miller has explained why the testimonies were such an effective action:

> To build a political force that could not be resisted, advocates had to emphasize and make visible what was different about the experiences of women; they had to make these experiences too horrendous to ignore. ... The campaign took a classic feminist tool—ending silence—and coupled it with another classic feminist tool—intimate story telling by individual women. By these means, activists overturned myths: rape doesn't happen in marriage, rape always "happens" in war.[53]

Additionally, an NGO women's caucus effectively lobbied government delegations at the World Conference on Human Rights, held from June 14 to 25, repeating the successful strategy that Bella Abzug initiated at the 1992 UN Conference on the Environment and Development in Rio. According to observers, "women made up half of the 3000 NGO participants [at the HRC] ... and were the most organized and vocal group of NGOs."[54] The women's caucus not only highlighted the issue of violence against women, but it broadened the conference discussion to include economic and development issues that violated women's human rights as well. As the women's caucus at the 1992 UNCED had emphasized links between global issues, the 1993 HRC Women's Caucus insisted "development, democracy and human rights are inextricably related." Caucus lobbyists urged government delegates "to recognize that human rights, true democracy and peace are incompatible with poverty and exploitation of which women are the greatest victims, and to affirm and propose initiatives and mechanisms to implement political, civil, social, economic and cultural rights and the right to development." A second women's caucus made up of government delegates and representatives of UN agencies including the UN

Development Fund for Women (UNIFEM), the UN Population Fund and the UN Children's Fund and the Division for the Advancement of Women also met daily at the HRC to monitor these linked issues in conference document debates. Throughout the NGO forum and at the UN conference, feminist communications specialists organized extensive media coverage of women's actions.[55]

All these activities produced some feminist results.[56] The conference documents that 171 government delegations signed, the Vienna Declaration and Program of Action, agreed to address violence against women, specifically "systematic rape, sexual slavery and forced pregnancy" that occurred during conflicts, and to define the gender violence as human rights violations. Most importantly, the delegates agreed that women's human rights are "an inalienable, integral and indivisible part of universal human rights." Conference delegates also supported the Declaration on the Elimination of Violence Against Women (DEVAW) that held governments responsible for identifying and eliminating violence against women, whether it was perpetrated by public or state authorities or by private entities, and not to accept cultural or religious traditions as license to commit gender violence with impunity.[57] UN member governments adopted the Declaration at the September 1993 UN General Assembly. In March 1994 the UN appointed a Special Rapporteur, Radhika Cooaraswamy, to investigate underlying causes of violence against women as well as specific complaints regarding violations of the DEVAW that were brought to her office. Moreover, because new understandings about what constituted violations of women's human rights were agreed upon at the HRC, the International Criminal Tribunal for the Former Yugoslavia that began operations in 1995 "respond[ed] to women's demands … [and] began to prosecute rape and sexual violence as war crimes and crimes against humanity." This precedent was followed after 1996 when the International Criminal Tribunal for Rwanda finally commenced and also prosecuted rape as a war crime.[58]

The U.S. Government's Response to the Feminist Agenda at the HRC

At the World Conference on Human Rights and in the months that followed, the Clinton Administration recognized and promoted women's rights as part of its support for global human rights. At the HRC, Secretary of State Warren Christopher addressed the world powers speaking for the U.S. government. Christopher's main foreign policy goal was to secure global support for a strengthened UN office on Human Rights to be headed by a High Commissioner, which was achieved. But he also voiced strong U.S. support for the feminist women's rights agenda: "Violence and discrimination against women don't just victimize individuals; they hold back whole societies by confining the human potential of half the population. Guaranteeing human rights is a moral imperative with respect to both women and men. It is also an investment in making whole nations stronger, fairer, and better. Women's rights must be advanced on a global basis."[59]

In September 1993, in his report on the HRC to the House Committee on International Relations, Assistant Secretary of State for Human Rights and Humanitarian Affairs John Shattuck explained more fully the administration's position in support of women's rights and the actions that that the administration had already taken. Shattuck asserted that the U.S. delegation to the UN World Conference on Human Rights had worked closely with women's groups "to promote a substantial women's rights agenda." With U.S. Ambassador to the Commission on the Status of Women Arvonne Fraser on the U.S. delegation, this was likely the case. Fraser had directed the USAID Women in Development office during the Carter Administration and led the NGO International Women's Rights Action Watch in the 1980s. Shattuck also described the global tribunal that feminists had organized at the NGO forum and noted that the testimonies had "emphasiz[ed] the truth of the simple but often ignored slogan: 'Women's rights are human rights'." Shattuck thus used and affirmed the language of the global feminist movement. Various positions that the U.S. delegation had promoted at the conference were also in line with the feminist agenda such as: "systematic integration of women's issues into UN human rights programs," "training of UN personnel to ensure sensitivity and competence in addressing gender-based abuses," "appointment of more women to positions of responsibility at the UN," "adoption of a UN Declaration on Violence Against Women" and appointment of "a UN Special Rapporteur on Violence Against Women."[60]

John Shattuck also announced that the State Department would revive the practice of addressing violations of women's rights in its annual human rights reports on countries that received U.S. foreign aid, a policy established during the Carter Administration that had lapsed in practice. As he explained, "U.S. embassies are now instructed to report in greater detail any evidence of systematic physical abuse of women, governmental attitudes toward such abuse, and the extent of governmental effort to curtail abuses. Although human rights violations against women have never been ignored in the reports, they are now significantly highlighted." In regard to USAID programs that focused on global women's needs for education, health care and job training, some of these programs, Shattuck asserted, would also "include legal rights education." In defining violations of women's human rights Shattuck also used global feminist language in asserting the U.S. government's position on female genital mutilation, that it was "both harmful to women's health and as a violation of their right to physical integrity." He also announced that the United States had supported the creation of the International War Crimes Tribunal for the former Yugoslavia with the intent to prosecute wartime rapes as violations of the Geneva Conventions. Shattuck confirmed that women's human rights were universal, inalienable and indivisible and that "culture and tradition cannot excuse gross and systematic violations of human rights." Shattuck stated explicitly: "The Clinton Administration regards promoting the cause of women's rights as a key element of our overall human rights policy."[61]

After the HRC, NGOs pressed the State Department to maintain focus on liberally-defined women's rights issues, including reproductive rights. Population Action International (PAI) led by Robin Chandler Duke appealed directly to Ambassador Warren Zimmermann, the last U.S. Ambassador to serve in united Yugoslavia in the 1980s, to persuade USAID to send contraceptives and other supplies to fulfill women's reproductive healthcare needs in Bosnia. U.S. emergency relief shipments had commonly overlooked these needs even though the U.S. Centers for Disease Control had recognized that: "Women's health needs are largely unmet in Bosnia. Local doctors report that contraceptive services are in high demand and that counseling and support services are widely needed. In most areas, hospital records indicate that therapeutic abortions have increased while birthrates have decreased during the war. In Sarajevo, still-births as a fraction of all births have increased 64%, premature births have increased 143%, and average birth weight has declined 19% from before the war."[62] Following PAI's appeal, by December 1993, USAID began supplying reproductive health care supplies and contraceptives to refugee centers.[63]

When the State Department released its country-by-country human rights reports in February 1994, John Shattuck and Timothy Wirth held a press conference to reaffirm the government's commitment to global women's human rights and reproductive rights: "We have placed increased emphasis this year in the report—and in our policies—on the protection of the rights of women, including issues such as rape, female genital mutilation, treatment of women in the workplace, marginalization of women in the political process, and the rights of women to freely and responsibly choose the number and spacing of their children."[64] Shattuck and Wirth acknowledged that women's organizations had lobbied for more attention to violations of women's rights in the country reports, but they also asserted that "This administration has been committed on women's issues from day one, focusing on family leave, children, and health care." In a *New York Times* interview, president of the National Organization for Women Patricia Ireland praised the administration's rhetorical shift supporting women's human rights since the HRC, but she also pressed for practical changes in U.S. government programs and operations to address women's needs and rights, at home and abroad.[65] Dorothy Q. Thomas, Director of the Women's Rights Division at Human Rights Watch, agreed. After spending years working with feminist and human rights activists to make global violations of women's human rights "visible" to the United Nations and to the U.S. government, her response to publication of the U.S. human rights country reports was direct and to the point: "I have reached a point beyond visibility. I am interested in accountability. I am interested in what we do now that the extent of the scope, nature and egregious character of women's human rights violations are available to all of us in startling and probably more detailed form than we ever wanted to be exposed to."[66]

Due to appeals from feminist NGOs and their allies in the Congressional Caucus for Women's Issues the Fiscal Year 1994 Foreign Relations budget authorization included a section titled "Women's Human Rights Protection." [67] The section asserted: "It is the sense of Congress that the Department of State should designate within the appropriate bureau a special assistant to the Assistant Secretary to assure that women's human rights issues are considered in the overall development of international human rights policy."[68] This authorization allowed the State Department Global Affairs bureau to establish the Office of International Women's Issues (OIWI) in 1994, which became the mechanism for feminist women at the State Department and for NGOs to broadly elaborate U.S. global gender policy. Initially the OIWI focused on gender policy in reference to the 1995 UN Fourth World Conference on Women. Later, it engaged in a wide range of global women's rights and women's empowerment projects. Dorothy Thomas recalled how these events unfolded in 1993 and 1994:

> We argued strenuously for the creation of the Office on International Women's Issues, and worked closely with several Congressional leaders to get it established and to ensure that it would have the mandate (and constituency) to integrate attention to women's issues across the Department and, more generally, into U.S. foreign policy. We, along with other women's and human rights groups, highlighted to Congress and State the kinds of gender-specific human rights abuses the U.S. might both investigate and raise with governments and encouraged them

> strongly to do so. Our advocacy raised a number of serious issues affecting women including un-remedied domestic violence, sex discrimination in employment, education and criminal justice, trafficking in women, custodial sexual abuse and wartime violence. The OIWI became a key leverage point within the U.S. government to develop policy and practice that was more responsive to women's needs and significantly more respectful of their rights.[69]

The First U.S. Women's Foreign Policy Office: The Office of International Women's Issues

Looking back at the history of the Office of International Women's Issues in 2009, Dorothy Thomas noted, "Our sense has always been that [the OIWI] would have benefitted over the years from much more substantial political and material support than it ever received."[70] Nonetheless, the OIWI, created in mid-1994, had an important State Department sponsor, Undersecretary of State for Global Affairs Timothy Wirth, who established the office under his portfolio and appointed its first leader at the rank of senior coordinator.[71]

In retrospect, Wirth's appointee, Gracia Hillman, a political activist whose area of expertise was voting rights issues and who was employed as executive director at the League of Women Voters when she was invited to head OIWI in 1994, was not a politically astute choice. Hillman did not have a background in foreign policy, or an understanding of institutional politics at the State Department or particularly strong associations with feminist NGOs. Prior to working with the League of Women Voters, she had directed the Congressional Black Caucus Foundation and the National Coalition on Black Voter Participation. Yet in November 1994 she joined an established and well qualified team of liberal feminists working with the Global Affairs bureau as it drafted positions for the U.S. delegation to the Fourth World Conference on Women, where women's human rights were a central issue of government concern. Other members of this team included Director Margaret Lycette, USAID Office of Women in Development; Ambassador Sally Shelton Colby, USAID; Depurty Assistant Secretary Felicia Stewart, Office of Population Affairs, Department of Health and Human Services; Senior Coordinator Ellen Marshall, Bureau for Population, Refugees and Migration Issues, State Department; Ambassador Arvonne Fraser, the UN Commission on the Status of Women; Kathleen Hendrix, Office of International Organization Affairs, State Department; and Theresa Loar, the Global Affairs bureau, State Department, among others.[72]

Theresa Loar was appointed to head another office that opened at the State Department in June 1994, the UN conference secretariat. A career foreign service officer, Loar had served in U.S. embassy and consul posts abroad in the 1980s and had worked at State Department country desks in Washington in the 1990s. She joined the Global Affairs bureau in June 1993 and began coordinating logistical arrangements and gathering research for U.S. policy positions for the 1994 and 1995 UN conference delegations. Undersecretary Timothy Wirth was focused on the environment and population, his strongest policy interests, and he and Vice President Al Gore took the lead in preparing U.S. policy positions for the International Conference on Population and Development to be held in September 1994 in Cairo. Theresa Loar consequently focused on global gender policy issues including women's reproductive rights and women in development, and laid the groundwork for the upcoming September 1995 Fourth World Conference on Women to be held in Beijing.[73]

Like Hillman, Loar did not come into the State Department from the feminist NGO world but she knew State Department politics. She developed a liberal feminist perspective over the years that she was associated with the UN conference secretariat and when she directed the President's Interagency Council on Women that formed in August 1995. She also coordinated global gender policy development with Gracia Hillman at the OIWI. When Hillman left government service in 1996, Loar was appointed senior coordinator of OIWI and led the office throughout Bill Clinton's second presidential term. Through those various positions Loar developed expertise as a "gender policy entrepreneur." Political scientist Jacqui True has defined the characteristics of gender policy entrepreneurs that accurately describe Loar's role in the Clinton Administration's State Department, as the following chapters will document:

> Gender policy entrepreneurs are able to see how proposing particular innovations could alter the nature of policy debates. They strive to see problems and issues from a range of perspectives including the perspectives of differently situated groups of women and men. As individuals they are socially adept and able to mix in a variety of social and political settings to acquire valuable information and use their contacts to pursue policy change for gender justice. Gender policy entrepreneurs may make different arguments to different groups while keeping the overall story consistent. They are strategic team builders in the sense that they think about the type of coalition best able to support their issue or a series of issues over time. Gender policy entrepreneurs

> often lead by example, creating prefigurative forms of the policy innovations they seek to introduce more broadly.[74]

Loar and Hillman consulted frequently with feminist activists as they prepared U.S. conference delegations, and as the State Department and USAID generally drew on NGOs' expertise during the Clinton Administration's tenure in office. The administration's post-ICPD report explains how representatives of feminist, healthcare, environmentalist and population-focused NGOs were involved in Cairo conference activities; not just in larger numbers than ever before but in substantive ways, too, these NGOs "played an important role in drafting conference documents":

> The administration actively sought the input of citizens and organizations in the development of its new policies. State Department representatives participated in town meetings from coast to coast and conducted meetings encouraging participation in document drafting. Continuous outreach for input has been at the crux of U.S. preparations. The increased international involvement of citizen groups signals an important shift—from top-down imposition of "population control" measures to community-based programs that are crafted to respond to the needs of individuals and families.[75]

NGO consultations continued in preparations for the Beijing Fourth World Conference on Women as well. Theresa Loar credits Timothy Wirth with leading the shift in practice at the State Department to include more NGO representatives on UN conference delegations in efforts to expand generally public interest in foreign policy making:

> I think that a big part of U.S. participation, when Tim Wirth was the Undersecretary of State for Global Affairs, was leading the efforts for the U.S. involvement in this conference. He had a real interest in bringing NGOs into the process; and I think it was a lasting contribution that he made to the U.S. government. It spilled into the State Department, because he really opened up the doors in the State Department to NGOs. The State Department didn't like it one little bit.[76]

Unlike some career Foreign Service Officers who resisted the new inclusiveness, Loar embraced the challenges of the democratic and pluralistic process. Loar recalled her first foray into United Nations' politics, when she first began meeting and working with feminist NGO activists, coordinating the various parties involved in the Cairo ICPD preparations:

> The Clinton Administration's point of view was supporting free access for women all over the world to family planning, and to be able to determine the number, the timing, and the spacing of their children. That was something that was a clear policy, and shaped a lot of the U.S. government's participation in the conference. Of course, that got misinterpreted by many who said that it was promoting abortion or some who saw it as not going far enough. They were a huge domestic issue—abortion and reproductive rights, and you put it in the UN context, and it's a really potent mix. But it drew members of Congress who were very concerned about the issue. There were others who were very concerned about just placing women at the center of development. That was another U.S. goal: looking at empowering women and strengthening women's roles within the families; and then that became another issue—what a family is. And we had some very strong involvement by the Vatican in this, and the Vatican working with and reaching out to all kinds of Islamic countries, who you wouldn't think would be on the same side as the Vatican on any issue, which was surprising to me! It was a real brew of domestic politics brought onto the UN stage. I thought my participation was helpful, because it helped me to see and to manage this set of issues. While we had much broader issues coming up in the Beijing conference, it was helpful to see some of the very successful and smart things that were done, and to look at some of the things that pose particular challenges that would need to be addressed the next time around.[77]

Feminist Activism at the ICPD

Feminist activists did not need to be persuaded to join U.S. government preparations for the UN-sponsored International Conference on Population and Development. Many feminists such as Bella Abzug who led the Women's Environment and Development Organization (WEDO) and Adrienne Germain who led the International Women's Health Coalition (IWHC) were experienced UN conference lobbyists. Their organizations among many other feminist NGOs had particularly strong interests in interjecting their ideas and strategies to reaffirm the 1993 HRC agreements regarding women's empowerment and women's human rights in order to shape global government agreements on controversial issues such as women's reproductive rights at the ICPD. These issues became the focus of many conference discussions on sustainable and effective development strategies and global population growth.[78]

Significantly, the State Department invited Bella Abzug to serve on the U.S. delegation to ICPD in spite of, or perhaps because of, her forceful and polarizing presence.[79] Abzug's vocal advocacy for feminist policy positions on women's reproductive rights and a range of other development and environmental issues contributed to the United States' high visibility at ICPD preparatory meetings and in Cairo. Theresa Loar recalled the particular strengths that Abzug brought to all her causes:

> She was really a very warm person too, [although] that wasn't really her public persona. But she was very warm, very dedicated to standing up for women. Even if you didn't agree with her particular point of view or with the way she expressed it, you couldn't help but be won over by her real driving drive to help women be heard and break through channels, and to really make sure that women's needs were on the agenda. No one has come along who was like that within the UN system [or] in the U.S. NGO community who has really had an effect like that. She was really unique in that way, and it was interesting having her on our delegation because she wasn't someone you managed.[80]

Certainly Abzug was adept at employing multiple strategies that Karen Beckwith has defined as "common among feminist movements," working both autonomously and in tandem with the U.S. government, utilizing feminists who were positioned inside the government as well as outside, working independently and applying coalitional strategies with other social movements (such as the environmental movement, the human rights movement, the women in development movement and women's health and reproductive rights movement of the 1990s) and utilizing the power of discursive politics to change policy makers' attitudes and embed feminist language in government policy.[81]

In the end, feminist language infused the ICPD government treaty, or the Program of Action, and credit is due to a vigorous NGO women's caucus, in which Bella Abzug also played a key leadership role.[82] Abzug and her WEDO colleagues organized an active women's caucus at every ICPD preparatory meeting and at the Cairo conference. The caucus expanded the governments' discussion of "family planning" to include provisions in the conference document addressing women's reproductive rights and health, sexual rights and "fundamental freedoms for women, including advancing gender equity, equality and the empowerment of women, eliminating violence against women, and ensuring women's ability to control their own fertility."[83]

4.2 Rubina Lal (India), Carmen Ricon Cruz (Mexico) and Amina Samb (Nigeria) on the panel "From Vienna to Beijing: the Cairo Hearing on Reproductive Health and Human Rights." International Conference on Population and Development, Cairo, Egypt, September 1994. Courtesy of the Center for Women's Global Leadership.

The women's caucus coordinated global NGO activism at the ICPD. The women's caucus "Writing Analysis Group" drafted text for the Program of Action that governments and NGOs alike debated at three UN Preparatory Committee meetings held between 1991 and 1994, and finally approved at the Cairo conference. Women's caucus organizers (with Abzug and the women of WEDO foremost among them) kept a global network of NGOs and feminist supporters abreast of key UN meetings, the positions of key governmental leaders and UN officials and the ever-evolving language of the international conference treaty, the Program of Action.[84] In spite of the wide-ranging coordination, a major point of contention at the ICPD concerned the Program of Action language that was linked to abortion, in conference treaty "paragraph 8.25" affirming women's reproductive rights. This controversy revealed rifts within the global feminist movement, and between feminists and national governments, as the following section explains.[85]

The Clinton Administration's Response to the Feminist Agenda at ICPD

From the time the Clinton Administration took office, the administration's views on global population policy and women's empowerment were closely aligned, although not identical, with the positions of feminist activists.[86] At the first ICPD preparatory meeting that the new administration attended in May 1993, Undersecretary of State Timothy Wirth announced the radical turn around in the U.S. government's global population policy that feminists, population policy

NGOs, UN agencies and many national government delegations welcomed.[87] President Clinton had decided to reverse the Reagan/Bush population policy, to fund global family planning initiatives and UN population agencies and to support abortion rights for women in nations where abortion was legal, including the United States. In the view of some analysts, the Clinton Administration's transformed population policy "helped to create a more favorable climate for feminist activism" throughout the Cairo conference process.[88] In May 1993 Undersecretary Wirth announced:

> [W]e are committed to help promote international consensus around the goal of stabilizing world population growth through a comprehensive approach to the rights and needs of women, to the environment, and to development. … The President has reversed the so-called Mexico City policy, lifting restrictions that prohibited some family planning organizations from receiving U.S. funding because of abortion-related activities. He has mandated a reorganization of the State Department to reflect the greater priority we are giving to population as a major global issue. He has called for a restructuring of our foreign aid programs to promote development more effectively. And he has requested a $100 million increase in population assistance for [Fiscal Year] 1994. … An additional step will be taken by the U.S. Government. I am pleased today to reconfirm the Clinton Administration's intention to contribute to the UN Fund for Population Activities.[89]

The assembled meeting broke into applause.[90] In further remarks that global feminists particularly welcomed, Wirth continued to discuss women's health and their unequal status as linked concerns of the U.S. government:

> Overall, we must take a broader approach to sexual and reproductive health. We must recognize that advancing women's rights and health and promoting family planning are mutually reinforcing objectives. Even more fundamentally, all barriers which deprive women of equal opportunity must be removed. Universal educational opportunities, especially for girls and women, are an essential precondition for economic empowerment.[91]

In his carefully calculated statement regarding the issue of abortion Wirth's remarks also ignited intense political opposition from domestic representatives of the U.S. Religious Right and global powers including the Vatican, predominantly-Catholic Latin American nations and predominantly-Islamic Middle Eastern nations, as he dropped the concluding bombshell in regard to the most disputed issue of the conference:

> Difficult as it is, we must also discuss thoroughly the issue of abortion. Recent international meetings have drawn attention to the human tragedy of illegal and unsafe abortion. It is estimated that as many as a quarter of maternal deaths, ranging from 50,000 to 200,000 annually, are due to this cause, almost all in developing countries.
>
> International consensus has yet to be developed on the proper and feasible role of governments and public policy in this area. The abortion issue should be addressed directly with tolerance and compassion rather than officially ignored while women, especially poor women, and their families suffer. The U.S. Government believes the Cairo conference would be remiss if it did not develop recommendations and guidance with regard to abortion. *Our position is to support reproductive choice, including access to safe abortion.*[92] [Emphasis added]

The Clinton Administration had defined its position on abortion: that it should be "safe, legal, and rare." The administration was also explicit in stating that it did not promote abortion in other countries, or, as Vice President Al Gore elaborated, "We believe that decisions about the extent to which abortion is acceptable should be the province of each government within the context of its own laws and national circumstances. … [But in the United States] our administration believes that the U.S. Constitution guarantees every woman within our borders a right to choose, subject to limited and specific exceptions. We are unalterably committed to that principle. But let us take a false issue off the table—the United States has not sought, does not seek, and will not seek to establish any international right to an abortion. That is a red herring."[93]

These U.S. positions were consistently pursued throughout the two-year-long ICPD preparatory process[94] and at the conference meetings in Cairo,[95] even though the administration suffered domestic political fallout. Socially conservative "pro-life" politicians within the Republican Party criticized the administration's lack of "family values."[96] Global opponents of abortion rights led by the Vatican challenged the administration's "feminist" goals and motives that sought "to sanction a current lifestyle in minority circles of certain opulent societies." Critics asserted that "terms in the [ICPD treaty] like 'reproductive health' and 'reproductive rights' introduce the idea of, 'in effect, abortion on demand' as a proposed international right to be established by the gathering."[97]

The ICPD conference treaty included paragraph 8.25, a "single paragraph in a 133-page document [that] held up the conference for three days and required the creation of a working committee to resolve the matter in two days." The offending paragraph dealt with abortion as a women's health concern and called for access to family planning to prevent unwanted pregnancies and for safe abortions in countries where abortion was legal.[98] However, as Marilen Dangulian explained the competing views on the meaning of paragraph 8.25:

> For the Islamic countries, the Holy See and its allies, 8.25 was more than a gangrenous lesion, it was a cancerous growth that had to be excised and burned. For most women's groups, it was an affirmation of their reproductive rights which constituted the bedrock of their self-determination. For development activists, it was a gadfly, a red herring that deflected the course of the conference from the issue of development or under-development.[99]

Some feminists at the women's caucus objected when language from the 1984 International Population Conference held in Mexico City was inserted at the opening of paragraph 8.25, "In no case should abortion be promoted as a method of family planning," because the stricture had been used by some governments (such as the U.S. government during the Reagan and Bush Administrations, among others) to justify withholding funds from family planning clinics that provided abortion counseling or performed abortions, among their services. Nonetheless, the language was included "to placate the Holy See and its allies."[100] Although it did not achieve those results, ICPD delegates adopted the amended Program of Action.[101]

Feminist Critiques of the Clinton Administration's Positions at the ICPD

Many feminist NGOs considered the ICPD Program of Action to be a watershed document, representing "a giant leap for womankind,"[102] because it endorsed the concept of women's "reproductive rights" and it committed the 181 government signatories and UN agencies to fund programs to support women's reproductive health, to expand women's education and to raise women's legal, social and economic status.[103] In the view of many, the Program of Action made "women the central focus of population policies,"[104] which was considered a progressive development by those who fought for years to get demographers and other population experts to acknowledge women's needs and interests in policy and state programming.[105] Indeed, the Clinton Administration held this view.[106] Yet as the ICPD ended, questions remained about its true consequences for women worldwide:

> But what does "central focus" mean? That women have become instruments to stabilize population growth rates? Or that, by focusing all efforts on empowering women through education, functional literacy, and gainful employment, they may just decide not to give birth, and in doing so, bring down fertility rates? Or that women will gain effective access to reproductive and sexual health, education, literacy and all the social services to which they are entitled—regardless of whether or not these will cause a decline in population growth? How governments implement the ICPD Program of Action will show what they mean by "central focus."[107]

Feminist NGOs from the global North and South appreciated the shift that the ICPD treaty represented, from previous population planners' focus on "controlling" population growth with sometimes coercive family planning measures in order to promote global economic development. Yet they also criticized the "underlying conviction" at the base of the Program of Action "that meeting the basic needs of the world's poorest people, especially women, will empower them to gain control over their own lives and livelihoods, and it is the most effective means of promoting equitable economic growth, human rights and sustainable development." In the aftermath of the ICPD, feminists continued to challenge U.S. and Western governments that adopted neoliberal economic policies to integrate women into the global capitalist economy, where women were paid the lowest wages and where "their incomes are marginal at best." The Clinton Administration's belief that jobs were the solution to all development and poverty problems, in the United States and in the world, did not in fact meet peoples' needs when "the jobs that are available mostly do not pay a family wage or a living wage and … many of our neighbors live hand to mouth, unable to save, unable to create any assets toward some kind of economic security."[108]

Mayra Buvinic, president of the International Center for Research on Women, observed in her annual report for 1994, "In the early 1990s, a renewed concern for poverty reduction and the human dimensions of development swept across the mainstream agencies. This pendulum shift helped to bolster the ability of the women's movement to shape new population policies and programs at the UN population and development conference held in Cairo this past September." Looking to the future, however, she asserted that "Many challenges lay ahead. The first is to strengthen further and expand the constituency of women-based NGOs so that they can ensure implementation of gender programs. A second challenge is to get development planners to focus on women's productive, not just reproductive roles" and to address the widespread issues of women living in poverty.[109]

Feminist NGOs voiced these criticisms as the Clinton Administration and activists prepared for two UN world conferences scheduled to take place in 1995: the World Summit for Social Development and the Fourth World Conference on Women. To be sure, feminist NGOs such as WEDO and Development Alternatives for a New Era (DAWN) linked the series of UN conferences in the 1990s, beginning with UNCED in 1992, and continuing with the 1993 HRC, the 1994 ICPD and the 1995 world conferences, because their thematic focuses had a critical impact on women's lives and status, as well as on the lives and status of other underprivileged peoples. Feminist NGOs solidified these links through their women's caucuses and, after 1994, through a monitoring network they called "Women Watching ICPD" that exerted political pressures on world governments to maintain progressive gains for women and to keep moving forward.[110] Feminist NGOs from both the global North and South worked together to influence the outcomes of UN conferences at mid-decade. In the process of coming together at these 1995 global forums their influence on the Clinton Administration's global gender policy was never greater, as chapter five explains.[111]

---

[1]William Jefferson Clinton, "Family Planning Grants." In January 1993, the Clinton Administration reversed U.S. policy that the Reagan Administration established at the 1984 UN World Conference on Population and lifted restrictions that prohibited some family planning organizations from receiving US funding because of abortion-related activities. See also: History of the Department of State during the Clinton Presidency.

[2]Warren, "Department of State Reorganization"; History of the Department of State during the Clinton Presidency.

[3]Baker, "U.S. Foreign Policy Priorities and FY 1991 Budget Request"; Christopher, "Budget Priorities for Shaping a New Foreign Policy."

[4]History of the Department of State during the Clinton Presidency. See also: Wirth, "Statement at Confirmation Hearings."

[5]William Jefferson Clinton, "A New Era of Peril and Promise."

[6]Meyer, *Security, Economics and Morality in American Foreign*, p. 138.

[7]Christopher, "New Steps Toward Conflict Resolution in the Former Yugoslavia"; Christopher, "NATO and US Foreign Policy."

[8]Shattuck, *Freedom on Fire*, pp. 117, 160-4; Albright, "UN Security Council Adopts Resolution 1010 on Bosnia"; William Jefferson Clinton, "Success of the NATO Air Campaign in Bosnia."

[9]Meyer, *Security, Economics and Morality in American Foreign Policy*, p. 269.

[10]William Jefferson Clinton, "The Balkan Proximity Peace Talks"; William Jefferson Clinton, "U.S. Support for Implementing The Bosnian Peace Agreement."

[11]Meyer, *Security, Economics and Morality in American Foreign Policy*, pp. 139-41.

[12]Ibid. p. 336, n. 76. According to Warren Strobel, *Late-Breaking Foreign Policy, The News Media's Influence on Peace Operations* (Washington DC, United States Institute for Peace, 1997), p. 153. Deputy Secretary of State Strobe Talbott dismissed "the CNN Effect" on U.S. policy.

[13]Amanpour, "Newseum War Stories."

[14]Meyer, *Security, Economics and Morality in American Foreign Policy,* p. 120. "The fighting killed tens of thousands, forced hundreds of thousands of people from their homes, and disrupted political, economic, and social structures to such an extent that one could rightfully describe Somalia in the 1990s as a 'failed state.'"

[15]Ibid. pp. 120-4.

[16]Ibid. p. 268.

[17]"Profile: Jean-Bertrand Aristide."

[18]"Fair Haven for Haitian Refugees." "The huge tide of Haitians fleeing the chaos and terror after last September's coup caused the U.S. to abandon normal principles of political asylum. At first, many Haitians were forcibly returned. Then the Administration allowed people picked up in leaky boats to be processed at the Guantanamo Bay naval base. But in May, contending that the base had reached capacity, Mr. Bush ordered the Coast Guard to intercept all refugee boats and turn them back without screening any of the passengers."

[19]William Jefferson Clinton, "The Crisis in Haiti, U.S. Interests in Haiti."

[20]Meyer, *Security, Economics and Morality in American Foreign Policy,* pp. 131-3.

[21]Shattuck, *Freedom on Fire,* p. 109.

[22]"Rwandan Violence." The administration recognized and condemned the outbreak of violence in Rwanda that violated negotiated ceasefire agreements, but the genocidal character of the violence was not yet apparent in early 1993.

[23]Moose, "The Crisis in Rwanda: U.S. Response."

[24]Meyer, *Security, Economics and Morality in American Foreign Policy,* p. 127. See also: Shattuck, *Freedom on Fire,* p. 16. U.S. Assistant Secretary of State for Human Rights and Humanitarian Affairs John Shattuck identified "a logical progression [in U.S. intervention policy] from Rwanda to Haiti to Bosnia. ... Rwanda in the early spring and summer of 1994 exemplified a U.S. policy of catastrophic disengagement heavily influenced by the killing of U.S. troops in Somalia the previous fall. Haiti in the fall and winter of 1994-1995 represented an early step toward a policy of containing human rights wars, although domestic political pressures required the multiregional force that intervened in Haiti to exit prematurely, and precluded any sustained follow-through. The U.S. approach towards Bosnia in the fall of 1995 demonstrated a more effective and longer-term commitment to linking diplomacy with the use of military force, after three years of American dithering while ineffective European and UN peacekeeping had failed to control the conflict and stop the human rights atrocities."

[25]Christopher, "Resumption of Mid-East Peace Negotiations."

[26]Meyer, *Security, Economics and Morality in American Foreign Policy,* pp. 102, 105-07.

[27]Weatherford and McDonnell, "Clinton and the Economy: The Paradox of Policy Success and Political Mishap," p. 406.

[28]Ibid. pp. 415, and n. 23., 420, 422.

[29]Morrison, "The Clintons Go to Washington, A Healthy Move?", p. 350.

[30]Weatherford and McDonnell, "Clinton and the Economy," p. 412, quoting Bert A. Rockman, "Leadership and the Clinton Presidency" in Colin Campbell and Bert A. Rockman, eds., *The Clinton Presidency: First Appraisals* (Chatham, NJ: Chatham House Publishers, 1996).

[31] See for example: Tolchin, "Women as Policy Makers: They can make a difference"; USAID, "The Participation Forum, Topic: Participation and Gender," November 17, 1994, KT, box 7.

[32]Hirschmann, "Democracy and Gender: A Practical Guide to USAID Programs."

[33]Mayoux, "Gender Equity, Equality, and Women's Empowerment: Principles, Definitions and Frameworks."

[34]Douglas, "What About Bosnia?"; "An International Appeal: Word Out of Bosnia"; "Catherine A. MacKinnon to represent Croatian, Muslim wartime rape survivors," p. 3; "Bosnia: 20,000 Women Raped," p. 5; "Taking Our Lives Into Our Own Hands" Special 50th Issue *The Tribune* (April 1993), IWTC, Acc. # 93S-60, box 2.

[35]Equality Now, Annual Report, 1992-93.

[36]Hamilton, "International Women's Rights Campaign: Women's Rights are Human Rights," p. 2.

[37]Mertus, *War's Offensive on Women*, p. 7.

[38]Ibid. p. 16.

[39]"Seventh Report on War Crimes in the Former Yugoslavia."

[40]"U.S. Assistance for Victims of Violence in the Former Yugoslavia."

[41]Rhonda Copelon, "Gendered War Crimes: Reconceptualizing Rape in Time of War," in Peters and Wolper, eds. *Women's Rights/ Human Rights: International Feminist Perspectives,* p. 205.

[42]Mertus, *War's Offensive on Women*, pp. 28-30, 36.

[43]Alice Miller, Phone Interview with Author, May 26, 2010.

[44]Mertus, *War's Offensive on Women*, p. 19.

[45]Copelon, "Gendered War Crimes," in Peters and Wolper, eds. *Women's Rights/ Human Rights: International Feminist Perspectives,* 198.

[46]Hamilton, "International Women's Campaign: Women's Rights are Human Rights," p. 2.

[47]"Violence Against Women Violates Human Rights" *The Tribune* Special 50th Issue (April 1993), IWTC, Acc. # 93S-60, box 2; Jutta Jochim, "Shaping the Human Rights Agenda: The Case of Violence Against Women," in Meyer and Prugl, eds. *Gender Politics in Global Governance*, p. 154.

[48]Jochim, "Shaping the Human Rights Agenda," in Meyer and Prugl, eds. *Gender Politics in Global Governance*, pp. 142-3. See also: "Making Women's Rights part of the Global Human Rights Agenda, " *Libertas Newsletter of the International Center for Human Rights and Democratic Development* 2: 3 (June 1992), CWGL, United Nations World Conference Files, 1993-1996, box 1; International Women's Rights Action Watch [IWRAW], "Report of the IWRAW Working Session: Vienna, January 16-17, 1993," IWTC, Acc. #00S-8, box 4.

[49]Miller, "Sexuality, Violence Against Women, and Human Rights," p. 20.

[50]True, "Mainstreaming Gender in Global Public Policy,"369. True cites Sonia Alvarez, "Advocating Feminism: The Latin American Feminist NGO 'Boom'," *International Feminist Journal of Politics* 1, no. 2 (1999) and Catherine Eschle, *Global Democracy, Social Movements, and Feminism* (Boulder, CO: Westview Press, 2000).

[51]"Women should Claim the Global Agenda as Their Own," [Interview with Charlotte Bunch] *UNIFEM News* 1, no. 2 (June 1993), KT, box 8.

[52]"Report of the Global Tribunal on Violations of Women's Human Rights, Submitted to the World Conference on Human Rights, Vienna, 14-25 June 1993," Delivered by Charlotte Bunch, Director, Center for Women's Global Leadership and Florence Butegwa, Uganda, Women in Law and Development in Africa, CWGL, United Nations World Conference Files, 1993-1996, box 2. The international panel of judges issued the following statement after hearing the women's testimony: "These violations remain both unremedied and unrecognized as discriminatory or as an affront to women's human dignity. ...We note with dismay that international human rights law has not been applied effectively against injustices women experience solely because of their gender. We hereby affirm the principle of universality that protects all humanity, including women. Universal human rights standards are rooted in all cultures, religions and traditions, but those cultural, religious and traditional practices that undermine universality and prove harmful to women cannot be tolerated."

[53]Miller, "Sexuality, Violence Against Women, and Human Rights," p. 25.

[54]Friedman, "Gendering the Agenda," p. 320.

[55]"Women's Human Rights" *The Tribune* Vienna, June 1993, IWTC, Acc. # 93S-60, box 2.

[56]Riding, "Rights Forum Ends in a Call for a Greater Role by UN": "Women declare victory. 'The key factor has been the unity of women at the conference,' said Roxanne Carrillo, an official of the United Nations Development Fund for Women, referring to the strong presence of independent women's groups here. 'We strongly believe this alliance is the key to what we are celebrating today.'"

[57]Jochim, "Shaping the Human Rights Agenda," in Meyer and Prugl, eds. *Gender Politics in Global Governance*, pp. 149-50. This Declaration had been under discussion and in development by women's international organizations, the UN Division on the Advancement of Women, and the UN Commission on the Status of Women since the mid-1980s.

[58]Antrobus, *The Global Women's Movement*, pp. 91-3; 118-19; Copelon, "Rape and Gender Violence: From Impunity to Accountability in International Law"; Day, "Downstairs at the UN Human Rights Meeting," p. 6; Mertus, *War's Offensive on Women*, pp. 97-9; Pettman, "Global Politics and Transnational Feminisms" in Ricciutelli, Miles, and McFadden, eds. *Feminist Politics, Activism & Vision*, p. 52.

[59]Christopher, "Democracy and Human Rights: Where America Stands."

[60]Shattuck, "Violations of Women's Human Rights."

[61]Ibid.

[62]Robin Chandler Duke to Warren Zimmermann, Director, Bureau for Refugee Programs, Department of State, October 22, 1993, RCD, box 1.

[63]Robin Chandler Duke to Beatriz Rosales, Senior Program Officer, Threshold Foundation, December 17, 1993, RCD, box 1; Robin Chandler Duke, "Bosnia Diary", c. September 1994, RCD, box 2.

[64]Wirth and Shattuck, "Opening statements from a press briefing on the annual human rights report."

[65]Greenhouse "State Department Finds Widespread Abuse of Women, Stark Picture is Painted."

[66]Dorothy Thomas, Director, Women's Rights Project, Human Rights Watch, "Report of International Women's Month at the World Bank," March 1994, SIGI, box CONF 13.

[67]Mayra Buvinic, "The President's Message: Looking Ahead, Looking Back," International Center for Research on Women, Annual Report, 1994; "Resolution from the Women's Caucus of the Third Global Structures Convocation on US Action needed for Immediate and Effective Integration of Women's Human Rights into United States Foreign Policy", February 6, 1994, CWGL, IV World Conference on Women, Beijing, China 1995, box 4.

[68]Foreign Relations Authorization Act 1994; Section 137, "Women's Human Rights Protection," *Congressional Record* 140,1994, February 2, 1994.

[69]Dorothy Q. Thomas e-mail to author, July 14, 2009.

[70]Ibid.

[71]Loar, The Association for Diplomatic Studies and Training Foreign Affairs Oral History Project.

[72]"Focus on Population and Development: Follow-up on Cairo Conference," U.S. Department of State Bureau of Public Affairs *Bulletin*, September 5-13, 1994, RCD, box 2.

[73]Loar, The Association for Diplomatic Studies and Training Foreign Affairs Oral History Project.

[74]True, "Mainstreaming Gender in Global Public Policy," p. 379.

[75]"Focus on Population And Development: The U.S. and the UN International Conference on Population and Development."

[76]"U.S. Gears Up for UN Conferences," Women's Environment & Development Organization, *News & Views* 7, no. 2 (September 1994), IWTC, Acc. #95S-69, box 11. WEDO asserted that it and thirty other feminist NGOs meeting in Washington DC in June 1994 had exerted decisive pressure on Timothy Wirth that led him to reorganize the Global Affairs division in regard to preparations for the International Conference on Population and Development and the Fourth World Conference on Women. This reorganization included establishing the UN conference secretariat, hiring Theresa Loar as coordinator, and establishing the Office of International Women's Issues. See also: Martha Alter Chen, "Engendering World Conferences: The International Women's Movement and the UN," in Weiss and Gordenker, eds., *NGOs, the UN, and Global Governance,* p. 149: "In particular the U.S. delegation made every attempt to understand the concerns of women from the developing world. Over half its delegates were from NGOs, including the vice president of the International Women's Health Coalition and the U.S. co-chair of WEDO. The U.S. delegation was led by Undersecretary of State Tim Wirth, who held a daily press briefing at the NGO forum, not at the official conference hall, as an expression of his openness to NGO concerns."

[77]Loar, The Association for Diplomatic Studies and Training Foreign Affairs Oral History Project.

[78]"WEDO Fact Sheet on Women's Caucus"; Irene Tinker, "Nongovernmental Organizations: An Alternative Power Base for Women?" in Meyer and Prugl, eds., *Gender Politics in Global Governance,* pp. 99-100; Moghadam, *Globalizing Women*, pp. 117-18; Chen, "Engendering World Conferences," in Weiss and Gordenker, eds., *NGOs, the UN, and Global Governance,* pp. 147-8.

[79]Adrienne Germain who was well-respected and had been working as a women's health and human rights advocate for over a decade also served on the U.S. conference delegation.

[80]Loar, The Association for Diplomatic Studies and Training Foreign Affairs Oral History Project.

[81]Beckwith, "Mapping Strategic Engagements: Women's Movements and the State," pp. 318-20, 327.

[82]Chen, "Engendering World Conferences," in Weiss and Gordenker, eds., *NGOs, the UN, and Global Governance,* p. 149. Chen includes the comments of the International Women's Health Coalition [Adrienne Germain] regarding the impact of the Women's Caucus at the ICPD: "The underlying basis for consensus was created by the constituency most concerned—women. For the first time, a wide range of representatives of women's organizations from every region of the world were central to the negotiation of an international population document. Working together with a common purpose, women engaged at every stage of conference preparations and at every level to gain access to negotiations. Gradually, through the conference preparations, governments and international agencies recognized women as legitimate players. ... At numerous points throughout the process ... when language accepted by the majority of governments and NGOs was threatened by a handful of delegations, women were the ones who mobilized to protect the emerging consensus. Because women have been affected by population policies and programs, they emerged as an unassailable moral force." See also: Higer, "International Women's Activism and the Cairo Conference" in Meyer and Prugl, eds., *Gender Politics in Global Governance*, p. 135.

[83]"Reproductive Rights are a Topic of NGO-Delegate Dialogue at Cairo Population Conference," Women's Environment & Development Organization, *News & Views* 7, no. 2 (September 1994), IWTC, Acc. #95S-69, box 11.

[84]Abzug, "To Women's NGO Caucus Members."

[85]Danguilan, *Women in Brackets*, p. 85.

[86]Warren M. Hern, "The Role of Abortion in Women's Health and Population Growth," To the NGO Forum 94, [ICPD], September 5-13, 1994, RCD, box 2. "During the election campaign of 1992, Bill Clinton actively sought the support of pro-choice groups and strongly supported reproductive freedom. Hillary Rodham Clinton was highly visible in these efforts. By January 24, 1993, Clinton had reversed a wide variety of Reagan-Bush administration domestic policies that had been aimed at restricting reproductive choice, and he nullified the Mexico City policy. He appointed U.S. Senator Tim Wirth as a Counselor in the Department of State with a portfolio to include population policy. Wirth had a strong record of outspoken support for reproductive freedom as a member of the House of Representatives and as a Senator Subsequent policy statements by Wirth and Clinton have consistently expanded this support, including a recent

statement by Wirth that the goal should be the availability of fertility control methods to every couple on the planet who wants them."

[87]Danguilan, *Women in Brackets,* pp. 8-9. Marilen Dangulian identifies a coalition she terms the "population establishment" that would have welcomed Wirth's announcement. These entities included: "a transnational coalition of national governments (mainly the US, Japan, UK, Germany, Canada, and France), multilateral institutions, [UN agencies, particularly the United Nations Population Fund (UNFPA), World Bank and the International Monetary Fund], bilateral institutions (United States Agency for International Development, Canadian International Development Assistance, and Japanese International Cooperation Agency), private population organizations (International Planned Parenthood Federation or IPPF, Population Council, Population Crisis Committee, Rockefeller, Ford, MacArthur), consultant firms (Futures, Options), environment and conservation groups which blame increasing population growth rates for environmental destruction (Sierra Club, among others), and mostly U.S.-based academic institutions (East-West Center, University of Chicago, University of North Carolina)."

[88]Higer, "International Women's Activism and the Cairo Conference," in Meyer and Prugl, eds. *Gender Politics in Global Governance,* p. 137.

[89]Wirth, "U.S. Statement on Population and Development." See also: Warren M. Hern, "The Role of Abortion in Women's Health and Population Growth," RCD, box 2. The George H. W. Bush Administration had opposed funding for the UN Fund for Population Activities (UNFPA) "because of the controversy concerning China's abortion policies, and the House of Representatives repeatedly refused to appropriate $15 million for that program."

[90]Ellen Marshall, phone interview with author, August 18, 2009. See also: Hobart Rowen, "$100 Million More for Family Planning."

[91]Wirth, "U.S. Statement on Population and Development."

[92]Ibid.

[93]Gore, "The Cairo Conference: Defining an Agenda of Hope, Opportunity, and Progress."

See also: Gore, "Remarks at the opening session of the UN International Conference on Population and Development."

[94]Timothy Wirth, "Women, Population and Development: Toward Consensus and Action," March 30, 1994, RCD, box 2; Timothy Wirth, "Population and Sustainable Development: Defining an Agenda."

[95]Timothy Wirth, "U.S. Goals at the Cairo Conference."

[96]Loar, The Association for Diplomatic Studies and Training Foreign Affairs Oral History Project.

[97]Alan Cowell, "Vatican Says Gore is Misrepresenting Population Talks." See also: Danguilan, *Women in Brackets,* p. 87.

[98]"The ICPD Program of Action, Chapter 8: Health, Morbidity and Mortality": "In no case should abortion be promoted as a method of family planning. All Governments and relevant intergovernmental and non-governmental organizations are urged to strengthen their commitment to women's health, to deal with the health impact of unsafe abortion as a major public health concern and to reduce the recourse to abortion through expanded and improved family planning services. Prevention of unwanted pregnancies must always be given the highest priority and all attempts should be made to eliminate the need for abortion. Women who have unwanted pregnancies should have ready access

to reliable information and compassionate counseling. Any measures or changes related to abortion within the health system can only be determined at the national or local level according to the national legislative process. In circumstances in which abortion is not against the law, such abortion should be safe. In all cases women should have access to quality services for the management of complications arising from abortion. Post-abortion counseling, education and family planning services should be offered promptly which will also help to avoid repeat abortions."

[99]Danguilan, *Women in Brackets,* p. 85.

[100]Ibid. p. 96.

[101]"Reproductive Freedom at the UN: The Cairo Conference, A Program of Action for Reproductive Rights?" Center for Reproductive Law and Policy, International Program, October 28, 1994, IWTC, Acc. #95S-69, box 11. "Anti-choice forces, represented by the Holy See, Malta, Ecuador, and Argentina argued that all abortions were unsafe for the fetus. The phrase 'unsafe abortion' they argued, was this redundant."

[102]Chen, "Engendering World Conferences," in Weiss and Gordenker, *NGOs, the UN, and Global Governance*, p. 147. See also: "Reproductive Freedom at the UN: The Cairo Conference, A Program of Action for Reproductive Rights?" IWTC, Acc. #95S-69, box 11.

[103]"Overview of Conference Aims, Background, International Conference on Population and Development, September 5 – 13, 1994."

[104]Danguilan, *Women in Brackets,* p. 119.

[105]Higer, "International Women's Activism and the Cairo Conference," in Meyer and Prugl, eds. *Gender Politics in Global Governance,* pp. 123, 138. "The preeminence of women's issues was, by all accounts, the hallmark of the Cairo conference. Cairo's World Programme of Action formulated a new definition of population policy that emphasized the empowerment of women and downplayed the demographic rationale. It also articulated a broadened concept of family planning that placed such programs within a larger context of comprehensive health services (McIntosh and Finkle 1995, 223). The Cairo conference indeed has come to symbolize a women-centered approach to population policy. Many observers attribute this shift in emphasis to the influence of women's health activists (e.g. Cohen and Richards 1994, 223; Crane and Isaacs 1995; McIntosh and Finkle 1995, 235-9; and Sen 1994)."

[106]Gore, "Defining a Global Approach Toward Stabilizing the World Population."

[107]Danguilan, *Women in Brackets,* p. 119.

[108]Statement of the National Congress of Neighborhood Women in preparation for the Beijing Fourth World Conference on Women quoted in: "Development at the Crossroads: Women in the Center," Alt-WID Resource Center *Bulletin*, No. 41, August 1995, CWGL, IV World Conference on Women, Beijing, China 1995, box 5.

[109]Mayra Buvinic, "Looking Ahead, Looking Back," International Center for Research on Women, Annual Report, 1994.

[110]"US Gears Up for UN Conferences," Women's Environment & Development Organization, *News & Views* 7, no. 2 (September 1994), IWTC, Acc. #95S-69, box 11; Chen, "Engendering World Conferences," in Weiss and Gordenker, *NGOs, the UN, and Global Governance*, p. 149.

[111]Pettman, "Global Politics and Transnational Feminisms" in Ricciutelli, Miles, and McFadden, eds., *Feminist Politics, Activism & Vision*, p. 54: "North-South divides were central in early international women's conferences, but by the mid-1990s Bina Agarwal could argue that 'among women's groups there is a growing recognition of the importance of forging strategic links. One could say 'romantic sisterhood' is giving way to strategic sisterhood for confronting the global crisis of economy and policy'."

5

U.S. Commitments to Global Women

American feminists worked hard to shape the Clinton Administration's policies and platform positions at the March 1995 World Summit for Social Development and the September 1995 UN Fourth World Conference on Women, as this chapter explains. The administration's participation in the World Summit disappointed many feminist activists who condemned the administration's continuing adherence to neoliberal economic policies and military policies that negatively impacted global populations—especially women. Nonetheless, the administration also offered up new USAID programs that feminists supported. U.S. delegation leaders Hillary Clinton and Al Gore announced new foreign aid partnership roles for NGOs and new education and development funds directed to global women. In spite of their pointed criticisms of U.S. economic and foreign policies at the World Summit, liberal feminist NGOs continued their energetic lobbying of Clinton Administration officials regarding these and other issues on the government agenda at the UN Fourth World Conference on Women held in Beijing, China. Working with the State Department conference secretariat, the Office of International Women's Issues and other U.S. government offices, as well as through ideological campaigns waged in the mainstream and feminist media, feminist activists influenced the substance of the U.S. government's Commitments to Women, announced in Beijing.

Among those Commitments, the formation of the President's Interagency Council on Women (PICW) in August 1995 was especially significant in advancing feminist goals and feminist practices within U.S. government institutions. The PICW director, Theresa Loar, and PICW members, all high-level cabinet officers, played critical roles defining specific gender policies and programs that the cabinet agencies implemented to fulfill the Commitments to Women in the years following the Beijing conference. These new policies and programs initiated institutional changes in U.S. government operations that benefitted U.S. and global women. The PICW also maintained regular consultations with feminist NGOs after the Beijing conference ended, throughout 1996 and beyond.

In another significant development, First Lady Hillary Clinton emerged as a highly visible global promoter of women's human rights at the Fourth World Conference on Women. Although her concern for the wellbeing of vulnerable women and children had long been on public record, Hillary Clinton adopted the women's rights language of the feminist movement in her Beijing conference speeches and applied feminist principles in her global advocacy for women in the years following the conference. Since 1995 Hillary Clinton has continued to be recognized as a feminist leader throughout the world.

1995: A Momentous Year

In 1995 the United Nations Organization celebrated its fiftieth anniversary. In 1945, the victorious World War II Allies—the "United Nations"—had established a global security treaty and global financial system that in many ways had institutionalized the unequal division of power between the relatively stable, technologically and economically developed nations of the global North, and the relatively insecure, underdeveloped nations of the global South. During this anniversary year, the U.S. government and governments throughout the world participated in two major United Nations meetings that highlighted the global body's expanded influence in regard to defining social and cultural relationships, as well as its continuing political and economic importance: the World Summit for Social Development and the Fourth World Conference on Women.

Within the United States domestic politics influenced the Clinton Administration's participation in these two global gatherings. Mid-term election results in November 1994 had challenged the Clinton Administration's leadership and the Democratic Party's progressive social policies and long running federal government fiscal policies. Republican Party politicians had run for office pledging support for a "Contract with America" to cut taxes and reduce the size and reach of the federal government.[1] With the 1994 electoral victories, they gained a voting majority in both the House of Representatives and the Senate.[2] As they took office in 1995 the newly-elected Republicans, mostly male, undercut numerical gains made by progressive women candidates who had been elected to national offices in 1992. They vowed to reduce domestic social welfare spending, to challenge civil rights for homosexuals and to overturn abortion rights for U.S. women, among other political aims.[3] Republican politicians also interjected their conservative social and political agendas into U.S. foreign policy. They sought deeper cuts in foreign aid budgets and pushed to include their conservative social agenda in U.S. platforms developed for the 1995 global UN meetings. These Republican interventions consumed a great deal of State Department and USAID energy as administration foreign policy makers struggled to justify new foreign aid allocations and U.S. global treaty positions at the UN conferences.[4]

As conservative U.S. politicians pressed to rollback progressive gains for women in regard to U.S. domestic and foreign policy, in the global arena backlash from fundamentalist forces also occurred. Religious and politically right-wing constituencies challenged women's freedom of choice in regard to their bodies as well as recent gains that women had made in expanding their decision making power within the family, the capitalist economy and in governments worldwide.[5]

Responding to these challenges, U.S. and global feminists stressed "unity" among women's organizations, whether those NGOs were based in the global North or the South, in regard to women's participation in the 1995 UN meetings.[6] They advocated for "linked activism" among organizations focused on various issues in order to leverage their combined political power and maintain the progressive concessions women had won from global governments at previous United Nations conferences in 1992, 1993 and 1994.[7] For feminist women working in NGOs based in the United States and elsewhere, the connections between the 1990s UN conference themes and global women's status and security were clear. Their efforts to focus government conference delegations on women's needs and rights were both extensive and effective as they utilized the mechanism of the NGO women's caucus.[8] Each of the UN conferences of the 1990s took years of preparation—for UN member governments, the UN secretariat and its specialized agencies as well as for the global social movements and the NGOs that mobilized global policy making power on their behalves. In regard to the 1995 World Summit on Social Development and Fourth World Conference on Women, preparations for both global meetings were well underway among all interested parties by early 1993.

The World Summit on Social Development

The UN General Assembly voted in December 1992 to convene the World Summit on Social Development in Copenhagen, Denmark in March 1995. The week-long Summit brought together 117 heads of state, delegations from 186 UN member states, and representatives from over 800 NGOs to address rising levels of global poverty and stalled social and economic development, all within the context of protecting and enhancing human rights. In addition to setting goals to reduce poverty and promote development worldwide, the Summit also sought to soften the punitive effects of neoliberal structural adjustment policies that global financial institutions applied. These goals were outlined in government agreements adopted at the World Summit: the Copenhagen Declaration on Social Development and the Copenhagen Program of Action.[9]

During the 1990s the world had experienced various positive consequences of economic globalization. The number of democratically elected governments, the volume of global trade and the global wealth of nations had all increased. Nonetheless, not everyone shared in these benefits. More than a billion of the world's population lived in abject poverty and the majority of the world's poor were women. There was a growing disparity in wealth between the developed nations of the global North and developing nations of the global South—the richest fifth of the world's population controlled 82 percent of the world's income, while the poorest fifth of the world received 1.4 percent of the world's income.[10] These persistent failures of the existing development models and structural adjustment programs that capitalist First World nations and international financial institutions promoted cried out for systemic changes at the state, market and household levels of the economy.[11]

The United Nations Department for Policy Coordination and Sustainable Development took charge of organizing the World Summit's preparatory committee meetings, consultations with development experts and NGOs and government Summit sessions. World Summit General Secretary Juan Somavia from Chile convened the first of three preparatory meetings in January 1994 that brought together government delegations, representatives of UN agencies, the World Bank, the World Trade Organization, the International Monetary Fund and international NGOs.

During preparatory meetings Undersecretary of State for Global Affairs Timothy Wirth articulated the Clinton Administration's World Summit goals to "humanize" and reform the existing financial system. Specific Clinton Administration proposals followed familiar themes that the administration had promoted in regard to addressing weaknesses in the U.S. domestic economic policy, these were: to "advance a global discussion on creating more and better jobs," to "reinforce and strengthen global resolve to eradicate the most abject forms of poverty in the poorest countries by early in the next century" and to "highlight the critical need to empower women." Undersecretary Wirth asserted that "Economic adjustments should be planned to put people first. We expect governments and the international financial institutions to accord high priority to identifying and reducing policies which hurt the poor, and to promote instead policies which enhance the earning power of poor people."[12]

An NGO women's caucus spearheaded by Bella Abzug, Charlotte Bunch and Sonia Correa and their organizations, the Women's Environment and Development Organization (WEDO), the Center for Women's Global Leadership (CWGL) and the Development Alternatives with Women for a New Era (DAWN), was active at all preparatory meetings as well as at the Summit.[13] Not surprisingly, the women's caucus'es criticisms of the global financial system were more pointed and their proposed remedies were far more radical than the reforms the Clinton Administration and most other national governments put forth. The women's caucus met daily when the Summit convened and consistently directed attention to the negative gendered impacts of neoliberal economic policies on women. The women's caucus called on global financial institutions to cancel debts for impoverished nations. They joined the United Nations Children's Fund (UNICEF) and the UN Development Agency in advocating for what became known as the "20: 20" formula, calling on nations to devote 20 percent of national budgets and 20 percent of foreign aid budgets to social development programs. Representing the women's caucus, Bella Abzug spoke at the Summit on March 8, International Women's Day, and announced the "180 Days/180 Ways Women's Action Campaign" to build a global lobby for women's empowerment and gender justice in anticipation of the Beijing Fourth World Conference on Women. The women's caucus also worked with over six hundred NGOs to draft the Copenhagen "Alternative Declaration" that outlined global social activists' "wide-ranging criticisms of a neo-capitalist system that favors giant corporations and gender inequalities."[14]

An NGO forum took place parallel to the World Summit from March 3 to 12, attended by 12,000 NGO representatives. Here, too, an NGO women's caucus were active participants who organized forum meetings, such as the "Women Reclaim the Market" roundtable. At this session, feminists proposed an alternative vision to neoliberal capitalist market values in which exchange of goods and services would take place primarily to meet human needs rather than primarily to increase corporate profits. They challenged foundational capitalist profit motives that allowed "sex markets" and "arms markets" to flourish among other global markets.[15]

5.1 Peggy Antrobus, Noeleen Heyser, Mariana Williams, and Soma de Souza, panel at the World Summit for Social Development, NGO Forum, Copenhagen, Denmark, March 1995. Courtesy of the Center for Women's Global Leadership.

In the hope of repeating the impact that the Global Tribunal on Violations of Women's Human Rights had on mobilizing sympathetic public opinion at the 1993 World Conference on Human Rights, on March 7, the CWGL and DAWN co-convened a "Hearing on Economic Justice and Women's Rights" at the NGO forum. In particular, the feminists' testimonies criticized the U.S. government. The U.S. government was "a major contributor and loudest voice at the World Bank and the International Monetary Fund." Therefore, the U.S. government was responsible for ongoing structural adjustment policies that penalized the developing nations and the world's poorest peoples.[16] The women's testimonies also condemned the gendered effects that U.S. foreign policies had on particular populations of global women. For example, U.S. economic sanctions on Cuba had jeopardized the health and welfare of Cuban women and children; U.S. military bases in the Philippines and elsewhere contributed to increasing incidences of trafficking in women and forced prostitution in the Asia-Pacific region. Within the United States' borders, the proposed welfare system overhaul outlined in the Republicans' Personal Responsibility and Work Opportunity Act was condemned for its racial and gender biases.[17] The feminist NGOs also criticized U.S. government's treatment of illegal immigrants, increasing national levels of poverty and domestic violence and the deteriorating criminal justice system throughout the country. In all these ways, feminist NGOs challenged the gender biases and far-reaching consequences of U.S. economic and foreign policies as well as those policies of other First World nations that attended the World Summit. Their immediate impact on U.S. global gender policy is revealed in the speeches that Hillary Clinton and Al Gore delivered at the World Summit.

U.S. Policy Pronouncements and Aid Pledges at the WSSD

Unlike many other world governments whose heads of state personally attended the World Summit on Social Development, President Bill Clinton sent the first lady and the vice president to address mounting global social crises at the United Nations gathering. To be sure, these emissaries, Hillary Clinton and Al Gore, had global stature. The world recognized Hillary Clinton as a leading advocate for women and children's welfare and Al Gore as an environmental policy expert and strong supporter of sustainable development principles.

Hillary Clinton delivered two important addresses at the World Summit that advocated for increased investments in women and girls in order to promote global development and women's human rights. On March 7, Clinton outlined a multi-faceted approach to development, combining government investments in social programs, partnerships with NGOs and private investment directed at meeting the needs of the world's poorest populations. Clinton also asserted that governments "will have to respect basic human rights, and that includes the rights of women and workers to be protected from exploitation and abuse. They will have to create conditions that encourage individual initiative and a vibrant civic life." In her remarks to the Summit leaders Clinton listed the valuable contributions made by NGOs. NGOs represented civil society. They mobilized government action, proposed "innovative solutions to problems" and monitored government progress.

Clinton also highlighted the progressive potential of private investments in social development achieved through microcredit financing. She singled out Muhammad Yunus, founder of the Grameen Bank in Bangladesh, for praise. Yunus had successfully used microloans as a means of promoting social and economic development, especially among women, at the local village level. Clinton particularly noted the important benefits of educating women and girls. Educating women and girls promoted gender equality and protected their rights as human beings; educated women and girls lifted their families and communities out of poverty.[18]

5.2 Bella Abzug and Hillary Clinton, panel at the World Summit for Social Development, Copenhagen, Denmark, March 8, 1995. Courtesy of the Women's Environment and Development Organization.

On March 8, Hillary Clinton focused her remarks on the government contribution to the social development equation. She announced that the U.S. government would direct $100 million to education initiatives for women and girls in Latin America, Asia and Africa over the next ten years. The USAID allocation was based on the assumption that "No single factor contributes to the long-term health and prosperity of a developing nation—or any nation—more than investing in education for girls and women."[19] Hillary Clinton articulated the Clinton Administration's response to the feminist NGOs' "20: 20" proposal to fund social development programs. The administration had set goals for the education initiative to strive for "a 20% increase in girls' primary school completion rates or a 20% increase in the number of women who are functionally literate in the project areas in each country within 10 years." She noted that "A key element in this initiative is that it will be women, organized by NGOs, who will take the leadership in this effort. This new program also will assist women in developing their own capacities for improving the education of their children, including their daughters."[20]

Al Gore followed Hillary Clinton and addressed the World Summit on March 12. He announced USAID's "New Partnerships Initiative" to disperse 40 percent of development aid money through Nongovernmental Organizations, including those based in the U.S. that worked with global populations as well as locally-based NGOs in underdeveloped nations.[21] In 1995 the U.S. development aid allocation was $10 billion,[22] and NGOs were already responsible for dispensing approximately 13 percent of total overseas development assistance.[23] Additionally, USAID would "empower small businesses and entrepreneurs to drive economic growth" through strategies such as microcredit financing because the Clinton Administration believed "that permanent gains can occur only if we encourage free markets and individual initiative."[24] Gore asserted that working in these ways to encourage development through local initiatives would also serve the third objective of the New Partnerships Initiative: "To help nations bolster democracy at the local level."[25] The New Partnerships Initiative also placed "special priority on activities that engage and empower women."[26]

Some feminist NGOs appreciated the U.S. government's vocal support for the principle of equal rights for women and its economic support and vote of confidence in the ability of NGOs to design programs that could address the development needs of the world's poorest peoples at the local level. But neither Hillary Clinton nor Al Gore proposed systemic changes in global financing or capitalist free trade markets. Nor did they propose plans to halt the rise in violent conflicts and militarization that crippled and destabilized many developing countries. In her remarks to the World Summit Bella Abzug raised these important considerations that the NGO women's caucus had identified and that most world governments in attendance, including the U.S. government, had not adequately addressed. She again demanded fundamental changes in state budget priorities including significant reductions in military spending and application of the 20:20 formula to social spending. Abzug ended her remarks with a call to action:

> As we speak of initiatives, let us pledge that this summit will be remembered as the high-water mark on the decades of greed. That from this day forward, we will act to reclaim our communities and rein in renegade financial systems and markets.[27]

In the end, the NGOs' persistent lobbying and consciousness-raising arguments yielded some limited but significant results in the final Summit agreements. Government delegations did not renounce global gender agreements made at previous UN conferences and the Copenhagen Declaration on Social Development included an explicit statement that the women's caucus proposed: "We acknowledge that social and economic development cannot be secured in a sustainable way without the full participation of women and that equality and equity between women and men is a priority for the international community and as such must be at the centre of economic and social development."[28] Several nations cancelled the debts of developing nations. The Netherlands and

Norway adopted the 20: 20 funding formula for social development. The United States committed $100 million to support girls' education programs. Bella Abzug asserted that women's NGOs were primarily responsible for achieving these results. In the Summit's aftermath, Abzug, who appreciated incremental changes even as she advocated for revolutionary transformations, summed up her optimistic view: "Especially for women the world over, Copenhagen was a small but decisive step forward in the Sisyphean struggle for equity and equality."[29]

The UN Fourth World Conference on Women

In 1991 the UN Commission on the Status of Women called on the UN Economic and Social Council to convene a Fourth World Conference on Women. The purpose of women's conference was to assess progress that UN member nations had made toward reaching the goals set at the last UN Decade for Women conference held in Nairobi in 1985: to promote "equality, development and peace for all women everywhere," and that had been outlined in the Nairobi conference treaty, the Forward Looking Strategies for the Advancement of Women to the Year 2000. The UN CSW members, advised by international women's NGOs, determined that holding a fourth women's conference before the year 2000 was necessary to negotiate a new global treaty, whereby governments agreed to "more concrete and quantifiable" steps to raise women's economic, legal, political and social status and to eliminate all gender-based discriminations against women before the end of the millennium.[30] In October 1991 the UN General Assembly adopted a resolution to hold the women's conference in September 1995 and accepted the People's Republic of China's offer to host the conference and the NGO forum.

Between 1993 and 1995 conference Secretary General Gertrude Mongella from Tanzania arranged regional preparatory meetings and conference sessions with government delegations, expert advisers and NGOs. Mongella negotiated site arrangements with the host country, the People's Republic of China, and its local arrangements committee, the All-China Women's Federation, for conference and press facilities. She also worked with an NGO forum organizing committee and helped the NGOs negotiate through contentious forum site arrangements with the PRC.[31] The NGO forum committee faced tremendous logistical and political challenges, including the PRC government's decision to move the NGO forum site thirty-five miles outside of Beijing to Huairou several months before the women's conference opened. In the end, approximately 30,000 people attended NGO Forum 95: Looking at the World through Women's Eyes. They represented 185 nations and included 5,000 Chinese participants. The UN government conference held in Beijing was attended by some 17,000 participants from 189 nations, making the Fourth World Conference on Women and NGO Forum 95 the largest world gathering of women ever held in history.[32]

Beyond the myriad opportunities that the Fourth World Conference on Women and NGO Forum 95 offered for global networking that strengthened and expanded social movements, feminist NGOs sought to increase their political impact on policy making at the United Nations and in their home countries.[33] During the two years leading up to the Beijing conference and in the year that followed, U.S. feminist NGOs generally succeeded in swaying the heated domestic political debates regarding the conference in their favor and in positively influencing the Clinton Administration's gender policies, with some notable exceptions as the following pages explain.

Feminist NGOs Prepare for the Beijing Conference

Feminist NGOs influenced U.S. global gender policies formulated in conjunction with the Beijing Fourth World Conference on Women because they were well-informed and organized, they had clear goals and they knew how to identify and work with allies inside the Clinton Administration.[34] As feminist NGOs outlined their goals in early 1994, first and foremost, they pressured the Clinton Administration to pay more attention to the United Nations' meetings and to foreground global women's needs and gender equality principles in official U.S. conference positions. They pressed the administration to allocate more government resources to the UN meetings. They sought and gained a new office within the State Department focused exclusively on UN conference preparations.[35] Feminist NGOs also exerted their influence on the Clinton Administration in regard to determining who would serve on the U.S. delegation to the Fourth World Conference on Women. They pushed for the inclusion of women who represented diversity in class, race and sexual orientation and who reflected the entirety of the population in multicultural America, in addition to making appeals for specific women to be included on the U.S. delegation.[36] (See Appendix D)

Globally feminist NGOs framed the Fourth World Conference on Women as a "Conference of Commitments" and pressured national governments, including the U.S. government, to outline specific steps that they would take to reach gender equality, development and peace goals set for the year 2000.[37] By March 1995 feminist NGOs including the Center for Women's Global Leadership, the International Women's Health Coalition, the International Women's Tribune Centre and the

Women' Environment and Development Organization among many others, drafted a list of commitments to lobby for with national governments. The NGOs sought pre- and post-conference meetings with governments in order to draft specific national plans of action to meet the Beijing Platform for Action agreements. In terms of government spending priorities, they demanded 5 percent immediate reductions in government military spending, with further reductions to take effect annually thereafter. They sought gender equity in all government operations. They pushed for government pledges that 50 percent of all poverty eradication funds and social development aid would be directed to women's needs. They called for integration of "gender analyses" in all government policies, meaning that all policies would specify the differential impacts, positive and negative, on men versus women. They pushed for gender balance in all government appointments and inclusion of women in all government peace keeping efforts. Finally, they sought immediate ratification of the United Nations Convention on the Elimination of All forms of Discrimination Against Women (CEDAW) that would legally bind governments to enforce all these specified gender equity provisions, and more, within their borders.[38]

Among all the government commitments that global feminist NGOs sought in their pre-Beijing lobbying efforts, within the United States CEDAW ratification was a particularly controversial and highly politicized issue. President Jimmy Carter had signed CEDAW in 1980, however, political opponents of the convention in both the Democratic and Republican parties thwarted U.S. ratification of the treaty throughout the 1980s. They claimed that CEDAW provisions forced nations to adopt laws that bound them to radical feminist egalitarian standards and practices that intruded into all private family relations and into the private marketplace, in addition to regulating all public government operations.

After President Clinton took office in 1993 U.S. feminists and a coalition of moderate and liberal Republican and Democratic senators who supported the women's rights convention saw a political opportunity to achieve ratification. They pressed the State Department to review the international convention and send it to the Senate for ratification along with any recommended "reservations, understandings or declarations" attached to the treaty obligations. In September 1994 the Senate Foreign Relations Committee reviewed the treaty along with the Clinton Administration's reservations and advice. The committee then sent the convention to the Senate-at-large for a vote, but the vote was tabled until after the November 1994 elections. In the view of some analysts, if the Clinton Administration had been able to arrange a CEDAW ratification vote in the Senate before the elections were held, it might have passed.[39]

After November 1994, a Republican Party majority presided over Senate. Senator Jesse Helms, who fiercely opposed CEDAW, took his place as Chairman of the Senate Foreign Relations Committee. Helms refused to hold hearings on CEDAW ratification throughout Clinton's tenure in office.[40]

Throughout 1994 and 1995 feminist NGOs pressed for ratification of CEDAW among other U.S. government commitments to women in anticipation of the Beijing conference. These NGOs wielded significant influence within the Clinton Administration. In the United States, WEDO's guiding force, Bella Abzug, was among the most visible, powerful and persistent feminist advocates who pressured the Clinton Administration to dedicate resources to the Beijing conference and to consult with NGOs on U.S. platform positions. Publicizing the women's conference in the boldest terms gained media attention, and Abzug used the attention to make feminist demands: "'We're not going to Beijing to beg or ask—we're going to present our bill—and we expect it to be paid,' she said…. 'We're going to create a movement from the bottom—hitting the top and then going back to the bottom—where people say "you promised to do it, now you better do it!' she said."[41] Because of her prominence Abzug was a lightning rod for criticisms from conservative Republican politicians who not only denounced Abzug's feminist ideology but also attacked the Clinton Administration for conferring with Abzug on global gender policy issues.[42] Nonetheless, Abzug found that the Clinton Administration opened more doors to feminist NGOs than previous U.S. administrations, although this did not prevent her from appealing to President Clinton for even great access to policy makers and for higher priority assigned to the UN conference preparations among the State Department's many other operations.[43]

The Clinton Administration's Preparations for the Beijing Conference

In spring and summer of 1994, Arvonne Fraser, U.S. ambassador to the UN Commission on the Status of Women, and Karen Nussbaum, director of the Women's Bureau at the Department of Labor, organized a series of meetings held in each of the ten federal districts to elicit input from American women's organizations on the issues that were most important to them in order to draft U.S. platform positions for the Beijing Fourth World Conference on Women.[44] Due to Arvonne Fraser's past experiences working with the USAID Women in Development office in the 1970s and with feminist NGOs in the 1980s she supported wide participation in the platform drafting process. She also aimed to build popular support for U.S. participation at the women's conference among the general American public. She had experienced firsthand the negative impact of organized political resistance to U.S. participation in UN forums from conservative politicians, governments and fundamentalist activists. At the annual UN CSW meeting held in March 1994 the United States had lost its long-held membership seat on the commission. The Clinton Administration's delegation was voted off the CSW because of its liberal population policies, including support for global family planning initiatives and for access to safe abortions for women in countries where abortion was legal.[45]

In June 1994 the State Department established an office dedicated to UN conference preparations that American feminist NGOs had called for, led by Foreign Service Officer Theresa Loar.[46] Initially, the office concentrated on preparations for the International Conference on Population and Development and for the Beijing Fourth World Conference on Women. In regard to the Beijing conference, from mid-1994 onward Theresa Loar organized meetings for women's NGOs at the State Department in order to gather even more input in drafting U.S. platform positions for conference documents.[47] Loar's office also facilitated American participation at the conference in China. Loar worked to secure visas for the thousands of American representatives of NGOs and political lobby groups of all political persuasions that attended the Beijing conference and Huairou NGO Forum 95. Loar worked closely with State Department embassy staff in China and with Chinese government representatives in the United States negotiating conference sites and facilities. She also worked with Gracia Hillman who joined the State Department's Global Affairs bureau in fall 1994 when Office of International Women's Issues (OIWI) was established in response to NGO and congressional requests for an office focused on women's human rights.[48]

Gracia Hillman, senior coordinator of the Office of International Women's Issues, had been given the broad mandate to "integrat[e] the advancement of women into U.S. foreign policy,"[49] and to serve as "the State Department's principal liaison with domestic nongovernmental organizations that are concerned with international women's rights and the role of women in development."[50] This mandate differed somewhat from the goal that women's human rights activists had set when they lobbied members of congress and the administration to create the OIWI in the fall of 1993. At that time, feminist NGOs envisioned an office that would "work to ensure the full integration of women's human rights into U.S. policy." By redefining the mandate of the OIWI, and, in the view of some NGOs, weakening the mandate, the State Department had "undercut its effectiveness" in ensuring that U.S. foreign policy would consistently champion women's human rights globally and would sanction governments that violated women's rights through U.S. trade and aid policies.[51] These NGOs continued to press the State Department to return to the original goals set for the office and specifically to:

> strengthen the technical and financial capability of this office to coordinate among [State Department] functional and regional divisions, as well as across federal agencies to address, for example: violence against women, sex discrimination, women's political participation, protection of women's human rights, equality, and access to education. The Senior Coordinator should have a key advisory role in the development of U.S. policy toward the International Criminal Court, and UN peacekeeping, peacemaking, and peace building activities.[52]

Gracia Hillman had no particular background in women's human rights issues; her previous professional experience and expertise were focused on voting rights issues, although she had done some contract work for the State Department in 1993 providing political training for women in Kenya who wanted to run for government office. When she accepted the position at OIWI she understood her focus was to be on women's human rights issues, but, as she recalled later, "I would say 80 percent of my work ended up being on the preparations for the [Beijing] conference." This was due, in part, to diminishing congressional support for the office after the November 1994 elections and decreased funding generally for U.S. participation in UN conferences. Therefore, Gracia Hillman and her small, under-resourced Office of International Women's Issues and Theresa Loar's UN conference secretariat combined their efforts and worked together. Hillman recalled that a major part of her job at the State Department was "doing general outreach to the NGOs," listening to their views on issues and explaining how those views would be integrated, or not, into official U.S. government positions regarding the Beijing conference documents, rather than any specific focus on women's human rights issues in regard to U.S. foreign policy.[53] Nonetheless, women's human rights became a major topic of government and NGO debate at the Beijing conference and human rights language was included in the conference treaty, the Platform for Action.[54] Moreover, the U.S. government, prompted by feminist NGOs, became a leading proponent of women's human rights in Beijing.

The PRC Government and Human Rights: Controversies That Threatened to Derail the Women's Conference

Women's human rights became a particular focus at the Beijing Fourth World Conference on Women, in part, because the conference took place in the People's Republic of China and the PRC government had earned a notorious reputation for widespread human rights abuses. Globally, human rights activists and global governance monitors criticized the PRC for violating the human rights of workers, political dissidents, prisoners, minority populations, Tibetan independence advocates, homosexuals and women. Women's rights advocates were especially critical of the PRC's coercive anti-natal "One Child" population policy.[55] Additionally, the Chinese government's suppression of the 1989 pro-democracy demonstrations and the decision to order the People's Liberation Army to clear the protests in Tiananmen Square in Beijing in 1989 that had resulted in the deaths of thousands of demonstrators—an incident known internationally as the "Tiananmen Square Massacre"—was fresh in the world's memory. The UN decision to hold the women's conference in China was controversial, and many Americans objected strongly to U.S. participation because it might be interpreted as a sign of the U.S. government's approval for China's record of brutal human rights abuse. In May 1995 Republican Congressman Benjamin Gilman proposed legislation to cut government appropriations that funded the U.S. delegation to the conference unless the Chinese government guaranteed various human rights protections and accredited several NGOs whose visas had been denied by the Chinese government due to political objections.[56] Feminist NGOs and human rights activists also faced the dilemma of whether to participate in the Beijing conference because of the message it might send, but the majority believed that the global meeting focused on women's rights issues was too important to stay away.[57]

Sensitive to these criticisms, the People's Republic of China tried to minimize political protests during the women's conference. Certainly, the PRC sought global recognition for the great strides it had made in modernizing China's economy and raising the national wealth and standards of living of many of its citizens since the late 1970s when the government had turned away from exclusive reliance on a centralized socialist development model and embraced some capitalist development strategies. China had opened to foreign investment and trade during the 1980s and 1990s. It had applied to join the World Trade Organization. Moreover, the PRC government had instituted some domestic democratic reforms that allowed Chinese people more economic freedom of choice (while continuing to control the political arena and to censor artists, filmmakers and writers). The nation's leaders were proud of their country's accomplishments and sought to showcase China's transformations to the world. Hosting the UN Fourth World Conference on Women presented this opportunity. However, when developments that the PRC government may not have anticipated occurred, the PRC clumsily tried to reassert its control and touched off global controversies and that involved the United States government.

In March 1995 the PRC government abruptly changed the site for the women's conference NGO forum from the Beijing Workers Sports Complex that was located in central Beijing in close proximity to the UN government conference site to a site in Huairou, thirty-five miles outside Beijing that was still under construction.[58] Officially, the Beijing Workers Sports Complex facilities had "structural problems" that could not be resolved before the forum convened.[59] Unofficially, feminist NGOs and the U.S. government believed that the PRC government had realized that the tens of thousands of activists who planned to attend the NGO forum would unleash chaos into their controlled state environment by staging public protests in Beijing. Theresa Loar, who spent a great deal of time negotiating for U.S. NGOs and for the U.S. government's participation at the women's conference, believed that when China's Premier Li Peng, a "hardline" leader who had ordered the suppression of the protesters in Tiananmen Square in 1989, attended the World Social Summit in Copenhagen and saw the unruly NGOs, he pulled back from welcoming thousands of social and political activists into Beijing.[60] Nonetheless, after lodging the U.S. government's objections to the venue change, Loar's office began to set up an information center at the new NGO forum site to assist all Americans who would be attending the forum in addition to organizing a hospitality room for Americans at the U.S. Embassy in Beijing. The U.S. Embassy hospitality room served as a meeting point for NGOs and the U.S. delegates who attended the UN conference meetings, and it was the location of the U.S. government's daily NGO briefings.[61]

Will She or Won't She? Hillary Clinton's Attendance at the FWCW

From the earliest stages of planning for the Fourth World Conference on Women feminist NGOs wanted First Lady Hillary Clinton to lead the U.S. delegation.[62] Symbolically, the first lady's attendance would signal the administration's strong support for the women's conference gender equality goals. Hillary Clinton's presence would draw more media attention to the conference, as well. Many feminists believed that without a strong U.S. delegation in attendance, global agreements defining women's rights that had been negotiated in Vienna and Cairo would be cast aside in Beijing. The Vatican and delegations from predominantly Catholic and Islamic nations had already proposed language for the Beijing conference documents to allow nations to compromise previous women's rights agreements if they conflicted with local cultural practices and religious beliefs. These proposals undercut previous government agreements in support of women's reproductive rights, human rights, rights to health care, inheritance rights, rights to pursue public roles beyond motherhood and protections for women based on their sexual orientation. The conservatives' proposals had not been overruled at the conference preparatory meetings and nearly 40 percent of the language of the government treaty, the Beijing Platform for Action, was still under negotiation as the conference opened on September 4.[63] Even though some feminists may have disagreed with Hillary Clinton's positions on particular issues or with the strategies for women's advancement that she supported,[64] she was a recognized advocate for women and children. Individuals and NGOs alike pressed her to head the U.S. delegation.[65]

Controversies over China's human rights record, however, prevented the U.S. government from committing the first lady's attendance although Hillary Clinton was named as honorary chair of the U.S. delegation in June 1995.[66] In July, these controversies took center stage when the People's Republic of China arrested human rights activist Harry Wu, a naturalized U.S. citizen who had spent nineteen years in a Chinese prison labor camp during the Maoist era. When Wu re-entered the PRC in June 1995 he was on a mission to expose the ongoing human rights abuses in China's labor camps and planned to film camp conditions. Arrested soon after he crossed into Chinese territory, Wu was charged with espionage, punishable by execution. Congressmen and Senators from both the Republican and Democratic parties called on the Clinton Administration to secure Wu's release[67] and to cancel the U.S. delegation's participation in the Beijing women's conference.[68] Other politicians and political commentators thought the U.S. delegation should go forward but objected to Hillary Clinton's appearance at the conference.[69]

5.3 Hillary Rodham Clinton meeting with Gertrude Mongella, Marjorie Margolis-Mezvinsky, Ambassador Madeleine Albright, Melanne Verveer, Theresa Loar and others. Prep committee meeting for the Fourth World Conference on Women, New York City, March 23, 1995. Courtesy of the William J. Clinton Presidential Library.

In a statement to the U.S. House of Representatives, Ambassador to the UN Madeleine Albright, chair of the U.S. delegation, answered the administration's critics. She advocated in favor of U.S. participation at the Fourth World Conference on Women in order to promote human rights in Beijing:

> The Clinton Administration will use the conference to bolster the view that women should be considered full partners in their communities and nations; to gain broad support for halting discrimination against girls; to combat the despicable notion that rape is just another tactic to war; and to undermine the truth that violence against women is no one's prerogative—it is a crime that we all have a responsibility to condemn, prevent, punish and stop,...
>
> It just does not make sense, in the name of human rights, to boycott a conference that has, as a primary purpose, the human rights of more than half the people on earth.[70]

Albright made it clear that the administration would not back away from its record of support for women's human rights established at the Vienna and Cairo UN conferences as she drew the battle lines:

> we are determined that there be no stepping back from the principle ratified in the 1993 Vienna Declaration and Plan of Action that "the

> human rights of women and the girl child are an inalienable, integral and indivisible part of universal human rights."…
>
> [and] the administration intends to hold firm in Beijing to the commitments made at the 1994 UN Conference on Population and Development in Cairo regarding reproductive health and rights. That agreement recognizes the right of couples and individuals to decide freely and responsibly the number, spacing and timing of their children and to have the information and means to do so free from discrimination, coercion and violence.[71]

Throughout the Harry Wu affair, many feminist NGOs and feminists in U.S. government service pressed the administration to keep its commitments to women and urged Hillary Clinton to lead the U.S. delegation.[72] U.S. Ambassador to the UN Human Rights Commission and the U.S. delegation's vice chair Geraldine Ferraro publicly advocated for Hillary Clinton's presence at the conference in an editorial published in the *New York Times*. Because Ferraro was a Clinton Administration appointee, it seems likely that she expressed the official view. Although she avidly pressed for Harry Wu's release, Ferraro, like Madeleine Albright, asserted that the United States should not boycott the conference, which would only hurt the linked cause of women's human rights:

> Those who are pushing for Washington to boycott are trying to keep away the leader in the United Nations on human rights in China and human rights for women. We cannot afford to take a chance that the world will back away from the agreements reached in Cairo and in Vienna the year before. That's what the Chinese government wants. We owe it to the world's women to attend, especially to the 5000 Chinese women who plan to be there. They will return to their cities and villages to spread the word about problems that are taboo in public discussion: coerced abortion, female infanticide, forced sterilization, domestic violence. If the American delegation fails to go to Beijing, who wins? Not Harry Wu. Not women. Not the United States. Only China's hard-liners will have reason to cheer if we stay home.[73]

According to historian Taylor Branch's account of his conversations with President Clinton, Hillary Clinton also wanted to go to China. As the conference neared she prepared a speech that championed respect for women's human rights everywhere rather than one that focused narrowly on criticizing China. However, in a surprise move that followed a month of tense negotiations with the U.S. government, the PRC government suddenly expelled Harry Wu from China on August 25 after convicting him of being in possession of state secrets and sentencing him to a fifteen-year prison term.[74] When the PRC government released Harry Wu "that made it easier for the president to weather attacks on Hillary's trip from both the political left and right."[75] It also allowed the administration to overcome objections emanating from the National Security Council and the State Department Bureau of East Asian and Pacific Affairs, where the dominant opinion held that attending a global conference in China was not in U.S. national interests.[76] Nonetheless, the decision-by-default to send the U.S. delegation led by Hillary Clinton to the Fourth World Conference on Women in Beijing was a decision where global women's interests prevailed.

U.S. Commitments to Women at the Fourth World Conference on Women

With Harry Wu's release and the first lady's attendance at the Beijing conference assured, feminist NGOs welcomed President Clinton's announcement of the formation of the President's Interagency Task Force on Women in a ceremony at the White House Rose Garden held on August 26, Women's Equality Day. The task force, made up of high-ranking leaders of presidential cabinet agencies and co-chaired by Hillary Clinton and Secretary of Health and Human Services Donna Shalala, was to all oversee all efforts within federal government offices to fulfill the U.S. Commitments to Women that would be formally presented at the Fourth World Conference on Women.

More so than at previous UN conferences where government treaties had pledged to guarantee women's human rights and address women's needs but had taken little action to fulfill those pledges, at the Fourth World Conference on Women feminists throughout the world pushed governments to make public "commitments" and to establish mechanisms of "accountability" in order to carry out the Beijing Declaration of principles and the Platform for Action treaty agreements.[77] The Beijing Declaration reaffirmed the pledges UN member governments had made in the Convention on the Elimination of All forms of Discrimination Against Women, the Nairobi conference Forward Looking Strategies and in the Rio, Vienna and Cairo conference documents to define women's human rights and empower women. The Declaration concluded "we hereby commit ourselves as Governments to implement the following Platform for Action."[78]

The lengthy and detailed Platform for Action finalized in Beijing outlined a blueprint for government action to remove legal and social obstacles to women's "full participation on the basis of equality in all spheres of society, including participation in the decision-making process and access to power."[79] The Platform included actions to address "twelve critical areas of concern": first and foremost, to eliminate violence against women, perpetrated by the state or otherwise; to involve women in economic and social development programs and to establish poverty eradication programs; to protect women's reproductive rights; to protect women's and girls' human rights; to work toward general and complete disarmament; to ensure women's and girls' equal access to education and healthcare, including reproductive and sexual healthcare; and to ensure women's equal access to economic resources such as land, credit, and technology. In order to implement and monitor their commitments, governments were to develop mechanisms to promote women's advancement in all these areas.[80]

In the months leading up to the Beijing conference U.S. NGOs and activists had specifically criticized the United States' record of unfulfilled promises to women:

> The United States has not fulfilled its promise, thus far ignoring the recent International Conference on Population and Development (ICPD) recommendations made to eliminate inequalities between men and women, to eliminate violence against women and children, to increase accessibility to reproductive health care. The United States, which has built an international image of superiority and power through technological advancement and military prowess, still suffers from serious domestic inequities, discrimination, [and] lack of education. Instead of trying to utilize the recommendations of the ICPD legislators here try to end affirmative action, implement harmful and cruel 'welfare reform,' and limit women's reproductive choices.[81]

In response to these criticisms and in response to all the input received in the previous two years' preparation for the women's conference, the Clinton Administration had devised a list of U.S. Commitments to Women to fulfill the overall goals of the Beijing Platform for Action. Specifically, the United States government committed to establish the President's Interagency Task Force on Women as a year-long federal government body that would coordinate the implementation of all other U.S. Commitments and would exchange information with NGOs. After Bill Clinton's re-election in 1996, the task force became the President's Interagency Council on Women (PICW), a "permanent" council that operated until President Clinton left office in 2001. The U.S. government also committed to establish the Office on Violence against Women within the U.S. Department of Justice in order to reduce domestic and other forms of violence against women through stricter laws and better training of law enforcement agencies. The U.S. Department of Labor committed to work with employers and other organizations to establish workplace policies to better balance work and family responsibilities. The Treasury Department committed to coordinate a Federal Microenterprise Initiative that would fund poor women entrepreneurs and expand women's access to credit. The Department of Health and Human Services committed to a range of women's health initiatives including gender-specific health research such as breast cancer research, as well as programs dedicated to treating women's health problems throughout women's lifespan, poverty-related diseases and HIV/AIDS. The White House pledged to renew its efforts to achieve Senate ratification of CEDAW. In regard to U.S. global gender policy, the U.S. Agency for International Development also launched new programs to promote women's political participation and women's legal rights in AID-recipient nations, in addition to continuing programs to support women's and girls' education and microlending programs in impoverished countries.[82]

These U.S. Commitments to Women did not address all the concerns that U.S. and global feminists raised in their many meetings with Clinton Administration representatives or all of the "twelve critical areas of concern" that the Platform for Action identified. In particular, there were no U.S. commitments to promote global disarmament or to involve women in conflict resolution and peace building efforts around the world, including those in Somalia, Rwanda or Bosnia where the United States military was involved in UN efforts to end the brutal and genocidal warfare.[83]

Hillary Clinton and U.S. Global Gender Policy in Beijing

At the time of the Fourth World Conference on Women and in its aftermath, U.S. and global feminists attached tremendous symbolic and substantive meaning to Hillary Clinton's presence and to the speeches she delivered at the UN government conference in Beijing and at the NGO forum in Huairou.[84] Hillary Clinton addressed the UN conference plenary in Beijing on September 5, and then addressed the NGO forum at the Huairou International Convention Centre the following day, September 6.[85] The main event, Clinton's address to the UN conference plenary, secured her global stature as a leader among women's human rights advocates. Clinton used the global feminist movement's arguments to explain the incontrovertible necessity of convening a Fourth World Conference on Women:

> The great challenge of this conference is to give voice to women everywhere whose experiences go unnoticed, whose words go unheard. Women comprise more than half the world's population, 70% of the world's poor, and two-thirds of those who are not taught to read and write. We are the primary caretakers for most of the world's children and elderly. Yet much of the work we do is not valued—not by economists, not by historians, not by popular culture, not by government leaders.[86]

5.4 Hillary Rodham Clinton addressing the United Nations Fourth World Conference on Women plenary session, Beijing, People's Republic of China, September 5, 1996. Courtesy of the William J. Clinton Presidential Library.

Hillary Clinton presented herself as one who could give feminist "voice" to the needs and aspirations of women who shared some universal concerns:

> Those of us who have the opportunity to be here have the responsibility to speak for those who could not. As an American, I want to speak for those women in my own country, women who are raising children on the minimum wage, women who can't afford health care or child care, women whose lives are threatened by violence, including violence in their own homes. I want to speak up for mothers who are fighting for good schools, safe neighborhoods, clean air, and clean airwaves; for older women, some of them widows, who find that, after raising their families, their skills and life experiences are not valued in the marketplace; for women who are working all night as nurses, hotel clerks, or fast food chefs so that they can be at home during the day with their children; and for women everywhere who simply don't have time to do everything they are called upon to do each and every day.[87]

All these U.S. women and women around the world deserved their full dignity and their rights as human beings without compromise:

> The international community has long acknowledged and recently reaffirmed at Vienna that both women and men are entitled to a range of protections and personal freedoms, from the right of personal security to the right to determine freely the number and spacing of the children they bear. No one—No one should be forced to remain silent for fear of religious or political persecution, arrest, abuse, or torture.[88]

Clinton asserted that "It is time for us to say here in Beijing, and for the world to hear, that it is no longer acceptable to discuss women's rights as separate from human rights," as some governments and some human rights activists continued to make a distinction.[89] Abuses of women's human rights that Hillary Clinton enumerated in her plenary address—female infanticide, trafficking in women, dowry killings, "honor" killings, rape of women (in wartime or otherwise), domestic violence, female genital mutilation, forced abortions or forced sterilizations—were all violations of women's human rights. Clinton's speech repeated what many feminists had long asserted,[90] but her words captured global governments' attention as no women's rights activists' had before her:[91]

> If there is one message that echoes forth from this conference, let it be that human rights are women's rights and women's rights are human rights, once and for all.[92]

During the rest of her tenure as first lady, Hillary Clinton focused on advocating for women's human rights and amplifying women's voices in all realms of society, public and private. Clinton's address to the Beijing conference plenary exemplifies the power of discursive politics. Over the years since the UN Decade for Women, repetition of the slogan "women's rights are human rights" by feminists working inside and outside governments had transformed "the 'universe of political discourse' so that ... new (feminist) issues [found] agenda access," in the United States and throughout the UN system.[93]

Certainly, Clinton's speech had its detractors, especially among global feminists who recognized the disconnect between Clinton's words and much of the history of U.S. foreign relations.[94] Liberal feminists inside U.S. government such as Theresa Loar at the State Department, however, believed that Hillary Clinton's speech in Beijing contributed to a rising "feminist" consciousness among governments around the globe. Loar also believed that that Clinton's words signaled a shift in the gender-blind culture of U.S. foreign relations that was already underway and that held progressive implications for the future of U.S. gender policy:

> I think the Beijing conference had a huge effect in policy development. I think it was a watershed event that led to a number of things. A year later I was in a senior position at the State Department focusing on women's human rights and foreign policy. So I was in a position to see what was happening in other parts of the world as follow-ups to this conference and to stay in touch with a number of the delegates and ministers for women, and ministers in other areas that I had worked with. And, our embassies were starting to do some reporting; and also all the ministers for women of other countries and delegates I had worked with would come in to see me. So I would regularly hear from people what they were doing after this conference. … I think that dialogue, all of that, was still around a year later in October of 1996 when the Taliban moved into the capital of Afghanistan and said that girls can't be educated, and women can't walk outside the home without being accompanied by a male. I think, I know, I wouldn't have been able to play the role I played, and I don't think our government would have responded the way we did if we had not had this conference ahead of time.[95]

Perhaps more important than the content of her speech on September 6 at NGO Forum 95, the first lady's presence at the forum was appreciated because it demonstrated the importance that the Clinton Administration attached to the work of NGOs and to global women's aspirations for equality.[96] As she praised the assembled activists, a largely American audience who overflowed a 1200-seat auditorium,[97] Hillary Clinton noted that "Time and time again, we have seen that it is NGOs who are responsible for making progress in any society…. [I]t is clear that it is the NGOs who have charted real advances for women and children. It is the NGOs who have pressured governments and have led governments down the path to economic, social, and political progress, often in the face of overwhelming hostility."[98]

5.5 Hillary Rodham Clinton addressing a panel organized by the World Health Organization and the UN Voluntary Fund for Women (UNIFEM) at the Fourth World Conference on Women, Beijing, People's Republic of China, September 6, 1995. Courtesy of the William J. Clinton Presidential Library.

5.6 Bella Abzug, Ambassador Madeleine Albright, and Conference General Secretary Gertrude Mongella at the UN Fourth World Conference on Women, Beijing, People's Republic of China, September 1995. Courtesy of the Women's Environment and Development Organization.

This symbolic solidarity with the NGOs, whose members had variously "been subjected to surveillance, harassment, intimidation, confiscation of materials and restrictions on freedom of expression and association" by the Chinese government,[99] was also expressed by the U.S. delegation chair, Madeleine Albright, when she visited Forum 95 and spoke at a forum session.[100] Moreover, in spite of continuously rainy weather and the long and inconvenient van rides from the city to Huairou, U.S. delegation members visited the Forum 95 site each day of its operations, August 30 to September 4. Several U.S. delegation members also joined a forum panel on women and politics. Overall, more than 7000 American women attended the Huairou NGO Forum 95.[101]

Global Mechanisms: Holding the World Bank Accountable to Women

In addition to holding national governments accountable to the commitments they made to women at the Beijing conference, feminist NGOs also utilized the conference forums to demand that the global financial system dominated by Western governments be held accountable for the hardships inflicted on global populations. Just as they had argued forcefully at the March World Summit, feminist NGOs held the World Bank, the International Monetary Fund and other global lenders responsible for perpetuating women's economic inequality, among other global problems. Throughout the 1980s and through the mid-1990s on the advice of these global financiers, state-run industries were privatized, centrally planned economies gave way to free market driven production and government spending on social programs was dramatically cut back in favor of theories that postulated private company profits would "trickle down" to benefit all members of society.

Structural adjustment policies based on these theories, however, had failed to grow economies in underdeveloped nations and resulted in even greater global disparities in income distribution and development and an expanding proportion of the global population living in poverty that were mostly women and children.[102] Consequently, at the Beijing conference in a more organized way than ever before, global feminist NGOs sought to extract pledges from global financial institutions to alleviate women's economic disadvantages embedded in structural adjustment lending and development policies and organized to monitor the global banks' progress in fulfilling those pledges. These feminist NGOs echoed criticisms made by a range of anti-World Bank activists who, in 1995, upon the fifty-year anniversary of the UN and the establishment of the global financial system, had launched a campaign "Fifty Years is Enough."[103]

Some global feminist NGOs focused on achieving an "equitable" distribution of social development money in order to "empower" poor women. Consequently, some NGOs supported microcredit programs that the Clinton Administration and other national governments promoted. These programs intended to put money directly into the hands of impoverished women, or would-be local businesswomen, as Mohammed Yunus and his Grammen Bank had done with much success in Bangladesh.[104]

Other feminist NGOs focused their attention on the largest global banks and investors and on governments' lending and development policies. These were the goals of the "Women's Eyes on the World Bank Campaign,"[105] championed by global feminist organizations such as Development Alternatives with Women for a New Era who decried the growing "wealth of nations" at the cost of the "poverty of women."[106] Global feminists circulated a petition at the Beijing conference that was presented to World Bank president, James Wolfensohn, who had been nominated by President Clinton and had stepped in to fill the Bank's leadership position in July 1995.[107] Wolfensohn spoke at the Beijing women's conference, which he attended in order to "undo negative perceptions of World Bank activities." He announced that the World Bank would invest $2 billion over five years on global education initiatives, with $900 million of each year's investment dedicated to educating girls.[108]

Wolfensohn's Beijing speech also included arguments that global feminist NGOs had made for years:

> I need no persuading that women are absolutely central to sustainable development, economic advance, and social justice. … Despite progress over the last two decades, the harsh reality is that women are nonetheless more likely to be under-nourished, under-educated, over-worked and underpaid, than their male partners. They are also more likely to be poor: of the 1.3 billion people living on a dollar a day or less, 70 percent are women. … Women themselves are key to development—the primary agents of change in their communities.[109]

In addressing these global inequities, he invited women to judge him on the record he intended to establish at the World Bank, hiring women for high-level leadership positions and "ensuring that women are not hurt by structural adjustment programs" by being "vigilant and more sensitive to arguments which relate to disproportionate adverse effects on women." Wolfensohn pledged to direct a greater proportion of funds from the World Bank's International Development Association (IDA) to microcredit lending to women entrepreneurs and to increase investments in girls' education that would "be augmented by investments in immunization, nutrition, safe water and sanitation, and other measures to address the needs of the world's poor children." Wolfensohn concluded his address with a remarkable invitation to women: "And as you leave Beijing, please know this: the World Bank stands with you. We will commit our finance and our energy as an advocate and a partner in the fight for equity. If you have ideas, share them with us. If you have initiatives where our experience or assistance can be relevant, let us know. You can count on us."[110]

Wolfensohn's remarks proposed no fundamental changes to restructure the global capitalist system. Instead, he offered palliative measures that addressed the immediate needs of some global women. After the Beijing conference, the World Bank's Women in Development Unit of the Social Programs and Sustainable Development Division ensured that loan recipients integrated gender analysis and equity considerations into their funded programs. Regional departments of the Bank hired "gender specialists" to monitor operations, and the Bank established an External Gender Consultative Group as the mechanism for NGOs to provide feedback. These initiatives allowed for feminist input into World Bank lending policies and operations, but it remained unclear whether any feminist transformations in policy development or program implementation occurred under Wolfensohn's presidential tenure.[111] Moreover, feminist NGOs that chose to work with the World Bank, consulting with the organization and designing aid programs for the World Bank IDA, often found that their own goals were co-opted, "inevitably reshaped by their relationship with the World Bank." NGOs, it could be argued, sought to "influence programs and institute policy shifts without sufficient clout to implement them."[112]

In contrast, a more positive conclusion can also be drawn here. The growing presence of feminist women holding leadership positions in intergovernmental organizations such as the World Bank would eventually and inevitably change the organization's culture, politics and policy priorities. This was certainly the view of Mayra Buvinic, president throughout the 1980s and early 1990s of the International Center for Research on Women, a Washington DC-based feminist NGO that focused on global development policy. Buvinic left the ICRW to work with the InterAmerican Development Bank in 1996 and has directed the Gender and Development division at the World Bank since 2005.[113] Bella Abzug also expressed this view when she spoke at the Beijing conference regarding the impact that feminist women would have working from positions inside powerful government and financial institutions: "I think women will change the nature of power rather than power changing the nature of women. Women don't want to be mainstreamed into a polluted stream; they want to change the stream—they want to make it fresh; they want to make it clean; they want to make it flow in new directions."[114]

Bringing Beijing Home: The President's Interagency Council on Women

Prior to the Beijing conference feminist NGOs had worked together to ensure that national governments made specific commitments to achieve women's equality "in law and in fact."[115] When the conference concluded U.S.-based NGOs immediately launched concentrated efforts to ensure that the U.S. government implemented its pledges. Interviewed by the press and asked to comment on the meaning of the "Conference of Commitments" and the Beijing Platform for Action signed by 189 governments, Bella Abzug replied "It's a contract—a contract with the world's women and it has to be honored."[116] Organizations such as Abzug's Women's Environment and Development Organization widely publicized the U.S. Commitments to Women announced in Beijing. WEDO monitored the U.S. government's progress through its own publications and through campaigns such as its "Contract with the Women of the USA."[117] WEDO called on elected officials to enact the U.S. Commitments and to reject the premises of the Republican Party's "Contract with America" that, WEDO argued, was in fact a "Contract *on* America."[118]

WEDO also publicized national governments' progress worldwide through its "Commitment Scoreboard" campaign.[119] InterAction, a consortium of NGOs focused on development, publicized the U.S. Commitments on its organization websites. Amnesty International circulated pamphlets explaining the U.S. Commitments and suggested political actions to ensure government follow-through. In a major theme of the post-Beijing feminist activism in the United States, local and state-wide campaigns around the country called for ratification of the Convention on the Elimination of all Forms of Discrimination against Women. Although the U.S. Senate never ratified CEDAW as the law of the nation, individual states and cities, prodded by feminist activists, symbolically ratified the UN convention within their jurisdictions. Universities and women's organizations across the nation hosted follow-up meetings to share their personal experiences and to explain conference documents. "Bringing Beijing Home" and "Beijing and Beyond" conferences and programs took place nation-wide.[120]

The President's Interagency Council on Women, chaired by Secretary of Health and Human Services Donna Shalala and supported by Hillary Clinton's involvement as honorary chair, continued the forward momentum to carry out U.S. Commitments to Women within the presidential cabinet agencies. Melanne Verveer, the first lady's chief of staff, coordinated Hillary Clinton's attendance at PICW meetings whenever possible. Theresa Loar was appointed to direct the PICW secretariat. She was aided by her deputy director Kathleen Hendrix and a small staff that occupied an office at the White House.

Theresa Loar was keen to chart progress toward fulfilling the U.S. Commitments and to share U.S. government actions with feminist NGOs. She held monthly PICW meetings that were open to all interested organizations and frequently published government progress reports.[121] As Loar recalled her motivations in organizing the work of the PICW, she strove for "transparency" as the key to establishing the PICW's legitimacy among feminist NGOs and among the administration's anti-feminist critics as well:

> I wanted to set out the principle that Tim Wirth pioneered when he was Undersecretary. This was that you wanted to build constituencies with the work that you were doing, and you also want people to understand what you're doing so your work was transparent. If they have some input, they can criticize or they can tell you you're right or wrong. But, you've done it in a transparent way so people know where you're going. And so we held these briefings every month and when we came back from Beijing, we continued holding those; so it was this very open way of continuing to talk to this whole NGO community. [122]

In the year following the Beijing conference Loar encouraged government cabinet agencies to take concrete, measurable steps toward fulfilling their individual bureau commitments. She provided ideas regarding gender equity policies and program implementation when needed, and she suggested collaborations among agencies. She documented the results in order to demonstrate to skeptics within the U.S. government that efforts to promote women's equality were worthwhile and that results were achievable and to demonstrate to feminist NGOs that the government was sincere in its efforts to promote women's equality.[123] Toward these ends, in November 1995 the government added an eighth commitment to its Beijing pledges to pursue women's equality goals through the PICW and the departments of Justice, Labor, Treasury, Health and Human Services, State, USAID and the White House—the Department of Education pledged to "take action on a range of issues to remove barriers [to educational opportunities] facing girls and women of different backgrounds, including girls and women with disabilities, those of low income, and those from ethnic and racial minorities."[124]

Some of the government agency actions were symbolic. For example, the Women's Bureau at the Labor Department announced an initiative in November 1995 called the "Working Women Count Honor Roll" that provided certificates of recognition to employers who took steps to improve working conditions for female employees and who could demonstrate that they were "improving the lives of women workers in concrete ways." While this government campaign was symbolic, the Women's Bureau goal was to support progressive private sector initiatives.[125]

Other government agency actions had far-reaching impact in regard to protecting global women's human rights. The United States Immigration and Naturalization Service, for example, issued guidelines that, for the first time, formally recognized gender-based violations such as domestic violence, rape or female genital mutilation as potential grounds for asylum, in addition to recognizing violations of human rights based on race, religion, nationality, membership in a particular social group or political opinion that could be claimed by male or female asylum seekers.[126]

In March 1996 USAID Administrator Brian Atwood announced a major reorientation of the agency's development aid allocation and programs to "reflect the central role of women in development." The USAID's Gender Plan of Action pledged to conduct gender analyses of all existing and newly-proposed AID programs, to reallocate funds to address gender issues, to evaluate results of programming by taking gender impact into consideration and to hire program officers or reassign program and project development officers with specific job duties to address gender issues throughout the agency, not just confined to the Women in Development office. The Gender Plan of Action also incentivized WID projects with a new Performance Fund and established a WID fellowship "to help build a technical cadre to support the integration of gender issues in development."[127]

The existence of the President's Interagency Council on Women that promoted these government policy changes, large and small, was in itself significant. As Linda Tarr-Whelan, the newly-appointed U.S. ambassador to the UN Commission on the Status of Women, explained in her opening statement at the annual March 1996 CSW session "For the first time, the United States has created a formal mechanism especially for implementation and follow-up. … Time is short and the task before us great. The United States is determined to waste no time and the President's Council has begun the work of implementation now. It is our goal to institutionalize as much change as possible." Certainly, Washington's political climate was volatile and new program initiatives vied for limited government funds. The U.S. Commitments to Women would have to be implemented "within existing resources, through refocusing, reordering priorities, thinking creatively."[128]

In regard to the State Department's support for the U.S. Commitments to Women, Gracia Hillman and her staff at the Office of International Women's Issues attended the PICW monthly meetings through the fall of 1995 and early spring of 1996.[129] However, Hillman resigned her position in April 1996. The position of senior coordinator remained vacant and the office dormant until late 1996, when Theresa Loar was appointed to lead the OIWI.

Although the OIWI did not play an active role at this time, highest-level State Department leaders continued to assert the primacy of women's human rights in their public foreign policy addresses. In March 1996, Undersecretary of State Timothy Wirth highlighted the Administration's concern for "the human rights of women and the advancement of their status." He asserted that women's human rights violations cataloged in the annual reports of U.S. embassies around the world were abuses "that President Clinton has particularly identified as a problem that we must end." Wirth also praised the leadership displayed by the U.S. delegation to the Beijing conference, especially singling out Hillary Clinton's address to the global conference delegates and her strong statement that "women's rights are human rights."[130]

As U.S. Ambassador to the UN Madeleine Albright campaigned around the country to pressure Congress to pay up on past-due funding pledges to the United Nations and to reject further cuts in future UN contributions, she also highlighted U.S. participation at the Beijing conference as one example of the way the United States had demonstrated its global leadership at UN forums: "All Americans can take pride in the message Mrs. Clinton brought to Beijing—a message that applies both in the United States and overseas—a message that says that the physical abuse of women must stop; that the life of a girl should be valued equally with that of a boy; that there should be equal access to education, health care, and the levers of economic and political power; and that women's rights are neither separable nor different from those of men." These global human rights principles, Albright asserted, needed the media and public attention that a global forum mobilized to prompt government action: "The Women's conference could not solve these problems overnight, but it could—and did—outline a plan for addressing them."[131]

Secretary of State Warren Christopher spoke at the State Department's International Women's Day commemoration in March 1996 and he, too, used the language of feminist activists to assert: "Where women's rights are not protected, human rights are not secure. Where women are not educated about their health, their families suffer along with them. Where women play no role in protecting the environment, it does not get protected. But where women enjoy equal rights and equal protection, all society progresses. That is why this administration is committed to bringing women's issues into the mainstream of American diplomacy."[132]

These statements from Clinton Administration leaders were necessary to build political support for incorporating feminist concerns into U.S. foreign and domestic policy making. Throughout President Clinton's tenure in office, the Republican Party actively opposed the administration's gender policies and the Republican majority in Congress threatened to impose crippling budget cuts to foreign aid and diplomacy budgets along with further reductions in funding for domestic social programs.[133]

The PICW's First-Year Anniversary

The national teleconference called to assess "America's Commitment: The UN Conference One Year Later" linked groups of women across the nation who listened to reports from the first lady, cabinet members serving in the PICW and feminist NGO leaders regarding progress made toward implementing the U.S. Commitments to Women announced in Beijing. Without much of a budget to run an on-site national conference, the idea of a teleconference fulfilled the goal to create a widely shared experience facilitated through new technology.[134] Hillary Clinton's involvement in the national teleconference, broadcast from Washington DC on September 28, 1996, was critical to the administration's efforts to build a national constituency of support for its domestic and global gender policies,[135] as was the involvement of Secretary Donna Shalala, Ambassador Madeleine Albright and Ambassador Geraldine Ferraro, among other popular administration leaders.[136] Feminist NGOs, too, helped the PICW to plan and publicize the teleconference and they rallied widespread participation.[137] NGOs reported on local activism and organized "Speak Out" sessions to share their evaluations of the U.S. government's record of implementing its Commitments to Women.[138] Many American women had been politicized during the years of activism preceding the Fourth World Conference on Women. Their awareness of both the national and global feminist movements was greater than that of previous generations of American women. Women across the nation demonstrated a high level of interest in the teleconference. Organizations hosted teleconference events at 800 local sites across the country,[139] and an estimated 70,000 people participated nationwide.[140]

Clearly, for many American feminists and global women involved in the Beijing conference process and in the post-conference Commitments campaigns Beijing had "made a difference" in their lives as it affirmed women's dignity and human rights.[141] Feminist women were asserting their rights to speak out and define the nation's global gender policies. However, they needed a receptive partner in the White House to support legal measures and to move forward institutional policies and practices that were friendly to women's interests. The prospects for continued feminist influence on federal government gender policies and operations, and the fate of the President's Interagency Council on Women and the State Department Office of International Women's Issues, depended on the outcome of the November 1996 presidential election.

---

[1]Gayner, "The Contract with America: Implementing New Ideas in the US."

[2]Republicans gained 54 seats in the House of Representatives for a 54.4% voting majority and gained 6 seats in the Senate for a 53% voting majority.

[3]Douglas, "Election 1994: Revenge of the White Guys," p. 2.

[4]Atwood, "U.S. Foreign Assistance Program Reform"; Loar, The Association for Diplomatic Studies and Training Foreign Affairs Oral History Project.

[5]Antrobus, *The Global Women's Movement*, pp. 114-15; Mantilla, "NWSA Getting a Global Perspective," p. 8; "Stepping Stones from Copenhagen to Beijing," *DAWN Informs* (March 1995), IWTC, Acc. #00S-8, box 9; Riley, "The Invisible Agenda."

[6]Tinker, "Nongovernmental Organizations: An Alternative Power Base for Women?" in Meyer and Prügl, eds. *Gender Politics in Global Governance*, pp. 100-01. See also: Mantilla, "NWSA Getting a Global Perspective," p. 8. "[Nawal el Saadawi concluded a keynote address to the 1994 National Association of Women's Studies annual meeting] by saying that we face two challenges: internal powers and fanatic religious groups. To successfully counter these powers we must fight together and work together. We must network with women from all over the globe. We need globalization from below to fight the globalization from above."

[7] "Cairo—Copenhagen—Beijing: A Common Agenda," Invitation for Luncheon and Panel, The Academy for Educational Development, Washington DC, December 14, 1994, IWTC, Acc. #00S-8, box 3.

[8] Women's Environment & Development Organization, *News & Views* 7, no. 2 (September 1994), IWTC, Acc. #95S-69, box 11. Susan Davis, Executive Director of WEDO, explained feminist NGOs' goals in pursuing the Women's Caucus strategy at each of the UN world conferences: "By linking Women's Caucuses, we are trying to prevent collective amnesia."

[9]"Report of the World Summit for Social Development."

[10]Riley, "The Invisible Agenda."

[11]"Summary of the 1994 World Survey on The Role of Women in Development," *Women,* Published by the United Nations Department of Public Information, c. September 1995, IWTC, Acc. #00S-8, box 9.

[12]Wirth, "Making the Social Summit Work: The U.S. View."

[13]Sonia Correa, "Gender Perspectives on the Social Summit: Challenges, Risks and Breakthroughs" *DAWN Informs* 3 (1995), IWTC, Acc. #00S-8, box 9; Moghadam, *Globalizing Women*, pp. 115, 119. See also: "The Women's Caucus

Statement, The World Summit for Social Development, Compilation of Comments and Suggestions on the Overview Report of the Secretary General and Working Papers Prepared During PrepCom I," February 10, 1994, IWTC. Acc. #95S-69, box 11: "The Women's Caucus, comprised of 100 women and men from 23 countries from every region, met daily during the first PrepCom. Four Task Forces on each of the core issues prepared detailed analyses and recommendations which were synthesized by the Caucus."

[14]"Summary of the 1994 World Survey on The Role of Women in Development"; Moghadam, *Globalizing Women*, 120; Antrobus, *The Global Women's Movement,* p. 88; Bella Abzug to Women's Caucus Member, "Women's Caucus Post PrepCom III," February 15, 1995, IWTC, Acc. #95S-69, box 11; Bella Abzug to "Dear Friend," March 6, 1995, IWTC, Acc. #00S-8, box 3.

[15]Anne Sisson Runyan, "Women in the Neoliberal 'Frame'," in Meyer and Prügl, eds. *Gender Politics in Global Governance*, 218.

[16]Susan T. Fried, "Women's Human Rights at the World Summit for Social Development," *AWID News* 9, no. 4 (August 1995), KT, box 5.

[17]Gayner, "The Contract with America: Implementing New Ideas in the US." See also: "Taking it Out on Women and Children," *Sister to Sister/S2S*, Newsletter of the Women of Color Resource Center 1, no. 4 (Winter 1995), IWTC, Acc. #00S-8, box 2. The Personal Responsibility and Work Opportunity Act included provisions for "prohibiting welfare going to mothers under the age of 18, halting the increase of benefits for mothers each time they had additional illegitimate children, and cutting welfare spending."

[18]Hillary Rodham Clinton, "Remarks at special event to World Summit for Social Development in Copenhagen, Denmark."

[19]Hillary Rodham Clinton, "Announcement of U.S. Initiative to Expand Girls' and Women's Education in the Developing World." See also: "Fact Sheet: The United States Boosts Girls' and Women's Education Worldwide." "USAID will allocate $11.7 million in Fiscal Year 1995 for this initiative, as part of its $125-million basic education program. Over the next decade, USAID's initiative will target about 12 countries in Africa, Asia, and Latin America. The principal goal of the initiative is to achieve higher school completion rates for girls. … In countries where governments have invested in primary and secondary education of girls and women, this investment has been repaid many times through higher economic productivity, greater participation of women in the modern labor sector, lower infant and maternal mortality rates, improved child nutrition and family health, longer life expectancy, and lower fertility rates. Recent research has demonstrated that investments in the education of girls and women may well yield a higher return than any other investment in a country's development."

[20]Hillary Rodham Clinton, "Announcement of U.S. Initiative to Expand Girls' and Women's Education in the Developing World."

[21]Gore, "Remarks at UN World Summit for Social Development."

[22] Robert S. Hirshfield, "Washington comes down on behalf of NGOs," *The Earth Times* (March 31-April 4, 1995), KT, box 6.

[23]Wirth, "Making the Social Summit Work: The U.S. View."

[24]Gore, "Remarks at UN World Summit for Social Development." See also: "Focus on Population and Development: Follow-up on Cairo Conference, USAID Programs."

[25]Gore, "Remarks at UN World Summit for Social Development."

[26]Fact Sheet: "The New Partnerships Initiative—Strengthening Grass-roots Political and Economic Institutions." See also: "Focus on Population and Development: Follow-up on Cairo Conference, USAID Programs."

[27]"Speeches by Non-Governmental Organizations at the World Summit for Social Development, Bella Abzug, Women's Environment and Development Organization," Copenhagen, March 6-12, 1995, SIGI, box CONF 11.

[28]"Report of the World Summit for Social Development."

[29]Bella S. Abzug, "The Glass Half-Full: Looking at some of the 'Courageous Initiatives'," *The Earth Times* (March 15-31, 1995), KT, box 6.

[30]International Women's Tribune Center '95 Preview *Bulletin*, no. 1 (April 1993), IWTC, Acc. #93S-60, box 2.

[31]Ibid. and *Women on the Move,* no. 7 (1995), publication of the Division for the Advancement of Women, Secretariat of the Fourth World Conference on Women, IWTC, Acc. #00S-8, box 9.

[32]"United Nations: U.S. Participation in the [FWCW]," Report to Congressional Requesters, Government Accounting Office (GAO), February 16, 1996, KT, box 9.

[33]Antrobus, *The Global Women's Movement,* p. 114.

[34] See for example: Susan Davis and Mim Kelber, Women's Environment and Development Organization to "Dear Friend," September 1, 1994, IWTC, Acc. #95S-69, box 11; Amnesty International, "Equality by the Year 2000? Amnesty International's recommendations for the Fourth UN World Conference on Women's Platform for Action," September 1994, IWTC, Acc. #00S-8, box 5; Sarah Moten, National Council of Negro Women "NGOs Establish US Network for the Fourth World Conference" On the Road to Beijing (October 1994), CWGL, IV World Conference on Women, Beijing, China 1995, box 1; Charlotte Bunch and Niamh Reilly to "Friends," December 1, 1994, CWGL, IV World Conference on Women, Beijing, China 1995, box 1; "Cairo—Copenhagen—Beijing: A Common Agenda" Invitation for Luncheon and Panel, The Academy for Educational Development, Washington DC, December 14, 1994, IWTC, Acc. #00S-8, box 3; "Beijing and Beyond: A domestic organizing, funding, and communications initiative sponsored by the Ms. Foundation for Women," c. July 1995, CWGL, IV World Conference on Women, Beijing, China 1995, box 4.

[35]Women's Environment & Development Organization, *News & Views* 7, no. 2 (September 1994), IWTC, Acc. #95S-69, box 11.

[36]See for example: Charlotte Bunch to President Bill Clinton, January 25, 1995, CWGL, IV World Conference on Women, Beijing, China 1995, box 6.

[37]Friedman, "Gendering the Agenda," p. 325.

[38]"A Pledge to Gender Justice: A Call for Commitment to the Agenda for Equality for Women at the Fourth World Conference on Women and Beyond," *The Earth Times* (March 15-31, 1995), KT, box 6. See also: International Women's Health Coalition, Draft of proposal "World Conference on Women: U.S. Commitments on Reproductive Rights and Health," July 21, 1995, CWGL, IV World Conference on Women, Beijing, China 1995, box 4.

[39]"Focus on Population and Development: Follow-up on Cairo Conference, USAID Programs."

[40]Hoff Sommers, "Feminism by Treaty"; Feminist Majority Foundation, "Global Women's Rights: CEDAW."

[41]InterPress Third World News Agency Press Release, Jaya Dayal, "Women: 180 Countdown to Beijing," March 13, 1995, IWTC, Acc. #00S-8, box 3.

[42]Letter to President Bill Clinton from Representative Christopher Smith, Chairman, Subcommittee on International Operations and Human Rights Committee on International Relations and Congressman Henry Hyde, Chairman Committee on the Judiciary and Member Committee on International Relations, January 19, 1995, CWGL, IV World Conference on Women, Beijing, China 1995, box 6.

[43]Bella Abzug to President Bill Clinton, May 16, 1994, CWGL, IV World Conference on Women, Beijing, China 1995, box 6.

[44]"On the Road to Beijing: The UN Fourth World Conference on Women: Action for Equality, Development and Peace," April 1994, published by the Women's Bureau, U.S. Department of Labor, IWTC, Acc. #95S-69, box 11. See also: Sharon Kotok, Global Conference Secretariat, U.S. Department of State, "On the Road to Beijing: Development of the Platform for Action," October 1994, CWGL, IV World Conference on Women, Beijing, China 1995, box 1.

[45]Letter to President Clinton from Representative Christopher Smith, Chairman, Subcommittee on International Operations and Human Rights Committee on International Relations and Congressman Henry Hyde, Chairman Committee on the Judiciary and Member Committee on International Relations, January 19, 1995.

[46]History of the Department of State during the Clinton Presidency. According to the State Department, recognition of "the central importance of women's issues for U.S. foreign policy" and the need for "an administrative mechanism to provide input to the policy process" within the Global Affairs Bureau led by Undersecretary of State Timothy Wirth prompted the opening of the UN conference secretariat. See also: Kathleen Hendrix, "On the Road to Beijing: State Department Establishes Global Conference Secretariat," October 1994, CWGL, IV World Conference on Women, Beijing, China 1995, box 1.

[47]"Women Thinking Globally, Acting Locally," Official U.S. Preparatory Meeting for the United Nations Fourth World Conference on Women, November 15, 1994, IWTC, Acc. #95S-69, box 11.

[48]Loar, The Association for Diplomatic Studies and Training Foreign Affairs Oral History Project.

[49]History of the Department of State during the Clinton Presidency.

[50]U.S. State Department, Office of Global Affairs, biography of Gracia Hillman, Senior Advisor for International Women's Issues released September 22, 1995.

[51]"The Women's Rights Project," Human Rights Watch *World Report 1995* (New York, 1996), pp. 354-5.

[52]"Draft Compilation of Recommendations from Human Rights NGOs in the Washington Working Group on Women Directed at Strengthening U.S. Commitment to Protect Women's Human Rights in the U.S. and Internationally," July 26, 1995, SIGI, box CONF 12.

[53]Gracia Hillman, Phone Interview with Author, June 22, 2009. See also: "Report on Donor's Meeting, The Ford Foundation/ Women and Philanthropy, on UN Fourth World Conference on Women," February 15, 1995, KT, box 7: "Gracia Hillman discussed the new position, which she has filled for three months, as Senior Coordinator for International Women's Issues at the U.S. Department of State. She is responsible for incorporating women's issues into foreign policy and acts as a liaison between the State Department and U.S. NGOs on Beijing. Her responsibilities include coordinating the participation of U.S.

agencies in the March PrepCom on Beijing, and facilitating discussions on how U.S. progress, plans, etc., jibe with the draft Platform for Action."

[54]Kristen Timothy and Marsha Freeman, "IWRAW The CEDAW Convention and the Beijing Platform for Action: Reinforcing the Promise of the Rights Framework" January 2000, CWGL, Beijing +5, box 1: "Beijing was the first global conference in which women in development issues were closely and explicitly linked to women's human rights. The Platform for Action also is the first global political agreement in which the CEDAW Convention is clearly reflected. The Beijing Platform for Action mentions "rights" approximately 500 times and includes human rights as one of the twelve Critical Areas of Concern. Signatories called for restraint from violating women's human rights and placed new emphasis on vigorous "promotion" and "protection" of rights. The Platform for Action 'upholds' the CEDAW Convention (para 7) and notes that since 1985 there had been many 'violations' of and failure to protect all human rights and fundamental freedoms of all women, and their civil, cultural, economic, political and social rights including the "right to development" (para 42). The Platform calls for protection of a wide range of rights including: the right to education; right to economic resources including property rights (para 166c); right to equal pay for equal work or to work of equal value (para 165a); freedom of association and the right to organize (para 1661 and 175c); workers' rights (para 178a); right to collective bargaining (178h); the right to participate in government (para 181)."

[55]Kristen Timothy, "Walking on Eggshells at the UN" in Fraser and Tinker, eds. *Developing Power,* pp. 59-60. See also: Dawson, "When Women Gather: The NGO Forum of the Fourth World Conference on Women Beijing, 1995," p. 8.

[56]Global FaxNet # 12, International Women's Tribune Center. New York, May 19, 1995, SIGI, box CONF 11. "The provision spells out a number of requirements to be met by China and certified by the US State Department before funds could be released to pay the way for the US delegation to Beijing. These criteria include proof that no NGO seeking accreditation be granted to the conference is denied admission based on its political or ethnic affiliation; that accreditation be granted to at least one representative from Tibet and Taiwan; and that China grant visas to all NGO representatives who have applied on time. The bill appears part of a campaign by Republican lawmakers to strong-arm Beijing into cleaning up its human rights record."

[57]Mantilla and Kraus, "On the Road to Beijing,"1: "While Human Rights Watch has reservations about the Fourth World Conference on Women being held in Beijing due to China's poor record on human rights, they have decided to support the conference because of its potential importance to women around the world. While in China, however, they will be monitoring for human rights violations by the Chinese surrounding the conference such as jamming radio broadcasts or arresting peaceful demonstrators." See also: "Women war resisters protest Beijing," p. 8.

[58]*Beijing Agender* [publication of South African Women and Men], Issue 2 (May 1995), IWTC, Acc. #00S-8, box 9: "According to an NGO assessment, not only is the Huairou site remote but it also lacks satisfactory accommodation for delegates; its meeting rooms, spread out over a radius of 6 km, can only hold a total of 9,430 persons, and it has no facilities for the disabled."

[59]"Information concerning the change of site for the NGO Forum on Women," [c. April 1995], prepared for NGOs by NGO Forum Planning Committee, IWTC, Acc. #95S-69, box 11.

[60]Loar, The Association for Diplomatic Studies and Training Foreign Affairs Oral History Project.

[61]Ibid. See also: Friedman, "Gendering the Agenda," p. 324.

[62]Women's Environment & Development Organization *News & Views* 7, no. 2 (September 1994), IWTC, Acc. #95S-69, box 11.

[63]Roberts, "Beijing Fourth World Conference on Women"; Jaya Dayal, United Nations [press release] "Women: UN Human Rights Czar says Beijing Draft Weakens Human Rights," July 25, 1995, CWGL, IV World Conference on Women, Beijing, China 1995, box 2.

[64]For example, many feminists did not share Hillary Clinton's belief that the micro-credit strategy she strongly supported would 'lift' women in developing nations out of poverty.

[65]Loar, The Association for Diplomatic Studies and Training Foreign Affairs Oral History Project.

[66]"White House Names Leaders of US Delegation," *On the Road to Beijing* (June 1995), CWGL, IV World Conference on Women, Beijing, China 1995, box 1.

[67]"Free Harry Wu."

[68]Republican U.S. Senators and Congressman [Newt Gingrich, Robert Dole, Benjamin Gilman, Christopher Smith, Alfonse D'Amato] to President Clinton, July 13, 1995, SIGI, box CONF 12: "In our view, it would be wholly inappropriate to participate in any international conference in the People's Republic of China while an American citizen is being unjustly detained by the Chinese government. … Accordingly we urge you to announce that the United States government will not participate—at any level or in any fashion—in the upcoming conference as long as Harry Wu is detained in China. Anything less would send a tragic signal of disregard for the human rights of an American citizen." See also: "Meeting of the Subcommittee on International Operations and Human Rights, on the subject of the Beijing Conference on Women," July 18, 1995, KT, box 7.

[69]Binder, "2 Republican Senators Caution Hillary Clinton on China Trip." See also: "Meeting of the Subcommittee on International Operations and Human Rights, on the subject of the Beijing Conference on Women," July 18, 1995, KT, box 7; Press release from Congresswoman Nancy Pelosi, "Representative Nancy Pelosi, Subcommittee on International Operations and Human Rights, Hearing on the Fourth World Conference on Women," July 18, 1995, CWGL, IV World Conference on Women, Beijing, China 1995, box 3.

[70]Statement by Ambassador Madeleine K. Albright, U.S. Permanent Representative to the United Nations to the Subcommittee on International Operations and Human Rights, House Committee on International Relations, U.S. House of Representatives, August 2, 1995, CWGL, IV World Conference on Women, Beijing, China 1995, box 2. See also: Albright, "Charting Further Gains in the Status and Rights of Women."

[71]Statement by Ambassador Madeleine K. Albright, U.S. Permanent Representative to the United Nations to the Subcommittee on International Operations and Human Rights, House Committee on International Relations, U.S. House of Representatives.

[72]Fax from Ms. Foundation re "Action in Support of U.S. Participation in Beijing," and press release "Ms. Foundation for Women Calls for US Support for Conference on Women," July 18, 1995, CWGL, IV World Conference on Women, Beijing, China 1995, box 4; Fax re "Should Hillary Go to Beijing? Yes! Says Charlotte Bunch," August 18, 1995, CWGL, IV World Conference on Women, Beijing, China 1995, box 6. For a contrary view, see: Letter from Human Rights Watch to Hillary Clinton, August 16, 1995, CWGL, IV World Conference on Women, Beijing, China 1995, box 6: "As long as Mr. Wu is in detention, we believe it would be highly inappropriate and counterproductive for you to go to Beijing. Your presence would make a mockery of U.S. concerns about Mr. Wu, and the controversy surrounding your participation would divert attention from the important business of the conference."

[73]Ferraro, "Women's Rights, Human Rights."

[74]"The Harry Wu Opening."

[75]Branch, *The Clinton Tapes*, pp. 288-9.

[76]Loar, The Association for Diplomatic Studies and Training Foreign Affairs Oral History Project.

[77]Bella Abzug, "Women Have Great Expectations," *The Earth Times: Beijing Women's Conference Daily,* August 30, 1995, IWTC, Acc. #00S-8, box 9.

[78]Roberts, "Beijing Fourth World Conference on Women."

[79]Ibid.

[80]The United Nations Fourth World Conference on Women, Platform for Action.

[81]"U.S. Women of Color Statement on the Status of Women", Prepared by the U.S. Women of Color Delegation to the United Nations Fourth World Conference on Women, August 1995, CWGL, IV World Conference on Women, Beijing, China 1995, box 4.

[82]Maran, "After the Beijing Conference: What will be done?"; U.S. Department of State, "United States Commitments Announced at the Fourth World Conference on Women", Beijing, China, September 1995, SIGI, box CONF 13.

[83]See for example: Charlotte Bunch, NGO Forum Opening Plenary, August 31, 1995, IWTC, Acc. #96S-34, box 1; Winnie Byanyima, Constituent Assembly Women's Caucus, Uganda, Opening Plenary Session, "Global Forces and Their Impact on Women, An African Perspective," August 31, 1995, IWTC, Acc. #96S-34, box 1.

[84]See for example: Joan Holmes, "The Global Phenomenon of Women's Leadership," in Lee and Clauson-Wicker, eds. *Voice of Women*, p. 37; Alyse Nelson, Interview with Author, Washington DC, November 26, 2006.

[85]Hillary Clinton also addressed Conference sessions organized by the World Health Organization and the United Nations Development Fund (UNIFEM). See: Hillary Rodham Clinton, "Health Care Security for Women and Girls: An International Priority," and "Women's Economic Empowerment Zone." In her address to the World Health Organization Forum, Clinton affirmed U.S. support for investments in healthcare for women and girls as part of national and international development strategies and she asserted that at FWCW preparatory meetings "the United States took the lead in highlighting the importance of a comprehensive approach to women's health." She also confirmed agreements that the U.S. and 180 other world governments made at the Cairo International

Conference on Population and Development, or the so-called "Cairo Consensus," including "the basic right of all couples and individuals to decide freely and responsibly the number, spacing, and timing of their children and to have the information and means to do so." Stressing individual choice and protections of women's health, she repeated the U.S. government position that some feminists had objected to in Cairo, "in no case should abortion be promoted as a method of family planning." In her remarks at the UNIFEM panel, Clinton expressed her strong support for microcredit used as a community development strategy that benefitted women and society: "But the fact is: give a woman a seed, and she will plant it, she will water it, nurture it, then reap it, share its fruits, and finally, she will replant it. In this way, step by step, the world's poorest women are leading their families, their communities and their countries to a better future. When we help these women to sow, we all reap."

[86]Hillary Rodham Clinton, "Remarks to the United Nations Fourth World Conference on Women, Plenary Session."

[87]Ibid.

[88]Ibid.

[89]Charlotte Bunch, "NGO Forum Opening Plenary," August 31, 1995, IWTC, Acc. #96S-34, box 1. Charlotte Bunch directed the Center for Women's Global Leadership and spoke at the NGO Forum 95 Opening Plenary Session. She recounted how women's human rights advocates had been making these arguments for years, but continued to face resistance to their explanations:"Many of us have worked over the last few years to transform the definitions and interpretations of human rights so that they will recognize the reality of the violations that women experience every day. The original terminology of human rights, as we know it today, came from the experience of the white, propertied, European/American male who did not need to worry about violence in the family or poverty because those were not his problems. His human rights needs, where he felt his humanity was most violated, were in relation to the state, in terms of matters such as his right to freedom of religion and freedom of speech."

[90]Charlotte Bunch, "After Twenty Years We Have Global Recognition," in Lee and Clauson-Wicker, eds. *Voice of Women*, pp. 18-19.

[91]Wirth, "Report to the President from the United States delegation to the United Nations Fourth World Conference on Women." See also: Loar, The Association for Diplomatic Studies and Training Foreign Affairs Oral History Project.

[92]Hillary Rodham Clinton, "Remarks to the United Nations Fourth World Conference on Women, Plenary Session."

[93]Beckwith, "Mapping Strategic Engagements," p. 326.

[94]*Ancient Wisdoms New Visions: Reflections of Indigenous Women on the Fourth World Conference on Women, Change,* [Philippines] VI: 2 & 3 (June-December 1995), IWTC, Acc. #00S-8, box 9. For example, a group of indigenous women from the Philippines could speak from national experience when they claimed: "So when Hillary Rodham Clinton came to Beijing and blasted at the human rights violations of China, human rights activists applauded her. They conveniently forgot the role played by the United States in perpetuating the most repressive military dictatorships in many Third World countries. If this is what depoliticizing human rights means, it is about time to rethink and be more critical of how phrases like 'universality of human rights' or 'women's rights are human rights' are being misused."

[95]Loar, The Association for Diplomatic Studies and Training Foreign Affairs Oral History Project.

[96]Seona Smiles, "The Medium and the Message," *The Earth Times: Beijing Women's Conference Daily,* September 7, 1995, IWTC, Acc. #00S-8, box 9.

[97]"The real story of Beijing," p. 1.

[98]Hillary Rodham Clinton, "Advancing the Progress of Women."

[99]"Statement from the Women's Human Rights Caucus: Concerns about the Openness at the NGO Forum and Recommendations for Future UN Conferences," September 8, 1995, CWGL, IV World Conference on Women, Beijing, China 1995, box 2. See also: "The real story of Beijing," p. 1.

[100]Albright, "Remarks before the International Leadership Forum for Women with Disabilities."

[101]Wirth, "Report to the President from the United States delegation to the United Nations Fourth World Conference on Women, Beijing, China, September 4-15, 1995."

[102] *Markers on the Way: The DAWN Debates on Alternative Development, DAWN's Platform for the Fourth World Conference on Women*, September 1995, IWTC, Acc. #00S-8, box 8; Gita Sen, Development Alternatives for Women in a New Era (DAWN), Indian Institute of Management, "The Forces Shaping Women's Lives," Opening Plenary Session, August 31, 1995, IWTC, Acc. #96S-34, box 1. See also: Charlotte Bunch, NGO Forum Opening Plenary, August 31, 1995, IWTC, Acc. #96S-34, box 1.

[103]Irene Tinker, "Nongovernmental Organizations: An Alternative Power Base for Women?" in Meyer and Prugl, eds. *Gender Politics in Global Governance*, p. 93.

[104]Maran, "After the Beijing Conference: What will be done?"

[105]"Women's Eyes on the World Bank, A Global Campaign to Transform the Bank to Meet Women's Needs," IWTC, Acc. #00S-8, box 2.

[106]"Women's Eyes Watch the World Bank," Leadership and Development in the Americas, *Directions: Partners of the Americas* September/October 1996, IWTC, Acc. #00S-8, box 8.

[107]Moghadam, *Globalizing Women*, pp. 120, 122.

[108]Maran, "After the Beijing Conference: What will be done?"

[109]James D. Wolfensohn, President, The World Bank, "Women and the Transformation of the 21st Century," Address to the Fourth World Conference on Women, September 15, 1995, KT, box 6.

[110] Ibid.

[111]Moghadam, *Globalizing Women*, pp. 138-9. See also: "Beyond Promises: Governments in Motion, One Year After the Beijing Conference," Report published by WEDO with support from UNFPA, UNICEF, Ford Foundation, the Ministry of Foreign Affairs of Norway, the Finnish International Development Agency, and the Netherlands Organization for International Development Organization, c. September 1996, IWTC, Acc. #00S-8, box 8: "The World Bank's Progress One Year After Beijing … Despite some encouraging motions toward greater gender sensitivity and responsiveness to women's issues, clear evidence of concrete changes in Bank programs has yet to be found. Anecdotal reports … suggest the degree to which any particular Bank effort reflects top management's stated commitment depends on the individual commitment of staff involved. In other words, the rhetorical priority now placed on gender has yet to be institutionalized into standard Bank practice. It appears to have focused greater

attention on gender and women's concerns in certain activities, but much remains to be accomplished."

[112]These points were made by Paul Nelson, a Washington DC activist quoted in Tinker, "Nongovernmental Organizations: An Alternative Power Base for Women?"in Meyer and Prugl, eds. *Gender Politics in Global Governance*, p. 93.

[113]Mayra Buvinic, Interview with Author, World Bank, Washington D.C., September 23, 2009.

[114]Bella Abzug, "We Won't Be Mainstreamed into a Polluted Stream," in Lee and Clauson-Wicker, eds. *Voice of Women*, p. 15.

[115]"From Beijing, a Platform for Action and a clear mandate for women's progress," *Women* Published by the United Nations Department of Public Information, c. November 1995, IWTC, Acc. #00S-8, box 9.

[116]Bella Abzug, "We Won't Be Mainstreamed into a Polluted Stream," p. 13.

[117]"Contract With Women of the USA," IWTC, Acc. #00S-8, box 2.

[118]Excerpts from Bella Abzug's speech at the closing UN General Assembly, "Women Going Forward: Envisioning a Feminist Future," p. 18: "Extremists in the Republican Party and the Congress of USA are endangering the continuation of a democracy in the country. That's what it really is. It's not just how serious it is cutting Medicare, environment, education, all of these things. It's not that they want to lower the taxes for rich people placing the burden on poor people by throwing them off all kinds of programs which are desperately needed and are the tradition of America. They coerce mothers to work, deny their children, and balance the budget by cutting student loans and summer jobs, earned income tax credits, head start, child nutrition, health for the poor, and other programs which effect low income people women, youth and children. They're deregulating environmental requirements which will plunge us into a morass of environmental degradation. What about the male military megalomania? That male megalomania that insists on depriving us of the harvest of what should happen after the cold war is over." See also: Bella Abzug, "We Won't Be Mainstreamed into a Polluted Stream," p. 14.

[119]"Keeping the Promises. Holding Governments and International Agencies Accountable: Monitoring Strategies for Advancing Women's Agendas. A WEDO Workshop Report," September 10-12, 1996, IWTC, Acc. #00S-8, box 8.

[120]Suzanne Kindervatter, Director of the Commission on the Advancement of Women, "Government Commitments Presented in Plenary Sessions at the Fourth World Conference on Women in Beijing," November 8, 1995, IWTC, Acc. #00S-8, box 2; Maran, "After the Beijing Conference: What will be done?"; Tarr-Whelan, "Opening Statement."

[121]"Follow up on U.S. Commitments Made at the UN Fourth World Conference on Women Beijing, China, September 4-15, 1995, January 24, 1996"; "U.S. Follow-up to the UN Fourth World Conference on Women, Synopsis of May 1996 Report" and "U.S. Government Follow-up to the U.N. World Conference on Women, Update on Key Initiatives, September 1996," The President's Interagency Council on Women Archives. See also: [full report] "The President's Interagency Council on Women, U.S. Follow-up on the UN Fourth World Conference on Women," IWTC, Acc. #00S-8, box 2.

[122]Loar, The Association for Diplomatic Studies and Training Foreign Affairs Oral History Project.

[123]Ibid.

[124]"Follow up on U.S. Commitments Made at the UN Fourth World Conference on Women, Beijing, September 4-15, 1995, November 7, 1995," The President's Interagency Council on Women Archives.

[125]"Join the Honor Role Valuing Women's Work,"*AWID The Newsletter of the Association for Women in Development* 9, no. 5 (November 1995), IWTC, Acc. #00S-8, box 9.

[126]International Women's Rights Action Watch, *The Women's Watch* 9, no. 3 (January 1996), KT, box 9.

[127]Atwood, "Gender Plan of Action." See also: "The Gender Plan of Action: Federal Programs Benefiting Women and New Initiatives as follow-up to the UN Fourth World Conference on Women, May 1997," The President's Interagency Council on Women Archives.

[128]Tarr-Whelan, "Opening Statement."

[129]The President's Interagency Council on Women, "U.S. Follow-up on the UN Fourth World Conference on Women," Section on "Foreign Policy and Foreign Affairs," IWTC, Acc. #00S-8, box 2.

[130]Christopher, Wirth, and Shattuck, "Promoting Human Rights Reflects U.S. Ideals, Advances Interests."

[131]Albright, "The UN: What's in it for the U.S.?"

[132]Christopher, "International Women's Day: Celebrating Remarkable Achievements."

[133]Memo "Population Action International: International Advocacy Program," May 21, 1996, and memo "House Foreign Operations Subcommittee Markup FY 1997," May 22, 1996, RCD, box 2; Christopher, "American Diplomacy and the Global Environmental Challenges of the 21st Century" and "The International Affairs Budget: Large Returns From a Small Investment," and "Focus on Diplomacy: The State Department at Work, The Foreign Affairs Budget And Assistance."

[134]Loar, The Association for Diplomatic Studies and Training Foreign Affairs Oral History Project.

[135]Hillary Rodham Clinton, "The UN Women's Conference One Year Later."

[136]"Women Speak Out Across the USA on their own National Action Agenda," WEDO *News & Views* 9, nos. 3-4 (November-December 1996), IWTC, Acc. #00S-8, box 9.

[137]"Contract with Women of the USA" brochure, IWTC, Acc. #00S-8, box 2.

[138]"Contract with Women of the USA," *off our backs*, p. 9.

[139]Soon-Young Yoon, "Beijing + One," *The Earth Times* August 31-September 14, 1996, KT, box 9.

[140]Loar, The Association for Diplomatic Studies and Training Foreign Affairs Oral History Project.

[141]"Leadership and Development in the Americas," *Directions: Partners of the Americas* September/October 1996, IWTC, Acc. #00S-8, box 8.

6

The "Vital Voices" Initiative

This chapter examines the evolution and expansion of the Clinton Administration's focus on global women through its foreign policy agencies as Bill Clinton was re-elected and served his second term in office. During the fall run-up to the November 1996 presidential election and in the election's immediate aftermath, U.S. foreign policy offices grappled with ongoing regional conflicts that brought women's human rights issues to the center of U.S. government attention. In Afghanistan, the fundamentalist Islamist Taliban regime seized power following long years of civil conflict that had been fueled and stoked by the United States' and the Soviet Union's Cold War era interventions. The Taliban's egregious attacks on the human rights of Afghan women and girls elicited outrage from feminists and human rights activists who pressed their allies inside the Clinton Administration to elevate principles over pragmatism in devising the U.S. government's response.

Human rights activists also called on the Clinton Administration to lead the campaign for gender justice in regard to international efforts to reconstruct post war Rwanda and Bosnia. Genocidal civil wars had torn apart Rwanda and Bosnia and Herzegovina during Bill Clinton's first term in office. At that time, the Clinton Administration had been slow to apply the necessary diplomatic pressure and military force to end the brutal ethnic slaughters and gendered violence against women that characterized both conflicts. A second term in office gave Bill Clinton a second chance to lead international coalitions in establishing International War Crimes Tribunals for the Former Yugoslavia and Rwanda and in reconstructing peaceful democratic nations out of those broken and divided societies. Feminists and human rights activists again pressed their cases with receptive administration allies to punish violations of women's human rights in the war crimes tribunals and to foreground women's needs when allocating postwar reconstruction aid to Rwanda and Bosnia.

President Clinton's second term foreign policy team led by Secretary of State Madeleine Albright enhanced the State Department's focus on global gender policy. Following Secretary Albright's leadership, the State Department adopted feminist arguments to push the International War Crimes Tribunals to indict and prosecute Serbian and Rwandan leaders who had ordered mass rapes and other sexual assaults on women. However, competing political imperatives prevented the administration from signing the Rome Statute to establish a permanent International Criminal Court in 1998, an institution that U.S. and global feminist activists believed would promote human rights norms that would universally benefit global populations. Nonetheless, the U.S. government contributed significantly to UN postwar reconstruction funds established to aid Bosnia and Rwanda and directed attention and resources to meet women's needs in ways that partially addressed feminist concerns.

Secretary Albright's leadership in promoting women's human rights was assisted by Theresa Loar, appointed to lead the State Department's Office of International Women's Issues (OIWI) in October 1996, a position Loar held in addition to her duties directing the staff of the President's Interagency Council on Women. Under Loar's leadership, the OIWI's role and influence within the State Department expanded significantly, especially after the OIWI coordinated the first "Vital Voices: Women in Democracy" conference with the first lady's office at the White House and the U.S. Embassy in Austria in July 1997. This conference program adapted the Clinton Administration's democracy promotion goals to serve liberal feminists' interests. At the same time, liberal feminists' interests were adapted to serve the Clinton Administration's global capitalist development goals. Relationships among liberal feminist NGOs, academics, businesswomen, their State Department allies and global women partners deepened as the subsequent "Vital Voices: Women in Democracy Initiative" continued throughout President Clinton's second term in office with meetings held in Northern Ireland, Uruguay, Iceland, Trinidad and Nigeria, from 1998 through 2000.

Changes in the State Department Leadership Enhance U.S. Global Gender Policy

With Bill Clinton's re-election in November 1996 feminists and human rights activists were among those assured that the "sea change" in U.S. foreign policy rhetoric emanating from the White House and the State Department would continue for the next four years. Throughout his first term in office and as he prepared to move forward into the new term, President Clinton had often voiced his strong support for human rights as a cornerstone of U.S. democracy promotion policy and he emphasized democracy promotion as a key element to achieving U.S. national security and economic prosperity goals. While some among the foreign policy establishment and in the Republican Party opposition espoused *real politick* views and dismissed the "hopeful" but ultimately "unworkable" policy position "that fostering democracy overseas promotes American national security because democratic countries do not start wars with each other,"[1] President Clinton and his first term foreign policy team leadership, Secretary of State Warren Christopher, Undersecretary of State Timothy Wirth, and Assistant Secretary of State John Shattuck, believed otherwise. They had often asserted that "defense of human rights" was a "fundamental" American interest.[2] In the words of President Clinton, "Promoting democracy and human rights reflects our ideals and reinforces our interests. It's a fundamental pillar of our foreign policy. History shows that nations where rights are respected and governments are freely chosen are more likely to be partners in peace and prosperity."[3]

Moreover, the Fourth World Conference on Women held in Beijing in 1995 had heightened awareness among the American public and among government officials regarding widespread violations of women's human rights, even if some State Department career officers did not believe that women's rights belonged among the ranks of "serious national security issues."[4] Here, too, the president and his first term leadership had consistently signaled strong support for women's human rights and women's empowerment in numerous foreign policy statements. As the president asserted at a December 1996 White House ceremony in honor of Human Rights Day, "Beijing's message was as clear as it was compelling. We cannot advance our ideals and interests unless we focus more attention on the fundamental human rights and basic needs of women and girls. … We are putting our efforts to protect and advance women's rights where they belong—in the mainstream of American foreign policy."[5] Human rights and women's rights activists applauded the administration's rhetoric, but they also sought institutional change and human rights protections that went beyond what some described as the "ad hoc" approach.[6]

Bill Clinton's re-election brought two significant personnel changes that moved the U.S. government forward in integrating and institutionalizing women's human rights considerations into foreign policy making in ways that had not happened during the administration's first term in office. First and foremost, President Clinton appointed Madeleine Albright as the nation's first female secretary of state. Albright shared the president and first lady's convictions that promoting human rights and human security worldwide was the best way to ensure the national security and prosperity of the United States, and that advancing women's status and defending women's human rights were necessary to achieving U.S. global security goals.[7] The secretary's views were supported by other strong-minded women who held important cabinet leadership posts and whose offices reinforced U.S. global gender policy: Janet Reno at the Department of Justice, Alexis Herman at Labor, Donna Shalala at Health and Human Services and Carol Browner at the Environmental Protection Agency.

President Clinton's selection of Madeleine Albright to lead the State Department, rather than a more "conventional" male candidate such as George Mitchell or Richard Holbrooke who were also considered for the secretary of state appointment, represented a symbolic advance for American women into high-ranking political leadership positions. To be sure, Albright had established her foreign policy credentials serving as U.S. ambassador to the United Nations during Clinton's first term in office. Before stepping into that highly-visible government post as ambassador, Albright had been a long-time resident of Georgetown and was a "Washington insider."

Madeleine Albright had taught international relations at Georgetown University's School of Foreign Service as a specialist in Russian and Central and Eastern European politics and had directed Georgetown's Women in Foreign Service Program.[8] As ambassador to the UN, Albright was intimately involved with the United States-United Nations-NATO alliance's diplomatic negotiations in the Balkans. She supported Bill Clinton's decision to launch a U.S.-led NATO military operation to end the genocidal conflict in Bosnia in August 1995 and she participated in the international negotiations that led to the peace accords signed in Dayton, Ohio in November 1995. Among Albright's many other contributions during the conflict resolution process, she had pushed the peace negotiators in Dayton to acknowledge that mass rapes of women had been perpetrated as a weapon of war, and she pushed for rape to be included among the enumerated war crimes to be prosecuted in the UN War Crimes Tribunals established for Bosnia and Rwanda. Albright also proposed that post-conflict police and judges in Bosnia undergo training to deal with victims of rape and other sex-related crimes.[9] When she led the U.S. delegation to the Beijing women's conference in September 1995, Albright's vocal support for a central role for women in transforming global relationships foreshadowed the "creative and unorthodox" approach to diplomacy that she would bring to the State Department throughout her tenure from 1997 to 2001:

> As we approach the new century, we know that we cannot build the kind of future we want without the contribution of women. And we know that, around the world, women will only be able to contribute to our full potential if we have equal access, equal rights, equal protection, and a fair chance at the levers of economic and political power. This isn't rocket science or something that is even more difficult, like child-rearing; it is simple common sense. We know from experience, after all, that when women have the knowledge and power to make our own choices, the cycle of poverty, in which too many countries remain ensnared, can be broken. Birth rates stabilize; environmental awareness increases; the spread of sexually transmitted diseases slows; and socially constructive values are more likely to be passed on to the young.[10]

Another significant second-term personnel change occurred when Theresa Loar was brought back into the State Department in October 1996 to lead the Office of International Women's Issues. Loar's experiences from 1994 through 1996, coordinating U.S. participation at the Beijing conference and directing the President's Interagency Council on Women at the White House, had made her an effective advocate for U.S. government actions to promote global women's equality and women's human rights. Above all else she had learned from her government service, Loar was a pragmatist who understood that the key to successful feminist policy advocacy within the federal government was to demonstrate positive and concrete results. These successes built up support for new feminist proposals and feminist methods of work within the ranks of government and among the American public. As chapter five has explained, Loar published frequent PICW progress reports that identified the new gender policies adopted by federal agencies and that charted their progress toward successful implementation.

Loar also knew how to frame the administration's gender policies in non-threatening ways for those who were suspicious of, or opposed, any policy changes associated with a "feminist agenda." She realized early on in her work preparing for the Beijing conference that she needed to persuade political opponents that the conference themes and U.S. policy positions were not "anti-family." Growing up in a Catholic family and as a wife and mother herself, Loar used her own personal example to defuse anti-feminist critics. She opened her office doors and listened to opponents of reproductive rights, even though these critics did not diminish the administration's support for women's reproductive choices. She secured visas and credentials for socially conservative NGOs and for feminist NGOs alike who wanted to attend the Beijing conference.

6.1 The President's Interagency Council on Women, Washington DC, January 22, 1999. **Back row from left to right**: Ellen Lazar, Treasury; Jennifer Luray, White House Women's Office; Sylvia Baca, Interior; Scott Busby, National Security Council; Virginia Canter, National Endowment for the Humanities; Constance Dunham, Office of the Comptroller of the Currency; Nancy Hendry, Peace Corps; Carole Becraft, Navy; Bonnie Campbell, Justice; Anita Botti, State; Jan Piercy, World Bank; Ambassador Sally Shelton-Colby, U.S. Agency for International Development; Ambassador Betty King, U.S. Mission to the United Nations; Dr. Nancy Valentine, Veterans Affairs; Joyce Kravitz, United States Information Agency; Ambassador Craig Johnstone, State; Jill Long Thompson, Agriculture; Lidia Soto-Harmon, State; Elaine Shocas, State; Frankee Greenberg, Environmental Protection Agency; Dr. Susan F. Wood, Health and Human Services. **Seated from left to right**: Sarah Kovner, Health and Human Services; General Claudia Kennedy, Army; Secretary Madeleine K. Albright, State; First Lady Hillary Rodham Clinton; Secretary Donna Shalala, Health and Human Services; Melanne Verveer, The White House; Deputy Secretary Kitty Higgins, Labor; Theresa Loar, State.

Courtesy of the William J. Clinton Presidential Library.

Loar also identified and promoted the common ground. She recognized that nearly all who attended the women's conference opposed violence against women and would support U.S. government policy to end the violence in all its forms. In the aftermath of the conference, the Office on Violence Against Women led by Bonnie Campbell at the Justice Department became one of the administration's greatest feminist policy accomplishments that aided women in the United States through new, tougher criminal laws, enforcement mechanisms and victim services. The 1994 Violence Against Women Act and the new Justice Department office that it authorized were viewed as models for other nations that also sought to address the widespread problem of violence against women in their own societies.[11] Under Loar's direction, the PICW continued progress toward fulfilling the U.S. Commitments to Women in the federal government cabinet agencies. These efforts generally—with the exception of sexual and reproductive health policies and programs—received bipartisan and widespread popular support. In a gesture intended to promote the idea that the administration's gender policies were well within the mainstream of U.S. popular opinion, the PICW designed a logo for its one-year follow-up national teleconference that featured a mother and daughter silhouetted against an American flag. Certainly, the use of this particular logo pandered to the administration's anti-feminist critics, but the intent was to build up a wide base of support for a range of progressive and feminist-friendly federal policies.[12]

Theresa Loar brought her pragmatic and goal-oriented liberal feminist sensibilities to the work of the Office of International Women's Issues following her appointment in October 1996. Loar initially had no staff assigned to her at the State Department, just a chair and a desk, but she brought in four White House interns who had worked on PICW projects and who had security clearance. Loar was at home in the State Department and she and her interns were eager to move women's rights issues onto the U.S. foreign policy agenda. Soon after setting up the office, Loar decided to publicize reports on women's rights issues that were included in the daily cables received from U.S. embassies abroad in the monthly State Department newsletters and in the public information the department released to interested NGOs. This information was usually summarized in the annual human rights reports. As embassy staff abroad realized their reports would get more attention in Washington, reporting increased.

Loar also began hosting monthly briefings at the State Department for NGOs and instituted an open door policy for NGO representatives, as well as for other State Department bureau officers, all with the intent of building visibility and support for the OIWI. Moreover, after the Senate confirmed Madeleine Albright's appointment as secretary of state in January 1997, Albright also took on the position of chair of the President's Interagency Council on Women, as Loar continued to direct the PICW secretariat from her office at the State Department. Consequently, with Madeleine Albright's attention directed to the PICW's and the OIWI's work, and to global women's rights issues generally, the Office of International Women's Issues' activities and stature within the State Department expanded greatly during Theresa Loar's four years as OIWI senior coordinator.

As President Clinton's second term began, "advancing the status of women" was not only a recognizable U.S. foreign policy theme, it became a "mission." In the words that Secretary Albright repeated often, "Advancing the status of women is not only a moral imperative; it is being actively integrated into the foreign policy of the United States. It is our mission. It is the right thing to do, and, frankly, it is the smart thing to do."[13] That mission affected State Department operations overseas as well as diplomacy emanating from Washington DC.[14] It was especially evident in defining U.S. government relations with the Taliban government in Afghanistan, U.S. support for the International War Crimes Tribunals established for the Bosnian and Rwandan wars, U.S. postwar reconstruction assistance for the two crippled states and the "Vital Voices: Women in Democracy" initiative, among other global gender policy issues that will be discussed in chapter seven.

U.S. Policy toward the Taliban: Affirming Afghan Women's Human Rights

Within days of Theresa Loar's return to the State Department to re-open the Office of International Women's Issues in October 1996, the fundamentalist Islamist Taliban regime took control over Afghanistan's central government. Loar reacted immediately and viscerally to the Taliban's public proclamations banning women and girls from attending schools and universities, forbidding women from working outside the home or from venturing out into any public spaces for any reason without a male escort and requiring all women to cover their bodies completely in traditional burqas.[15] The Fourth World Conference on Women and the ongoing focus of her government work to advance gender justice and women's empowerment globally had raised Loar's consciousness to the assault on women's human rights that the Taliban policies represented, especially since the Taliban imposed brutal physical punishments on all who violated the edicts. The Taliban's harsh laws violated Loar's sense of justice and triggered her empathy toward Afghan women. However, at the time she spoke out to denounce the Taliban's women's human rights abuses and launched a campaign within the State Department to prevent the U.S. government from recognizing the new Afghan government until it restored women's rights and freedoms, Loar had no real knowledge of the history of Afghan political and religious conflicts over the past decades or of the U.S. government's interventions in those armed conflicts.[16]

Throughout the first half of the twentieth century traditional Afghan tribes confronted Western governments that sought to colonize and organize Islamic Afghanistan into a "modern" nation. Some Afghans had embraced Western goals to secularize and modernize Afghan society and political institutions. Other Afghans resisted any challenges to traditional Islamic culture and religious laws. After World War II ended and the Cold

War rivalry between Western democracies and the Soviet Union ensued, global security policy imperatives dictated foreign interventions in all regions of the world, including central Asia. Western nations and the Soviet Union vied for influence over Afghanistan's modernizing projects.

The Afghan nation experienced uneven socio-economic development during the Cold War era. In consequence, a cultural and ideological split occurred. In the more modern cities, less conservative mores prevailed. Women and girls were educated along with men and boys, and women could move about fairly freely and some could choose whether to wear the burqa or not. In the more traditional and still-tribal-dominated rural areas of the country, women and girls were not educated and were secluded within the home. In 1979, a radical Soviet-funded and socialist-inspired People's Democratic Party of Afghanistan (PDPA) launched the Great Saur Revolution and took over the national government. Like other Soviet socialist revolutionaries the PDPA declared Afghan women's equality with men, thus "freeing" women to work and study outside the home and to participate in public life. Traditional groups resisted these modernizing changes that were imposed throughout the nation with force. Civil war ensued. Throughout the 1980s, the Soviet Army invaded Afghanistan and fought alongside the PDPA while the United States funded and armed various rural tribal warlords and anti-Soviet coalitions.

During that last Cold War era decade, many traditional, fundamentalist Afghans fled the country and sought safety in UN refugee camps in Pakistan and Iran. Refugees organized traditional patriarchal tribal societies in these camps, isolating women in the private sphere of the family and imposing strict laws governing all aspects of women's behavior as mothers, wives and daughters. As the civil war dragged on without resolution, the Soviet Union withdrew its Army in 1989. Various Afghan coalitions continued fighting each other for control of the nation.[17] The PDPA government fell in 1992. Without the threat of Soviet influence in the region expanding, the U.S. government also cut back funding for anti-socialist factions and declared itself "neutral" in Afghan's civil war. After 1992, the U.S. government promoted a UN-brokered settlement among all warring parties.[18] The U.S. position remained unchanged through the summer of 1996.[19] Eventually two major contenders for power, the "Northern Alliance" of regional warlords and the "Taliban" fundamentalist Islamists who had organized their military campaign in the Pakistan refugee camps, emerged to wage the final struggle. The Taliban claimed victory over the Northern Alliance in October 1996 when they seized control of Kabul, the nation's capital.

Afghanistan's years of warfare and continuous struggle between "modern" and "traditional" factions violated the human rights of the entire population, but the conflict had affected men and women in distinctly gendered ways. Julie Mertus[20] has cataloged these differences in her study of *War's Offensive on Women*, published in 2000:

> Despite the way the Taliban exert control over women by removing their right to employment, education, and mobility, and despite the egregious human rights abuses it commits against them, the Taliban cannot be blamed for all their suffering. The effect of long years of war, poverty, poor nutrition, inadequate health care, stress, fear, and depression have created untold misery for everyone in Afghanistan, especially for women. More men were killed and disabled in the fighting, but women were the victims of the relentless shelling of homes and markets and countless land mine injuries.
>
> Afghan women bore enormous hardships through the conflicts, including gender violence and physical and mental torment in many forms. One study reports that more than 76 percent of women's deaths during the war were due to aerial bombings. Another study describes the lifelong trauma Afghan women suffer as a result of "multiple rape, forced prostitution, slavery and other forms of gender-related violence." Urban women, accustomed to moving about without restrictions, were devastated by the edicts. Severe depression led to some suicides. International health workers reported a number of women brought to hospitals after ingesting caustic soda—a painful but common means of suicide among women. Cultural stigma and religious prohibitions caused most cases to go unreported; some deaths are recorded as accidental. Depression also plagues men who feel ashamed of their inability to support their families. Some react to the stress by lashing out at their wives and children.[21]

Theresa Loar and her State Department colleagues had varying degrees of knowledge regarding Afghanistan's history and U.S. involvement in the Afghan wars of the 1980s and 1990s. Consequently, they reacted to the rise of the Taliban government in very different ways. Loar and various women's rights- and human rights-focused NGOs reacted to the bald disregard for women's humanity and believed that protection of Afghan women's human rights should determine U.S. policy toward the Taliban. Loar promoted non-recognition of the Taliban by the United States and other world governments, clear and forceful statements condemning the Taliban's women's human rights abuses and an immediate end to all U.S. aid to Afghanistan that flowed through Taliban government channels. Loar found a State Department ally in Nicholas Burns, spokesman and acting assistant secretary of state for Public Affairs, who advised Secretary of State Warren Christopher and gave press briefings throughout the fall of 1996. According to Loar, Burns, too, was affected by the global focus on women's human rights that the Beijing conference and Hillary Clinton's conference plenary speech had brought to light, and Burns willingly delivered strong statements condemning the Taliban's human rights abuses in his daily press briefings.[22]

The rhetorical groundwork for the defense of Afghan women's human rights had already been laid throughout the Clinton Administration's first term in office. In October, U.S. Ambassador to the UN Commission on the Status of Women Linda Tarr-Whelan repeated foreign policy principles that the administration had championed at the United Nations: the United States valued inclusive and pluralistic democracy, social and political equality for women and empowerment of women through education and participation of in the economy. The U.S. government respected women's human rights and opposed all forms of violence against women.[23] Also in October, Madeleine Albright, then U.S. ambassador to the UN, labeled the Taliban's edicts "medieval" and asserted that the women's human rights violations could not be "justified or defended."[24] Human rights activists called on the Clinton Administration to take actions that would give some substantive meaning to these words as they rallied to the Afghan women's cause.

Others in the State Department including Lee Coldren, the lead political officer for Pakistan, Afghanistan and Bangladesh, and Robin Raphel, assistant secretary for South Asian Affairs, were not convinced that women's human rights should take primacy in defining U.S. policy toward Afghanistan. They viewed the Taliban as one of many political factions that violated Afghan's human rights. The press quoted Lee Coldren asserting that "'even if the Taliban disappeared tomorrow, you would still have one of the greatest human rights disasters in the world,' in Afghanistan because of the anarchy there and the complete breakdown of law and order." Coldren and Raphel argued that the Taliban had brought some stability to the region and that the U.S. government should remain neutral and should engage the Taliban in negotiations rather than isolate the regime from the global community. Moreover, they argued that the United States should not cut off humanitarian aid or attach conditions to aid, which would further hurt the Afghan people.[25]

Yet another element also factored into the Clinton Administration's Afghan policy formation process. The Union Oil Company of California (UNOCAL) had been trying for several years to negotiate a trans-Afghanistan oil pipeline. UNOCAL's executive officer, Marty Miller, who had shared intelligence on Afghanistan with the CIA, was in Kabul when the Taliban took over the country. Miller also advised the administration that the United States should remain neutral in its policy toward the Taliban. Zalmay Khalizhad, a former U.S. ambassador to Afghanistan, Iraq, and the United Nations, and Robert Oakley, a former U.S. ambassador to Pakistan, both consulted for UNOCAL, and both advised the Clinton Administration to "re-engage" with the Taliban.[26] By 1998, however, UNOCAL's pipeline deal dissolved. Nonetheless, throughout the first years that the Taliban held power, in 1996 and 1997, UNOCAL representatives lobbied the Clinton Administration to modify its policy of resistance to the regime.

In her ongoing efforts to promote transparency in government operations and to give access to "people who had every legitimate right to be in this building expressing their views to policymakers," Theresa Loar brought human rights activists including Marjorie Lightman who had co-founded the Washington DC Women's Working Group on International Human Rights and T. Kumar from Amnesty International, in for a meeting at the State Department. She hoped that Lee Coldren, the State Department expert on Afghan politics, would discuss U.S. policy with the activists and would listen to the human rights community. However, the meeting soon devolved into a shouting match between the activists and the "realistic" foreign service officer. Loar's efforts proved to be a "complete disaster."[27]

Nonetheless, Loar drew on external support from feminists and human rights activists and on internal support from her allies at the State Department, including the Undersecretary of State for Global Affairs Timothy Wirth and the director of Policy and Resource Planning at the Population, Refugees, and Migration bureau Allan Jury.[28] Loar also used her insider positions as senior coordinator of OIWI and director of the PICW to bolster U.S. policy to condemn the Taliban's abuse of women's human rights, to ostracize the Taliban government in UN forums and to deny any U.S. aid delivered to Afghanistan through any Taliban government channels. These policies were in place even as U.S. aid for educating Afghan women and girls was dispersed in Pakistan's refugee camps, and emergency food aid for Afghanistan was delivered through United Nations' agencies, from 1996 through 2000.[29] In public pronouncements using feminists' language and arguments Loar insisted: "We are facing in Taliban-controlled Afghanistan one of the worst examples of the treatment of women in history. Women are not merely discriminated against. It is worse than that. They have been brutalized and made 'invisible' by the edicts and punishment inflicted on them simply for being women. This is wrong and must stop. This also points to another reason it is so important that [the Convention on the Elimination of all forms of Discrimination Against Women] be ratified. CEDAW provides a standard to judge situations just like this."[30] As Loar recalled in an oral history interview that took place in 2001,

> We tried to draw attention to this as often as we could. We also tried to send a signal to the community outside the government that we understood the situation, and that we were not going to recognize this government. However, I don't know if those words were ever spoken publicly by any official, "that we would not recognize the Taliban." But at the end of the day, we didn't.[31]

Among the NGO community, the Feminist Majority Foundation (FMF) had launched a concerted and ultimately influential media and lobby campaign that denounced the Taliban's "gender apartheid" policies.[32] FMF President Eleanor Smeal testified before Congress in October 2001 that "In both 1999 and 2000, officials at the U.S. State Department told us that we had successfully mobilized a U.S. constituency on a foreign policy issue and that they had received more mail from Americans on restoring women's rights in Afghanistan than on any other foreign policy issue."[33]

Throughout President Clinton's second term in office, the president,[34] the first lady[35] and secretary of state[36] denounced the Taliban government for its violations of women's human rights. The U.S. government continued to deny formal diplomatic recognition and aid to Taliban-ruled Afghanistan, while funding education for Afghan girls in refugee camps and sending humanitarian emergency food aid through UN agencies and American and international NGOs.[37] The U.S. government also tried to lead the international community in condemnation of the Taliban's human rights violations and introduced several resolutions at the United Nations to that effect.[38]

No further actions were taken by the U.S. government during the Clinton Administration's tenure and the humanitarian crisis in Afghanistan worsened as a drought also decimated food crops.[39] Human rights activists, American feminists included, believed that their interventions supported important human rights principles and therefore had value. In contrast, from the perspective of some Afghan people, the activists' principles had little positive impact on their lives. In a study published in 2000, Julie Mertus reported on devolving conditions throughout Afghanistan:

> Today the pernicious poverty and other effects of the ongoing civil war remain the principal problems for [Afghan] women. Everything must be weighed in light of extreme deprivation. Food stalls in Kabul and in other areas display seasonal vegetables but people do not have the

> financial resources to purchase adequate food supplies. Most men and women are jobless. Families have sold nearly all of their household belongings. The longer people live in such poverty the worse their health becomes. Tuberculosis is increasing, with 70 percent of the cases among women. Each year Afghanistan sinks lower on the UN Development Index. The life expectancy is estimated at 44 years for women. The material mortality rate is the second highest in the world (nearly 1700 per 100,000 live births). Family planning and reproductive health services are rare. One quarter of all children die before the age of five, and literacy rates for females are estimated 13 percent in urban areas and 3 to 4 percent in rural districts. Some NGOs believe that the literacy rate has actually fallen in the past three years. Land mines injure more than eight thousand people each year, mostly civilians, including women and children.[40]

International aid programs did not develop coordinated sanctions or impose conditions on aid that might have pressured the Taliban to amend their assault on human rights.[41] Many Afghan women shunned the increased media', donor agencies', and human rights activists' attention to their plight as "victims" of the Taliban's abuse after years of being kept from the public sphere. They wanted and needed emergency aid, but rejected human rights campaigns originating among Western activists who did not consult with Afghan women and who used stories of Afghan women's suffering for political purposes that the women did not determine.[42]

Rwanda and Bosnia: Understanding Rape as a War Crime

During the Clinton Administration's second term in office, complex women's human rights issues in postwar Bosnia and Rwanda also brought to the forefront the problems of defining a "feminist" foreign policy and a "feminist" response to crises experienced by global women. In the 1997 to 2000 period, most of the global attention elicited from governments, aid donors, media and feminist activists alike focused on Bosnia and Herzegovina situated in Southeastern Europe, rather than on Rwanda in Sub-Saharan Africa. In part this was due to renewed Serbian violence directed at Kosovo, a Muslim-majority province located within Serbia. The war in Kosovo and the U.S. and UN responses will be discussed in chapter seven. Nonetheless, by 1997, genocidal conflicts in Bosnia and Herzegovina and in Rwanda had settled into uneasy peace and the United Nations had established two international tribunals to investigate and prosecute crimes against humanity that included crimes of sexual violence.

In the summer and fall of 1992, government, media and feminist reports had focused world attention on Serbia's genocidal ethnic cleansing policy underway in Bosnia and Herzegovina. The policy that Bosnian Serb leader Radovan Karadzic formulated and that the Serbian government led by Slobodan Milosevic supported was intended to eradicate Bosnia's Muslim population and reunite Bosnia with Serbia. Serbian soldiers committed mass rapes of Bosnian Muslim women as a weapon of war to carry out the official ethnic cleansing campaign. By December 1992, the UN Security Council issued Resolution 798 that "for the first time in history … condemns wartime rape, calling the rapes taking place in the former Yugoslavia 'massive, organized, and systematic.'" In February 1993, UN Security Council Resolution 808 established an international tribunal to prosecute crimes against humanity committed in the former Yugoslavia since 1991.[43]

Women's human rights activists were key advocates that persuaded the United Nations to establish the International Criminal Tribunal for the former Yugoslavia (ICTY)—the first such war crimes tribunal established since the Nuremburg and Tokyo Tribunals prosecuted those who committed genocide and other crimes against humanity during World War II. In the mid-1990s, feminist activists successfully campaigned for the ICTY to recognize rape and other forms of sexual violence as war crimes and made sure that these gendered crimes were not dismissed as "by-products of war." Feminists also ensured that a "gender perspective"[44] infused all aspects of the ICTY's operations. They lobbied to include women as judges, prosecutors and witnesses, and they influenced the tribunal's decisions regarding who would be indicted and tried as war criminals.

According to one report on the influence feminist activists had wielded over the ICTY proceedings, "Prosecutor Richard Goldstone, for example, claims that if women had not been involved with the Tribunal in its early years, there might not have been any indictments for gender-based crimes."[45] The New York-based feminist NGO Equality Now claimed it had contributed crucial arguments ensuring "inclusion of crimes of sexual violence in the investigation and prosecution of war crimes in the former Yugoslavia and in Rwanda." Equality Now made influential appeals to the president and chief prosecutor for ICTY "regarding the rules of evidence relating to rape, and particularly the defense of consent." Equality Now activists argued successfully that there could be no "consent" in wartime circumstances when rape was used "to spread political terror," unlike rape that occurred under "normal" circumstances.[46]

Equality Now also exerted strong pressure on the ICTY that led to the indictments of Radovan Karadzic, leader of the Bosnian Serbs, and Ratko Mladic, commander of the Bosnian Serb Army, in 1995,[47] even though Karadzic and Mladic were not arrested and put on trial until 2008 and 2011, respectively. These indictments, among others, of those who committed rapes and of those who commanded the rapists were critically important to feminists making a case that "systematic" rape—"committed as part of a widespread or systematic attack against any civilian population on national, political, ethnic, or racial grounds"—was a heinous war crime.[48] Feminists also argued successfully that these war crimes must be prosecuted in order for justice to be served:

> Nor is it enough for the Tribunal statute simply to recognize rape as a crime; those responsible for rape and related crimes must be charged and prosecuted in accordance with bias-free standards and recognized procedure. This is essential if the women of Bosnia are to be recognized as full subjects, as well as objects, of this terrible victimization, and if the international attention focused on Bosnia is to have meaning for women subjected to rape in other parts of the world.[49]

The feminists' arguments also influenced the organization of the International Criminal Tribunal for Rwanda (ICTR), established in 1995. The ICTR tried ethnic Hutu war criminals who perpetrated a mass extermination campaign against an ethnic Tutsi population killing over 800,000 people in a three-month-long bloodbath from April to June 1994, and who had massacred "up to one million Tutsis and moderate Hutus … in what was clearly a campaign of genocide" throughout the war that began in 1990.[50] Due to "extensive documentation" produced by human rights activists, media and filmmakers, the ICTR also prosecuted the widespread incidence of rape—an estimated 250,000 to 500,000 women and girls were raped during the 1994 genocide[51]—although these prosecutions were somewhat delayed. According to the Human Rights Watch Women's Rights Project that in 1996 was "focused particularly" on monitoring the ICTR:

> The lack of indictments in Rwanda was largely due to a lack of political will among those responsible for the investigations. There was a widespread perception among tribunal investigators that rape was somehow a 'lesser' or 'incidental' crime not worth investigating. Some at the Rwanda tribunal also held the mistaken view that Rwandan women would not come forward to talk about rape.[52]

As feminist NGOs monitored the tribunal, the ICTR created a "sexual assault committee" specifically to investigate rapes and other sexual violence. When Canadian judge Louise Arbor became the chief prosecutor of both the ICTR and ICTY, she pledged that "allegations of sexual assault would be vigorously investigated and prosecuted."[53] Moreover, when Jean-Paul Akayesu, the Hutu mayor of a Rwandan community where Tutsis had sought refuge and where mass rapes were documented, was arrested and charged with committing crimes against humanity including crimes of sexual violence, he was "the first non-military leader [convicted] for rape crimes committed in an internal armed conflict."[54] This was due to global feminist activism on the part of NGOs such as the Coalition for Women's Human Rights in Conflict Situations, formed by Human Rights Watch Women's Rights Project and some eighty other NGOs[55] along with Equality Now that had successfully redefined rape in international law.[56]

Feminists and human rights activists influenced the Clinton Administration's responses to these conflicts in two important ways. First, they gained the administration's support for establishing the two International Criminal Tribunals; second, they influenced the administration's post-conflict aid policies and programs in Bosnia and Rwanda. During Bill Clinton's first term in office, his decisions to intervene militarily to stop the genocide in both Bosnia in August 1995, and Rwanda in July 1994, were so long delayed that the administration had earned widespread criticisms from human rights advocates, feminists, conscientious officials and scholars alike.[57] Nonetheless, in 1993, the Clinton Administration had responded to feminist arguments that women's human rights had been violated by the sexual violence that occurred during these conflicts and the administration demonstrated its understanding of the feminist argument that "systematic rape was being used as a weapon of war."[58]

The Clinton Administration was an early advocate of establishing International Criminal Tribunals for both Bosnia and Rwanda. From 1993 onward UN Ambassador Madeleine Albright led these efforts within the administration.[59] When she became secretary of state in January 1997 Albright continued her vocal support for the International Criminal Tribunals: "We will maintain our strong backing for the UN war crimes tribunals for Rwanda and the Balkans. After all the horror of this century, history will not forgive us if we do not strive to hold accountable perpetrators of ethnic cleansing, mass rape, and other atrocities. Our proposed contributions to the UN's peacekeeping activities include continued support for these tribunals."[60] In October 1996, Warren Christopher announced the U.S. contribution to the ICTR: $650,000 out of a total $5,650,000 pledged internationally.[61] During 1996 and 1997, U.S. government representatives met with ICTY and ICTR officials to ensure that that prosecutors were "trained in issues of sexual violence against women" and the U.S. government funded NGO-led workshops to train tribunal investigators.[62] In March 1997 First Lady Hillary Clinton visited the Rwanda Tribunal held in Arusha, Tanzania where she sat in on one of the training sessions for those working with victims of sexual violence. Hillary Clinton vowed "We will do our utmost to see to it that the war criminals who practiced them—who subjected women and children to sexual abuse and violence—will be investigated, prosecuted, and punished with the full force of the law."[63]

Although the international community created these tribunals to prosecute war crimes including the crime of rape, women who had been raped often found it monumentally difficult to come forward and testify against their accusers. Jasmina Kuzmanović, a Croatian reporter, has written about some of the hurdles challenging Bosnian women of all ages, from teenage girls to elderly women, who had been raped and in some instances impregnated by Serbian soldiers. She explained that women were "silent victims," forced to remain silent by their patriarchal culture that was deeply shamed by their violation. More often than not, women silenced themselves due to feelings of shame. Or, women believed that the men in their families were the "true" victims of human rights abuses including massacres, imprisonment and torture, because governments, international human rights conventions and criminal courts had recognized those crimes against humanity for many years.[64] Consequently, according to a report on "Women's Participation in the International Criminal Tribunal for the Former Yugoslavia" published in 2004:

> Although Bosnian women have served as witnesses, investigators and advocates, their participation in the activities of the ICTY has been rare and is declining as the Tribunal continues to lose the confidence of the population it was established to serve. … Though Bosnian women's groups helped to locate and prepare many ICTY witnesses, the Tribunal has failed to develop fully its relationship with these organizations.[65]

The International Criminal Court: Traditional Political Imperatives Prevail

The Clinton Administration had generally agreed with feminist activists' support for the establishment of the International Criminal Tribunals for the former Yugoslavia and Rwanda. In the view of feminists, those tribunals represented breakthroughs in international law that promoted gender justice because they prosecuted perpetrators of rape as a weapon of war, among other enumerated war crimes against humanity. The ICTR had determined that rape was a form of genocide, based in part on evidence provided by the World Health Organization that estimated that 15,700 women and girls had been raped in Rwanda in 1994. The ICTY had also charged Serbian soldiers who established "rape camps" where women and girls were held as sex slaves and repeatedly raped by soldiers, with committing crimes against humanity.[66] Acts committed during these two wars presented clear human rights violations.

The U.S. government, however, disagreed with feminist activists who supported the 1998 Rome Statute that established an International Criminal Court. While the ICC promised to prosecute "systematic" rape, sexual slavery and forced pregnancy committed during wartime as crimes against humanity,[67] the U.S. government believed that the Rome Statute was too broad. It would have allowed charges of war crimes against any government that was a party to the treaty, without allowing for a United Nations Security Council veto when those charges were made against "the vital efforts of the United States and others" that deployed soldiers to promote international peace and security.[68]

The U.S. government believed the ICC would devolve into a political tool used by factions to compromise national sovereignty. In contrast, feminist supporters of the ICC believed it could become "a tool to fight against impunity for gender justice," used to prosecute wartime rape, as well as human traffickers, or those who enforced "sexual apartheid" policies like the Taliban.[69] While President Clinton argued that the U.S. government had negotiated for the International Criminal Court in good faith, it could not support the Rome Statute without provisions for a UN Security Council veto. Moreover, if the administration had signed the Rome Statute along with 120 other nations in 1998, the treaty would have required U.S. Senate ratification. That ratification was not likely to have taken place given the U.S. political context of the late 1990s.

Working with NGOs: Reconstruction and Reconciliation Projects

In Bosnia during the war and in its immediate aftermath, the U.S. government and private donor aid that was funneled through international channels and local women's NGOs primarily provided emergency relief and psychosocial counseling services for women who had been raped and otherwise traumatized. After 1996, "reconstruction and reconciliation" projects received most of the foreign aid.[70] Initially, the U.S. government dispersed funding to NGOs through the USAID and through the State Department Bureau of Population, Refugees and Migration (PRM). After it was established in 1996, much of U.S. aid flowed through the United Nations Bosnian Women's Initiative (BWI).[71]

"Reconciliation" projects attempted to forge relationships among women from various ethnic groups that were previously at war with one another and to bring them together in multi-ethnic organizations so that they could work on problems that were common to "all women," such as concern for children's welfare. According to cultural anthropologist Elissa Helms, in the postwar period international donors "especially targeted women for projects of ethnic reconciliation and the re-establishment of cross-ethnic communications." Generally, Western donors shared the beliefs that "women are 'naturally' more interested in peace, more tolerant of ethnic differences, and more willing to engage in dialogue and compromise to diffuse conflicts." Because of their own gender biases, many Westerners, feminists and non-feminists alike, believed "that women were against the war, which was decided on by men, and are therefore innocent (passive) victims, incapable of hatred and nationalism."[72] Yet in funding reconciliation projects that reinforced gender role stereotypes, the U.S. government and other Western donors often undermined their own efforts. The Westerners sought to "empower" women and to involve them in community-building projects, yet they concurrently de-politicized and disempowered the region's women by promoting essentialist ideas about women's gentle natures.[73] Delphi International's "Star Project" was one example of a fairly successful large-scale reconciliation project that brought together "non-nationalistic and multiethnic women's organizations" for networking, vocational training and other common projects.[74] Generally, however, reconciliation projects failed to overcome ethnic divisions fueled by years of brutal warfare and "most local women's NGOs in many parts of Bosnia continue to be composed predominantly of one ethnic group."[75]

"Reconstruction" projects that Western governments and donors sponsored focused on ways to involve women in economic development, primarily through funding microenterprises run by local women entrepreneurs. Among others in the Clinton Administration, First Lady Hillary Clinton often praised the strategy of microcredit lending to women in order to alleviate poverty and to rebuild communities.[76] Various liberal feminist NGOs such as Women's World Banking and the International Coalition for Women and Credit shared Hillary Clinton's enthusiasm for microcredit programs as a means to empower women in underdeveloped societies.[77] According to economic theory, microcredit financing directed to impoverished women would provide those women with an independent source of income and would reduce their dependence on their husbands or on other male family members. Economic independence and working in the public realm of society would expose women to a variety of liberal ideas and values and would create opportunities for women to develop social and other support networks beyond their families. Presumably, women would then become more assertive of their own rights. Additionally, if women's business endeavors were successful economically, their status would rise in the eyes of their communities and of their male family members.[78] Secretary Madeleine Albright, another Clinton Administration microcredit enthusiast, also asserted that "economists will tell you that especially in the developing world income controlled by the mother is many times more likely to be used to promote the health and education of children than income controlled by the father."[79] Certainly, many feminist economists and other microenterprise critics challenged these optimistic projections and assumptions.[80] Nonetheless, U.S. government postwar reconstruction programs in Bosnia and Rwanda adopted the microcredit lending strategy.

The U.S. government provided by far the largest share of the voluntary contributions to the UN Bosnian Women's Initiative (BWI) which focused on developing microenterprises, "providing women with business development loans and skills training and ensuring them access to resources like daycare, legal services, and education."[81] As the UN BWI was established, the U.S. government contributed $5 million and the Danish government contributed $155,000. By March 1997, the U.S. government had contributed an additional $1 million.[82] With these international funding priorities clear, unless they became self-sustaining, "to survive in Bosnia, [most] NGOs have had to jump on the women's microenterprise and income generation bandwagon."[83]

In 1995, the State Department also pledged $1 million to the UN Rwandan Women's Initiative (RWI), which pursued some of the same goals as the aid programs in Bosnia.[84] In Rwanda, foreign aid efforts were directed "to protect and advance the rights of women who have been torn from their homes, to provide them with access to reproductive health services and to help them start new businesses. These programs promote the reintegration of women into the economy through training programs, legal assistance, and support for microenterprise projects."[85] During her trip to Africa in March 1997, Hillary Clinton addressed a group of Rwandan women and announced that USAID money would specifically focus on women's needs: "You may know that in November of 1996, the United States announced a new USAID program with funding of about 153 million dollars. The vast majority of that assistance will be spent on reconciliation issues, reintegration and humanitarian aid to returnees. The program targets aid to women via the Women in Transition Program. … USAID is attempting to focus as much as possible on female heads of households and to assist you in the overwhelming task of caring for the many children orphaned as a result of this genocide."[86]

Clinton Administration representatives consistently articulated essentialist notions that "women" could best promote reconciliation in post-conflict states; they also supported egalitarian goals to raise global women's status and promote women's rights by integrating women leaders into governments and women workers into local economies. For example, Phyllis Oakley, assistant secretary for Population, Refugees and Migration at the State Department, defined "Women's Role in the New Age of Globalization" in spring 1997. She asserted that "I have seen in the Great Lakes region of Africa hundreds of Rwandan women from the Hutu and Tutsi ethnic groups working side-by-side to prevent a repeat of the genocidal violence which has caused so much suffering in that country." In the same speech, Oakley promoted programs to empower women so that they could better contribute to postwar economic reconstruction: "Women are prepared to be full partners in sustainable development, but they need education, decent health care, including reproductive health care, access to credit, and protection from violence. They need the knowledge and the power to make their own choices."[87] These essentialist ideas and egalitarian goals could not co-exist without tensions. Nonetheless, these ideas and goals fueled the Clinton Administration's postwar projects in Bosnia and Rwanda as well as the administration's "Vital Voices: Women in Democracy Initiative" that Ambassador Swanee Hunt at the U.S. Embassy in Austria, the first lady and her chief of staff at the White House, and the Office of International Women's Issues Senior Coordinator Theresa Loar established in 1997.

The Vital Voices: Women in Democracy Initiative

U.S. and global feminist activism and the Clinton Administration's responses from 1993 onward had laid the groundwork for the first Vital Voices conference that took place in Vienna, Austria in 1997, although it was U.S. Ambassador to Austria Swanee Hunt who first proposed this event promoting women's equal participation in governing and developing their communities. Hunt was a member of the Dallas, Texas Hunt family, whose fortune was made in the oil industry. Swanee and her sister Helen broke away from the family business and had used their resources to support various humanitarian organizations and progressive causes. Swanee Hunt was living in Colorado in the 1980s when she got involved in Democratic Party politics and met the Clintons. She supported

Bill Clinton during the 1992 presidential campaign, and Clinton appointed Hunt as U.S. ambassador to Austria in 1993.[88]

Based in Vienna, Swanee Hunt was in close proximity to Bosnia and other former Soviet satellites that were the so-called New Independent States in transition to democracy. By her own accounts, Hunt became aware of the ways that regional political and social conflicts impacted women through her duties as U.S. ambassador, flying with food supplies into Sarajevo during a Serbian siege of the city in 1994.[89] Susan Crais Hovanec, a career foreign service officer serving with Ambassador Peter Galbraith at the U.S. Embassy in Croatia, whose work focused on reporting on the Bosnian war and the ensuing humanitarian crisis, also raised Hunt's consciousness in relation to the problems of Balkan women. Crais Hovanec introduced Hunt to regional women activists who came to her with their appeals for peace and reconstruction of their societies.[90] Hunt subsequently hosted conversations with these women at the ambassador's residence in Vienna. Hunt's embassy aide, Sarah Gauger, recalled the emotional meetings that took place:

> There are stories that you probably read in [Swanee Hunt's] books of these small gatherings that we hosted at the Embassy where we would maybe have twenty people or so. We would bring them across the border on a bus and they would sit on separate sides of the bus and there wouldn't be any conversation, or very tense conversation, and then we had them together at the Embassy for several days. We had a UN psychologist and coalition builder there. We had a space, a safe space where people could—without being watched, without being listened in on—could really talk and discover what their similarities were, and discover that what they were working for was democracy, and discover that what they wanted—what they all shared—was this desire for safe communities. And so these were transformative gatherings.[91]

Hunt became convinced that women's participation was necessary to ensure the success of peace building efforts in their communities. She aimed to include their voices in the peace deliberations led by male policy makers in their nations and in Washington DC:

> After some 35 trips throughout the new democracies, it became even more clear to me that women's voices were essential to the healthy evolution of these societies. The women who spoke were articulate, they had ideas, and they had energy. The problem was not that women were silent. Often one of them sounded like a whole choir. The question was, who was listening? Over several weekends in 1996, I invited small groups of women from Croatia, Ukraine, and Bosnia, to spend three days in my Vienna residence, putting together plans of how they could

> strengthen their voices back home. They explored leadership styles, talked about families, sang folk songs, and pushed through barriers of misunderstanding.[92]

Following preliminary discussions with regional women, Ambassador Hunt and her staff developed plans for a forum that would bring together women of privilege from the West, who were leaders in government, nongovernmental organizations, academia and businesses, with women leaders from Central and Eastern European "emerging democracies" to share ideas and strategies for women's advancement and civil society development. In the early stages of organization Hunt bore the brunt of the costs associated with the meeting, her staff provided the logistical support and Hunt invited her friend Hillary Clinton in order to raise the event's profile. Secretary of State Madeleine Albright was also invited, but a NATO Summit in Madrid prevented her from attending the first Vital Voices conference held in Vienna, July 9-11, 1997. Nonetheless Albright sent her greetings and asserted "we know that, in this region and around the world, women will only be able to contribute our full potential if we have equal access, equal rights, equal protection and a fair chance at the levers of economic and political power."[93]

Hillary Clinton sympathized with Hunt's plans. Due to the rousing speeches she delivered at the 1995 Beijing conference, Clinton was beloved by women worldwide who saw her as someone who stood up for women and children.[94] During her world travels Hillary Clinton represented the administration and promoted women's empowerment through democratic and economic participation in developing and post-conflict states. She often repeated the phrase that "women's rights are human rights" in international forums and she was a well known advocate for funding microcredit enterprises for the world's poorest people—usually women.[95] Clinton's chief of staff, Melanne Verveer, was also a strong advocate for these global women's issues, and she supported and cheered on the first lady.[96]

Feminist women who held strategic positions inside the administration supported Hillary Clinton's decision to attend Hunt's forum in Vienna. Nonetheless, the first lady's involvement changed the nature of the meeting. The State Department and National Security Council set standards for selecting participants, vetted the issues that would be discussed and pushed for concrete outcomes to result from the women's discussions.[97] As the event planning progressed, Theresa Loar, who coordinated exchanges between Washington and Vienna, seized upon the Vital Voices conference as a model program to promote women's involvement in building democracy and strong economies in

Eastern Europe and elsewhere. By repeating the Vital Voices program in various sensitive global regions, the newly reorganized Office of International Women's Issues became integrally involved in one of the State Department's primary post-Cold War democracy promotion missions. Susan Crais Hovanec explained: "I think Theresa and Hillary and Swanee were strategically very clever and Swanee's coming up with Vital Voices as a way to help Bosnian women gave the whole Office [of International Women's Issues] traction, and substance, really when it needed it. It was critical. There was a critical need."[98]

Later, it became popular perception that Hillary Clinton and Madeleine Albright had founded the Vital Voices initiative. To be sure, they promoted the programs in their public addresses and through their attendance many subsequent Vital Voices events.[99] Nonetheless, it was OIWI Senior Coordinator Theresa Loar who took the spark of Swanee Hunt's idea and quickly recognized that her office could play a more meaningful role and gain institutional stature at the State Department if the event was successful:

> It was a struggle to get the State Department to see this conference as something more than a gathering to support women. It was a big deal to get a cable out to say that 'promoting women's roles and building democracy is one of the elements of U.S. foreign policy.' I remember it was Jim O'Brien in Secretary Albright's office who was my ally and allowed me to get clearance to get the cable out, because it wasn't enthusiastically received. It was seen as [the pet project of] an ambassador, and a political appointee ambassador to boot, who was leaving [her] post and wanted to pull some women together for a conference. It wasn't well received despite all of Swanee's good efforts. ...When Swanee had asked me to become involved, I wanted to [add] the foreign policy components to it; so that was a big effort to do that.[100]

European women at the highest levels of leadership also became involved in the Vital Voices conference as the planning moved forward. Emma Bonino, European Union (EU) Commissioner for Humanitarian Affairs, Anita Gradin, EU Commissioner for Justice and Home Affairs, Jaroslava Moserová, Senate Vice-President of the Czech Republic, Vesna Pešić, President of the Civic Alliance in Belgrade, Maria Rauch-Kallat, General Secretary of the Austrian People's Party, and Anastasia Posadskaya-Vanderbeck, Open Society Institute Director of the Regional Women's Program, were all members of the Vital Voices conference steering committee that Swanee Hunt chaired and Theresa Loar coordinated. The Steering Committee invited 300 women from the United States, and Eastern, Western and Central Europe. Many of these women were also leaders in their fields—politicians, businesswomen, educators, lawyers, judges, journalists and NGO activists. High-profile participants included former Italian Foreign Minister Susan Agnelli, CNN reporter Christianne Amanpour, former U.S. Congresswoman Marjorie Margolies-Mezvinsky who had also served as deputy-chair of the U.S. delegation to the Beijing conference, U.S. Supreme Court Justice Sandra Day O'Connor and many other luminaries who held influential positions with national and international stature. They met to discuss their personal experiences and strategies for advancing women to leadership positions in politics, law and business with aspiring leaders. With an eye to the future, by design, 10 percent of the invited guests were young women under age thirty. Meeting in large plenaries and small discussion groups, all the participants were encouraged to tell their stories, to share their leadership and development strategies and to leave the conference with plans to put those strategies into action.[101]

When Hillary Clinton addressed the women gathered in Vienna she cheered on the transition to democracy in the former socialist states, and she affirmed the need for women's voices to be heard in peace negotiations and in governing their new societies. She also urged women to network with one another across the professions, the business world, government service and academia as the Vital Voices conference brought women together to forge activist alliances. She asserted that USAID programs also aimed to promote women's activist networks. USAID's strategy was to disperse funds through NGOs "that are working to protect the environment, or improve health services or spark economic development, teaching children basic democratic values, working to create that area between the market and the government crucial to the continuation and progress of democracy." She announced $3 million new U.S. government funds that would be directed to global women's programming.[102] Over the next few years, as Hillary Clinton preached the gospel of women's empowerment at subsequent Vital Voices conferences, the State Department establishment also grew to appreciate the Vital Voices initiative. A State Department history of the Clinton presidency praised the initiative's accomplishments and pronounced it "one of the most innovative" of the administration's democracy promotion programs.[103]

6.2 Hillary Rodham Clinton addressing the Vital Voices: Women in Democracy Conference, Vienna, Austria, July 11, 1997. Courtesy of the William J. Clinton Presidential Library.

The name "Vital Voices: Women in Democracy" provided the overall theme of the Vienna conference: to promote women's equality through their involvement in the governing and running of their societies in influential, decision-making ways, with the underlying assumption that "women" were a democratizing force. This idea had been a long running discursive theme among feminists internationally from the World War II era onward, who had often argued that a "true" democracy did not exist unless all adult members participated and women were included in the public realm, so the theme resonated with male and female policymakers.[104] This became one conceptual frame of the 1997 Vienna conference and for all that followed, that women were "necessary" political actors in democratic societies.[105] Moreover, the "essential connection between voice and empowerment" became a rhetorical theme running through Hillary Clinton's public addresses from July 1997 onward.[106] Political scientist Jacqui True has noted that language has unique power to shape convictions and spur action. Conceptual frames play crucial roles in efforts to achieve measurable social and institutional change:

> Words and concepts literally make it possible to think and to see what was previously unthinkable or hidden. Powerful slogans such as 'democracy without women is no democracy', 'women's rights are human rights and human rights are women's rights', 'sexual

> harassment' and 'violence against women' have changed reality by changing the way we see and think about the world around us. … Words and meanings emerging from second wave feminist theorizing can now be found in laws and policies, where they are subject to interpretation and contestation as well as implementation.[107]

A second conceptual frame also directed this and subsequent Vital Voices conferences. Since the UN Decade for Women and even before that, women in development organizations argued that it was "necessary" to support women's productive contributions in order for developing societies to fully realize their economic and social potential.[108] Rather than limiting or excluding women's participation in the formal capitalist economy which only slowed down economic development, or from civil society-building initiatives that created the stable conditions necessary for economic development, it was far more beneficial to bring women into the public realm as full partners. This conceptual frame coincided with USAID Women in Development office efforts throughout the 1990s. USAID/WID programs targeted women in developing countries with programs that recognized their "critical role" in achieving economic and social development. USAID/WID supported gender equality measures that enabled women's economic participation such as "legal reform and access to education, credit and health care," including assistance for "family planning" (i.e. contraceptives) and various "advocacy" training programs to prevent violence against women among others.[109] Women were defined as "economic drivers" who could make great contributions to national and international development if they were allowed to do so. Coinciding with this conceptual frame, Vital Voices conference organizers included many Western and European businesswomen, entrepreneurs and NGO activists who had been involved in women in development advocacy at various UN and regional gatherings.[110]

Although feminist goals inspired the Vital Voices conferences, and feminist government insiders organized and implemented Vital Voices programs, the programs also served U.S. government national security interests in aligning the New Independent States of the post-Cold War world with the West's "broader neoliberal structural adjustment agenda." Vital Voices conferences included representatives from countries that were deemed "emerging democracies" with "transitioning capitalist economies" who cooperated with Western goals internationally.[111] This combination of feminist and instrumental goals shaped the 1997 conference and all subsequent Vital Voices conferences that the State Department Office of International Women's Issues organized through the duration of President Clinton's second term. In Belfast, Northern

Ireland, for example, the Vital Voices conference that took place in October 1998 intended to strengthen goals of the April Peace Accords that the Clinton Administration helped to negotiate.[112] Hillary Clinton attended the conference, co-sponsored by Northern Ireland's Secretary of State Marjorie Mowlam, and announced "over $2 million in public-private partnerships to support the Vital Voices objectives, including media training, mentoring and economic development projects for women."[113]

The OIWI sponsored a Vital Voices conference in Montevideo, Uruguay in 1998 where the first lady addressed 400 women from thirty-four Latin American nations and public-private partners—represetnatives of businesses, governments and NGOs—all committed resources, training and skills aimed at implementing the conference action plans to promote women's further advancement in their nations' political institutions where some progress had been made by women during the 1990s, and into their nations' economies, as well.[114] The OIWI also organized Vital Voices meetings in 1999 held in Reykjavik, Iceland for women from the Baltics, Scandinavia, and Russia,[115] in Port of Spain, Trinidad and a roundtable in Istanbul, Turkey, that "brought together women leaders working to foster democracy in the areas of economics, politics, human rights and the law, representing the countries of Turkey, Kazakhstan, Kyrgyzstan, Tajikistan and Uzbekistan."[116] Before the administration left office, the Vital Voices initiative organized a final meeting in Nigeria in 2000 "to strengthen democracy in Nigeria and highlighted the key issues facing women in the region, such as HIV/AIDS and its impact on African women."[117] The Vital Voices initiative sought to mainstream gender perspectives into U.S. democracy promotion programs, to strengthen relationships between the U.S. government and women's NGOs and to direct more USAID funds to global women's programs.[118] Progress toward this funding goal was especially successful in the regions of Eastern Europe and the former Soviet states, as these areas of the world had been targeted for increased U.S. foreign aid since early in the 1990s.[119]

In addition to the economic aid directed to women through the efforts of the Vital Voices initiative, the program also produced a less-quantifiable result. The women who attended and met with high-profile U.S. and global women leaders felt validated by the attention and moral support they received from the Vital Voices organizers and from each other. Theresa Loar recounted a Vital Voices "success story" in her testimony before the House Committee on International Relations in May 2000:

> An example of an emerging woman leader who has benefited from the Vital Voices Initiative is Nadine Perrault, a human rights leader in Haiti. After attending the Vital Voices of the Americas conference in October 1998, she returned home to Haiti and formed a Vital Voices of Haiti Association. This Association of some 100 women worked with other women in Haiti to strengthen their role in the political, economic and social progress of their country.
>
> Their work quickly spread throughout the Caribbean and in October 1999, women from 14 Caribbean countries came together in Trinidad to launch a Vital Voices of the Caribbean Initiative. They focused on raising awareness of and combating domestic violence and the creation of a women's leadership institute of the Americas. As a result of this experience, five women decided to run for elected office in Haiti. Because of the political situation there, many of these women have suffered threats against their lives and the safety of their families. The Vital Voices of Haiti Association is serving as a support network for these political candidates.[120]

The Washington DC foreign policy establishment may not have appreciated these results, but participants found them significant nonetheless. Hillary Clinton explained the value that global women attached to the Vital Voices meetings:

> In Romania and Russia, I've heard the voices of women struggling to recreate a civil society where they had only known authoritarian rule and there had been no tradition of democracy. They are attempting to be sure that their voices are heard and their contributions recognized. In Northern Ireland, I've heard the voices of Catholic and Protestant women who've never been in the same room together before, but who now sit down and talk about what they have in common and how they can work across sectarian lines. In Guatemala and El Salvador, I sat with women who'd been on opposite sides of the civil wars that have only recently ended there. I remember listening to one woman who had been a guerilla leader, sitting next to the sister of the president of the country, and they both talked about how they would have never known of one another if they had not been brought together to recognize that they did indeed share common goals—not only a common humanity but as women—a commitment to a better, more peaceful future. Many women around the world are finding their voice in new ways. And as we stand here together we have to do all that we can to make sure that those voices are amplified, their stories are heard and told.[121]

Between July 1997 and January 2001 when the Clinton Administration left office and the Vital Voices initiative transitioned to a nongovernmental organization, the women involved used the state in order to promote liberal feminist gender equality and women's empowerment goals. Some feminist critics dismiss the liberal feminist message of programs like the Vital Voices initiative because the women who participated in the Vital Voices conferences including U.S. government officials, U.S. women's NGOs and global women leaders and activists, did not acknowledge the anti-feminist elements inherent in Western liberal democratic theory, in the global neoliberal capitalist system or in the "coercive" and militarized state that sponsored these events. However, feminists such as political scientist Jane S. Jaquette has argued that is a misguided position to take: "[F]ew feminists defend the state, although it is the only social institution with the legitimacy, scope and credibility to deliver any of the goods feminist seek, from reproductive rights to affirmative action or the recognition that engaging meaningfully in the public sphere provides."[122] Jane Mansbridge concurs. Mansbridge has asserted that feminists who want to change the state should engage with the state: "Given that states will not disappear in the near future, what stance should we take toward them? My answer is: wary usage. State power will be used against women, just as other forms of power are used against women, unless we intervene. One response is to establish barriers, such as constitutional or internationally enforceable rights, to certain kinds of invasions by state power. Another is to make states more likely to act in the interests of women."[123] With more feminists engaged in foreign policy making during the Clinton Administration through the Office of International Women's Issues and through other avenues, the U.S. government's record demonstrated that the state was, in fact, more likely to act in the interests of global women than it had been under previous administrations.

According to Theresa Loar, there was conscious effort to avoid discussion of the "'dark side' of women's issues" at the Vital Voices conferences.[124] These events were intended to generate positive messages for and about women governing their countries and developing their economies and communities. The Vital Voices initiative became an important component of the work of the Office of International Women's Issues. In addition, under Loar's leadership the office also focused on fundamental women's human rights issues asserting women's bodily integrity, as the next chapter explains.

---

[1]Lippman, *Madeleine Albright and the New American Diplomacy*, p. 285.

[2]Christopher, "Commemorating Human Rights Day": "As Secretary of State, I have insisted that our foreign policy be grounded in what are America's fundamental interests. I have no doubt in my mind—I never have had any doubt—that defense of human rights is one of those fundamental American interests. It's

not peripheral, it's central, and I owe to John Shattuck, I think, just a word, that I believe he has done more than any other Assistant Secretary of State. Of course, we all build on the achievements of our predecessors, but I think John has done more than any of his predecessors in making human rights part of the mainstream of American foreign policy."

[3]Clinton, "Remarks by the President at Human Rights Day Event."

[4]Lippman, *Madeleine Albright and the New American Diplomacy*, p. 285.

[5]Clinton, "Remarks by the President at Human Rights Day Event."

[6]Gedda, "Albright Champions Women's Rights"; International Center for Research on Women, Annual Report, 1996: "'There has been a sea change in the rhetoric,' says Regan Ralph of the Washington-based Human Rights Watch. But, she says, 'The institutions that are supposed to back up the rhetoric are way behind.' To the extent that there are programs, she says, 'they are small and the approach is ad hoc.'"

[7]Lippman, *Madeleine Albright and the New American Diplomacy*, pp. 31-2, 294.

[8]Ibid. pp. 7-9, 13.

[9]Gedda, "Albright Champions Women's Rights"; International Center for Research on Women, Annual Report, 1996. See also: Lithander, "Engendering the Peace Process, A Gender Approach to Dayton and Beyond." According to Lithander, Madeleine Albright raised these issues in the Dayton peace negotiations as others have documented, but according to some critics, the Dayton Peace Accords nonetheless "fall short of the demands from Beijing and other human rights treaties, not because they do not stipulate the protection of fundamental human rights and freedoms, including equality and a clear condemnation of discrimination based on gender, but because it is gender neutral. If the Dayton Peace Accords had absorbed the principle of these instruments, women of Bosnia and Herzegovina, and civil society as a whole, would have benefitted from it to a much larger extent than what became a reality. As women's special interests and needs are not taken into consideration in the Dayton Peace Accords, gender awareness in general has been lacking in the implementation process."

[10]Madeleine Albright quoted in Lippman, *Madeleine Albright and the New American Diplomacy*, pp. 31-2.

[11]"The President's Interagency Council on Women: Follow-up on U.S. Commitments Made at the UN Fourth World Conference on Women, Beijing, China," January 24, 1996, CWGL, Beijing +5, box 1. In January 1996 the Department of Justice Violence Against Women office announced the first grants available for training of law enforcement and criminal justice system personnel, and for enhancement of victims' services. The Violence Against Women Act of 1994 authorized $1.6 billion over five years to hire more prosecutors, improve domestic violence training for prosecutors, police officers, and health and social services professionals, provide for more shelters, counseling services, and research into the cause of violence against women as well as public education campaigns. The VAW office established a 24-hour nationwide Domestic Violence Hotline.

[12]Loar, The Association for Diplomatic Studies and Training Foreign Affairs Oral History Project.

[13]Albright and Hillary Rodham Clinton, "Remarks at special program in honor of International Women's Day, Department of State."

[14]Albright and Hillary Rodham Clinton, "Media Roundtable."

[15]Loar, The Association for Diplomatic Studies and Training Foreign Affairs Oral History Project; Mertus, War's Offensive on Women, p. 53.

[16]Loar, The Association for Diplomatic Studies and Training Foreign Affairs Oral History Project.

[17]Mertus, *War's Offensive on Women*, pp. 53-7.

[18]"Pre-transition Council for Afghanistan."

[19]Raphel, "U.S. Interests in and Policy toward Afghanistan": "The interests of the United States in Afghanistan remain largely as they have been since the fall of the communists in 1992."

[20]Julie Mertus is Professor and Co-director of the Master's program in Ethics, Peace, and Global Affairs at American University.

[21]Mertus, *War's Offensive on Women*, p. 58.

[22]Loar, The Association for Diplomatic Studies and Training Foreign Affairs Oral History Project.

[23]Tarr-Whelan, "Statement," October 29, 1996: "We cannot forget the commitments we made in Beijing. The United States is concerned about human rights in Afghanistan, particularly the status of women and girls. Directives which keep women out of the workplace and keep young girls out of school are morally wrong, economically counterproductive and politically unwise. In addition to violating women's human rights, actions that deny women and girls the equal right to education and employment, and the right to participate equally in political life are self-defeating. You cannot run a modern economy without women. Restrictions on Afghan women and girls limit the ability to dig out from over a decade of war, to rebuild the country, and to establish a sense of national unity."

[24]Pitts, "U.S. Condemns Human Rights Violations in Afghanistan."

[25]Ibid.

[26]Coll, *Ghost Wars*, pp. 215, 364-5.

[27]Loar, The Association for Diplomatic Studies and Training Foreign Affairs Oral History Project.

[28]Ibid.: "I was very concerned [about aid to Afghanistan]. … If you were excluding girls and women from the distribution channel for food, and from education, and from basic needs, are we, as a country, and all the other donor countries going to ignore that and go on as though it was business as usual? And Allan had the opinion that we shouldn't, and he didn't. … Allan was really supportive of this and really wanted to go to the donor meetings, saying that, 'It's not business as usual. The United States is going to have to look at how we distribute aid and what kind of assistance we give, because we're not going to turn over the same kind of stuff to the Taliban, and we're going to have to figure out how we can maneuver this to make sure that women and girls get a fair shake and maybe develop some new things because now they're being excluded from the basic services they had before.' … When Allan wasn't around, or if there was someone meeting at the UN, it required monitoring of all the different mechanisms, all the different ways that policies develop that were affecting this country. It was a tremendous challenge, and ultimately we moved in the right direction."

[29]"Highlights of the State Department Activities to Promote the Advancement of Women";"America's Commitment: Federal Programs Benefiting Women and New Initiatives as follow-up to the UN Fourth World Conference on Women, May 1997"; "1999 Up Date: America's Commitment:

Federal Programs Benefitting Women and New Initiatives as Follow Up to the UN Fourth World Conference on Women, Supporting Women and Girls in Afghanistan"; "America's Commitment: Women 2000, A Five Year Review of Federal Programs Benefitting Women and New Initiatives as Follow-Up to the UN Fourth World Conference on Women", The President's Interagency Council on Women Archives.

[30]Loar, "Statement on Women in Afghanistan"; Loar, "Statement Before the House Committee on International Relations."

[31]Loar, The Association for Diplomatic Studies and Training Foreign Affairs Oral History Project.

[32]Laville, "Gender apartheid? American women and women's rights in American foreign policy," in Johnstone and Laville, eds. *The US Public and American Foreign Policy*, pp. 88-91.

[33]Ibid., p. 87.

[34]Clinton, "An Historic Commitment to International Human Rights."

[35]Hillary Rodham Clinton, "United Nations International Women's Day Speech on Women's Rights": "We can point to many problems around our world today where women—for reasons of history, culture, discrimination, prejudice—are used to lift up patriarchy, are used really as objects in order for others to exercise power. There probably is no more egregious and systematic trampling of fundamental rights of women today than what is happening in Afghanistan under the iron rule of the Taliban."

[36]Lippman, *Madeleine Albright and the New American Diplomacy*, 303; Albright, "Advancing the Status of Women in the 21st Century"; Albright, "Address to the Roslyn Carter Distinguished Lecture Series"; "Women and Girls in Afghanistan".

[37]"Update to federal Programs Benefitting Women and New Initiatives as Follow-up to the UN Fourth World Conference on Women," April 1998 Supplement, CWGL, Beijing +5, box 1: "The United States is neutral toward the various Afghan factions fighting in that country, but our neutrality does not extend to violations of international norms of behavior. We condemn Taliban human rights violations, particularly against women and girls. The United States has taken a leadership role in the region and in the United Nations to promote peace in the region. ... The United States has a commitment to providing humanitarian assistance to women and girls of Afghanistan. United States officials play a key role in making the issue of assistance to women in Afghanistan a major focus of the Afghanistan Support Group. In 1997 the United States contributed $24.6 million to the UN High Commission on Human Rights, the International Committee of the Red Cross, and the World Food Program to run a variety of programs that directly benefit Afghan women and girls. This was nearly a quarter of the total for the UNHCHR and ICRC programs. The United States recently called for a UNHCHR investigation of reports of violence against women and girls in refugee camps in Pakistan. Due to the United States efforts, an investigation is now underway. United States funding supports UNHCHR procedures to provide protection to women and girls in refugee camps. The United States is committing up to $2.5 million in new funds for women's grassroots organizations in Pakistan and for training to improve the skills of women in Afghanistan."

[38]Linda Tarr-Whelan, "Statement to the Forty-fourth session of the United Nations Commission on the Status of Women," February 29, 2000, CWGL, Beijing +5, box 3.

[39]Inderfurth, "The Taliban: Confrontation or Engagement?"; Albright, "Remarks at 6 + 2 Meeting on Afghanistan."

[40]Mertus, *War's Offensive on Women*, p. 59. For more information on the war's impact on Afghan women see also: Statement by Ravan Farhadi (Afghanistan), United Nations Press Release, "UN Adopts Political Declaration, 'Further Actions and Initiatives', Assembly President Notes 'No backward movement' on language of Beijing," June 9, 2000, CWGL, Beijing + 5, box 9.

[41]Mertus, *War's Offensive on Women*, pp. 62-3. CARE, Oxfam, and Save the Children periodically suspended aid programs when the Taliban reneged on negotiated agreements to distribute aid to women and girls. UNICEF refused to fund schools when girls were banned. The World Health Organization and International Red Cross cooperated with Taliban authorities in order to deliver health and other emergency aid. For its part, "the Taliban took advantage of the lack of a coordinated approach among the UN family, as it did among NGOs. For both sets of actors, the Taliban delayed or refused permission for programs to operate, pressured agencies to hire relatives, and refused to meet with agency representatives, fully aware that such challenges would not provoke a concerted response."

[42]Ibid. p. 67.

[43]Mertus and Hocevar Van Wely, "Women's Participation in the International Criminal Tribunal for the Former Yugoslavia," p. vii.

[44]Mertus, *War's Offensive on Women*, p. xii: "A gender perspective emphasizes using the expertise of women and including women in central decision-making processes in all stages and aspects of humanitarian action. It promises transformative change by examining the socially constructed roles of men and women and exposing the very root of exploitation and domination of women. It challenges the institutions that perpetuate inequality."

[45]Mertus and Hocevar Van Wely, "Women's Participation in the International Criminal Tribunal for the Former Yugoslavia," pp. vii-viii.

[46]Rhonda Copelon, "Gendered War Crimes: Reconceptualizing Rape in Time of War," in Peters and Wolper, eds. Women's Rights, Human Rights, pp. 203-4.

[47]"International Criminal Justice: Holding Human Rights Violators Accountable," Equality Now Annual Report, 1996-1997.

[48]Rhonda Copelon, "Gendered War Crimes: Reconceptualizing Rape in Time of War," p. 203.

[49]Ibid. p. 207.

[50]Meyer, *Security, Economics and Morality in American Foreign Policy*, p. 125.

[51]UN Special Rapporteur to the Commission on Human Rights, "Report on the Situation of Human Rights in Rwanda," E/CN.4/1996/68, paragraph 16.

[52]"The Women's Rights Project," *Human Rights Watch Annual Report* 1996, p. 346.

[53]Ibid.

[54]McKinley, "UN Tribunal, in first such trail verdict, convicts Rwandan ex-Mayor of Genocide."

[55]"The Women's Rights Project," p. 351.

[56]"Women's Action Update: Kosovo—Forced Removal, Rape, Genocide," Equality Now Annual Report, 1998-1999.

[57]Meyer, *Security, Economics and Morality in American Foreign Policy*, p. 131: "Did the international community fail miserably to act in the face of genocide? Undoubtedly. Although there is plenty of blame to be shared by the UN Secretariat and Security Council, the Clinton administration must accept a greater share of the responsibility for it has a disproportionate amount of political, economic, and military influence in the UN and in the broader international community. Only the US government could have overcome the numerous obstacles to more forceful engagement. As one disgusted observer put it, 'US leaders harmed themselves and degraded the highest ideals of the human race by their inaction during Rwanda's genocide.'" See also: Shattuck, Freedom on Fire, pp. 17-8, 115-7, 140, 160-2.

[58]Sheffer, "Witness and Victim Protection in International Criminal Courts": "Are crimes of rape and other serious sexual assault violations of international humanitarian law? The answer is yes, whether one is examining the crime of genocide, crimes against humanity, or war crimes. While there has been and will be debate over precisely how to define crimes of sexual assault within the context of international humanitarian law, the United States will continue to exercise its leadership to ensure that these serious crimes are fully incorporated in the work of the ad hoc tribunals and in the jurisdiction of the permanent international criminal court. There has been an impressive amount of scholarly study of this subject, and I have come to know in my work some of the scholars and practitioners who have done path-breaking work in this field. One is Professor Rhonda Copelon of City University of New York Law School, whose work in the permanent court talks has proven instrumental in protecting women's rights. Another is Kelly Dawn Askin, a Visiting Scholar at Notre Dame Law School, whose new book, War Crimes Against Women, is a path breaking, comprehensive source of the law. Patricia Viseur-Sellers, until recently the gender adviser to the ad hoc international criminal tribunals, has helped put the issue of sexual assault at the forefront of the tribunals' work. We owe these individuals and many others whom I cannot hope to list tonight our gratitude and thanks."

[59]Shattuck, *Freedom on Fire*, p. 124: "In early 1993, the United States had begun to champion the creation by the UN Security Council of an International War Crimes Tribunal for the Former Yugoslavia. The leader of this effort was Madeleine Albright, then the U.S. ambassador to the United Nations, whose strong views on the Balkan crisis had been shaped in part by her own family's experience of having twice been forced to flee her native Czechoslovakia, first under the Nazis and later under the communists." See also: Albright, "UN Security Council Establishes International Tribunal for Rwanda"; Gedda, "Albright Champions Women's Rights."

[60]Albright, "Building a Framework for American Leadership in the 21st Century."

[61]"The Women's Rights Project," p. 347.

[62]"U.S. Government Follow-up to the United Nations Fourth World Conference on Women, Update on Key Initiatives, March 1997" and "America's Commitment: Federal Programs Benefiting Women and New Initiatives as follow-up to the UN Fourth World Conference on Women, May 1997," The President's Interagency Council on Women Archives.

[63]"Remarks and Commentary by First Lady Hillary Rodham Clinton, Africa," c. March 1997, RCD, box 2.

[64]Jasmina Kuzmanović, "Legacies of Invisibility: Past Silence, Present Violence Against Women in the Former Yugoslavia" in Peters and Wolper, eds. Women's Rights, Human Rights, pp. 57-61.

[65]Mertus and Hocevar Van Wely, "Women's Participation in the International Criminal Tribunal for the Former Yugoslavia," p. ix.

[66]Jason Topping Cone, "Why an International Criminal Court?," *The Earth Times* (April 17, 2000), CWGL, Beijing + 5, box 9.

[67]"UN CSW Framework for further actions and initiatives that might be considered during the special session, Women 2000: Gender Equality, Development and Peace for the Twenty-first Century, Report of the Secretary-General," E/CN.6/1999/PC/2, CWGL, Beijing +5, box 1.

[68]Sheffer, "Address on the 50th Anniversary of the UN Declaration on Human Rights."

[69]Jason Topping Cone, "Why an International Criminal Court?"; WEDO, "Women's Equality: An Unfinished Agenda. Women's Organizations Assess U.S. Government Actions on Implementing the Beijing Platform, 1995 – 2000," CWGL, Beijing +5, box 7.

[70]Mertus, *War's Offensive on Women*, pp. 29-31.

[71]Albright, "The United States Assistance to Post-Conflict Societies."

[72]Helms, "Women as agents of ethnic reconciliation?," p. 19.

[73]Ibid. p. 15. Elissa Helms, for example, has argued in relation to Bosnian women: "Women are charged with achieving the very political goals of ethnic reconciliation and refugee return, yet the essentialist constructions used to encourage women's peacemaking roles effectively marginalize them from formal political power."

[74]Mertus, *War's Offensive on Women*, p. 29.

[75]Ibid. p. 30.

[76]See for example: Hillary Rodham Clinton, "Remarks at the [Global] Microcredit Summit."

[77]International Women's Tribune Centre, The Tribune: A Women and Development Quarterly, No. 56 (April 1997), IWTC, Acc # 01S-03, box 1: "Because extending credit to people too poor to borrow from traditional banks can be a powerful tool for ending poverty, and because women comprise the majority of the world's poor, the establishment of services and facilities to make more microcredit available is high on women's agendas."

[78]Bayes, "Beneath the Surface: Microcredit and Women's Empowerment."

[79]Albright, "Advancing the Status of Women in the 21st Century."

[80]Dawkins Scully, "Micro Credit No Panacea for Poor Women."

[81]"The Women's Rights Project," p. 347.

[82]Mertus, *War's Offensive on Women*, p. 33. See also: "U.S. Policy Initiatives Related to Refugee Women." The Japanese Government, the Japanese Committee for Refugee Relief, and the European Community Humanitarian Office (ECHO) also contributed funds to the UN BWI.

[83]Ibid. p. 32.

[84]"The Women's Rights Project," p. 347.

[85]"America's Commitment: Federal Programs Benefiting Women and New Initiatives as follow-up to the UN Fourth World Conference on Women," May 1997, The President's Interagency Council on Women Archives.

[86]"Remarks and Commentary by First Lady Hillary Rodham Clinton, Africa," RCD, box 2.

[87]Oakley, "Address at Ewha Woman's University."

[88]Hunt, *Half Life of a Zealot.*

[89]Hunt, "Muslim Women in the Bosnia Crucible," p. 301.

[90]Hunt, *Half Life of a Zealot*, p. 287.

[91]Sarah Gauger, Interview with Author at the Institute for Inclusive Security, Cambridge, Massachusetts, March 12, 2009.

[92]Message from Ambassador Swanee Hunt in "We Are Listening," pp. 2-4.

[93]Albright, "Statement to Vital Voices: Women in Democracy"; Hunt, Half Life of a Zealot, 373; Sarah Gauger, Interview with Author, March 12, 2009; Susan Crais Hovanec, Phone Interview with Author, May 19, 2008.

[94]Albright and Hillary Rodham Clinton, "Remarks at a Special Program in Honor of International Women's Day,": "During the past four years, Hillary Rodham Clinton has become America's most respected and valued--albeit unofficial--Ambassador. She has advocated America's agenda of peace, democracy, economic growth and law from India to Indonesia, from China to Copenhagen, and from Ukraine to a memorable diplomatic and culinary experience in Ulan Bator. She brings to her assigned tasks enormous energy, brains, commitment and volumes of eloquence. Those of you who have done public speaking know how hard it can be to excite an audience, at least without getting into trouble. Imagine how hard it is when that audience comes from 150 different countries and when most of them are sitting there with earphones on, wires going every way, listening to emotionless and not always accurate translation. And yet, this woman, the honorary chair of our delegation, electrified precisely that kind of audience in Beijing."

[95]Anne F. Mattina, "Hillary Rodham Clinton: Using her Vital Voice," in Meijer Werthheimer ed. *Inventing a Voice*, pp. 426-7: "[Hillary Rodham Clinton's] official website archived a total of 284 speech texts, listed under broad subject areas: 45 percent centered on "Advancing Democracy," with fifty-nine of those texts on topics of "Human Rights" and "Women as Citizens." Other texts focused on the needs of families and children, particularly in the areas of health care and education reform. An examination of these texts clearly reveals Clinton's deep commitment to empowering women and bringing children's issues into the realm of public policy. Indeed, her political agenda is coherent and it is one she has maintained throughout her public life."

[96]Stephanie Foster, "Spotlight: Melanne Verveer," in O'Connor ed., *Gender and Women's Leadership,* p. 318; Melanne Verveer, Phone Interview with Author, May 27, 2008.

[97]Loar, The Association for Diplomatic Studies and Training Foreign Affairs Oral History Project: "She [Swanee Hunt] did a very exciting, energetic job of pulling people together and putting on this big-time conference of these 300 people in Vienna, Austria. She was putting together a steering committee, and she asked me, as the Senior Coordinator of International Women's Issues, and in the foreign policy part of my job, to serve on this steering committee and to engage the State Department. She also contacted the First Lady's office and asked Mrs. Clinton to come to this and speak. So the NSC got involved, because if Mrs. Clinton was going to speak at a conference on democracy, it was important that the foreign policy elements be right in line. That was actually a very important first step."

[98]Susan Crais Hovanec, Phone Interview with Author, May 19, 2008.

[99]Mattina, "Hillary Rodham Clinton: Using her Vital Voice," p. 426; Hunt, *Half Life of a Zealot*, p. 375.

[100]Loar, The Association for Diplomatic Studies and Training Foreign Affairs Oral History Project: "So when Swanee left government, we wanted to continue this model of bringing emerging women leaders and engaging our embassies, around the overlay of women in democracy, because I thought that was a very important way of presenting these issues to the State Department, to the general public and to other governments. Nobody could say they were really against democracy. So as I was saying, it was packaging the idea of women's human rights under the democracy umbrella, which is a very legitimate thing to do because democracy should be a delivery system for human rights and for women's human rights. It allowed us to move forward and engage broad sectors in this conference. It went from conference to initiative."

[101]"We Are Listening… Report of the Vital Voices: Women in Democracy Conference."

[102]Hillary Rodham Clinton "Remarks of the First Lady" in "We Are Listening," p. 20: "Today I have the honor of announcing that the United States will commit three million dollars next year to projects that will directly support the objectives of this conference. These funds, which are entirely new funds, will be reserved solely for efforts that help women enter and ascend the realms of politics, law, and business. Moreover, we will continue to see that women have full and complete access to the entire range of democracy and business programs that we support."

[103]"Promoting Democracy" and "Women's Issues," in "History of the Department of State during the Clinton Presidency."

[104]For an early expression of this idea, see: Kenyon, "Victories on the International Front." See also: Lovenduski, *Feminizing Politics*, p. 22.

[105]Loar, "Statement before the House Committee on International Relations"; "Message from Ambassador Swanee Hunt" and Hillary Rodham Clinton, "Response from the First Lady" in "We Are Listening," pp. 3 and 20.

[106]Mattina, "Hillary Rodham Clinton: Using her Vital Voice," pp. 426-31.

[107]True, "Mainstreaming Gender in Global Public Policy," pp. 374-5.

[108]Berkovitch, *From Motherhood to Citizenship*, 141-3; Jain, *Women, Development and the UN*, pp. 45, and 51-3; Garner, *Shaping a Global Women's Agenda,* pp. 200-2.

[109]Atwood, "USAID initiatives relating to Women and Gender 1990s, Gender Plan of Action"; Albright, "Remarks before the Vital Voices Conference."

[110]Report of the "Business and Beyond Track" in "We Are Listening."

[111]True, "Mainstreaming Gender in Global Public Policy," pp. 374, 379.

[112]Loar, The Association for Diplomatic Studies and Training Foreign Affairs Oral History Project: "When the women from Northern Ireland came to one of the St. Patrick's Day receptions at the White House, right after the Good Friday Peace agreements in 1998, they said they were very concerned that when the new government structures and new economic structures were to be developed, that they [women] would be pushed aside, and they needed some help in finding their voice and in articulating their message. The word 'voices' kept coming up, and out of that came, through the mysteries of how our country works [laughter], an agreement, and when President Clinton announced our U.S.

commitments to the peace accords, there was a line that said, 'and the U.S. government has agreed to host a Vital Voices conference in Northern Ireland to help women integrate themselves into the new structures,' and hence, we were going to hold a Vital Voices conference. And I'm not sure all the players involved in that from the NSC side quite understood how that happened, how this little Vital Voices piece got in there [laughter], but it happened, and it was all for good!"

[113]"1999 Up Date: America's Commitment: Federal Programs Benefitting Women and New Initiatives as Follow Up to the UN Fourth World Conference on Women," President's Interagency Council on Women Archives.

[114]Ibid.

[115]Hillary Rodham Clinton, "Remarks at the Vital Voices Conference on Women and Democracy, Reykjavik, Iceland." Hillary Clinton announced among many other NGO and private donor initiatives that emerged from the Reykjavik meetings: "I was delighted that Deputy Secretary Talbott announced the U.S. Government and the Nordic Bank will provide $2 million in microcredit to expand small businesses in Russia and the Baltics."

[116]"History of the Vital Voices: Women in Democracy Initiative" Vital Voices: Global Partnerships NGO web site. Accessed in 2010 at: http://vitalvoices.org/?q=node/3.

[117] Ibid.

[118]Albright, "Remarks before the Vital Voices Conference."

[119]Loar, The Association for Diplomatic Studies and Training Foreign Affairs Oral History Project.

[120]Loar, "Statement Before the House Committee on International Relations."

[121]Hillary Rodham Clinton, "United Nations International Women's Day Speech on Women's Rights."

[122]Jaquette, "Feminism and the Challenges of the 'Post-Cold War' World," p. 342. Jaquette also cautions feminists to beware of those who are not sufficiently critical of global capitalism: "I fully support efforts to give women greater economic power, but greater access to the market can never achieve anything like parity for women, who remain disproportionately responsible for sustaining families."

[123]Mansbridge, "Anti-statism and Difference Feminism in International Social Movements," p. 356. See also p. 359: "Feminists have a 'stake in a capable state.' It would be catastrophic to be so carried away by the theoretical virtues of civil society or by anti-state discourse as to deaden oneself to the practical need to work with the state to improve the lives of women."

[124] Theresa Loar, "On the Vital Voices Initiative," US State Department *Magazine* (March 1998): "…This effort demonstrates the kind of partnership the Office has worldwide with NGOs, which work effectively with their own governments to improve the lives of women and girls, Ms. Loar said. Her office focuses on far more than the "dark" side of women's issues. Enabling women to participate fully in the political lives of their countries builds a foundation for democracy and complements the United States' broader strategic, diplomatic and economic interests, observed the former career Foreign Service officer." See also: "Message from Ambassador Swanee Hunt" in "We Are Listening": "We did not address the important issue of women as victims, or even women's rights per se.

Instead we shared know-how on specific strategies to propel women forward in three areas: politics, law, and business."

7

Women's Bodies as a Policy Issue

Throughout the 1990s women's bodies were at the very center of cultural and political debates in the United States and in United Nations forums. All interested parties engaged in hotly contested arguments over whether women had the "right" to independent control over their bodies and their reproductive lives, or whether women's bodies should be subject to external controls emanating from government laws, religious commandments, or other cultural beliefs and practices. During President Clinton's second term in office, his administration's global gender policies generally demonstrated respect for women's bodily integrity, that is, "the inviolability of the physical body [that] emphasizes the importance of personal autonomy and the self-determination of human beings over their own bodies."[1] The administration's gender policies included provisions to promote global women's interests and to protect women's bodies that were generally in agreement with liberal feminist activists' understanding of global women's needs and desires.

This chapter examines the ways that Clinton Administration officials devised global gender policies that focused on women's bodies including policies on global women's health and reproductive rights, female genital mutilation, sex trafficking in women and violence against women in Kosovo as an ongoing ethnic conflict escalated into war. The Clinton Administration attempted to devise policies and to support legislation that responded to the needs and respected the interests of global women regarding these sensitive but urgent issues of concern. Conservatives on the Religious Right exerted strong political pressures on the administration throughout global gender policy making processes that addressed these issues.[2] Conservatives put forward their competing gender policy perspectives that privileged religious values and traditional cultural practices over individual rights in regard to women's status and male-female relationships. They argued that regulation of women's bodies fell within the private realm of the family. Or, they accepted government's role in protecting women's bodies from abuse in the public realm of society, while still rejecting government's role in guaranteeing women's autonomy and women's rights within the private family.

Clinton Administration officials attempted to steer a course between what was politically possible given the strength of the conservative Religious Right and its political champions within the Republican Party that maintained a legislative majority, and what would serve liberal feminist values that the administration generally supported through its well-established global gender policy themes: to promote opportunities throughout the world for women's involvement as full partners in democratic governance and in their economies, with equal access to education to give women and girls knowledge to make their own choices, equal access to credit and other resources for social and economic development, equal access to healthcare including reproductive care and family planning and protection from all forms of violence that violated women's human rights.[3]

The Clinton Administration and Women's Reproductive Rights

Women's reproductive rights had been a constant source of controversy in U.S. domestic politics ever since the Supreme Court had made a landmark decision in 1973, in the *Roe v. Wade* court case. The Supreme Court determined in 1973 that women had the right to safe and legal abortions to terminate pregnancies, subject to state-mandated restrictions and conditions, based on their constitutional right to privacy. As discussed in chapter two, some Christian conservatives and other religious fundamentalists considered women's reproductive rights guaranteed by *Roe v. Wade* to be attacks on the privileges reserved for the private realm of society, that is, attacks on the inviolability of the traditional family. In the 1970s, Christian conservatives established a Religious Right political constituency that over time gained voting power and support among Republican Party politicians.[4] In the 1980s and 1990s, Democratic Party politicians generally and Bill Clinton in particular opposed the Religious Right's and the Republican Party's attempts to overturn the Supreme Court's *Roe v. Wade* decision, along with other attempts to elevate traditional family prerogatives to the status of law or to allow other restrictions on women's individual rights.[5]

A related controversy regarding women's bodily integrity and individual rights had reached a critical juncture at the UN-sponsored International Conference on Population and Development in 1994. As discussed in chapter four, this controversy focused on whether or not U.S.

government foreign aid should be used to fund organizations that provided contraceptives and other family planning services or counseling to global women. At that time the Clinton Administration reiterated its support for women's access to a range of family planning services including safe abortions in countries where abortion was legal. The administration supported women's individual rights to make their own decisions regarding the number and spacing of their children in efforts to promote global women's empowerment.[6] The controversy over allocating U.S. foreign aid to fund global family planning programs dispersed through United Nations' agencies such as the UN Population Administration (UNPA) or through liberal feminist NGOs resurfaced during President Clinton's second term in office. It involved President Clinton and Secretary of State Madeleine Albright in a political tug of war with congressional Republicans.

When the Clinton Administration began its second term, Secretary Albright led the administration's efforts to reorganize the State Department. The administration wanted to close down the U.S. Information Agency and the Arms Control and Disarmament Agency and to give the secretary of state authority over the U.S. Agency for International Development that had operated as a separate foreign policy office ever since it was established in 1961. These changes were proposed in the interest of rationalizing the government's foreign policy making operations. The House of Representatives and the Senate approved bills outlining the proposed State Department reorganization by June 1997 in House resolution 1757 and Senate bill 903. However, as the bills passed through various committee reviews, two controversial amendments were attached to the bills' provisions: one placed restrictions on payments of back dues that the U.S. owed to United Nations' agencies (nearly one billion dollars by some estimates);[7] the other restricted U.S. funds for global family planning programs.[8]

In regard to the proposed amendment restricting funding for family planning programs, House Republicans led by Congressman Christopher Smith proposed prohibitions on all U.S. foreign aid to global family planning agencies that "performed or actively promoted abortions" among their services. These prohibitions would affect NGOs that provided a range of women's healthcare services as well as various aid-recipient foreign governments and UN agencies that provided women's reproductive healthcare services abroad. If any of these healthcare providers performed abortions among the range of reproductive services offered, those NGOs and agencies would be cut off from U.S. foreign aid, even if the funds for abortion services were obtained from separate and distinct funding sources and not from the U.S. government. Moreover, any healthcare providers that received U.S. government funds would also be subject to a "global gag rule" that prohibited them from conducting any lobbying or advocacy efforts to liberalize abortion laws in their countries. Healthcare providers would be prohibited from making public statements, distributing material, or sponsoring conferences that advocated for legalizing abortion or easing restrictive abortion policies.

Even before Congressman Smith proposed that these foreign aid prohibitions be attached to the State Department reorganization bills, congressional Republicans had already slashed U.S. funding for global family planning programs.[9] By the spring of 1997 U.S. foreign aid for family planning programs had been reduced by one-third of their 1995 levels and Congress had imposed various restrictions on the dispersal of funds to global population planning agencies. These funding cuts had been made based on the premise that reducing funds for family planning services would reduce the incidences of abortion worldwide. Many opponents of these U.S. funding cuts and restrictions argued that reductions in aid for family planning programs would in fact increase the number of unplanned pregnancies and therefore would increase the number of abortions performed globally. Nonetheless, Republican advocates and their conservative constituents, who supported cuts in foreign aid and the imposition of a global gag rule on family planning service providers, were unmoved.[10]

Although Secretary Albright advocated strongly for the proposed State Department reorganization and had pushed for payment of the U.S. government's past dues to the United Nations ever since she had served as U.S. ambassador to the UN, she also shared President Clinton's support for global family planning programs. Albright had often asserted that: "family planning is a vital international health issue. Women want to have choices, not only about what jobs we have, and how we live, but also about how we plan our families. These aspirations, by themselves, [should] be enough to warrant our support."[11]Albright tried to persuade Congress to separate the restrictions on foreign aid for family planning from the House and Senate bills that allowed for State Department reorganization and payment of UN dues before they came up for votes, but she failed in her efforts. In April 1998, U.S. Congress and the Senate passed reorganization and spending bills that included family planning funding restrictions. In consequence, President Clinton vowed to veto the bills when they were presented for his signature.

From April until October 1998 neither the Republicans who opposed foreign aid for family planning providers, nor the president, changed their positions. The stalemate between Congress, the Senate and the president remained in place even as Republican politicians waged an incendiary public campaign denouncing the president's position on global family planning aid. Representative Christopher Smith wrote in the *New York Times*:

> Without the Mexico City Policy [the U.S. population policy that restricted funds to global family planning services, in force 1984 to 1993], U.S. taxpayer dollars continue to enrich and empower foreign organizations that pressure developing countries to abandon their pro-life laws—the most egregious form of cultural imperialism. … Late last year Congress offered President Clinton a generous foreign aid package that included all his requests: $3.5 billion in credit for the International Monetary Fund, authorization of $926 million to the United Nations, a UN reform package and reorganization of the State Department. … President Clinton rejected everything. In the give and take of the legislative process, he was all take and no give. … If Clinton is truly concerned, he should listen to his foreign policy and economic advisers—and not his abortion advisers—in deciding what he perceives to be most important for the country.[12]

Senator Jesse Helms asserted that President Clinton's veto of the Senate bill that included restrictions of foreign aid to family planning agencies demonstrated "an astounding display of administration priorities. The White House chose to block this reform bill at the end of the first session of Congress after the House added a single provision protecting unborn babies from deliberate mass destruction."[13]

President Clinton claimed that he vetoed the bill "for several reasons, most importantly because the Congress has included in this legislation unacceptable restrictions on international family planning programs and threatened our leadership in the world community by tying our payment of dues to the United Nations and other international organizations to these unrelated family planning issues." He believed the restrictions would lead to "more unwanted pregnancies and more abortions, not fewer."[14]

In the midst of the controversy, the Women's Environment and Development Organization founded by Bella Abzug published a report titled "Mapping Progress: Assessing Implementation of the Beijing Platform," just prior to Abzug's death on March 31, 1998. The report included a section on the "International Family Planning Crisis" that focused on Washington politics and their pernicious effects on global women. The report asserted that:

> The Republican-controlled Congress, a body that was a strong supporter of voluntary population planning and health for nearly 30 years, has over the last two years reduced funds for international population

> planning programs. In 1996, Congress cut funds for population assistance by 35% and imposed complex spending restrictions, permitting release of funds in small monthly installments, which effectively reduced funding by 87%, from $583 million to just $72 million in that year. In 1997, Congress further cut funding and enacted unprecedented and cumbersome rules governing the release of funds. Most of these restrictions relate to trying to render ineligible for U.S. aid any overseas organization that may utilize non-U.S. government funds to provide abortions, including complications to post-abortion care.[15]

As the 105th congressional session ended in October 1998, the provisions for State Department reorganization were removed from the disputed House and Senate bills. State Department reorganization was attached to the Omnibus Consolidated and Emergency Supplemental Appropriations Act of 1999, which the president signed, and State Department reorganization, on the administration's terms, moved forward. On the same day, October 21, 1998, the president vetoed congressional bills that included provisions to pay the UN dues because those bills included further restrictions on foreign aid for family planning services.[16]

Leading the Office of International Women's Issues at the time, Senior Coordinator Theresa Loar made a strategic decision not to entangle the OIWI in this particular women's reproductive rights battle. She supported the administration's position on funding international family planning initiatives so that contraceptives and reproductive counseling would be available to women who could then make their own choices about whether to have children or how many children to have.[17] But she also determined that family planning and reproductive rights advocacy was not part of the OIWI's "mandate." Even though she was criticized by the political left and the right for this decision, she believed that:

> strategically it was the right thing to do; and I think we would not have made any of the progress on bringing people along on this agenda if we had included that as well. First of all, there was [already] a strong structure in our government, in many different places in our government, for dealing with that and for working on that issue. I was trying to look at the underdeveloped issues: violence against women; trafficking; women playing a role in moving towards democracy, and getting women to be part of that; and the women who really wanted U.S. partnership and wanted the U.S. to help them find their voice in their own country.[18]

The Clinton Administration and the Congressional Campaign to End Female Genital Mutilation

In 1996, the Office of International Women's Issues and the State Department became involved in a minor way in another controversial global issue that focused attention on women's bodies: the practice of female genital mutilation, or FGM. The government's response to this practice raised an issue where politics and culture again collided. Democratic congresswoman and liberal feminist Patricia Schroeder, a long-time advocate of federal government legislation to ban the practice of FGM in the United States, led an active public awareness campaign that finally won support from some of her congressional colleagues in the mid-1990s. By that time, global feminists and U.S. feminists had raised public awareness about widespread violence against women in general. U.S. feminists had also defined FGM as one particular expression of violence against women. Congresswoman Schroeder and her liberal feminist allies focused public attention on several immigrant women who had fled to the United States and sought asylum rather than submitting to FGM rituals practiced in their home countries. While these women faced long detentions by the Immigration and Naturalization Service (INS) and experienced many difficulties justifying their claims for asylum in immigration courts, congressional and feminist activists took up their cases as *causes célèbre*.[19]

The practice of FGM was not widely known or understood in the United States until feminist activists began shedding light on the practice and defined it as an abusive act that violated women's human rights during the UN Decade for Women from 1975 to 1985. Prior to the Decade for Women, United Nations agencies and Western governments considered FGM to be a "regional" issue, of concern only to countries where it was practiced in middle Africa, and in Yemen and Oman on the Arabian Peninsula.[20] Within those countries, FGM was practiced among certain ethnic groups and tribes whereby girls' genitalia were cut or removed to "prepare girls for womanhood." Among some ethnic groups the ritual cutting was performed on infants, but more commonly it was performed on girls between the ages of four and eight.[21] In the 1950s and 1960s UN agencies such as the World Health Organization and UNICEF refused to engage in any FGM eradication efforts because the issues at stake were deemed "cultural and social" rather than "medical."[22] However, African activists, many of them doctors and nurses, began to make counter-arguments that the practice of FGM posed serious health hazards to girls. Following the advice of these African women's health advocates, WHO and UNICEF changed their policies in the 1970s and 1980s. They began to call for the eradication of FGM.[23]

During these same decades of the 1970s and 1980s, Western European and U.S. feminists became aware of FGM practices. They condemned FGM as a violation of women's human rights; however, they often voiced their objections to FGM in culturally insensitive ways. They framed their FGM eradication campaigns as "rescue missions" intended to "save" African girls from "barbaric" practices. Therefore, African women often resented Western efforts to end FGM practices. In addition, African activists directed their own criticisms at Western women who underwent breast augmentations or otherwise "mutilated" their bodies to attain a culturally-determined beauty ideal.[24]

By the 1990s, however, a global feminist movement to eradicate FGM was underway. This global movement, led by African women, took into account the myriad social and cultural meanings of the practice, but it emphasized the immense and life-long physical and mental health issues that girls and women who had undergone FGM suffered and presented the campaign as a women's health crusade. Feminist members of the global eradication movement also asserted that the underlying aim of the practice of FGM was to exert patriarchal control over women's bodies. They challenged the practice as a means of challenging patriarchal power.[25]

In September 1996 U.S. Congress responded to the U.S.-based liberal feminist and global feminist FGM eradication campaigns. Congress passed federal legislation that defined female genital mutilation performed on girls under age 18 as a matter of custom or ritual to be a federal criminal offense under the provisions of the Illegal Immigration Reform and Immigrant Responsibility Act. The provisions banning FGM from being performed in United States' territory that went into effect in March 1997 also directed the Department of Health and Human Services to compile data on the physical and psychological health problems associated with FGM and to distribute information on those health issues to immigrant communities. The INS was also directed to provide information on the physical and mental health problems associated with FGM and to explain the criminal penalties for those who performed FGM on minors when it issued visas to immigrants. Finally, the federal law banning FGM in the United States also required U.S. directors of international financial institutions such as the World Bank and the International Monetary Fund to oppose any non-humanitarian loans to countries that had not taken measures to educate populations to end the practice of FGM within their borders.[26]

When Theresa Loar took up her new post as senior coordinator of OIWI in October 1996, Congress had just passed the federal law that criminalized FGM in the United States. Congressional sponsors of the law such as Patricia Schroeder and U.S. feminists felt triumphant. However, African women came to Loar to denounce the U.S. Congress's actions. Loar recalled the African women's angry reaction, "This [law] is not helpful to us, … our country's going to get less aid and fewer loans because this practice takes place in our country. Our government will be angry at us, and our people will suffer, and that's not helpful that you did that!" [27]

Loar decided to bring together the parties in conflict—U.S. activists who had lobbied for the legislation banning FGM and African women who felt betrayed by the U.S. government's actions—to talk out their differences and promote mutual understanding. Loar also invited Dr. Nahid Toubia, a Sudanese doctor whose credentials as a women's rights and women's health advocate were well established, to join the discussion held at the State Department. Toubia had advised the World Health Organization, other UN agencies and the Human Rights Watch Women's Rights Project on FGM eradication efforts. She had also held a faculty position at the Columbia University School of Public Health and had published essays examining the FGM issue from the African women's perspective.[28] Western and African women alike held Nahid Toubia in high regard.

This State Department meeting between the various feminist and activist parties yielded better results than the meeting Loar had arranged between human rights activists and the Department's South Asian bureau in the wake of the Taliban's assumption of power in Afghanistan, as recounted in chapter six. One of the African women told Loar, "I would never in a million years think I'd be sitting at the U.S. Department of State on a policy discussion of this [FGM], and I want to thank you, the U.S. government, for getting us space to talk about it." Consequently, Loar asserted that a greater degree of cooperation between the U.S. government and African women's organizations was achieved. She asserted that there was a "greater integration of awareness and education against FGM … in our health programs, through AID, and [in] our commitment to talk about it as a harmful health practice [as well as a human rights issue]."[29] The Clinton Administration established an interagency committee within the President's Interagency Council on Women to coordinate U.S. policy and law enforcement as it related to the 1996 federal law banning FGM. The interagency group included representatives from Health and Human Services, the Treasury Department, the INS, USAID and the Department of State.[30] Loar also consulted with African women and U.S. feminists regarding the ongoing discussions and work of the interagency group.[31]

The State Department and the OIWI did not take any further actions regarding the practice of FGM, although Madeleine Albright and Theresa Loar sometimes referenced FGM in their public addresses when they listed harmful practices that the Clinton Administration philosophically opposed in its support for women's empowerment and women's human rights.[32] Secretary Albright, in particular, referenced FGM with her often-repeated assertion: "Halting violence against women is a goal of American foreign policy around the world, where abuses range from domestic violence to dowry murders to mutilation and to forcing young girls into prostitution. Some say this is all cultural and there's nothing we can do about it. I say its criminal, and we each have a responsibility to stop it."[33]

Trafficking in Women: The Clinton Administration Recognizes the Problem

During the Clinton Administration's second term in office global gender policy makers focused on the problem of trafficking in women and that focus generated further heated cultural and political debates about women's bodies. The Office of International Women's Issues and the President's Interagency Council on Women both played leading roles in gathering research and formulating the administration's domestic legislative agenda and policy proposals. The OIWI and PICW also participated in the administration's collaborative work with allies at the United Nations to develop an international anti-trafficking protocol.[34] The Clinton Administration's support for anti-trafficking legislation and related executive branch actions from 1997 to 2000 raised fundamental questions and elicited some negative criticisms that administration officials may not have anticipated. However, these results were not so surprising given the volatile mix of feminist, non-feminist and anti-feminist policy makers and activists who were all concerned with the problem of trafficking in women at this time.

Representatives of feminist, non-feminist and anti-feminist constituencies disagreed on the causes, the nature and the scope of the problem of trafficking in women. In addition, they seriously disagreed about the laws and policies needed to remedy the problem. Nonetheless, Clinton Administration officials considered the outcomes of several years' study, negotiation, proposals for legislation and policy development: the Trafficking Victims Protection Act passed into law by Congress in October 2000 and the United Nations "Protocol to Prevent,

Suppress and Punish Trafficking in Persons, Especially Women and Children," signed by eighty-one nations in December 2000, to be significant legislative and moral triumphs for the administration and progressive steps forward that expanded protections for global women.[35]

Although the Clinton Administration did not begin to recognize the problem of trafficking in women and girls until after the 1995 UN-sponsored Fourth World Conference on Women held in Beijing, liberal feminists and human rights activists began their attacks on the global sex trafficking problem in the 1970s. At that time, a global sex industry that included both "forced" and "voluntary" prostitution was expanding.[36] One reason for the expansion of the global sex industry in the 1970s was related to the concurrent expansion of U.S. military bases in Southeast Asia and the Pacific that were a consequence of the ongoing war in Vietnam and other regional Cold War conflicts.[37] According to some statistics linking the growing U.S. military presence to increasing prostitution in the region that a feminist journal reported in 1994, "It is estimated that by the mid-80s the sex industries around bases in the Philippines generated more than $500 million. At the end of the war in Vietnam, Saigon had 500,000 prostituted women—this is equal to the population of Saigon before the war."[38]

The expanding global sex industry was also linked to economic development initiatives originating in Western industrialized nations that encouraged unindustrialized nations of the global South to develop their natural resources and native products for global consumption. Tourism was one such industry that brought Northern "First World" dollars to Southern "Third World" nations. "Sex" was "part and parcel of the tourist attraction." The global traffic in women and girls for sex purposes followed the money as women and girls from Third World nations were sold to buyers in First World nations. In the 1990s sex trafficking also became more prevalent in Europe as Soviet and Eastern European socialist governments dissolved. As discussed in chapter three, regional civil wars, global capitalist structural adjustment policies and political transitions at the end of the Cold War caused widespread social disruptions throughout the former Warsaw Pact nations. Many women in these formerly socialist states lost waged jobs as their social, political and cultural status also declined. In consequence, some women turned to prostitution to earn their livings or they were duped or coerced into the sex industry and were trafficked into Western European countries.[39]

Feminist activists who attended the UN-sponsored preparatory meetings for the 1995 Fourth World Conference on Women raised alarms regarding the rising numbers of women and girls involved in global sex trafficking operations.[40] Feminists claimed that sex trafficking violated women's human dignity and human rights and that "Trafficking is one of the most dire problems facing women today and it must be addressed and stopped."[41] To be sure, human trafficking operations also ensnared men and boys as well as women and girls, and trafficked human beings were not always trafficked for sexual purposes,[42] but the majority of feminist activists who engaged with governments and policy makers in the run-up to the 1995 Beijing conference focused on sex trafficking of women and girls and they framed the sex trafficking problem as a violation of women's human rights. This human rights framework initially focused attention on the detrimental physical and destructive psychosocial consequences of sex trafficking for women, and not necessarily on the social, economic and political causes that might have embroiled women in trafficking schemes in the first place. At the time, some activists expressed an alternate viewpoint that defined prostitution as a "profession" and called for the need to respect "the human rights of 'sex workers'." However, this was a minority view among those who engaged in policy advocacy with governments at the Beijing Fourth World Conference on Women and afterward.[43]

By the mid-1990s sex trafficking in women was included on the global feminist agenda as part of a broad discussion of women's human rights.[44] This was the way that First Lady Hillary Clinton referred to sex trafficking in her famous plenary address to the assembled government delegates at the Beijing conference. As Clinton listed numerous women's human rights violations she noted that women and girls were "sold into the slavery of prostitution" and that governments had to take action to address this abuse.[45]

In the years following the Beijing conference Hillary Clinton heard from global activists who described the insidious ways that sex trafficking affected women and girls in their home countries. For example, in November 1996 Hillary Clinton accompanied the president on state visits to Thailand, the Philippines and Australia. In Thailand, she visited a USAID-funded project run by an American Baptist missionary, Lauren Bethel, who was working with young girls and women who had been entrapped by prostitution, many also infected by HIV/AIDS viruses. The young girls' stories of their attempts to reclaim their lives moved Clinton.[46]

Clinton also met with Thai activist Dr. Saisuree Chutikul at Payup University in Chiang Mai. For years, Dr. Chutikul had advocated for aid to women and girls who had been victims of sexual exploitation and forced labor from high-level positions that she held within her own government and as Thailand's representative to several United Nations commissions.[47] Within her own country Saisuree Chutikul had led a crusade to enact and enforce stricter criminal laws and penalties for traffickers, who captured impoverished young girls from Thailand and neighboring Burma and then drugged and enslaved their victims in brothels. Dr. Chutikul recounted her experiences to the first lady and these stories also fueled Hillary Clinton's growing concern about the problem of sex trafficking.[48]

In the following year, at the Vital Voices: Women in Democracy conference held in Vienna in July 1997, Hillary Clinton also met with activists who worked with trafficked Russian and Ukrainian women and girls. Although the conference discussions had focused on promoting women's political and civil leadership roles, and on women's full participation in their economies in the post-socialist states of Eastern Europe and the former Soviet Union as chapter six explains, these activists pushed forward another agenda. Oksana Horbunova from the Ukraine, Marina Pisklakova from Russia and Martina Vandenberg, an American who had been living in Moscow, all worked with women who had been trafficked and otherwise sexually abused. They shared vivid stories about the "horror of women and children being sold into modern-day slavery" with Hillary Clinton.[49] Theresa Loar recalled the deep impression that the women's accounts made on Clinton at the Vital Voices meetings: "So when this issue of trafficking came up, and we saw Ukrainian women talking about this in this conference in Vienna and Russian government officials putting their hands up to say, 'It's overwhelming; we can't even address it,' it was clear that we needed to develop a [U.S.] government response to this."[50]

Hillary Clinton's chief of staff, Melanne Verveer, who accompanied Clinton to Vienna, also influenced Clinton's sense of urgency regarding the problem of sex trafficking as it affected Russian and Ukrainian women. A Ukrainian-American whose grandparents immigrated to the United States in the early twentieth century, Verveer was raised in an ethnic community in Pennsylvania where her family kept many of the Ukrainian cultural traditions alive. She empathized with the stories that anti-trafficking activists recounted in Vienna. Verveer also had a life-long interest in politics and international affairs and a background as a congressional legislative aide. She brought her political expertise and energy to the Clinton Administration's anti-trafficking initiatives that got underway in the fall of 1997.[51]

All these personal stories led to further investigations into the problem of sex trafficking by the Office of International Women's Issues at the State Department and the First Lady's Office at the White House. Clinton, Verveer and Loar, along with the men and women working in government offices and the NGO activists that they brought together through meetings with the President's Interagency Council on Women to address the global problem of trafficking in women and girls over the next several years, were pragmatists who looked for concrete solutions. Hillary Clinton expressed the administration's action-oriented approach to combatting the sex trafficking problem in an address at a meeting of the Organization for Security and Cooperation in Europe in Istanbul, Turkey in 1999:

> There were many Baltic and Nordic and Russian women leaders present [at the 1999 Vital Voices conference held in Reykjavik, Iceland]. And again the issue of trafficking was raised. ... But it wasn't just to wring our hands and trade the terrible stories we knew, but instead to develop and commit ourselves to [anti-trafficking] strategies. Because in the last several years, the trafficking of girls and women had finally come out of the shadows and moved into the spotlight and the glare of attention that we hope will lead to the strategies you've heard discussed actually being implemented.[52]

The Clinton Administration Develops Anti-Trafficking Strategy: "Prevention, Protection, Prosecution"

As director of the President's Interagency Council on Women, Theresa Loar assembled a team drawn from the various cabinet agencies whose wide-ranging areas of expertise were brought to bear on the human trafficking problem.[53] Anita Botti, a demographer who worked in the State Department Population, Refugees and Migration (PRM) bureau, led the interagency team that researched trafficking issues, consulted with NGO activists and met with the Organization for Security and Cooperation in Europe (OSCE) in order to study the European community's approach to ending human trafficking. Botti's investigations broadened the administration's concerns about sex trafficking of women and girls to encompass legislation, policies and government programs that addressed human trafficking for a range of purposes. Ultimately, Botti's research and consultations resulted in a variety of U.S. government-led anti-trafficking measures designed to address the "three P's": prevention, protection and prosecution. "Prevention" measures addressed systemic problems that created social and economic conditions that led to human trafficking. "Protection" measures aided victims of sexual abuse and other forms of exploitation and protected them from incarceration or deportation as illegal immigrants. "Prosecution" measures went after human traffickers, subjecting them to harsher criminal laws and more punitive penalties in order to deter them from breaking the law.[54]

While she worked at the PRM Botti had gained experience working with various migration issues. Botti knew that human traffickers often used the same routes as other border crossers. She knew that those who were trafficked for their labor as well as those who were trafficked for sexual purposes were often prosecuted under the same migration laws. She had contacts with activists and NGOs that had worked directly with illegal immigrants, such as faith-based organizations including Catholic Charities and the Lutheran's International Rescue Committee. She also had contacts among human rights organizations such as the International Human Rights Law Group, Human Rights Watch Women's Rights Division and Equality Now that were concerned with protecting immigrants' human rights.[55] Botti contacted all these nongovernmental groups to draw on their collective expertise and to elicit their advice on the range of human trafficking concerns.

In addition to these external sources of information Anita Botti also relied on internal government contacts and her insider's knowledge of the way that the federal government worked to design and implement effective anti-trafficking measures. Botti identified the various ways that the Departments of Justice, Commerce, State, the INS and the White House could all be effective in reducing human trafficking and addressing its social, political and economic consequences. Working through the President's Interagency Council on Women and its collaborative group meeting structure, Botti was able to explain the scope and urgency of the human trafficking problem to cabinet agency representatives and to explain in specific terms each agency's role in prevention, protection or prosecution efforts.[56]

In its efforts to investigate causes and propose solutions to the problem of human trafficking between 1997 and 2000, the Clinton Administration also formed alliances with European Union agencies such as the OSCE to investigate how European migration officials were dealing with trafficked victims as they crossed European borders. Administration representatives studied European efforts to educate potential trafficked victims to the dangers they faced, as well as measures that the EU took to educate border police and government officials regarding other deterrence measures.[57]

As the U.S. government's interagency "three P's" approach took shape in the winter of 1997 and spring of 1998, in March 1998 President Clinton publicly announced the administration's new anti-trafficking initiatives.[58] Among those initiatives, USAID allocated $10 million to fund NGOs abroad that specifically worked with trafficked populations or on other trafficking problems. In anticipation of broader international agreements, the U.S. government signed a bi-lateral agreement with the

Ukraine to jointly address human trafficking between the two nations. Theresa Loar and the PICW were formally charged to establish an interagency task force and to work with NGOs from "source, transit and destination countries" to develop "strategies for combating this fundamental human rights violation." In fact, these efforts led by Anita Botti were already underway. Attorney General Janet Reno was directed to focus on anti-trafficking prevention and prosecution measures within the United States' borders that included public education campaigns and law enforcement training.[59] Soon after President Clinton announced the administration's anti-trafficking initiatives in the United States, in April 1998 the U.S. government proposed the "Protocol to Prevent, Suppress, and Punish Trafficking in Persons, Especially Women and Children" as an addendum to the UN Convention Against Transnational Organized Crime. The United Nations Millennium General Assembly eventually adopted this Protocol in November 2000 and the United States and eighty other UN members signed on to the Protocol in December 2000.[60]

Although Anita Botti clearly understood the problem of human trafficking went far beyond sex trafficking, and Theresa Loar had been educated regarding the scope of the problem, some NGO activists and some congressional allies became engaged in anti-trafficking efforts because they understood a "simplified version" of the human trafficking problem as a problem of "sexual slavery."[61] Human rights activists were somewhat responsible for this over-simplification because the rhetoric used to describe trafficked "women in peril" effectively raised alarms among some NGOs on the Religious Right and among their conservative political allies in Congress. The rhetoric focused the conservatives' attention on a women's human rights issue, which seemed like a progressive development. However, women's human rights activists also recognized the dangers in using the "women in peril" rhetoric. Rights activists knew that all the attention paid to "trafficking primarily as a crime of male desire and forced sex" in fact essentialized women as sexual beings, rendered other forms of human trafficking less visible and deflected any critical examinations of global economic realities that fueled human trafficking.[62] Human rights activist Alice Miller called attention to this dilemma. She asked a key question that confounded feminist activists who worked with the Clinton Administration and with U.S. Congress on the global problem of trafficking in women and girls: "How do we ensure that our interventions focused on stopping harm against women do not unknowingly reinscribe and reinforce the idea that the most important thing about a woman is her sexual integrity?"[63]

Indeed, in the period between 1998 and 2000, congressional Republicans and Religious Right activists generally adopted an anti-trafficking stance that focused exclusively on protecting women's bodies. In addition, some organizations on the Religious Right and some organizations on the feminist far left made an unlikely political alliance. These allies on the conservative right-wing and on the radical left-wing both approached the problem of eradicating sex trafficking as part of a "moral crusade" to attack prostitution on a global scale. Zealous anti-prostitution "crusaders," whether right-wing or left-wing politically, tended to "rely on horror stories and 'atrocity tales' about victims in which the most shocking exemplars of victimization are described and typified." They tended to exaggerate the scale of the problem beyond what the empirical evidence would support, and they "consider[ed] the problem unambiguous: they are not inclined to acknowledge gray areas and are adamant that a particular evil exists precisely as they depict it."[64] The crusaders interjected their point of view into political debates with the assistance of human rights lawyer Sharon Payt, who worked for Republican Senator Sam Brownback. Payt mobilized a coalition of faith-based, human rights and feminist organizations to promote the moral crusade against prostitution. She displayed a "talent for bringing together groups from across the political spectrum [that] allowed her to use the U.S. Senate as a platform to respond to those heartbreaking stories … of women and girls disappearing in the former Soviet Union" in order to enlist congressional interest in anti-trafficking legislation.[65]

Hillary Clinton and Theresa Loar had initially become engaged with the problem of sex trafficking as it affected women and girls between 1994 and 1997. As Anita Botti conducted her investigations into the global trafficking problem, the Clinton Administration shifted focus to broader problems of human trafficking and developed an interagency approach to combat human trafficking combining elements of prevention, protection, and prosecution in policy and programs developed during 1998 and 1999. During these years the administration also accepted the European Union's perspectives that global organized crime networks engaged in human trafficking and that governments should focus their interventions on the traffickers as international criminals, which tended to emphasize prosecution efforts over prevention and protection measures. The European's perspectives were incorporated into the 2000 UN Protocol to Prevent, Suppress, and Punish Trafficking in Persons, Especially Women and Children.

As the definition of the problem of trafficking shifted, and the proposed legal and policy remedies were redefined, some of the Clinton Administration's critics coming from the political right and from the political left believed that the crucial focus on protecting women was neglected. These critics began to accuse the administration of supporting prostitution, as anti-trafficking measures diffused government attention from ending sex-trafficking for purposes of prostitution to other problems and crimes associated with human trafficking. In spite of the specific reference to "Prevent, Suppress and Punish Trafficking in Persons, *Especially Women and Children,*" in the title of the UN Protocol that the Clinton Administration proposed and supported, the administration felt compelled by its critics to release a statement:

> MYTH: The Protocol will legalize prostitution.
>
> FACT: The administration opposes prostitution in all its forms. The United States has perhaps the most far-reaching prostitution laws in the world. There are international human rights and humanitarian laws that fight exploitation and prostitution. We will not agree to a treaty that weakens existing prostitution laws here or around the world. In fact, the draft treaty clearly states that these international treaties--and the obligations they impose on participating countries--must remain unchanged. Despite what some have claimed, this treaty will not, in any way, undermine the 1949 UN Convention for the Suppression of the Traffic in Persons and of the Exploitation of the Prostitution of Others.[66]

Critics pointed out other failings of the Clinton Administration's anti-trafficking efforts, as well. Human Rights Watch praised the U.S. government for its support for a "markedly improved international protocol on trafficking of persons," but also asserted that the U.S. failed "to provide sufficient support for protocol provisions that would offer greater protections to victims of trafficking, such as psychological, medical, legal and financial assistance."[67]

Anita Botti also critiqued the Clinton Administration's policy measures that were intended to support U.S. domestic legislation in the Trafficking Victims Protection Act and to support of the United Nations Protocol. Botti asserted that:

> We worked very well on "protection" and on "prosecution," but the one area that continues to this day to be the one that eluded us has been "prevention," because it really does get into the component of globally trying to address the root causes, which takes into consideration, you know, how do you raise the status of women? How do you empower them? How do you give them alternatives so that they don't have the *need* to be looking to other countries for employment, or seeking somehow … to be without any resources, which is how these women were trafficked?[68]

Alice Miller, then associated with the International Human Rights Law group, agreed that the U.S. government did not address prevention issues very well. Moreover, she noted that, in practice, "only the most innocent of the innocent" women victims of sex trafficking were usually deemed worthy of protection by government agencies. Consequently, most U.S. government and international interventions and resources were directed at the less-controversial action, that is, prosecution of traffickers.[69]

Nonetheless, when U.S. Congress held hearings to investigate the problem of human trafficking in anticipation of voting on new legislation, Theresa Loar represented the Clinton Administration and testified before the House Subcommittee on International Operations and Human Rights and before the House Committee on International Relations. Loar presented the administration's findings and explained the rationale behind the "three P's" approach that the administration proposed to address prevention, protection of victims and prosecution of human traffickers.[70] She explained the global scope of the problem, that between one and two million women and girls were victims of human trafficking annually, and that 50,000 people were trafficked into the United States each year.[71] She defined the nature of human trafficking: "At its core, the international trade in persons is about coercion, deception, violence, and exploitation." She explained that sex trafficking was one form of human trafficking that was "first and foremost a human rights issue. But it is also a socioeconomic issue, a public health issue and a transnational crime issue." She asserted that "the trafficking industry is driven by poverty and economic desperation, most particularly among women and girls who have little or no access to economic opportunities, support services, or resources, including credit, land ownership and inheritance." Finally, she explained the administration's response to the problem: "a comprehensive and integrated policy framework that guides the development of our policies both domestically and internationally."[72]

In the end, congressional allies that included Republican Party Senator Sam Brownback and Representative Christopher Smith, and Democratic Party Senator Paul Wellstone and Representative Sam Gejdenson, all agreed with the administration's proposals and Congress and Senate moved forward and passed the Trafficking Victims Protection Act (TVPA) with near-unanimous bipartisan support in October 2000.[73] As Theresa Loar explained, all government and nongovernment actors agreed that human trafficking "is an inherent evil":

> Trafficking people into slavery denies them of their basic human rights, and we, as a country, have to stand up against it and treat people who

> were trafficked in the United States as victims and provide them with refugee services and help them. We have to aid in the prosecution of their traffickers. The United States has a responsibility to help countries around the world address this issue, to help them with prevention, protection, and prosecution. That's what the law [the TVPA] says."[74]

Some congressional supporters, however, sought to impose harsh economic sanctions on "sending" countries that did not combat trafficking within their own borders. Although the Clinton Administration opposed those sanctions because they might worsen economic conditions in developing nations and thus increase the numbers of people living in poverty who were vulnerable to trafficking,[75] the administration was forced to compromise its position to secure passage of the TVPA. Consequently, the State Department's annual Human Rights Country Reports were required to record the specific measures each government that received U.S. aid were taking to end human trafficking activity.[76] Even though U.S. legislation defined trafficking as "all acts involved in the transport, harboring, or sale of persons within national or across international borders through coercion, force, kidnapping, deception or fraud, for purposes of placing persons in situations of forced labor or services, such as forced prostitution, domestic servitude, debt bondage or other slavery-like practices,"[77] anti-prostitution activists from the right and left continued to insist that the anti-trafficking legislation passed by Congress in October 2000, and the UN Protocol adopted in December, minimized the problem of prostitution, as well as the problem of sex trafficking. These advocates argued that "Trafficking and sexual exploitation are intrinsically connected and should not be separated merely because there are other forms of trafficking; or because some countries have legalized [or] regulated prostitution and thereby want to censor any discussion of prostitution from regional and international policy agendas."[78] Political and ideological differences forced compromises among all the interested parties, but in the end the Clinton Administration believed the anti-trafficking legislation that Congress approved supported global women's interests.

The Kosovo War and the Clinton Administration's Response

Bloody ethnic warfare broke out in Kosovo in 1998 as Kosovar Albanians tried to secede from the Federal Republic of Yugoslavia. Like wars everywhere, this war had a specific and gendered impact on women.[79] Wartime rapes in Kosovo were commonplace, although some disputed whether those rapes were committed as part of a Serbian "ethnic cleansing" program intended to eradicate the Kosovo Albanian majority population.[80] The Clinton Administration's response to the Kosovo War in 1998 and 1999, as the leader of multilateral diplomatic efforts and ultimately of a NATO military response, paid special attention to women's needs and therefore earned some qualified praise from feminist NGOs.

In some respects, the administration's response to the outbreak of violence, in which Slobodan Milosevic's Serbian forces committed "horrendous human rights violations, violations of humanitarian law, and acts of punitive destruction on a massive scale,"[81] was determined by the decade-long history of warfare in the former Yugoslavia. The Clinton Administration had reluctantly and eventually led NATO forces in a humanitarian-inspired military mission to suppress the Bosnian Serb majority's genocidal policy of ethnic cleansing against Muslims in Bosnia and Herzegovina in 1995, as chapter four explains. Between 1993 and 1995 Madeleine Albright, then U.S. ambassador to the UN, had been among the administration's strongest advocates for armed intervention to stop the Serbian attacks on Muslim civilian populations. As chapter six explains, Albright also pushed for the prosecution of Serbian soldiers who raped Bosnian Muslim women and Serbian leaders who ordered the rapes in the International War Crimes Tribunal for the Former Yugoslavia. When the Kosovo Albanians led by the Kosovo Liberation Army (KLA), rose up against Serbian security forces in late 1997 and early 1998 in a bid to gain provincial independence from Serbian rule, Milosevic's Serbian Army cracked down with lethal force, "with entire families slain and whole villages destroyed in reprisal." Many of the victims were women and children.[82]

The out-sized Serbian response to the KLA rebel provocations caused Secretary of State Albright to announce in March 1998 that "we are not going to stand by and watch the Serbian authorities do in Kosovo what they can no longer get away with doing in Bosnia. …The time to stop the killing is now, before it spreads."[83] Nonetheless, it took Secretary Albright a year to mobilize an effective international military response to stop Milosevic's forces. In that year, hundreds of thousands of Kosovo Albanians were displaced from their homes—nearly 80 percent of the displaced were women and children[84]—and Serbian massacres of civilian populations routinely followed KLA attacks on Serbian police. Human Rights Watch reported on the gruesome war:

> In Serbia's attack on Kosovo, paramilitaries entered the homes of ethnic Albanians and raped women and girls in front of their families or outside in their gardens. Some paramilitaries told women they were expected to

> commit rapes as part of the campaign of ethnic cleansing. An unknown number of women and girls died after these attacks. In other instances, Serbian paramilitaries… demanded money from fleeing Kosovar Albanians, threatening to rape, kill, or torture those who would not comply…. While it appears that paramilitaries committed most of the rapes, Human Rights Watch also documented at least two cases in which regular Serb soldiers committed rape.[85]

Throughout the war, the United States sent humanitarian aid to Kosovar Albanians through State Department and United Nations agency channels. The U.S. funded refugee camps and supplied food and medical services with $150 million in aid money between January 1998 and March 1999.[86] In January 1999 Secretary Albright organized emergency peace talks that were held in Rambouillet, France, near Paris. The peace talks took place in February and March. In Rambouillet, Albright pushed for a ceasefire that would lead to further peace negotiations and a more permanent settlement of Kosovar Albanian's grievances. Both sides resisted Albright's and NATO's demands for a ceasefire, but in the end the KLA agreed to NATO's terms. Milosevic rejected those terms and war broke out again.[87] To bring Milosevic to heel, NATO forces began bombing Serbian targets on March 24. The bombing continued for seventy-eight days. In that time an estimated 1.5 million Kosovars fled from their homes. Kosovar rebels were publicly executed and their villages burnt to the ground; women were raped, men were tortured and imprisoned and children witnessed it all.[88] Following Russian diplomatic intervention with Serbia, Slobodan Milosevic finally agreed to a ceasefire in June 1999. According to the terms of the agreement, NATO ground forces moved into Kosovo to monitor the ceasefire and the KLA agreed to disarm in July 1999.[89]

As the ceasefire agreement went into effect the Clinton Administration quickly pledged aid to repatriate and resettle Kosovo refugees, with special funds dedicated to meet the needs of Kosovo refugee women. Human Rights Watch reported that in July 1999 the Clinton Administration pledged $10 million to the UN Kosovo Women's Initiative (KWI), a program of reconstruction and reconciliation similar to the UN programs established for women in postwar Bosnia and Rwanda. KWI programs were established in "record time"; they provided psychosocial counseling for Kosovo rape victims and funds that met other immediate needs of the women refugees and they provided microenterprise funds to help women rebuild their communities in the longer term. As Human Rights Watch reported, "While the KWI was criticized for being designed without sufficient NGO input, it was in fact a swift response to a dire situation."[90] As in other postwar situations when Western agencies and governments delivered foreign aid throughout the 1990s, local women and communities should have been making program decisions and leading the reconstruction process. However, Westerners were slow to turn over control even as aid givers sought to empower local populations.[91]

The Clinton Administration moved into its final year in office in 2000 with a significant record of responding to the needs of global women in ways that incorporated liberal feminist goals to establish respect for women's rights and to empower women and girls within their own communities. While the administration's record fell short of fulfilling all the liberal feminists' goals, progress was made on many policy fronts. The final chapter of this history of the Clinton Administration's global gender policy making sums up the administration's efforts and identifies some lessons for feminist activists and for future feminists in government service.

---

[1]"Feminist Issues: Women's Right to Bodily Integrity and Autonomy." See definition: "Bodily integrity is the inviolability of the physical body and emphasizes the importance of personal autonomy and the self-determination of human beings over their own bodies. It considers the violation of bodily integrity as an unethical infringement, intrusive and possibly criminal."

[2]Martin, "The Christian Right and American Foreign Policy," p. 74.

[3]See one articulation of these administration global gender policy themes: Oakley, "Women's Role in the New Age of Globalization."

[4]Martin, "The Christian Right and American Foreign Policy," pp. 68-70.

[5]Freeman, "Feminism vs. Family Values"; Warren M. Hern, "The Role of Abortion in Women's Health and Population Growth," NGO Forum 94, [International Conference on Population and Development], September 5-13, 1994, RCD, box 2.

[6]Wirth, "U.S. Statement on Population and Development"; Gore, "The Cairo Conference: Defining an Agenda of Hope, Opportunity, and Progress."

[7]Martin, "The Christian Right and American Foreign Policy," p. 74.

[8]Epstein, Nowels and Hildreth, "Foreign Policy Agency Reorganization in the 105th Congress."

[9]Martin, "The Christian Right and American Foreign Policy," pp. 74-75. In addition, "In 1998, social conservatives in the House of Representatives nearly blocked $18 billion in funding for the IMF, in part because the fund channels money to countries and organizations that regard abortion as an acceptable part of family planning or population control. ... In large measure because of opposition from the Religious Right, the United States did not contribute to the UN Population Fund in 1998, jeopardizing a program that provides contraceptives to nearly 1.4 million women in 150 countries."

[10]National Organization for Women, "105th Congress Voting Record Analysis." "A Rockefeller Foundation report, released prior to the vote, found that the $190 million cut in family planning assistance was estimated to result in

four million additional unplanned pregnancies, two million unplanned births, 134, 000 infant deaths, 8,000 deaths among women in pregnancy and childbirth, and 1.6 million abortions." See also: "A Key Vote on Family Planning." Quoting former Republican Senator Mark Hatfield to Representative Christopher Smith: "you are contributing to an increase of abortions worldwide because of the funding restrictions on which you insisted in last year's funding bill. It is a proven fact that when contraceptive services are not available to women throughout the world, abortion rates increase. … This is unacceptable to me as someone who is strongly opposed to abortion."

[11] Madeleine Albright quoted by Theresa Loar, "Statement before the House Committee on International Relations."

[12]Smith, "Foreign Aid and Abortion Overseas."

[13]Lippman, *Madeleine Albright and the New American Diplomacy*, p. 45.

[14]Ibid. p. 81.

[15]Women's Environment and Development Organization, "Mapping Progress: Assessing Implementation of the Beijing Platform," March 1998. See also: Women's Environment and Development Organization, "Women's Equality: An Unfinished Agenda. Women's Organizations Assess U.S. Government Actions on Implementing the Beijing Platform, 1995 – 2000," CWGL Beijing +5, box 7.

[16]Epstein, Nowels, and Hildreth, "Foreign Policy Agency Reorganization in the 105th Congress."

[17]Loar, "Statement before the House Committee on International Relations."

[18]Loar, The Association for Diplomatic Studies and Training Foreign Affairs Oral History Project.

[19]See for example: The 1994 case of Fauziya Kassindja, who fled to the US from Togo, "The Abolition of Female Genital Mutilation."; "The Campaign for Adelaide Abankwah: Gender-Based Political Asylum," Equality Now *Annual Report* 1998-1999.

[20]Berkovitch and Bradley, "The Globalization of Women's Status," p. 488.

[21]Nahid Toubia, "Female Genital Mutilation," in Peters and Wolper, eds. *Women's Rights, Human Rights*, pp. 225-6.

[22]Berkovitch and Bradley, "The Globalization of Women's Status," p. 489.

[23]Ibid. p. 490.

[24]Nahid Toubia, "Female Genital Mutilation," pp. 225, 232.

[25]Ibid. p. 232-5.

[26]Center for Reproductive Rights, "Legislation on Female Genital Mutilation in the United States."

[27]Loar, The Association for Diplomatic Studies and Training Foreign Affairs Oral History Project.

[28]"Contributors; Nahid Toubia" in Peters and Wolper, eds. *Women's Rights, Human Rights,* p. 366.

[29]Loar, The Association for Diplomatic Studies and Training Foreign Affairs Oral History Project.

[30]"The President's Interagency Council on Women: Follow-up on U.S. Commitments Made at the UN Fourth World Conference on Women, Update on Key Initiatives," March 1997, CWGL Beijing +5, box 1.

[31]Loar, The Association for Diplomatic Studies and Training Foreign Affairs Oral History Project.

[32]Loar, "Statement before the House Committee on International Relations."

[33]Albright, "Remarks before the Women's Legal Defense Fund Award Luncheon."

[34]Loar, "Statement before the House Committee on International Relations."

[35]"History of the State Department During the Clinton Administration," VII Global Affairs I.

[36]"Voluntary" prostitution is a highly contested concept.

[37]Kirk, Cornwell, and Okazawa-Rey, "Women and the U.S. Military in East Asia": "Sexual violence, sexual exploitation, thousands of fatherless Amerasian children, and health problems linked to environmental contamination are some of the damaging effects of the U.S. military presence in East Asia. Research conducted by a group called Okinawa Women Act Against Military Violence shows that U.S. troops in Okinawa have committed more than 4,700 reported crimes since 1972, when Okinawa reverted to Japanese administration. Many of these were crimes of violence against women. ... Sexism and militarism have commonly excluded feminine attributes and the perspectives and concerns of women. Sexism is central to a militarized masculinity, which involves physical strength, emotional detachment, the capacity for violence and killing, and an appearance of invulnerability. Male sexuality is assumed to be uncontrollable and in need of regular release, so prostitution is built into military operations, directly or indirectly, with the agreement of host governments."

[38]Mirkinson, "Red Light, Green Light: The Global Trafficking of Women."

[39]Ibid. See also: Emek M. Uçarer, "Trafficking in Women: Alternate Migration or Modern Slave Trade?" in Meyer and Prügl, eds. *Gender Politics in Global Governance*, pp. 233-4.

[40]"High Level Regional Preparatory Meeting for the Fourth World Conference on Women, Economic Commission for Europe, Vienna, "Vienna NGO Forum 94 Call to Action," UN Document: E/ECE/RW/HLM/L.4/Add.4, October 18, 1994, SIGI, box CONF 11; "A Modern Form of Slavery: Positive Moves Towards the Ending of the Trafficking of Burmese women and girls into Thai Brothels," *International Women's Development Agency: Report to Associates and Friends,* No. 29 (November 1994), IWTC, Acc # 01S-03, box 1.

[41]Mirkinson, "Red Light, Green Light: The Global Trafficking of Women," quoting Filipina activists at the March 1994 UN FWCW Preparatory Meeting held in New York City.

[42]Uçarer, "Trafficking in Women," p. 232: "According to the definition recently formulated by the International Organization for Migration (IOM), trafficking occurs when an international border crossing involves a facilitator who may provide information, fraudulent or stolen travel and identity documents, legal and illegal transportation, lodging and transit points, guided crossing of borders, and reception and employment in the country of destination. In addition, money or some other form of payment changes hands. Finally, entry and/or prolonged stay in the country of destination is often—but not always—illegal (International Organization for Migration 1996c, 2). Defining trafficking along these lines squarely frames it as a migration issue, implying that the trafficked individual is neither necessarily exploited in the country of destination nor trafficked and kept against her will."

[43]Ibid. p. 236. See also: Sayce, "Violence, abuse and women's citizenship,": "This international conference on Violence, Abuse and Women's Citizenship was held in Brighton, the United Kingdom, November 10-15 [1996]. ... Speaker after speaker denounced the Beijing conference declaration for omitting prostitution

per se from its consideration of violence against women. … The redefinition of prostitution as sex work, and pimps as business managers, is supposed to dignify the women. It merely dignifies the industry. The conference organizing committee made no apology for the position taken throughout on prostitution: to be unreservedly opposed to it."

[44]Uçarer, "Trafficking in Women," p. 240.

[45]Hillary Rodham Clinton, "Remarks to the United Nations Fourth World Conference in Women Plenary Session."

[46]Loar, The Association for Diplomatic Studies and Training Foreign Affairs Oral History Project.

[47]Clinton, "The U.S. and Thailand: Making a Partnership Work for the Asia-Pacific." In his address to the Thai government leaders, President Clinton included a description of his wife's activities during the state visit: "The United States Agency for International Development helped launch the Thai Women of Tomorrow Project to assist young women in finding better prospects than the prostitution that puts their lives at risk. The First Lady visited that project the day before yesterday when she traveled to Chiang Mai to see the project started by faculty members at Chiang Mai University. Of course, this is important to try to turn these young women and their families away from destructive life habits. But as the First Lady has said all over the world, it is not enough to protect women and girls from those who would exploit them; we must all work together to open wide the positive doors of opportunity so that every person in every free society can contribute and share in its progress."

[48]Theresa Loar and Laura Ardito, "Women's Leadership in the Fight Against Trafficking," in O'Connor, ed. *Gender and Women's Leadership* Vol. I, p. 266.

[49]Loar and Ardito, "Women's Leadership in the Fight Against Trafficking," pp. 264-5.

[50]Loar, The Association for Diplomatic Studies and Training Foreign Affairs Oral History Project.

[51]Stephanie Foster, "Spotlight: Melanne Verveer," in O'Connor, ed. *Gender and Women's Leadership* Vol. I, pp. 318-20. Hillary Clinton is quoted in this biographical essay describing Melanne Verveer: "She helped to launch the Vital Voices Democracy Initiative … she nurtured it and helped it to grow into what it is today. … And she particularly helped to lead our commitment to end the intolerable scourge, the global crime of human trafficking."

[52]Hillary Rodham Clinton, "Combatting Human Trafficking."

[53]Loar, "Trafficking in Women: The Need for International Cooperation and a Multidisciplinary Response."

[54]Anita Botti, Phone Interview with Author, June 23, 2009.

[55]Ibid.; Alice Miller, Phone Interview with Author, May 26, 2010; Loar, The Association for Diplomatic Studies and Training Foreign Affairs Oral History Project.

[56]Anita Botti, Phone Interview with Author, June 23, 2009. See also: Loar, The Association for Diplomatic Studies and Training Foreign Affairs Oral History Project.

[57]Bureau for Population, Refugees and Migration, "Fact Sheet: US-European Joint Information Campaign to Prevent Trafficking in Women." See also: Aleinikoff, "Trafficking in Women: International Cooperation."

[58]Clinton, "Memorandum to the Secretary of State, Attorney General, Administrator of the Agency for International Development, Director of the United States Information Agency."

[59]Clinton, "Remarks by the President and First Lady on International Women's Day."

[60]"History of the State Department During the Clinton Administration," VII Global Affairs I.

[61]Miller, "Sexuality, Violence Against Women, and Human Rights," p. 30.

[62]Ibid. pp. 34, 36.

[63]Ibid. p. 39.

[64]Weitzer, "The social construction of sex trafficking," p. 448. During these years when the Clinton Administration developed anti-trafficking legislation and policy, and continuing on under the George W. Bush Administration that enforced the U.S. anti-trafficking law passed in 2000 after taking office in 2001, the moral crusaders who were most involved with the problem of sex trafficking and who pursued resolution of the trafficking problem as part of their anti-prostitution campaign were, coming from the political right, Focus on the Family, National Association of Evangelicals, Catholic Bishops Conference, Traditional Values Coalition, Concerned Women for America, Salvation Army, International Justice Mission, Shared Hope International, and Religious Freedom Coalition, and coming from the political left, the Coalition Against Trafficking in Women, Equality Now, the Protection Project, and Standing Against Global Exploitation.

[65]Loar and Ardito, "Women's Leadership in the Fight Against Trafficking," pp. 263-4.

[66]Loar, "Fact Sheet: UN Trafficking Treaty: Facts/Myths." See also: Loar, The Association for Diplomatic Studies and Training Foreign Affairs Oral History Project.

[67]Human Rights Watch *Annual Report* 1999, p. 452.

[68]Anita Botti, Phone Interview with Author, June 23, 2009.

[69]McPhedran, "Ali Miller on Key Strategies," p. 34. Quoting Alice Miller: "Governments have tended to take those steps which are easiest to carry out without having to change fundamental structures of inequality or economic oppression—punitive law enforcement rather than the protection of the human rights of those men, women and children who are forced to labor without pay."

[70]"Trafficking of Women and Children in the International Sex Trade."

[71]The source of the numbers of global human trafficking victims is unclear, but it was repeated often by the Clinton Administration. The number of victims trafficked into the United States each year (50,000) came from a CIA report. See: Hillary Rodham Clinton, "United Nations International Women's Day, Speech on Women's Rights"; Loar, The Association for Diplomatic Studies and Training Foreign Affairs Oral History Project; "About Trafficking in Women and Children, U.S. Government Definitions"; Frank E. Loy, "International Trafficking of Women and Children."

[72]Loar, "Statement before the House Committee on International Relations."

[73]Kara C. Ryf, "The First Modern Anti-Slavery Law," pp. 52-3. "The bill passed with overwhelming support obtaining a 371-1vote in the House and a unanimous 95-0 vote in the Senate. On October 16, 2000, President Clinton signed the bill into law."

[74]Loar, The Association for Diplomatic Studies and Training Foreign Affairs Oral History Project. See also: Loar and Ardito, "Women's Leadership in the Fight Against Trafficking," p. 264.

[75]"Trafficking of Women and Children in the International Sex Trade."

[76]Loar, The Association for Diplomatic Studies and Training Foreign Affairs Oral History Project; Ralph, "International Trafficking of Women and Children": "Senator Paul Wellstone has played a key role in mobilizing government efforts to combat trafficking in persons in a way that promotes and protects the rights of women and particularly trafficking victims. His leadership led to new legislation requiring the Department of State to increase and improve its reporting on trafficking in its annual *Country Reports on Human Rights Practices.* We hope that additional attention to this issue will help to close the gaps in the U.S. State Department's reporting on this subject."

[77]United States Committee for Refugees and Immigrants, "Trafficking in women and children: a contemporary manifestation of slavery."

[78]Raymond, "The New UN Trafficking Protocol," p. 499.

[79]Mertus, *War's Offensive on Women,* pp. 37-52.

[80]Sheffer, "Address on the 50th Anniversary of the UN Declaration on Human Rights."

[81]Ibid., David Sheffer quoting Assistant Secretary of State for Human Rights John Shattuck who reported on conditions he witnessed firsthand in Kosovo.

[82]Krieger, ed., "Kosovo War."

[83]Redd, "The Influence of Advisers and Decision Strategies on Foreign Policy Choices," p. 142.

[84]Mertus, *War's Offensive on Women,* p. 39.

[85]Human Rights Watch *Annual Report* 1999, p. 439.

[86]Albright, "U.S. and NATO Policy Toward the Crisis in Kosovo."

[87]Redd, "The Influence of Advisers and Decision Strategies on Foreign Policy Choices," p. 143.

[88]Mertus, *War's Offensive on Women,* p. 44.

[89]Krieger, ed., "Kosovo War."

[90]Human Rights Watch *Annual Report* 1999, p. 452.

[91]Mertus, *War's Offensive on Women*, pp. 50-1. Julie Mertus evaluated aid to post-war Kosovo and concluded that: "While many international organizations have expressed a desire to involve local women in the reconstruction process in Kosovo, very few local women hold decision-making positions. Moreover, women are conspicuously absent from the high level positions in the international bodies that control the fate of Kosovo. At a minimum, someone with particular expertise on gender issues should be leading a task force on protection issues affecting women and children. Instead of being marginalized outside the existing civil/military structures operating in Kosovo, this new task force should be part of the main power structure."

8

The Legacy of Clinton's Global Gender Policies

The Clinton Administration entered office at a critical point in global history. With the demise of the Cold War, the stultifying effects of the political, military and economic rivalry between the Soviet Union and the United States on all international relationships were fading away. In previous eras, local, national and regional borders had affected trade patterns, delineated economic and governing systems, slowed communications and marked cultural and religious differences. By the 1990s, a new era of globalization broke down those borders, disrupted intergovernmental relationships and fueled new social movements among populations that aspired to generate new respect for human rights and for the global environment. Clinton Administration foreign policy makers responded to the opportunities and challenges of the new era by adopting a broader global perspective when they defined what was necessary to achieve U.S. national security goals. In adopting this global perspective they directed government attention and resources to meet the needs and assert the human rights of various populations of U.S. and global women.

The Clinton Administration's last year in office coincided with the Special Session of the United Nations General Assembly "Women 2000: Gender Equality, Development and Peace for the 21st Century," held to assess progress in reaching the goals outlined in the Fourth World Conference on Women Platform for Action. This coincidence allowed the Clinton Administration to present its record in advancing the status of U.S. and global women to the UN member nations and to feminist nongovernmental organizations and activists. It provided feminists with the opportunity to assess the administration's record and to collaborate with feminist women who worked inside the administration once again, and to devise policy and programs that would serve U.S. and global women's interests and elevate women's status. This final chapter considers critiques of the Clinton Administration global gender policy as it was evaluated by feminists inside and outside U.S. government as the administration prepared to leave office. It also draws some lessons for those who seek to shape public discourse and to devise U.S. foreign policies in ways that will promote feminist and humanist values in the future.

Assessing the Clinton Administration's Global Gender Policy Record: The Beijing + 5 UN Special Session

The UN Special Session "Women 2000: Gender Equality, Development and Peace for the 21st Century," more commonly known as the "Beijing + 5" Special Session, was held in New York City from June 5 – 9, 2000. Official delegates representing 148 governments and over 2000 representatives of 1036 global NGOs attended these meetings.[1] The Clinton Administration sent its delegation led by Secretary of State Madeleine Albright to report on the U.S. government's progress in implementing the U.S. Commitments to Women made in Beijing.

In the year leading up to the UN Special Session the President's Interagency Council on Women and its working group that included Ann Lewis, counselor to the president, Lidia Soto-Harmon, deputy director of the PICW and Kathleen Meyer, a PICW staff member, took the lead in preparing the U.S. government's report. The PICW also collaborated with U.S. and international feminists who mobilized once again to shape the UN Special Session agenda and to pressure governments to fulfill the commitments made to women at the 1995 Beijing conference.[2] Over the five years since the Beijing conference, the PICW had held quarterly meetings with briefings for NGOs and published regular reports on U.S. government actions to address its commitments to women. In preparation for the Beijing + 5 meetings, the PICW hosted thirteen regional conferences attended by feminist NGOs and community organizations across the United States to gather their perspectives on the U.S. government's policies related to the needs and goals of women and girls.[3] Utilizing this input, the PICW published its summation report, "America's Commitment: Women 2000," that recounted the U.S. government's record of accomplishments in advancing women's status and ending discriminations against women and proposed new initiatives for future government action.[4] The government's goal was to present its record in the most positive terms to demonstrate to women's organizations and to other UN member governments how U.S. domestic and global gender policy had improved the lives of women since the Clinton Administration took office.

The PICW also formed a United States host committee with feminist activists in New York City to facilitate meetings among global NGO visitors and to organize briefings with the U.S. delegation during the Special Session. (See Appendix D) This host committee assisted global women in navigating the United Nations' meetings. The host committee held an opening ceremony at the UN plaza where UN women leaders, Clinton Administration officials and various celebrities spoke to the assembled NGO delegates and raised the media profile of the Special Session. The committee also sponsored NGO panels and discussions held at local universities. In addition, the U.S. government provided the NGOs with meeting space at the U.S. Custom House where global feminist activists met and networked with one another.[5]

Secretary Madeleine Albright was particularly proud of the transformations in U.S. global gender policy that had been made at the State Department in the years since the Beijing conference.[6] As the spokesperson for the administration at the Beijing + 5 Special Session,[7] and continuing at speaking engagements throughout the administration's last year in office, Albright recounted the administration's gender policy accomplishments. She asserted that "Efforts to advance the status of women can never again be confined to the back waters or side channels of American interest. They must be—and I am proud to say they have become—part of the mainstream of U.S. foreign policy. Helping women to move ahead is the right thing to do, and—believe me—it's also the smart thing to do, because we know that despite the great strides made in recent decades, women remain an underdeveloped and undervalued human resource."[8]

At a forum hosted by the White House Project in September 2000 Albright told the assembled group of political women "After 63 male Secretaries of State, I have been determined to make a difference."[9] Albright and her Clinton Administration State Department colleagues were responsible for increasing the descriptive and substantive representation of women in U.S. foreign policy making from 1993 to 2000. Moreso than in previous administrations, women had been appointed to high ranking leadership positions within the State Department. Secretary Albright had consistently raised women's rights issues with male government leaders and engaged in unprecedented meetings with women leaders during her official visits to the Balkans, Central Europe, Africa and Latin America.[10] Albright also noted that the administration had established the President's Interagency Council on Women that focused the attention of highest-level cabinet officials on implementing programs to fulfill the U.S. Commitments to Women made at the Beijing conference. In 1994 the State Department had created the Office of International Women's Issues and in 1999 Senior Coordinator Theresa Loar had collaborated with Craig Johnstone at the State Department's Office of Resources, Plans, and Policy to establish a strategic plan for the OIWI that helped assure the OIWI's institutional permanence by tying its "objectives related to women's issues to key U.S. national interests, including economics and prosperity, democracy and human rights, law enforcement and humanitarian response."[11] The Vital Voices initiative, for one example, served the U.S. government's democracy promotion and global economic development goals. Since 1993, U.S. embassy Human Rights Country Reports had included sections devoted to women's human rights abuses that noted instances of violence towards women. The U.S. non-recognition policy toward the Taliban government in Afghanistan and the administration's anti-trafficking initiatives were tangible expressions of the government's support for global women's human rights.

The State Department's Bureau of Population, Refugees and Migration, mindful that over 80 percent of the world's refugees were women and children according to the UN High Commissioner for Refugees, consequently allocated "a significant amount of its funding to programs that address the needs of women and the girl child" and directed resources towards the problems of "violence against women, trafficking in women, empowerment of women and control in decision-making."[12] USAID had implemented the 1996 Gender Plan of Action that had mainstreamed gender considerations into all its sustainable development and other aid programs, personnel policies and staff trainings. USAID initiated aid programs to increase global women's access to credit through microenterprise projects; more than 80 percent of the estimated 3.4 million recipients of microenterprise aid in Fiscal Year 1998 were women. USAID funded global education initiatives "to close the gap between girls' and boys' access to basic education." The administration had directed aid to support family planning and reproductive health care, insofar as aid allocations determined by Congress had allowed. For example, USAID directed resources to fund maternal health and nutrition, HIV/AIDS, and family planning and reproductive health programs in over twenty-five countries. Overall, "between 1994 and 1998, the Agency spent almost $500,000,000 per year, on average, in improving women's status around the world. In [Fiscal Year] 1999, $605,000,000 was obligated."[13]

Nonetheless, Secretary Albright recognized areas where the U.S. global gender policy had fallen short and failed the world's women.

Reflecting her own departmental priorities, Madeleine Albright regretted the U.S. failure to pay the back dues it owed to United Nations agencies including the UN Population Fund. She also regretted the drastic cuts that had been made in U.S. aid to global family planning programs during President Clinton's second term in office. The Clinton Administration had been unable to persuade the Republican-majority Congress to pass more generous appropriations bills for these global initiatives that would have empowered women worldwide by giving them more control over their own bodies. The administration had also failed to persuade the U.S. Senate to ratify the Convention on the Elimination of all forms of Discrimination Against Women, the international bill of women's rights. Albright had argued that CEDAW ratification was not only the right thing to do based on the principle of women's equality, but it would have reinforced global norms by subjecting the U.S. government's human rights record to the same standards and scrutiny that 165 states had already accepted. Secretary Albright and Senior Coordinator of the Office of International Women's Issues Theresa Loar spoke out often in support of CEDAW but failed to move Senate opponents of the treaty to bring the treaty forward for a ratification vote.[14]

To be sure, feminist organizations made their own evaluations of the Clinton Administration's record in fulfilling the U.S. Commitments to Women made in Beijing in 1995. In addition to participating in the PICW-sponsored regional conferences, U.S.-based feminist NGOs also organized independently to mobilize women's participation and maximize feminist women's influence at the UN Special Session. Charlotte Bunch at the Center for Women's Global Leadership, June Zeitlin at the Women's Environment and Development Organization and Francoise Girard at the International Women's Health Coalition, among others, put out the call to global women's human rights, reproductive rights and women's health activists to identify pressing issues and to articulate common demands to government leaders at the Beijing + 5 Special Session.[15]

Feminist NGOs pushed UN agencies and national governments as they had at previous UN world conferences for more "accountability." Measures to improve accountability would include more gender research and gender analysis of the impact of government policies on women, as well as persudaing governments to set specific targets and benchmarks in order to expand and protect women's rights and status.[16] As a result of many discussions, feminist NGOs placed particular emphasis on women's economic empowerment and criticized governments for ignoring the detrimental effects of economic globalization and political restructuring on the lives of global women at the Beijing + 5 meetings.[17] Feminist

NGOs also criticized governments for failing to include women, who experienced war and suffered war's consequences in different ways than men, in national and international peace making and peace keeping initiatives.[18]

A coalition of feminists from various U.S.-based NGOs including InterAction, Baha'i of the U.S.A., the National Council for Research on Women, Women's Environment and Development Organization and Women Waging Peace, among others, developed their own "Report Card" evaluating the administration's policies and programs.[19] The Report Card graded the U.S. government's initiatives in the twelve gender policy areas identified as areas of "critical need" in the Beijing Platform for Action. Although many of the feminists' criticisms focused on the U.S. government's failures in terms of addressing the needs of U.S. women through its domestic policy and programs, in regard to global gender policy the following critiques were most relevant.

The U.S. government earned a "C" grade in relation to education and training for women and girls, although "Programs in selected developing countries to promote girls' educational access and women's literacy are commendable." The government's programs were rated "C minus" overall in regard to women's health issues. Although the government had made "impressive investments in research and prevention" of various diseases that particularly jeopardized women's health including HIV/AIDS and breast cancer research, "reproductive rights are in jeopardy" especially overseas, where, in the Fiscal Year 2000 budget, Congress once again imposed a "global gag rule" that restricted funding for global family planning services. In its programs addressing women and violence, globally, the government earned a "C plus." In one positive development in this area the government earned praise for its coordinated interagency approach to addressing the problem of trafficking of women and girls. The U.S. government had also focused world attention on the Taliban's violations of human rights that particularly affected women in Afghanistan. However, although the U.S. government had promoted the International Criminal Tribunals for the former Yugoslavia and Rwanda that addressed gendered war crimes against women, the administration had failed to sign on to the permanent International Criminal Court Convention, rejecting, again, global scrutiny that might condemn the United States' wartime conduct.

For the area of women in power and decision-making the Clinton Administration earned a "B" because of the "dramatic increase" in the number of women that President Clinton had appointed to high-level positions in government. President Clinton also earned a "B" for creating the President's Interagency Council on Women, an institutional mechanism that monitored U.S. government implementation of the U.S. Commitments to Women from 1995 to 2000 but that had no institutional permanence and would be dissolved when Bill Clinton left office.

The government's general lack of support for sustainable development policies and environmental policies that particularly impacted women's health earned a grade of "D," as did the government's lack of support for "the girl child" as demonstrated by Congress' failure to ratify the UN Convention on the Rights of the Child.

In the important area of military policy, feminist interventions made little impact. The U.S. government failed to sign a Comprehensive Nuclear Test Ban Treaty and had increased its Fiscal Year 2000 defense budget. Overall, the U.S. government failed to lead world government efforts to involve more women in conflict resolution negotiations or in peace keeping missions.

The feminists' Report Card rated the government with a "C minus" on women and the economy, noting generally that "globalization exacerbates gender inequalities" before enumerating specific economic disadvantages that affected U.S. women. These critiques of the negative impacts of economic globalization on women also related to the lowest grade the U.S. government received, an "F" for failing to address the increasing levels of world poverty and the increasing numbers of Americans living in poverty in the United States, of which women and children made up the great majority.[20]

The U.S. government was not alone among Northern developed nations in its efforts to avoid discussions of global military operations, conflict resolution policies and global macroeconomic policies at the Beijing + 5 Special Session. Nonetheless, feminist NGOs asserted that it was these areas of global concern that had the greatest impact on the lives of women and girls. They argued that women had to be included in relevant military and economic policy making bodies at all levels.[21] A coalition of like-minded feminist NGOs formed an Economic Justice Caucus at the UN Special Session and issued a Declaration for Economic Justice and Women's Empowerment to government delegates that asserted:

> Our primary point is that the entire review of the Platform for Action is too limited if it focuses on national implementation to the exclusion of the broader macro-economic picture in which nation's operate, and the international institutions that are setting the rules of the global economy. We state that women's equity and equality cannot be achieved within the current neo-liberal economic model that is anti-women and anti-people. ... We are disappointed that the talking points below make little reference to the global economy and women's economic human rights.[22]

Northern governments of the First World that set global capitalist economic policies and that established favorable conditions for transnational corporations that controlled most of the world's resources, however, generally considered these topics to be beyond the province of gender equity or women's human rights discussions at the Beijing + 5 Special Session. Moreover, in its closing statement to the UN Special Session General Assembly, the Clinton Administration asserted without irony that:

> [The U.S. government] wanted to disassociate itself from paragraphs 29, 30, and 135 (i) [of the Special Session closing document] dealing with globalization and economic issues. Those paragraphs characterized globalization and debt as significant obstacles to achieving gender equality. National governments had primary responsibility for social and economic development and for ensuring the equality of women. *Most aspects of equality for women had no direct link to international economic and financial issues*.[23] [Emphasis added].

With macroeconomic policies de-emphasized at the UN government assembly review meetings, "Mission delegates [were] more easily influenced by the Vatican and U.S. anti-abortionists who do systematic lobby work geared to New York UN missions."[24] This frustrated feminist activists who believed that the delegations' focus and media's focus on the ever-controversial issue of women's reproductive rights would allow governments to ignore the "devastating impact on women of globalization, structural adjustment, global debt, and new trade relationships under the WTO and regional accords." The focus on women's reproductive rights would give the Religious Right "a big victory by setting the [Special Session] agenda."[25]

Indeed, the U.S.-based Religious Right spent a great deal of time lobbying the world government delegations at the preparatory meetings and at the June Special Session to abandon their support for women's reproductive rights as agreed upon in the 1994 International Conference on Population and Development and the 1995 Fourth World Conference on Women conference treaties.[26] A "self-titled 'pro-family' coalition" led by Christian Right activist Austin Ruse and made up of organizations such as the Catholic Family and Human Rights Institute, the Mormon World Family Policy Center and the Christian Evangelical Family Research Center held their own Beijing + 5 preparatory meetings. They organized an "NGO Caucus for Stable Families" that lobbied government delegations with suggestions for the Beijing + 5 document language.[27] "Pro-family" NGOs believed that the combined influence of "feminism, the sexual revolution, gay rights, and liberalism" were destroying the "traditional" family and "traditional" female roles, i.e. "motherhood." Religious Right advocates argued that they were the "true protectors of women" who would "liberate" women from their jobs so they would be "free to raise children."[28] These conservative NGOs had learned effective organizing tactics such as the conference caucus from the liberal feminist NGOs. They adopted the liberal feminists' rights-based arguments and language focused on "liberation." In consequence, the conservative coalition won over converts among the delegations from Argentina, Nicaragua and several Islamic states.[29]

Additionally, but with less-satisfactory results, twenty-four Republican congressmen wrote to the U.S. Ambassador to the United Nations Richard Holbrooke to express their "great alarm" at the discussions of women's reproductive issues at the Beijing + 5 meetings, where some NGOs were asserting women's right to safe abortions and access to medical training for abortion providers. As the conservative congressmen wrote to Holbrooke, "This violates the Cairo Program of Action and the Beijing Platform of Action both of which called for fewer abortions." They objected strongly to the notion of "sexual rights" as asserted by some feminist NGOs, which they claimed was a "new and dangerous term, to which there are virtually no limits. … It will mean not just special rights for homosexuals but could mean the rights to sexual expression for children. Moreover, it may allow for the spread of prostitution … [And it represents an attempt] to remove parental rights, to denigrate the traditional family, and to force anti-family policies onto other nations."[30]

The U.S. government delegation did not retract the previous support for women's reproductive rights as they had been outlined at the UN conferences in Cairo in 1994 and Beijing in 1995. The delegation publicly reiterated its liberal position at the Beijing + 5 closing ceremony:

> Regarding the furtherance of women's rights, [the U.S.] Government has a firm position of non-discrimination on the basis of sexual orientation and considered that omission of such a position from the outcome document in no way justified such discrimination in any country. [The U.S.] delegation also fully supported the call in the Platform for Action for governments to recognize and address the health impact of unsafe abortions. Governments should recognize the implications of unsafe abortion. Even where abortion was legal, too many countries had not trained the providers to ensure that abortions were safe and accessible. It was a major health concern. On saving and protecting the health and lives of women, [the U.S.] Government would be guided by the consensus language of the document of the General

Assembly's special session on the International Conference on Population and Development (ICPD + 5).[31]

The *New York Times* reported that Hillary Clinton's role in establishing the U.S. delegation's positions was most influential: "Richard C. Holbrooke … said Mrs. Clinton had laid out the administration's position forcefully. 'It was Hillary's saying, do not erode the gains of Beijing,' he said."[32]

In spite of the Religious Right's interventions, the Beijing + 5 UN Assembly did not "backtrack on abortion, sexual rights, and family issues—the main targets of the conservative attack." Additionally, the governments attending the Special Session continued to affirm women's human rights and to denounce acts of violence against women. They pledged to reduce the numbers of women living in poverty and to "mainstream" gender considerations into global economic policy.[33] Government delegations adopted a "Political Declaration" and an outcome document entitled "Further actions and initiatives to implement the Beijing Declaration and Platform for Action."[34] As the leaders of the global feminist NGO Development Alternatives with Women for a New Era summed up the Beijing + 5 Special Session of 2000: "The storm is over and once again the feminist agenda has survived. But nothing indicates the work ahead will be less than it has been up to now. Rather, just as it has occurred in 1993, 1994, and 1995, the number and complexity of future tasks will necessarily expand."[35]

Moving Forward

In an essay aptly titled "Feminist Leadership for Feminist Futures" Shamillah Wilson articulated a most important lesson to be taken to heart by those who wish to see a new set of "feminist values," that are in fact humanist values, infused throughout government policy making and government operations. These values emphasize a compassionate concern with the welfare of others, social justice, equality, freedom and human reason, and these are the values that feminist activists working inside and outside government during the Clinton Administration tried to embed in U.S. global gender policy during the 1990s. Wilson's words explain the major conclusion that this history of the Clinton era illuminates. Feminist leadership is necessary to transform male-dominated and patriarchal governments, institutions and power structures that benefit a few at the expense of the rest of humanity:

> [A]s we contemplate the way forward, it is important to us to be clear that what we need is thoughtful action. But to change the rules, the very core of the social order, I firmly believe we need feminist leadership. According to Peggy Antrobus, what makes feminist leadership different from other forms of leadership is that it is transformational: 'with a passion for justice, a commitment to change things, beginning with oneself.'[36]

Although the governing record of feminist leaders who served in the Clinton Administration foreign policy making offices reveals the limits of their ability to make transformative changes within U.S. government, they succeeded in altering foreign policy rhetoric and they implemented some foreign policy and foreign aid practices that benefitted some global women. These progressive transformations, as qualified and circumscribed as they are, would not have occurred without the presence of feminist government officials, the government "insiders." Nor would they have occurred without sustained and strategic pressures applied by feminist activists working outside government who prodded their feminist counterparts and male allies working inside government offices. These feminist activist "outsiders" mobilized popular support for feminist goals through nongovernmental organizations. They utilized gender research to increase their effectiveness in transforming social attitudes and in proposing systemic political reforms.

Collaborations between feminist insiders and outsiders produced numerous progressive policy and program results as this history of gender and foreign policy making in the Clinton Administration recounts. Nonetheless, feminist insiders have been in the small minority of elected and appointed officials throughout the 1990s and into the new millennium. Established power structures that resist change have restricted feminist policy results. Feminist values have not transformed national war policies or global economic policies. A few palliative measures that aimed to "humanize" or "feminize" global economic systems, such as microenterprise lending programs that feminist insiders such as Hillary Rodham Clinton have touted, can sometimes improve economic prospects on an individual-by-individual basis. Yet these measures do not transform unfair global economic systems. Recent global treaties have affirmed in principle the need to involve women in United Nations peacemaking negotiations and peace keeping operations. The U.S. government has signed these treaties signaling its agreement with the need to involve women in peace building. However, even as the number of women involved in UN peace operations has increased, national war policies have not been transformed and the number of armed conflicts and incidences of violence against women during wartime have not been reduced in the few years that these global treaties have been in place.[37]

Despite the limited impact of feminist values on U.S. foreign policy making or on global governing bodies, the historic record confirms that if feminist women are *not present* inside power structures they *cannot advocate* for feminist values in policy making chambers where governing decisions are made. In response to those who would argue that feminist insiders are often coopted and used for anti-feminist purposes when they cooperate or collaborate with non-feminist institutions and organizations, yes, this danger is real. This consequence unfortunately has led some feminists to withdraw from non-feminist establishment power structures. Others have advocated a more fruitful course of action, that is, to increase the number of feminist women in powerful positions of leadership who will continue to advocate for feminist and humanist policy priorities from within the establishment. Linda Tarr-Whelan, for example, has argued that a critical mass of at least 30 percent of governing leadership positions should be filled by women. She makes this argument based on the value of equity and on practical considerations—increasing gender diversity in governing bodies directs more brain power to problem solving and more creativity to public policy making.[38]

One must consider that not all women are feminists, and therefore increasing the number of women in leadership positions may not radically transform institutions to adopt a feminist agenda. Nonetheless, the notion of achieving a critical mass of *feminist* women who hold positions of decision making power is an important concept for those who support transformational change. In order to achieve that critical mass of women holding office and wielding governing power within the United States, utilizing gender quotas provides one solution. Gender quotas increase the number of female candidates and in turn reduce the number of male candidates being elected into political office. Gender quotas can also expand women's participation in the political realm generally by producing a "role model affect" that inspires more women and girls to participate in politics. In other parts of the world where gender quotas have been utilized in political systems they can take the form of voluntary political party quotas, legislated candidate quotas or specific percentages of seats reserved for women in legislative bodies.[39]

A recent analysis performed by Harvard University scholars Rohini Pande and Deanna Ford in 2011 produced results that address many of the objections that are raised when gender quotas are discussed in the context of the U.S. political system. Their results confirm the benefits of utilizing gender quotas to increase the descriptive and substantive representation of women:

> Our review yields three broad conclusions. First, quotas can and do increase female leadership in politics and the corporate sphere. This provides *prima facie* evidence that the primary constraint on female leadership is not a lack of interest in leadership positions by women. Second, female leadership influences policy outcomes. The evidence for this is clearer in the policy arena where it reflects gender differences in economic status and work responsibilities. To the extent that equitable representation in policy-making is desirable, quotas are a good policy tool to achieve it. In politics, there is no evidence that such representation has come at the cost of efficiency. … Third, gender quotas do not seem to create a sustained backlash among citizens -- rather, evidence from political quotas suggests that voters use new information about how female leaders perform to update their beliefs about women.[40]

Gender quotas have been utilized effectively to increase women's participation in governing systems around the world.[41] U.S. feminists should publicize this new research in efforts to break down resistance to applying this gender equity mechanism in the United States.

In the late 1980s when Bella Abzug founded the Women's Foreign Policy Council, she explained her vision of the role that American women could play in U.S. foreign policy making. Although some historic changes have been realized, Abzug's vision continues to inspire feminist women's involvement in governing their societies.

> [T]he role of women in foreign policy is to create a different kind of structure that would enable women to secure a peaceful atmosphere, and also to change the prevailing thinking and perspective so that women can construct a world that will provide for equality, opportunity and social justice for their families and for themselves … we're no longer prepared to just hoot and holler from the sidelines. The failure of our own policies in this country, as evidenced by the Iran-Contra Affair, as evidenced by events in the Persian Gulf, as evidenced by a whole series of failures in the international economy indicates that it's time for a new, bold approach. And I think women can make a difference.[42]

Finally, until more feminist women are elected or otherwise enter government ranks, feminist and other progressive social movement activists must take the lead in demanding social justice within existing governing systems that still exclude many voices and amplify the voices of wealthy power holders that want to preserve the status quo. Democracy is an ongoing process.

[1]United Nations Press Release, "Adopts Political Declaration, 'Further Actions and Initiatives', Assembly President Notes 'No backward movement' on language of Beijing," June 9, 2000, CWGL, Beijing + 5, box 9.

[2]President's Interagency Council on Women, "Highlights from NGO Special Briefing, U.S. Department of State," July 13, 1999, CWGL Beijing +5, box 6; Email to "Nongovernmental Organization Partners for November 6 [1999] Women 2000 Conference in Delaware," November 4, 1999, CWGL, Beijing + 5, box 11.

[3]"Schedule of Quarterly Meetings and Briefings for NGOs," The President's Interagency Council on Women Archives. President's Interagency Council on Women, "America's Commitment: The United Nations Women's Conference, Women 2000, Beijing Plus Five, Domestic Regional Outreach Events," August 24, 1999, CWGL Beijing +5, box 6.

[4]"America's Commitment: The United Nations Women's Conference Women 2000, Beijing Plus Five," and Report: "America's Commitment: Women 2000," The President's Interagency Council on Women Archives.

[5]"Beijing + 5 Steering Committee, September 30, 1999 and "Final Report (Draft) Beijing Plus Five Host Committee," c. July 2000, CWGL Beijing +5, box 6; Center for Women's Global Leadership, Women's Environment and Development Organization (WEDO), "Beijing + 5 Review Process," n.d., CWGL Beijing +5, box 3.

[6]Albright, "Remarks on *America's Commitment,* Marking International Women's Day and Women's History Month."

[7]Albright, "Remarks at Special Session of the United Nations General Assembly on Women 2000: Beijing Plus Five."

[8]Albright, "Remarks at Symposium on Pacesetting Women of the 20th Century."

[9]Albright, "Remarks at White House Project Forum."

[10]Albright, "Remarks to the Women and Co. Foreign Executive Summit.": "And we have moved efforts to improve the lives of women and girls into the mainstream of U.S. foreign policy. Now, you might think that this wouldn't require new thinking. But it does. Because only about a quarter century ago, if you were a U.S. Foreign Service Officer, and got married, you were forced to resign. The whole atmosphere has obviously changed dramatically under President Clinton and Vice-President Gore, because, since 1993, women have been appointed to seven of the top ten positions in the Department of State. And we have found no problem in conducting diplomatic business with counterparts anywhere in the world--including the highly traditional Arab states. In fact, I have made a point of discussing women's rights with them at every opportunity, and found them quite open to discussion. And having just literally come back from Saudi Arabia, I can testify to the fact that when I, as a female Secretary of State, am treated with the highest respect."

[11]"America's Commitment: The United Nations Women's Conference Women 2000, Beijing Plus Five," 297. See also: "Institutionalizing Issues Affect Women" and "1999 Up Date: America's Commitment: Federal Programs Benefitting Women and New Initiatives as Follow Up to the UN Fourth World Conference on Women," May 1999, The President's Interagency Council on Women Archives.

[12]"America's Commitment: The United Nations Women's Conference Women 2000, Beijing Plus Five," p. 296.

[13]Ibid. pp. 330-2.

[14]Albright, "Speech at the California Women's Conference" and Loar, "Statement before the House Committee on International Relations, May 3, 2000": "This administration feels strongly that CEDAW must be ratified. Its ratification is an administration priority. The President, the First Lady and the Secretary of State have repeatedly called for its ratification. We have worked closely with NGOs in their quest for ratification of this treaty. ... CEDAW removes obstacles to women's full enjoyment of their rights. CEDAW does not create an international right to abortion. Rather it seeks to ensure equal access for men and women to health care services. It does not encroach on the principle of federalism or violate U.S. sovereignty. Rather it reinforces U.S. commitment to equality and human rights and serves to bolster existing domestic laws. It does not usurp parental role in child rearing. Rather it calls for protection of the interests of children. In countries that have ratified CEDAW, women have used it as a vehicle for positive change."

[15]E-mail Charlotte Bunch, CWGL, to various Women's International Organizations, "Beijing + 5 Organizing," November 9, 1999 and E-mail Francoise Girard, IWHC, to Charlotte Bunch and CWGL, "Re: Beijing + 5," November 22, 1999, CWGL Beijing +5, box 4.

[16]"NGOs for Women 2000: A Panel Discussion Beijing + 5, Setting Targets," November 22, 1999, CWGL Beijing +5, box 6; "Activities and Initiatives of Women World Wide," E-Newsletter *IWTC Women's GlobalNet* 134 (December 14, 1999), CWGL Beijing +5, box 4.

[17]Email Claire Slatter, DAWN to Charlotte Bunch, CWGL, "Re your email on plans and expectations for Beijing + 5," December 8, 1999, CWGL Beijing +5, box 4.

[18]Jason Topping Cone, "The Objective is a Women's Network," *The Earth Times* (April 17) and Robert E. Sullivan, "Waging Peace' at Carnegie Corporation," *The Earth Times* (June 8, 2000), CWGL, Beijing + 5, box 9.

[19]"Report Card on U.S. Federal Government Action for Women and Girls' Rights and Empowerment: An Assessment of the US Implementation of the UN Platform for Action." See also: WEDO, "Women's Equality: An Unfinished Agenda. Women's Organizations Assess U.S. Government Actions on Implementing the Beijing Platform, 1995 – 2000," CWGL Beijing +5, box 7 and WEDO, "Proposal: United States Shadow Report in Preparation for Women 2000," c. 1999, CWGL Beijing +5, box 2: "WEDO intends to compile a shadow report for the United States, which will applaud actions that carry out Beijing commitments and criticize inaction and policy changes that have a negative impact on women. We would also like to incorporate, where appropriate, recommendations for positive actions."

[20]NGO Working Session, "NGOs as Partners: On the Way to Accelerate Implementation of the Beijing Platform for Action," Prior to the ECE Regional Preparatory Meeting, January 17-18, 2000, CWGL Beijing +5, box 2. See: p. 8 Sub-Regional NGO Reports: "The U.S. report, presented by June Zeitlin, WEDO, ... underscores the major challenges remaining as follows, i.e. poverty and the economy. Despite the current economic growth, more women are working at low-pay or minimum wage levels, hold part-time or temporary jobs without health insurance and adequate affordable child-care. Specific policies must be adopted

to enable women to achieve economic self-sufficiency and to eliminate poverty, especially in light of steps to eliminate guaranteed welfare benefits and social support programs for poor women. The policies adopted must address the needs of all women with particular concern for racial and ethnic minorities and immigrant women. The U.S. must use its leadership position in the global economy to institute a gender analysis of macroeconomic policies of the World Trade Organization and other international institutions to ensure that women have access to private capital, technology, and natural resources." See also: McFeatters, "Looking Back So They Can Move Ahead": "Female-headed households make up two-thirds of those below the poverty line of $17,000 for a family of four," according to U.S. government statistics.

[21]"Women Building Peace: from the village council to the negotiating table," Campaign Update no. 1 (December 1999); Email Claire Slatter, DAWN to Charlotte Bunch, CWGL, "Re your email on plans and expectations for Beijing + 5", December 8, 1999, CWGL Beijing +5, box 4; Carol Barton, "North Shares Responsibility for Slow Progress in Beijing + 5," WomenAction [newsletter], June 9, 2000, CWGL, Beijing + 5, box 9; Lenora Todaro, "Going After Globalization: Feminists Trade Strategies for a Woman-Friendly Economy," *Village Voice* [on-line], June 14-20, 2000, CWGL, Beijing + 5, box 9.

[22]E-Mail Carol Barton, NGO Economic Justice Caucus, to CWGL, "Media Message Memo," May 26, 2000, CWGL Beijing +5, box 6.

[23]United Nations Press Release, "Adopts Political Declaration, 'Further Actions and Initiatives', Assembly President Notes 'No backward movement' on language of Beijing," June 9, 2000, CWGL, Beijing + 5, box 9. See also: Ambassador Betty King, U.S. Permanent Mission to the United Nations, "U.S. Reservations to Women 2000 Final Document," June 10, 2000, CWGL Beijing +5, box 6 and "Globalization: U.S. Government Interpretive Statement," Press Release, July 2000, The President's Interagency Council on Women Archives: "The United States would like to expand upon the statement delivered, on June 10, 2000, at the end of the special session of the general assembly devoted to the five-year review of efforts to implement the Beijing Declaration and Platform for Action. …Globalization is a fact, not a policy option. It is up to each nation to pursue policies that can help its people take advantage of the opportunities of globalization, so that all citizens, including women, will benefit. Sound national policies are the primary determinant of success in achieving the advancement of women, and indeed in achieving overall economic and social development. But developing countries should not face this task alone. The international community should provide encouragement and support, as appropriate, to help them build capacity and undertake the necessary reforms."

[24]Sonia Correa and Gita Sen, "The Beijing + 5 Trenches," (2001), KT, box 5.

[25]E-Mail Carol Barton, NGO Economic Justice Caucus, to CWGL, "Media Message Memo," May 26, 2000, CWGL Beijing +5, box 6.

[26]Jennifer Butler, Ecumenical Women 2000, "300 Religious Right Representatives Attend Beijing Plus Five Preparatory Committee Meeting," (Published by the Global Policy Forum), April 25, 2000, CWGL Beijing +5, box 6; Charlotte Bunch re-sending e-mail from Austin Ruse ['Pro-Family' Christian Right leader] to CWGL colleagues," December 10, 1999, CWGL Beijing +5, box 4.

[27]Friedman, "Gendering the Agenda," p. 326.

[28]Butler, "300 Religious Right Representatives Attend Beijing Plus Five Preparatory Committee Meeting."

[29]Rahul Singh, "Pro-life lobby gears up at women's meet," *The Earth Times* (June 8, 2000), CWGL, Beijing + 5, box 9.

[30]Rahul Singh, "Strong letter from the Right," *The Earth Times* (June 8, 2000), CWGL, Beijing + 5, box 9.

[31]Closing Statements Beijing + 5 Review, "Closing Statements GA/9725," c. June 2000: "Regarding the furtherance of women's rights, [the U.S.] Government has a firm position of non-discrimination on the basis of sexual orientation and considered that omission of such a position from the outcome document in no way justified such discrimination in any country. [The US] delegation also fully supported the call in the Platform for Action for governments to recognize and address the health impact of unsafe abortions. Governments should recognize the implications of unsafe abortion. Even where abortion was legal, too many countries had not trained the providers to ensure that abortions were safe and accessible. It was a major health concern. On saving and protecting the health and lives of women, [the US] Government would be guided by the consensus language of the document of the General Assembly's special session on the International Conference on Population and Development (ICPD + 5)."

[32]Crossette, "Hillary Clinton Wins Praise at UN Meeting on Women." See also: Rahul Singh, "Hillary Clinton Issues Call," *The Earth Times* (June 2000), CWGL, Beijing + 5, box 9.

[33]"Beijing + 5 Final," *Earth Negotiations Bulletin* (June 13, 2000), CWGL, Beijing + 5, box 9.

[34]United Nations Press Release, "Adopts Political Declaration, 'Further Actions and Initiatives', Assembly President Notes 'No backward movement' on language of Beijing," June 9, 2000, CWGL, Beijing + 5, box 9.

[35]Correa and Sen, "The Beijing + 5 Trenches," 2001, KT, box 5. See also: "Five Year Review of the Implementation of the Beijing Declaration and Platform for Action (Beijing + Five)" Section D, Outcome of the Special Session.

[36] Shamillah Wilson, ""Feminist Leadership for Feminist Futures," in Wilson, Sengupta and Evans, eds., *Defending our Dreams: Global Feminist Voices for a New Generation*, p. 226.

[37]"Gender Equality in UN Peacekeeping Operations," see UN Security Council Resolutions 1325 (2000); 1820 (2008), 1888 (2009) and 1889 (2009) (2010). For an overview of the United Nations' aspirational changes see "United Nations Peacekeeping, Gender and Peacekeeping."

[38]Tarr-Whelan, *Women Lead the Way: Your Guide to Stepping Up Leadership and Changing the World.*

[39]Pande and Ford, "Gender Quotas and Female Leadership: A Review," pp. 4 and 16.

[40]Ibid. p. 3.

[41]Ibid. Table 2: Political quotas, pp. 30-4.

[42]Opening Remarks by Bella Abzug, Informal Congressional Hearing on Women's Perspectives on US Foreign Policy, in "Women's Perspectives on U.S. Foreign Policy: Report of A Women's Foreign Policy Council Congressional Hearing," November 19, 1987, to the Committee on Foreign Affairs, U.S. House of Representatives, KT, box 7.

Appendix A: Interviews

Anita Botti, Phone Interview, June 23, 2009

Anita Botti, a Peace Corps alumna and foreign service officer since 1985, worked with the State Department bureau of Population, Refugees, and Migration in the Global Affairs bureau on "Refugee Admissions," helping war and conflict refugees to repatriate or resettle in safe locations, including resettlement to the United States. In 1997 until the end of 2000, she was assigned to work with the President's Interagency Council on Women to set up an interagency task force coordinating State, Labor, Commerce and Justice Department efforts on trafficking in women, where she participated in policy development that resulted in the administration's "three P's" approach: prevention (empowering women by promoting their economic independence), protection (of victims) and prosecution (of traffickers). These efforts coordinated with the work of the Office of International Women's Issues resulted in an Anti-trafficking Executive Order in 1998, and congressional legislation in 2000. Botti noted the importance of working with various NGOs who had long been active on refugee issues, and the significance of high-level and hands-on support from First Lady Hillary Clinton and her Chief of Staff Melanne Verveer to furthering the administration's anti-trafficking initiatives. In 2009, Botti joined the Office of Global Women's Issues as deputy director.

Charlotte Bunch, Phone Interview, May 5, 2010

Charlotte Bunch founded and directed the Center for Women's Global Leadership at Rutgers University and led the center's campaigns to focus on the global problems of violence against women and trafficking in women as human rights violations, from the late 1980s and throughout the decade of the 1990s, and beyond. She lobbied the UN to fund more women's NGOs to increase women's participation at the Human Rights Conference in Vienna in 1993, and she organized a global petition and public Tribunal focusing on violations of women's rights at the HRC that were key events in these campaigns. A scholar and activist, Bunch was inducted into the National Women's Hall of Fame in 1996 and was honored with the Eleanor Roosevelt Award for Human Rights by President Clinton in 1999. Nonetheless, rather than attaching importance to her own individual achievements or those of any other single Western feminist leader, Bunch noted the important paradigm shift that occurred in the 1990s facilitated by feminist activists throughout the world who were active since the UN Decade for Women ended in 1985, whereby the United Nations, governments and human rights organizations recognized that women's rights are human rights. Bunch also noted that, for the Clinton Administration, the implications of that paradigm shift began to impact U.S. policy at the 1994 International Conference on Population and Development and afterward. Although Bunch shared her feminist perspectives on gender policy issues with Theresa Loar and others in the Clinton Administration, she noted conflicts of interest arose when the U.S. government determined policies and implemented programs to address feminist issues.

Mayra Buvinic, Interview at World Bank Headquarters, Washington DC, September 23, 2009

Mayra Buvinic, PhD, an expert on "women in development" issues, was a founding member of the International Center for Research on Women (ICRW) and directed the center in its first twenty years of operation, from 1976 to 1996. Buvinic, Irene Tinker and others formed the ICRW following the International Women's Year Conference in Mexico City, with the goal of establishing a policy-oriented research and program development organization to direct USAID, Peace Corps, World Bank and private foundation donors' resources toward improving the economic status and welfare of Third World women and children. ICRW staff identify and design projects, and provide monitoring and evaluation services in the areas of women's access to credit; rural, urban, and regional development; small business development; vocational training; and health and nutritional services. Buvinic noted that collaborative relationships between the ICRW and USAID had formed to focus on women in poverty and HIV/AIDS issues by the late 1980s, and she also noted that openness and reciprocity between NGOs and government agencies increased when the Clinton Administration took office. First Lady Hillary Clinton brought high-level attention to women's rights and microcredit initiatives that involved women. The receptive political climate ushered in by the administration increased NGO partnerships with USAID, as NGOs provided research that justified policy and program changes, especially after the Beijing Fourth World Conference on Women. Buvinic also noted increased collaborations among NGOs working on gender and development issues facilitated by the umbrella organization InterAction. Yet she explained that frustration among NGOs grew by the end of the decade and into the 2000s because Beijing Commitments and the subsequent Millennium Development Goals have not been realized, especially in terms of improvement of reproductive health services or reducing maternal mortality rates in Third World countries. Moreover, the problem of evaluating the impact of aid programs and measuring "improvements in people's wellbeing" remains elusive. Buvinic moved to the InterAmerican Development Bank in 1996, and has directed the Gender and Development division at the World Bank since 2005.

Ellen Chesler, Phone Interview, October 23, 2009

Ellen Chesler began her professional career as a political activist who worked on campaigns in New York State to elect Carol Bellamy to office during the 1970s and 1980s and she met the Clintons at that time. When the Clinton Administration took office, Chesler worked with Hillary Clinton's communications director and speechwriter Lissa Muscatine. In 1995, Chesler attended the Beijing Fourth World Conference on Women with the International Women's Health Coalition that focused on funding leaders and grassroots organizations in the global South to improve women's and youth's reproductive health and to address other health issues. She noted the important roles that women from the global South played in leading the United Nations in addressing broad women's rights issues of health and security in the 1980s, and the ways that Hillary Clinton became a spokeswoman for these issues following the Beijing Conference. From 1997 to 2003, Chesler chaired the board of the International Women's Health Coalition working with Adrienne Germain, Joan Dunlop, and others to advocate for international health and population policy and promote women's equality and human rights. From 1997 to 2006, Chesler was senior fellow at The Open Society Institute where she directed the foundation's funding for reproductive health and rights policy development and programming initiatives. Working from these private foundations and NGOs, she collaborated with the first lady's office and the State Department on various women's empowerment initiatives in the 1990s, such as mobilizing media coverage for the Beijing

+ 5 UN Assembly Special Session in 2000. She noted the importance of collaborations between women in government, NGOs and funding foundations in the 1990s that together focused world leaders' rhetorical attention and new private resources on improving the lives of disadvantaged women, even as she noted budgetary and other impediments that inhibited the government's institutional change that were raised by conservative politicians. Bureaucratic inertia in agencies such as USAID also limited change. Chesler is the author of *Woman of Valor: Margaret Sanger and the Birth Control Movement in America* and numerous essays and articles on women's human rights, and has chaired the advisory committee of the Women's Rights Division of Human Rights Watch.

Susan Crais Hovanec, Phone Interview, May 19, 2008

A foreign service officer for over thirty years, Susan Crais Hovanec's interest in women's issues dates to the mid-1970s, when she learned about U.S. government preparations for the International Women's Year Conference in Mexico City and interned for the U.S. Conference Secretariat with Mildred Marcy, Catherine East and Jill Ruckelshaus in Washington DC. Joining the State Department in 1976, Crais Hovanec worked at the U.S. Embassy in Yugoslavia during the Cold War, where she continued to learn about women's lives in socialist states. During the mid-1990s, Crais Hovanec worked at the U.S. Embassy in Croatia with Ambassador Peter Galbraith. During the Bosnian War, she met U.S. Ambassador to Austria Swanee Hunt who shared Crais Hovanec's interest in women's welfare. With Hunt driving forward organization of the 1997 "Vital Voices: Women in Democracy" conference and funding the meetings in Vienna, Crais Hovanec was brought in from Croatia to direct event communications. During the George W. Bush Administration from 2003 to 2006, Crais Hovanec worked in the Office of International Women's Issues that continued operations due to Undersecretary of State for Global Affairs Paula Dobriansky's support. As someone who understood the State Department's internal politics, Crais Hovanec worked to raise the profile of the OIWI and established the "International Women of Courage" award to recognize international women leaders who worked to further women's human rights. She also contributed to the documentary "Afghanistan Unveiled," a film project conceived by Reza Deghati and the Afghan NGO "Aina," that was funded by the U.S. State Department. This project trained fourteen Afghan women to film and document their world.

Arvonne Fraser, Phone Interview, March 14, 2008

Coming out of liberal roots in the Minnesota Democratic Farm Labor Party in the 1950s and 1960s, Arvonne Fraser moved to Washington DC when her husband Donald Fraser was elected to U.S. Congress in 1963. Focusing on women's rights issues in Washington, Fraser led the Women's Equity Action League as president from 1972 to 1974, and led the upper Midwest Democratic Party campaign to elect President Jimmy Carter in 1976. Carter appointed Fraser to direct the Women in Development office at USAID in 1977, a position she held until the Reagan Administration took office in 1981. During her tenure as director of WID, she actively worked to engage NGOs with established inroads in developing countries with WID initiatives and to increase aid resources to benefit poor women. She attended the three UN Decade for Women conferences and was a member of official U.S. conference delegations in 1975 and 1980. During the 1980s, she organized and led the International Women's Rights Action Watch, and founded the Center for Women and Public Policy at the Hubert Humphrey Institute of Public Affairs. In 1993, Bill Clinton appointed Fraser as U.S. ambassador to the United Nations Commission on the Status of Women (CSW), a position she held through 1994. As U.S. ambassador to the CSW and a member of the State Department's Office of International Organization Affairs, Fraser worked with the U.S. Department of Labor Women's Bureau to host regional conferences across the United States to publicize the UN Fourth World Conference on Women among U.S. women's NGOs. With significant leadership experience working inside and outside government institutions, Fraser's political instincts sensitized her to the need for diplomacy. She also gained a thorough understanding of feminist interests in order to move a feminist agenda forward with government action, in national and international forums. She noted the benefits of establishing feminist networks within U.S. government and United Nations institutions that will work with NGOs. She believes feminists need to understand institutional rules and how they can work within systems to transform the systems.

Sarah Gauger, Interview at the Institute for Inclusive Security, Cambridge, Massachusetts, March 12, 2009

Sarah Gauger directs grant making and program operations at the Hunt Alternatives Fund established by Swanee and Helen Hunt, at the Institute for Inclusive Security. Gauger began working with Ambassador Swanee Hunt at the U.S. Embassy in Vienna in 1996, where she worked on special projects including developing U.S. support for the UN Bosnian Women's Initiative and for the 1997 "Vital Voices: Women in Democracy" conference that became a model for subsequent democracy promotion programs organized by the State Department's Office of International Women's Issues, from 1997 to 2000. Along with Swanee Hunt, Theresa Loar, Melanne Verveer, Valerie Gillen and Alyse Nelson, Gauger planned the 1997 Vital Voices conference to engage women leaders from Croatia, the Ukraine, Bosnia and other countries in Eastern Europe in conversations with Western leaders in order to develop strategies to advance women's political leadership and economic empowerment. Gauger noted the importance of elite leadership in providing inspiration and mobilizing resources to catalyze progressive social change. She has continued to work on various women's philanthropy initiatives with Swanee Hunt since the 1990s, to organize and promote "Women Waging Peace" and the Institute for Inclusive Security programs to improve the lives of women and girls, in local, national and global arenas.

Kathleen Hendrix, Phone Interview, December 5, 2006

With a background in journalism and a personal and professional interest in the U.S. women's movement, Kathleen Hendrix worked as a staff writer for the *Los Angeles Times* during the 1970s and 1980s. She reported on the UN Decade for Women conferences and the National Women's Conference in Houston for the *LA Times* before she joined the State Department as a speech writer in 1993 as a political appointee. At the State Department, Hendrix reconnected with Arvonne Fraser, also a Clinton appointee who led the U.S. delegation to the United Nations Commission on the Status of Women. With Fraser, Hendrix worked through the State Department's Office of International Organization Affairs to prepare the U.S. delegation and determine U.S. platform positions at the Fourth World Conference on Women. This work connected Hendrix to the global conference secretariat, then led by Theresa Loar, in the State Department's new Global Affairs division. In preparing for the Beijing conference and the International Conference on Population and Development, Hendrix noted the strong influence wielded by NGOs that worked on women's human rights issues, reproductive health issues and women and development issues. She singled out the Women's Rights Divisions of Amnesty International and Human Rights Watch, the National Spiritual Assembly of the Baha'i, International Human Rights Law Group, the International Center for Research on Women and the Women's Environment and Development Organization, as examples of NGOs that were especially influential in aiding the State

Department in drafting language for conference documents. She also noted the important role played by Madeleine Albright, then U.S. ambassador to the United Nations, in justifying U.S. participation in the Beijing conference to Republican Congressmen and Senators who objected to China's human rights record and to "feminist" language in the conference documents. After the Beijing conference, Hendrix went to work as Theresa Loar's deputy director at the President's Interagency Council on Women, developing programs to fulfill the U.S. Commitments to Women. In mid-1997, she began working on the Vital Voices: Women in Democracy Initiative with the Office of International Women's Issues, and continued to work as adviser to the Vital Voices Global Partnerships NGO after the Clinton Administration left office in 2001.

Gracia Hillman, Phone Interview, June 22, 2009

A political and community activist throughout the 1980s, Gracia Hillman worked through organizations such as the Congressional Black Caucus Foundation, the National Coalition on Black Voter Participation and the League of Women Voters before she was appointed as the first senior coordinator for the Office on International Women's Issues in 1994. Following an interview with Undersecretary of State for Global Affairs Timothy Wirth, she was hired to oversee OIWI activities with the broad and general mandate to promote international women's human rights and better integrate women's issues into foreign policy. During her tenure at OIWI, however, Hillman concentrated on preparations for the UN Fourth World Conference on Women, which she attended as a member of the U.S. delegation. Her efforts focused on outreach to nongovernmental organizations, arranging NGO credentials to attend the Beijing conference, and on justifying U.S. participation at the conference to a skeptical Republican-majority Congress that sought to cut funding for the delegation after the 1994 midterm elections. Hillman noted the important roles played by Hillary Clinton and Madeleine Albright whose influential support for U.S. participation in the Beijing conference kept conference preparations moving forward at the State Department. She also noted the infectious "spirit" of women's solidarity at the Beijing conference, the important focus that African women directed to problems and needs of girls, and dialogues between women with dramatically different cultural and religious backgrounds, at the conference site as well as at the NGO forum site at Huairou. Following the Beijing conference, Hillman left the State Department in 1996 to work for a private satellite technology company that broadcast literacy and health education information to countries in Africa and South Asia before she was appointed to the U.S. Election Assistance Commission by the George W. Bush Administration in 2003.

Suzanne Kindervatter, Phone Interview, August 25, 2009

With a background in international education and development issues, Suzanne Kindervatter had worked with women and girls in multiple countries at the Center for Development and Population Activities before joining InterAction in late 1993. InterAction is an alliance of U.S.-based international NGOs (now 190 members strong) that work on poverty alleviation, environmental sustainability and other policy advocacy positions, and on foreign assistance program development. Kindervatter joined InterAction's Strategic Impact Unit as NGOs and the U.S. government began planning for the Fourth World Conference on Women. This was a time, she noted, when UN agencies, national governments and the U.S, government in particular were open to collaborations with NGOs to determine conference agendas and conference document language, to a greater degree than in the past. NGOs formed interest groups among themselves (facilitated by NGO leaders like Bella Abzug who had a background in U.S. congressional caucusing strategy), to network and leverage their power at UN conference preparatory meetings. She noted as highlights of the Beijing conference the emotional validation felt by women who heard First Lady Hillary Clinton delivering her women's human rights address, and an open forum that World Bank President Jim Wolfensohn held with NGOs who criticized the World Bank's structural adjustment policies, and the concrete "commitments" to advance the status of women governments made at the conference. After the conference, Kindervatter and others at InterAction created the "commitments campaign" to monitor government progress in fulfilling public pledges and lobbied the Clinton Administration to continue the President's Interagency Council on Women through the Administration's tenure in office, and to promote government/NGO collaborations. Kindervatter noted that the 1990s were a historic moment when there was a political will among some world governments and the United Nations and its agencies to promote significant social change. At the time, that progressive political will was stronger than the reactionary forces pushing back.

Sarah Kovner, Phone Interview, November 10, 2010

As a long-time supporter of Democratic Party candidates and progressive and pro-choice politicians, Sarah Kovner worked as a political consultant on campaigns and with nongovernmental organizations, and served as a board member for the Coalition for Free Choice, the National Women's Political Caucus and the First Women's Bank from the 1970s onward. She was deputy director of the Clinton-Gore campaign in New York for the 1992 election. When Donna Shalala was appointed secretary of Health and Human Services, she hired Kovner as her special assistant, and Kovner worked at HHS throughout Clinton Administration's two terms in office. When the Clinton Administration took office, it immediately began to work on preparations for U.S. participation in the UN International Conference on Population and Development, scheduled for September 1994, and Kovner noted that collaborations among cabinet level agencies began at that time. Interagency collaborations continued throughout the Clinton Administration's tenure in office, and were especially active after the President's Interagency Council on Women was created in 1995. Kovner attended the PICW meetings representing the HHS, and the cabinet agencies reported out on what they had done to fulfill the U.S. Commitments to advancing the status of women at these meetings. During the mid-1990s, HHS directed its focus to women's health initiatives and developed a web site clearinghouse with information on women's health issues that was open to the public. HHS directed resources to breast cancer research and also coordinated its research and public education efforts with the offices of women's health in the Food and Drug Administration, in the Center for Disease Control, and in the National Institutes of Health. And HHS held many meetings with NGOs throughout these years. Kovner attended the ICPD in Cairo in 1994, and the Fourth World Conference on Women in Beijing in 1995 and believed that progressive developments vis-à-vis women came out of these conferences. She also noted the critical involvement of several U.S. government and NGO leaders promoting women's advancement at these conferences and otherwise, including Margaret Pollock and Sharon Kotok from the State Department, Bella Abzug and Susan Davis from Women's Environment and Development Organization and Adrienne Germain from the International Women's Health Coalition.

Tamara Kreinin, Phone Interview, August 10, 2009

In 1994, Tamara Kreinin, an expert on gender health issues, joined the Washington DC-based National Campaign to Prevent Teen Pregnancy to direct state and local affairs; in 2000, she went on to lead SIECUS, the Sexuality Information and Education Council of the United States. Kreinin now works with Timothy Wirth at the United Nations Foundation, where she is executive director of Women and Population and focuses on related issues of population, sexual and reproductive health and women's empowerment. She noted the critical impact of the 1994 International Conference on Population and Development in focusing world governments' (including the US government's) attention on women's wellbeing in a more holistic way than previously, integrating issues of women's reproductive health, women's economic status, and education in conference debates, and how these integrated discussions continued at the 1995 Fourth World Conference on Women. Kreinin also noted the Clinton Administration's support and funding for family planning initiatives and the important advocacy role played by Planned Parenthood of America led by Gloria Feldt in the 1990s, and how that support and funding ended when the George W. Bush Administration took office.

Laura Liswood, Interview at the Aspen Institute Offices of the Council for Women World Leaders, Washington DC, July 14, 2009

From a background in management and publishing, Laura Liswood is an expert on women's leadership development. She directed the Women's Leadership Project from 1992 to 1996, co-founded the Council on Women World Leaders with the former president of Iceland Vigdís Finnbogadóttir, and co-founded the White House Project in 1997 to train and advocate for women entering the elite ranks of political leadership. Liswood is also the author of several books and a documentary film focused on these topics. In 2000, the Clinton Administration appointed Liswood to a three-year term on the Defense Advisory Committee on Women in the Services (DACOWITS) that is concerned with recruiting and retaining women in the U.S. military. Liswood noted the confluence of international events in the 1990s that sparked her interests in advances for women generally and that led to more women entering the elite ranks of world government leadership. She also noted, however, that institutionalized discrimination against women and other traditionally unrepresented groups, such as racial minorities, continues to limit advances in countries worldwide. As someone who attended the first Vital Voices conference that the U.S. government organized in Vienna in 1997, she commented on the importance of U.S. government sponsorship that legitimized women's participation and aspirations and helped women who were attending these conferences justify their efforts to achieve public leadership positions in their native countries. These Vital Voices conferences could also serve as catalysts for more local women's organizing. She also noted that leadership at the top ranks of government sets the tone for supporting women's advancement.

Theresa Loar, Interview at the offices of CH2M HILL, Washington DC, November 28, 2006

Theresa Loar worked on marketing campaigns for advertising firms in New York City before she and her husband, a lawyer, joined the State Department as foreign service officers in 1986. Loar trained in Washington DC and held posts at the U.S. consulates in Mexico City and Seoul from the late 1980s until 1991, when she moved back to Washington and worked on Central American country desks until the Clinton Administration took office and established the Global Affairs division. At that point, Loar joined the Global Affairs bureau. In 1994, she headed a global conference secretariat within Global Affairs, and began to prepare for the upcoming International Conference on Population and Development and the UN Fourth World Conference on Women, conducting research, developing U.S. positions and reaching out to NGOs. When President Clinton formed the Interagency Council on Women to devise programs to implement the U.S. Commitments to advancing women's equality announced at the Beijing conference, Loar moved to the White House to direct the PICW. There she worked with leaders of cabinet agencies and with NGOs to design programs and to implement U.S. Commitments. In 1996, Loar was appointed senior coordinator for the Office for International Women's Issues at the State Department. Loar's tenure at the OIWI (held concurrently with her position as director of the PICW) lasted through Clinton's second term in office, and she played pivotal roles in relation to various global women's policy initiatives including U.S. policy toward the Taliban government in Afghanistan, the Vital Voices: Women in Democracy Initiative, and anti-human trafficking initiatives. Significantly, Loar's work at the OIWI had the support and engagement of First Lady Hillary Clinton and her White House Chief of Staff Melanne Verveer, Secretary of State Madeleine Albright and other senior staff at the Department of State that allowed her to make institutional and procedural changes at the department that would continue to direct attention to global women's issues. She discussed these developments, as well as the OIWI's engagement with the controversial issue of female genital mutilation and deliberate disengagement from controversial reproductive rights issues. When the Clinton Administration left office, Loar became founding president of the Vital Voices Global Partnerships NGO. She currently works for a global engineering and consulting firm where she is vice president of Global Strategies.

Ruth Mandel, Interview at the Eagleton Institute of Politics, Rutgers University, May 6, 2010

Ruth Mandel, Governor's Professor of Politics at Rutgers University, developed and directed the Center for American Women and Politics at the Eagleton Institute from 1971 to 1994; she currently directs the Eagleton Institute. In 1993, President Clinton appointed Mandel as vice chair of the United States Holocaust Memorial Council and she served the council in that capacity until 2005. As director of the Center for American Women in Politics, Mandel focused on the center's mission to increase knowledge about, and promote the effectiveness of, women's participation in U.S. politics. Mandel discussed the 1992 election phenomenon known as the "Year of the Woman" when the number of women elected to office doubled women's numerical representation in U.S. Congress, and more women entered Washington government offices through Clinton Administration appointments, as well. Invited by an associate of Swanee Hunt, Mandel attended the 1997 "Vital Voices: Women in Democracy" conference in Vienna, and summarized conference discussions on women's political leadership for the conference final report. She noted that these discussions about women's political participation attempted to bridge significant historical and cultural differences, but were not always successful. She also noted that the conference presented important networking opportunities for various women leaders. Mandel remarked on the electrifying impact of Hillary Clinton's presence at the conference and the ways that Hillary Clinton raised the visibility of global women's issues during the 1990s that had both substantive and symbolic impact.

Ellen Marshall, Phone Interview, August 18, 2009

Ellen Marshall worked on the Washington staff for Colorado Representative, then Senator, Timothy Wirth in the 1980s and early 1990s. Marshall joined Wirth's State Department staff when he was appointed Undersecretary of State for the Global Affairs division. There, she was senior coordinator in the bureau for Population, Refugees and Migration Issues, and helped to prepare U.S. conference platforms and served on U.S. government delegations to the International Conference on Population and Development, the World Summit on Social

Development and the UN Fourth World Conference on Women. Marshall noted that the ICPD marked a "sea change" in both the U.S. government and the United Nations, in terms of accepting new language in UN conference documents that supported women's sexual and reproductive health rights, taking the language beyond support for women's "access to family planning," and integrating gender-conscious population policy with women in development programs. These issues were debated and discussed with NGOs that gained much greater access to U.S. government delegations under Tim Wirth's leadership at the Global Affairs division. Wirth also engaged with Catholic leaders and conservative politicians and tried to focus the critics on broad areas of agreement within the ICPD and subsequent conference documents. Marshall noted the "chilling effect" of the 1994 midterm elections and the assumption of power by conservative congressional leadership that reduced funding for some more progressive aid and population programming initiatives, and that funneled aid and U.S. government energy into less controversial areas that may have had lesser impact on improving women's lives. Marshall left government service in 1996 and worked at the Audubon Society and UN Foundation in the late 1990s. Having developed expertise on international women's sexual and reproductive health issues, she is a partner at Good Works Group and consults on these issues with nonprofit organizations such as the International Women's Health Coalition, on communications, strategy, public policy and fundraising.

Alice Miller, Phone Interview, May 26, 2010

With a law degree and background in sexuality, gender, health and women's human rights issues, Alice Miller has worked in academe (at Columbia University Schools of Law, Public Health and International and Public Affairs; the Sexuality and Rights Institute, in Pune, India; the International School, Summer Institute on Sexuality, Culture and Society, Amsterdam, The Netherlands; and the University of California at Berkeley Law School), as well as with policy advocacy groups and nongovernmental organizations (such as Amnesty International, Human Rights Watch, the International Human Rights Law Group, the Women's Institute for Leadership Development and the U.S. Center for Reproductive Rights). As a student of Joan Fitzpatrick, Miller was introduced to women's human rights issues in the 1980s when these issues began to attract global attention. As she began work with Amnesty International in the late 1980s, Miller emphasized the intersection at that time of the women's human rights movement with various concurrent social justice movements, especially those critiquing neoliberal economic structures as they negatively impacted women's development that were initiated in the global South. She noted that these were critiques--focusing on economic justice issues within a women's human rights framework--that the Clinton Administration was not receptive to. However, in other areas, women's NGOs influenced the administration's foreign policy. Women's NGO activists (such as those in Amnesty International, Human Rights Watch, the National Spiritual Assembly of the Baha'i), advocated for an office focusing on women's human rights and pushed for inclusion of women's human rights reporting in the State Department Country Reports prepared by U.S. embassies abroad, that made women's human rights issues visible and that allowed women's NGOs to ask questions regarding women's human rights as matter of concern to U.S. foreign policy. Miller also noted that the Clinton Administration adopted positions regarding women's sexual and reproductive rights at the 1994 International Conference for Population and Development that were "relatively in line" with those of U.S. based women's rights groups, although there were problems with the administration's unwillingness to deal with economic development issues at the ICPD, as well. Miller discussed U.S. political opposition to ratification of the Convention to Eliminate All Forms of Discrimination Against Women and the Convention on the Rights of the Child, two conventions that were important to women's NGOs and that the Clinton Administration supported but could not move forward through the Senate ratification process. Finally, Miller noted that Theresa Loar consulted with women's NGOs on the administration's anti-trafficking initiatives at the end of the decade, and was receptive to the issues that NGOs raised in regard to language proposed for the U.S. anti-trafficking legislation.

Karen Mulhauser, Interview at the office of Mulhauser and Associates, Washington DC, September 22, 2009

Karen Mulhauser was the executive director of the National Abortion Rights Action League (NARAL), from 1975 to 1981, directed the Center for Education on Nuclear War and Citizens Against Nuclear War during the 1980s, and has been a consultant to nonprofit organizations (such as CARE, AWID, Women Thrive) and progressive political candidates and campaigns (including Eleanor Holmes Norton and Democratic Party presidential tickets), providing management assistance, strategic and program planning and evaluation, meeting planning and facilitation, fundraising and coalition building advice since the late 1980s. In 1989 Mulhauser founded the Women's Information Network to develop mentoring networks among women who hold senior positions in support of young women's professional advancement in Washington DC and to promote progressive social and political activism. WIN has been active throughout the 1990s and 2000s. Mulhauser noted several disturbing developments of in the last few decades, such as the negative and immobilizing effects that the development of "single issue politics," such as opposition to abortion, has had on various progressive issues, such as U.S. ratification of the Convention to Eliminate All Forms of Discrimination Against Women and support for reproductive health care. However, she also emphasized the concurrent growth of support for global girls' education opportunities which opened the door for women's global advancement. Mulhauser helped to organize a conference attended by government and NGO leaders on the topic of girls' education for the Academy for Educational Development that took place in Washington DC in 1997. In the 2000s, Mulhauser has continued to consult with USAID, helping USAID to leverage its policy influence with private foundation donors who provide more foreign aid monies than government sources.

Alyse Nelson, Interview at the offices of Vital Voices Global Partnerships, Washington DC, November 28, 2006

Alyse Nelson is the president and CEO of Vital Voices Global Partnership, the NGO that was created out of the Vital Voices: Women in Democracy Initiative established in 1997 by the Clinton Administration. As a college student, Alyse Nelson attended the UN Fourth World Conference on Women and NGO forum in Beijing and was inspired by First Lady Hillary Clinton's address to world governments and NGOs in support of women's human rights. Her enthusiasm for international women's issues continued when she met Theresa Loar and began to work on Loar's staff at the President's Interagency Council on Women in 1996 following the Beijing conference. Nelson was among the group of U.S. government women who organized the first Vital Voices: Women in Democracy conference held in Vienna in 1997. Following that first conference, Nelson worked on subsequent Vital Voices conferences and global women's leadership development programs with Loar at the State Department. In 2000, when the Clinton Administration prepared to leave office, Nelson helped to reorganize the Vital Voices program into a nongovernmental organization whose purpose continues to be hosting forums and leadership training with women in countries around the globe and to develop women's "social capital" through networking among women in business, politics and social movements. Nelson noted the importance of visible and charismatic leaders, such as Hillary Clinton, in building support for global women's empowerment, but she also noted that using "strategic" formulations to present women's empowerment goals in positive language can overcome male resistance (i.e. "investing in women is a smart investment"; women are not "victims" but "part of the solution" to social and political problems). Nelson praised Loar's ability to focus State Department attention on women's human rights issues by calling attention to the "mandate" created by Hillary Clinton and Madeleine Albright who promoted women's issues after the Beijing conference. With Loar's persistent encouragement, more senior officials in embassies and State Department bureaus began to ask questions about women, wove information about women into their speeches and included more content on women in their country reports. Nelson explained that the Vital Voices NGO is non-partisan, and it consciously worked to forge relationships with the George W. Bush Administration State Department with support from Undersecretary of State Paula Dobriansky from 2001 to 2009, as it continued to work with the Obama Administration beginning in 2009. Vital Voices continues to work with U.S. embassies to identify, support and train women leaders in their countries, which is presented as supporting U.S. democracy promotion goals, but it has also greatly expanded its partnerships with private foundation donors and with other NGOs.

Regan Ralph, Phone Interview, May 14, 2010

Beginning in 1992, Regan Ralph worked with the Women's Rights Division at Human Rights Watch, first with the division's director Dorothy Q. Thomas, and then as director of the division. At Human Rights Watch during the Clinton Administration tenure, she worked on campaigns to ensure that rape and sexual assault of women in conflict zones were prosecuted as war crimes, and to recognize gender-based persecution as legitimate grounds when refugees seek asylum. Ralph discussed the founding of the Office of International Women's Issues at the State Department, and the role played by the Women's Rights Division at Human Rights Watch that lobbied Congress to fund the office and helped to draft language for the Fiscal Year 1994 Foreign Aid Appropriations bill. She also noted the important role played by Theresa Loar in the second half of the decade, expanding the size and influence of the OIWI within the Department. At that time, Loar had the critical support of First Lady Hillary Clinton and Secretary of State Madeleine Albright who spoke about women's human rights issues "all the time," but Loar also funneled information from NGOs regarding global women's issues to senior leaders in the department and administration. Timothy

Wirth, Undersecretary of State for Global Affairs, had opened up the department generally to NGOs' perspectives on policy issues as the department prepared the U.S. delegation to the International Conference on Population and Development, and that led to a paradigm shift in the administration's understanding of "women's human rights," and to understanding that domestic violence directed against women was a violation of human rights, wartime rape and other violence against women was a violation of human rights, etc. NGOs provided research and prepared position papers, testified before congressional committees, visited State Department officials, helped draft legislation, and, ultimately had an impact on U.S. government policy rhetoric in the 1990s. Nonetheless, Ralph noted that in specific situations where violations occurred, dealing with specific governments, often the women's human rights rhetoric was not matched by U.S. government action. After leaving Human Rights Watch in 2001, she developed expertise in women's reproductive health and rights and was vice president for Health and Reproductive Rights at the National Women's Law Center in Washington D.C. in the 2000s. In 2009, Ralph founded and is executive director of the Fund for Global Human Rights, a grant making organization that connects donors with grass roots human rights organizations in Africa, South and Southeast Asia and Latin America.

Donna Shalala, Phone Interview, June 29, 2010

Donna Shalala entered government service from a career in higher education, as a political scientist with expertise in the political economy of state and local governments. After holding several faculty positions, Shalala served in Carter Administration from 1977 to 1980 as assistant secretary for Public Development and Research at the department of Housing and Urban Development. When Carter left office, she went on to serve as president of Hunter College in the 1980s, and was chancellor of the University of Wisconsin at Madison from 1987 to 1993. At that point, President Clinton appointed her to his cabinet as secretary of Health and Human Services, a position she held throughout Clinton's eight years in office. During those years, in addition to administering HHS programs, Shalala was co-chair of the U.S. delegation to the Fourth World Conference on Women and spoke on a panel sponsored by the World Health Organization on "Women and AIDS." She chaired the President's Interagency Council on Women from 1995 through 1996. Donna Shalala noted the strong contingent of feminist women who held leading cabinet positions in the Clinton Administration, as well as First Lady Hillary Clinton and her Chief of Staff Melanne Verveer, all beneficiaries of changes wrought by the U.S. feminist movement, who all provided strong support for a broad range of women's human rights. At HHS, Shalala was focused on promoting maternal and child health, women's education, and women's access to family planning options, in the United States and around the world. Through an interagency task force, Shalala worked with Attorney General Janet Reno addressing violence against women. As a board member of the International Women's Health Coalition, Shalala was open to NGOs' influence. During her tenure at HHS, an office was established to focus on women's health issues and government-funded women's health centers were established around the country. In 2001, Shalala became president of the University of Miami and she has continued public service with election to the Council on Foreign Relations, the National Academy of Education, the National Academy of Public Administration, the American Academy of Arts and Sciences, the American Philosophical Society, the National Academy of Social Insurance, the American Academy of Political and Social Science, the Institute of Medicine of the National Academy of Sciences. In 2007, President George W. Bush appointed Shalala to co-chair the Commission on Care for Returning Wounded Warriors; in 2008, President Bush awarded Donna Shalala the Presidential Medal of Freedom.

Wendy Sherman, Interview at the Offices of the Albright Group, Washington DC, July 17, 2009

Unlike the other women interviewed for this project, Wendy Sherman did not work specifically on "global gender policy" issues during the Clinton Administration. Trained in the field of social work, Sherman worked as chief of staff for Congresswoman Barbara Mikulski, and managed Mikulski's successful Senate campaign in 1987. Sherman went on to work for the Democratic National Committee in the late 1980s, and then as a political communications consultant in the private sphere during George Herbert Walker Bush's presidency. When Bill Clinton took office in 1993, Sherman went to work for the State Department with Secretary of State Warren Christopher, as assistant secretary of state for Legislative Affairs 1993 to 1996, where she promoted the administration's goals to obtain congressional support and funding for the former Soviet states, support for the Dayton Accords, and support for the North American Free Trade Act. After Madeleine Albright became secretary of state, she brought Sherman back into the State Department as counselor, at the rank of ambassador. Sherman advised Albright on a wide range of foreign policy and national security issues, and served as special advisor to President Clinton and policy coordinator on North Korea nuclear disarmament negotiations in 2000. Sherman noted that more women entered the ranks of foreign policy making in the 1990s partly as a consequence of the second wave of the U.S. feminist movement and the increasing number of women who had been promoted through the ranks of government. Secretary Christopher appointed women to positions in the State Department that women had not previously held (such as assistant secretary for Legislative Affairs), and Madeleine Albright's strong performance as U.S. ambassador to the United Nations and then as secretary of state proved women's competence in these highest leadership positions dealing with national security. As special advisor to the president and secretary of state in national security negotiations with North Korea in 2000, Sherman was still the only woman at the negotiating tables along with Japanese and Korean diplomats. Nonetheless, the presence of Sherman and Secretary Albright helped to confirm the feminist assertions that "every foreign policy issue is a women's issue." Sherman serves as undersecretary of state for Political Affairs in the Barack Obama Administration.

Linda Tarr-Whelan, Phone Interview, March 29, 2010

Trained as a nurse, Linda Tarr-Whelan has worked in the fields of management, labor negotiation and education, as well as health care. She entered government service during the Carter Administration as deputy assistant to Sarah Weddington for Women's Concerns at the White House and served at the Clinton-appointed ambassador to the United Nations Commission on the Status of Women from 1996 to 2000. Tarr-Whelan noted the importance of a receptive political climate in terms of advancing women's interests through government action. While the political climate was not receptive in the 1980s, when the Clinton Administration took office in 1993, the climate began to change. This was due, in part, to pressures from the women's constituency that elected Bill Clinton to office, from strong women representatives in U.S. Congress, from foundations such as the Ford Foundation that financially supported women's development projects, and also from the United Nations conferences held in the 1990s that mobilized women's NGOs and focused government attention on women's issues. In 1994, Tarr-Whelan became involved in U.S. preparations for the Beijing Fourth World Conference on Women. Although the 1993 Human Rights Conference and the 1994 International Conference on Population and Development established women's rights within a human rights framework, First Lady Hillary Clinton's speech at the Beijing conference "galvanized" governments' attention to women's human rights issues even as the language of policy makers was shifting to focus on women's "contributions" to development. At the UN CSW meetings Tarr-Whelan led the way in presenting the Clinton Administration's objections to the Taliban government in Afghanistan, because of the Taliban's violations of women's human rights. She also advocated on behalf of the Optional Protocol to the Convention on the Elimination of All forms of Discrimination Against Women (CEDAW), which established procedures for individual women or groups of women to lodge complaints with the monitoring Committee on the Elimination of Discrimination against Women, and for the committee to launch inquiries when governments have adopted the convention. As U.S. ambassador to the CSW, Tarr-Whelan supported the UN adoption of the Protocol even though the United States had not ratified the Convention. Also as US ambassador, Tarr-Whelan set the practice of holding daily briefings for NGOs when the CSW was in session that provided opportunities for NGOs from the United States and from other nations to share their perspectives with U.S. government policymakers. Tarr-Whelan is currently a senior fellow at Demos policy advocacy organization and is the author of *Women Lead the Way: Your Guide to Stepping Up to Leadership and Changing the World.*

Marie Wilson, Phone Interview, July 21, 2009

Marie Wilson, president of the Ms. Foundation from 1984 to 2004, founded the White House Project in 1998 to promote women's leadership in all realms of society, including the highest ranks of political leadership, in order to strengthen and fulfill the promise of democracy. Although her activism on behalf of women focused mainly on U.S. domestic policy, she became interested in microfinancing as a strategy to aid low income women and to promote women's economic literacy in the 1990s. Wilson's interest in linking national women's economic issues, especially in regard to unpaid work, to international women's issues grew with preparations for the UN Fourth World Conference on Women in the mid-1990s, which she attended as a NGO member of the U.S. delegation. Wilson noted the expanded collaborations among women's NGOs with the U.S. government, sharing research and debating platform positions on issues such as violence against women, microenterprise, immigration issues, etc. as the U.S. delegation prepared for the Beijing conference, and she noted the ways that the conference rallied U.S. women's strong support for Senate ratification of the Convention on the Elimination of All forms of Discrimination Against Women (CEDAW). This campaign, she explained, has not been successful because of the misconception that U.S. women face no barriers to entering the highest ranks of leadership and because strong women were very visible in the Clinton Administration cabinet and this led to conservative backlash that successfully pulled U.S. national politics to the right of the political spectrum. Wilson also discussed First Lady Hillary Clinton's leadership at the Beijing conference and Clinton's focus on women's human rights that came from issues promoted by NGOs and activist women such as Charlotte Bunch. Wilson also noted Madeleine Albright's leadership at the conference that focused attention on the rights of women with disabilities. Wilson believed the most important result of the Beijing conference in terms of the U.S. government was that it led to the establishment of the President's Interagency Council on Women that focused a gender lens on U.S. policies across the spectrum of the cabinet agencies. She also noted that international feminist activists began advocating for attention to "human security" after the Beijing conference, in terms of resolving violent conflicts and wars of the decade. She also shared that although she was not personally involved, the Ms. Foundation supported the State Department's Vital Voices: Women in Democracy Initiative. After 1998, Wilson directed her focus to the White House Project.

Melanne Verveer, Phone Interview, May 27, 2008

Melanne Verveer was chief of staff to First Lady Hillary Clinton in the 1990s but she had worked in public policy organizations and as a legislative staff aide in Washington DC prior to the Clinton Administration's tenure in office. A strong supporter of women's human rights and women's economic empowerment, two key themes in U.S. foreign policy of the 1990s, Melanne Verveer worked with the President's Interagency Council on Women from its inception in 1995, and coordinated Hillary Clinton's participation in the State Department's Vital Voices: Women in Democracy Initiative, from the time of the first Vital Voices conference held in Vienna in 1997, onward. When President Clinton left office, Verveer went on to lead the Vital Voices Global Partnerships NGO as its Chief Executive Officer, the position she held at the time of this interview. Verveer discussed the first lady's growing interest in global women's issues in the mid-1990s. These interests were driven by Hillary Clinton's support of microfinance strategies to aid low income women and by trips to South Asia and meetings with Muhammed Yunus and the women of SEWA, the Self-Employed Women's Association, in Islamabad, Pakistan. Because Hillary Clinton was so high-profile, the first lady's interests drove forward many government initiatives, such as the President's Interagency Council on Women that organized to support U.S. government Commitments to Women made at the UN Fourth World Conference on Women, and the Vital Voices Initiative. Vital Voices was first conceived by Hillary Clinton's friend, Ambassador Swanee Hunt who hosted the first conference that became a prototype for programs that followed in Northern Ireland, the Baltic States, etc., and the Initiative became an "all-consuming" interest for Hillary Clinton. Moreover, at the first Vital Voices conference, Clinton's interest in the problem of trafficking in women was sparked by Ukrainian women she met there and with whom she discussed the growing problem of sex trafficking in former Soviet republics and in Eastern Europe. This trafficking problem, too, became a focus of activism at the State Department's Office of International Women's Issues from 1998 to 2000. During George W. Bush Administration, Verveer continued to work with top officials at the State Department who engaged in global women's issues including Undersecretary of State for Global Affairs Paula Dobriansky who focused on anti-trafficking initiatives and on establishing public leadership opportunities for women in Afghanistan, and Ambassador Shirin Tahir-Kheli, who worked for Secretary of State Condoleeza Rice on Women's Empowerment in Middle Eastern Partnerships countries. At the time that this interview took place, during the Bush Administration's tenure in office, Verveer emphasized the fruitful collaborations between women's NGOs, business and other private partners and the U.S. federal government that continued to push forward a women's empowerment agenda. When the Barack Obama Administration took office in 2009, Verveer was appointed ambassador to the Office of Global Women's Issues (formerly the Office of International Women's Issues) at the State Department, led by Secretary of State Hillary Clinton. Among other organizations, Verveer is a member of the Council on Foreign Relations and the Women's Foreign Policy Group.

Appendix B: U.S. Delegation to the International Women's Year Conference

Delegation Leadership

Pat Hutar, U.S. Ambassador to UN Commission on the Status of Women, co-head
Daniel Parker, Administrator for the U.S. Agency for International Development, co-head
Jewel Lafontant, Deputy Solicitor General for the Department of Justice
Jill Ruckelshaus, Presiding Officer for the National Commission on the Observance of International Women's Year

Delegation Representatives

Virginia R. Allan, Deputy Assistant Secretary of State for Public Affairs
Ruth Clusen, President League of Women Voters
Arvonne S. Fraser, former President for the Women's Equity Action League
Joan Goodin, Assistant Director for the AFL-CIO International Affairs Department
Rita Hauser, U.S. Advisory Commission on International Educational and Cultural Affairs
Rita Johnston, Vice-Chair for the Inter-American Commission of Women
Joseph Jova, U.S. Ambassador to Mexico
Patricia Lindh, Special Assistant to the President for Women at the White House
Carmen Maymi, Director for the Department of Labor Women's Bureau

Virginia Trotter, Assistant Secretary for Education at the Department of Health, Education and Welfare
Barbara M. White, Alternate U.S. Ambassador for Political Affairs for the U.S. Mission to the UN

Congressional Advisers

Birch Bayh, U.S. Senator Indiana
Charles Percy, U.S. Senator Illinois
Bella Abzug, U.S. Representative New York
Margaret Heckler, U.S. Representative Massachusetts

Delegation Advisers

Ruth Bacon, Director for the U.S. Center for International Women's Year
Muriel Berman, Vice-Chair for the Women for Pennsylvania Bicentennial
Harrison Burgess, Bureau of International Organizations at the Department of State
Emily Carssow, Assistant Professor of Law at the University of Georgia
Catherine East, Deputy Coordinator for the International Women's Year Secretariat
Gilda Bojorquez Gjurich, National Commission on the Observance of International Women's Year
Mary Haselton, Bureau of Oceans and International Environmental and Scientific Affairs at the Department of State
Carl Hemmer, Bureau of Population and Humanitarian Assistance at the U.S. Agency for International Development
Shirley Hendsch, Bureau of International Organizations at the Department of State
Marion N. Javits, New York
Karen Keesling, Director of Women's Programs at the White House
Nira Long, Coordinator for Women in Development at the U.S. Agency for International Development
Mildred Marcy, Coordinator for International Women's Year Secretariat
Morag Simchak, Office of Labor Affairs at the U.S. Agency for International Development
Sally Warner, Bureau of International Organizations at the Department of State
Guy Wiggins, U.S. Mission to the UN

Appendix C: National Commission on the Observance of International Women's Year

Appointed by President Gerald Ford, serving from January 1975 to July 1976

Jill Ruckelshaus, Presiding Officer
Alan Alda
Ethel Allen
Anne L. Armstrong
Margaret Long Arnold
Elizabeth Athansakos
Barbara R. Berman
Patricia T. Carbine
Weston Christopherson
Mary Stallings Coleman
Audrey Rowe Colom
Helen K. Copely
Richard Cornuelle
Winfield C. Dunn
Casey Eike
Paula Gibson
Gilda Bojorquez Gjurich
Ella T. Grasso
Hanna Holborn Gray
Martha Griffiths
Katherine Hepburn
Lenore Hershey
Velma Murphey Hill

Patricia Hutar
Rita Zimmer Johnston
Ellen Groves Kirby
Dorothy Vale Kissinger
Clare Boothe Luce
William Crawford Mercer
Ersa Hines Poston
Sister Joel Read
Betty L. Smith
Mary Louise Smith
Annie Dodge Wauneka
Gerridee Wheeler
Congressional Representatives
Birch Bayh U.S. Senator Indiana
Charles H. Percy U.S. Senator Illinois
Bella S. Abzug U.S. Representative New York
Margaret M. Heckler U.S. Representative Massachusetts

Appointed by President Jimmy Carter, serving from March 1977 to March 1978

Bella Abzug, Presiding Officer
Ruth Abram, Executive Director Women's Action Alliance
Ethel Allan
Margaret Long Arnold
Elizabeth Athansakos
Betty Blanton
Liz Carpenter
John Mack Carter
Seymour Chassler
Ruth Clusen
Audrey Rowe Colom
Jane Culbreth
Harry T. Edwards
Casey Eike
Beverley Everett
March K. Fong Eu
Betty Ford
Bernice S. Frieder
Paula Gibson
Martha Griffiths
Gilda Bojorquez Gjurich

Dorothy Hawner
Rhea Mojica Hammer
LaDonna Harris
Lenore Hershey
Velma Murphy Hill
Koryne Horbal
Patricia Hutar
Mildred Jeffrey
Jeffalyn Johnson
Rita Johnson
Coretta Scott King
Ellen Groves Kirby
Dorothy Vale Kissinger
Mary Anne Krupsak
Margaret J. Mealey
Jean O'Leary
Clare Booth Luce
Mildred Persinger
Connie Plunkett
Ersa S. Poston
Cecelia DeBurciago Preciado
Clare Randall
Alice Rossi
Jill Ruckelshaus
Gloria Scott
Eleanor Smeal
Betty Smith
Jean Stapleton
Gloria Steinem
Ethel Taylor
Carmen Delgado Votaw
Annie Dodge Wauneka
Gerridee Wheeler
Addie Wyatt

Congressional Representatives

Birch Bayh U.S. Senator Indiana
Charles H. Percy U.S. Senator Illinois
Elizabeth Holtzman U.S. Representative New York
Margaret M. Heckler U.S. Representative Massachusetts

Appendix D: U.S. Delegations to UN World Conferences in the 1990s

Conference on Environment and Development, Rio de Janeiro, Brazil, June 3-14, 1992

(incomplete list)

Delegation Leadership

William Reilly, Administrator of the U.S. Environmental Protection Agency, chair and head

Curtis Bohlen, Assistant Secretary of State for Oceans and International Environmental and Scientific Affairs, coordinator

Ambassador Robert Ryan, Oceans and International Environmental and Scientific Affairs

Michael Young, Deputy Undersecretary of State for Economic Affairs, alternate head

Government Delegates

Carla Hills, Secretary of Housing and Urban Development

Congressional Representatives

Al Gore, U.S. Senator Tennessee

John Kerry, U.S. Senator Massachusetts

Timothy Wirth, U.S. Senator Colorado

George Miller, U.S. House of Representatives California

Nongovernmental Delegates

Michael K. Dorsey

World Conference on Human Rights, Vienna, Austria, June 14-23, 1993

(incomplete list)
Delegation Leadership
Warren Christopher, Secretary of State, chair and head
Timothy Wirth, Undersecretary of State for Global Affairs
John Shattuck, Assistant Secretary of State for Human Rights and Humanitarian Affairs
Arvonne Fraser, U.S. Ambassador to the UN Commission on the Status of Women

International Conference on Population and Development, Cairo, Egypt, September 5-13, 1994

(incomplete list)
Delegation Leadership
Al Gore, Vice President, chair and head
Timothy Wirth, Undersecretary of State for Global Affairs
Government Delegates
Phyllis Oakley, Assistant Secretary of State for Population, Refugee, and Migration
Ellen Marshall, Senior Coordinator for Population, Refugees and Migration
Edward S. Walker, U.S. Ambassador to Egypt
Congressional Representatives
John Kerry, U.S. Senator Massachusetts
Nongovernmental Delegates
Peggy McDowell Curlin, Center for Population and Development Activities
Bella Abzug, Women's Environment and Development Organization
Adrienne Germain, International Women's Health Coalition
Eleanor Hinton Hoyt, National Council of Negro Women
Susan Sechler, Pew Global Stewardship Initiative
Victoria Markell, Population Action International

World Social Summit for Development, Copenhagen, Denmark, March 6-12, 1995

(incomplete list)
Delegation Leadership
Al Gore, Vice President, chair and head

First Lady Hillary Rodham Clinton

Government Delegates

Ellen Marshall, Senior Coordinator for Population, Refugees and Migration

Melinda Kimble, Deputy Assistant Secretary for International Organization Affairs

Fourth World Conference on Women, Beijing, People's Republic of China, September 4-15, 1995

Delegation Leadership

First Lady Hillary Rodham Clinton, honorary chair

Madeleine K. Albright, U.S. Ambassador to the United Nations, chair and head

Donna Shalala, Secretary of Health and Human Services, co-chair

Carol Browner, Administrator of the Environmental Protection Agency, co-chair

Timothy Wirth, Undersecretary of State for Global Affairs, alternate head and alternate chair

Marjorie Margolies-Mezvinsky, former Member of Congress from Pennsylvania, deputy chair

Veronica Biggins, Executive Search Consultant, Heidrick & Struggles, former Assistant to the President and Director of Presidential Personnel at the White House, vice chair

Geraldine A. Ferraro, U.S. Ambassador to the UN Human Rights Commission, vice chair

Thomas H. Kean, President of Drew University, former Governor of New Jersey, vice chair

Government Delegates

Evan Bloom, Attorney Advisor for Department of State

Iris J. Burnett, Chief of Staff for U.S. Information Agency

Bonnie J. Campbell, Director for Department of Justice Violence Against Women Office

Mary Curtin, Human Rights Officer

Nils Daulaire, Deputy Assistant Administrator for U.S. Agency for International Development

Kathleen Hendrix, Special Assistant for the Global Conference Secretariat

Judith Heumann, Assistant Secretary for the Department of Education Special Education and Rehabilitative Services

Melinda Kimble, Deputy Assistant Secretary for International Organization Affairs

Sharon Kotok, Officer in Charge of International Women's Programs for International Organization Affairs
Sarah Kovner, Special Assistant to the Secretary of the Department of Health and Human Services
Madeleine M. Kunin, Deputy Secretary for the Department of Education
Ginger Lew, General Counsel for the Department of Commerce
Victor Marrero, U.S. Ambassador to the UN Economic and Social Council
Ellen Marshall, Senior Coordinator for the Bureau of Population, Refugees and Migration
Jean Nelson, Counselor to the Administrator of the Environmental Protection Agency
Karen Nussbaum, Director of the Department of Labor Women's Bureau
Jan Piercy, U.S. Executive Director of the World Bank
Sally Shelton, Assistant Administrator for the U.S. Agency for International Development
David Stewart, Assistant Legal Advisor for the Department of State
Bisa Williams Manigault, Advisor to the U.S. Mission to the UN

Nongovernmental Delegates

Laila Al-marayati, M.D., assistant professor at the University of Southern California School of Medicine; vice-chair for the Muslim Women's League
Maria Antionetta Berriozabal, U.S. delegate to the Inter-American Commission on Women, Hispanas Unidas
Myrna Blyth, editor-in-chief for the Ladies' Home Journal
Elizabeth J. Coleman, chairman of the board of directors and chief executive officer, Maidenform, Inc. and vice chair for the President's Export Council
Lynn Cutler, senior vice president for The Kamber Group
Felice D. Gaer, director for the Jacob Blausteen Institute for the Advancement of Human Rights of the American Jewish Committee
Adrienne Germain, vice president and program director for the International Women's Health Coalition
Arthenia L. Joyner, attorney for Stewart, Joyner, Jordan-Holmes
Sister Dorothy Ann Kelly, president for the College of New Rochelle
Dorothy V. Lamm, columnist for the Denver *Post*
Marilyn Monahan, secretary-treasurer for the National Education Association
San Juanita Munoz, youth delegate and fellow at the Carnegie Mellon University, Heinz School of Public Policy
Julia Taft, president and chief executive officer for InterAction, The American Council for Voluntary International Action

Linda Tarr-Whelan, president and chief executive officer for the Center for Policy Alternatives
Virginia Trotter Betts, president for the American Nurses Association
Susan Roosevelt Weld, professor of Chinese and Japanese Law at Boston College
Marie C. Wilson, president of the Ms. Foundation for Women

US Delegation to the Beijing + Five Conference, New York , New York, June 5-9, 2000

Delegation Leadership
Madeleine K. Albright, Secretary of State, chair
Donna Shalala, Secretary of Health and Human Services, co-chair
Richard Holbrooke, U.S. Ambassador to the United Nations, co-chair
Linda Tarr-Whelan, U.S. Ambassador to the UN Commission on the Status of Women, deputy chair
Betty King, U.S. Ambassador to the UN Economic and Social Council, deputy chair
Theresa Loar, Director of the President's Interagency Council on Women, director
Government Delegates
Katherine Blakeslee, Director of the Office of Women in Development at the U.S. Agency for International Development
Katherine Grove, Legal Advisor for the Department of State
Kathleen Hendrix, Advisor to the President's Interagency Council on Women
Judith Heumann, Assistant Secretary for the Department of Education Special Education and Rehabilitative Services
Sharon Kotok, Officer in Charge of International Women's Programs for International Organization Affairs
Sarah Kovner, Special Assistant to the Secretary of Health and Human Services
Geri Palast, Assistant Secretary of Labor for Congressional and Intergovernmental Affairs
Margaret Pollack, Director of the Office of Population, Bureau of Population, Refugees, and Migration
Avraham Rabby, Social Affairs Officer for the U.S. Mission to the UN
Lidia Soto-Harmon, Deputy Director for the President's Interagency Council on Women
Barbara Turner, Acting Assistant Administrator for the Office of Women in Development at the U.S. Agency for International Development.
Congressional Delegates

Barbara Lee, U.S. Senator California
Carolyn Maloney, U.S. Representative New York
Joseph Crowley, U.S. Representative New York
Nongovernmental Delegates
Caryl Garcia, Association for Women in Development
Kate Washburn, Women's Institute for Leadership Development (WILD) for Human Rights
Jane Smith, National Council for Negro Women
Ritu Sharma, Women's EDGE, The Coalition for Women's Economic Development and Global Equality

Beijing + 5 Host Committee

Committee Leadership
Carolyn Maloney, U.S. Representative New York, honorary co-chair
Ellen Chesler, Open Society Institute, co-chair
Sr. Dorothy Ann Kelly, President College of New Rochelle, co-chair
Promita Sengupta, coordinator
Government Members (ex-officio status)
Betty King, U.S. Ambassador to the United Nations
Sarah Kovner, Special Assistant to the Secretary of Health and Human Services
Ann Lewis, Counselor to the President, The White House
Theresa Loar, Director of the President's Interagency Council on Women
Linda Tarr-Whelan, U.S. Ambassador to the UN Commission on the Status of Women
Nongovernmental Members
Barbara Arnwine, Lawyers' Committee on Human Rights
Linda Basch, National Council for Research on Women
Kathy Bonk, Communications Consortium Media Center
Charlotte Bunch, Center for Women's Global Leadership
Leslie Calman, National Organization for Women
Miriam Chamberlain, National Council for Research on Women
Joan Dunlop, Rockefeller Brothers Fund
Felice Gaer, Jacob Blaustein Institute for the Advancement of Human Rights
Adrienne Germain, International Women's Health Coalition
Gilda Alacon Glasinovich, Alianza Latinamericana
Frances Kisslin, Catholics for Free Choice
Yolanda Moses, American Council on Education
Anne Mosle, Center for Policy Alternatives
Helen Neuborne, Ford Foundation

Rebecca Nichols, Conference of NGOs in consultation with UN Economic and Social Council
Kimberly Otis, The Sister Fund
Mary Purcell, International Federation of University Women
Anika Rahman, Center for Reproductive Law and Policy
Kavita Ramdas, Global Fund for Women
Julia Scott, National Black Women's Health Project
Emily Tynes, Communications Consortium Media Center
June Zeitlin, Women's Environment and Development Organization

Bibliography

"A Key Vote on Family Planning." *Washington Post*, February 1, 1997.

"About Trafficking in Women and Children, U.S. Government Definitions." http://secretary.state.gov/www/picw/trafficking/def.htm .

Abzug, Bella S. "To Women's NGO Caucus Members." August 5, 1994. http://www.iisd.ca/Cairo/womncauc.txt .

"AID Program for Integration of Women in Development: Strategies for Access to PPC/WID Assistance." USAID-WID, Fiscal Year 1989. USAID Development Experience Clearinghouse.

Albright, Madeleine K. "Address to the Roslyn Carter Distinguished Lecture Series." Atlanta, Georgia, December 3 1998.http://secretary.state.gov/www/statements/1998/981203.html.

———. "Advancing the Status of Women in the 21st Century." Remarks Upon Induction into the National Women's Hall of Fame, July 11, 1998. http://1997-2001.state.gov/www/statements/1998/980711.html.

———. "Building a Framework for American Leadership in the 21st Century." Statement before the House International Relations Committee, February 11, 1997. State Department *Dispatch*, (February 11, 1997).

———. "Charting Further Gains in the Status and Rights of Women." Remarks at the Center for National Policy breakfast, Washington DC, August 2, 1995. State Department *Dispatch* 6, no. 32 (August 7, 1995).

———. "Remarks at 6 + 2 Meeting on Afghanistan," United Nations, New York, September 15, 2000. U.S. Department of State. http://secretary.state.gov/www/statements/2000/000915a.html.

———. "Remarks at Special Session of the United Nations General Assembly on Women 2000: Beijing Plus Five." June 8, 2000. http://secretary.state.gov/www/statements/2000/000608.html .

———. "Remarks at Symposium on Pacesetting Women of the 20th Century." October 12, 2000. http://secretary.state.gov/www/statements/2000/001012a.html .

———. "Remarks at White House Project Forum." September 18, 2000. http://secretary.state.gov/www/statements/2000/000918a.html .

———. "Remarks before the International Leadership Forum for Women with Disabilities." Bethesda, Maryland, June 16, 1997. http://secretary.state.gov/www/statements/970616.html.

———. “Remarks before the Women’s Legal Defense Fund Award Luncheon.” June 13, 1997. http://secretary.state.gov/www/statements/970613a.html .

———. “Remarks before the Vital Voices Conference.” Washington, D.C., February 16, 2000. http://secretary.state.gov/www/statements/2000/000216a.html.

———. “Remarks on America’s Commitment, Marking International Women’s Day and Women’s History Month.” March 30, 2000. http://secretary.state.gov/www/picw/trafficking/mkage.htm .

———. “Remarks to the Women and Co. Foreign Executive Summit.” October 19, 2000. http://secretary.state.gov/www/statements/2000/001019.html .

———. “Statement to Vital Voices: Women in Democracy.” July 9, 1997. U.S. Department of State. http://1997-2001.state.gov/www/statements/970709b.html.

———. “Speech at the California Women’s Conference.” October 5, 1999. http://secretary.state.gov/www/statements/1999/991005a.html .

———. “The UN: What's in it for the U.S.?,” U.S. Permanent Representative to the United Nations Address to the Women’s Fund of the North Carolina Community Foundation, Raleigh, North Carolina, March 4, 1996. State Department *Dispatch* 7, no. 11 (March 11, 1996).

———. “The United States Assistance to Post-Conflict Societies.” Remarks at the U.S. Agency for International Development Conference on Promoting Democracy, Human Rights, and Reintegration in Post-Conflict Societies, Washington, DC., October 31, 1997. State Department *Dispatch* (December 1997).

———. “UN Security Council Adopts Resolution 1010 on Bosnia.” Statement by the U.S. Permanent Representative to the United Nations before the UN Security Council, New York City, August 10, 1995. State Department *Dispatch* 6, no. 34 (August 21, 1995).

———. “UN Security Council Establishes International Tribunal for Rwanda [SC Resolution 955].” Statement by the U.S. Permanent Representative to the United Nations before the UN Security Council, New York City, November 8, 1994. State Department *Dispatch* 5, no. 47 (November 21, 1994).

———. “U.S. and NATO Policy Toward the Crisis in Kosovo.” Statement Before the Senate Foreign Relations Committee, Washington DC, April 20, 1999. http://secretary.state.gov/www/statements/1999/990420.html .

Albright, Madeleine K. and Clinton, Hillary Rodham. “Media Roundtable.” (Hillary Rodham Clinton’s Closing Remarks). March 11, 1998. http://1997-2001.state.gov/www/statements/1998/980311.html .

———. “Remarks at special program in honor of International Women’s Day.” March 12, 1997. http://secretary.state.gov/www/statements/970312.html.

Aleinikoff, T. Alexander (Moderator). “Trafficking in Women: International Cooperation.” Carnegie Endowment for International Peace, Washington DC, September 29, 1997. http://www.carnegieendowment.org/1997/09/29/trafficking-in-women-international-cooperation/b4z .

Alonso, Harriet Hyman. Peace as a Woman’s Issue: A History of the US Movement for World Peace and Women’s Rights. Syracuse: Syracuse University Press, 1993.

Alston, Philip, ed. *The United Nations and Human Rights: A Critical Appraisal.* Oxford, UK: Oxford University Press, 1992.

Amanpour, Christiane. "Newseum War Stories: Christianne Amanpour." n.d. http://www.newseum.org/warstories/interviews/wmv/journalists/journalist movie.asp?id=23&anecdotenum=1&filename=bio_amanpour_1.
"An International Appeal: Word out of Bosnia." off our backs 22, no.10 (1992).
Antrobus, Peggy. *The Global Women's Movement: Origins, Issues and Strategies.* London: Zed Books, 2004.
Armitage, Richard. "Achieving National Consensus on the FREEDOM Support Act." Deputy Coordinator for Assistance to the Commonwealth of Independent States to Senate Appropriations Committee, May 6, 1992. State Department *Dispatch* 3, no. 19 (May 11, 1992).
"A Summary of the Proceedings at the Fourth Session of the UNCED Preparatory Committee." *Earth Summit Bulletin* 1, no. 27 (April 23, 1992).
Atwood, J. Brian. "USAID initiatives relating to Women and Gender 1990s, Gender Plan of Action." March 12, 1996. USAID Development Experience Clearinghouse. http://transition.usaid.gov/policy/ads/200/gplana96.pdf .
———. "U.S. Foreign Assistance Program Reform." Remarks at the Center for National Policy, December 14, 1994. State Department *Dispatch* 6, no. 1 (January 2, 1995).
Baker, James. "Efforts to Aid New Independent States at 'Defining Moment in History'." News Conference, April 1, 1992. State Department *Dispatch* 3, no. 14 (April 6, 1992).
———. "Securing a Democratic Peace." Secretary of State to Senate Foreign Relations Committee, April 9, 1992. State Department *Dispatch* 3, no. 15 (April 13, 1992).
———. "U.S. Foreign Policy Priorities and Fiscal Year 1991 Budget Request." Prepared Statement before the Senate Foreign Relations Committee, February 1, 1990. State Department *Dispatch* 1, no. 1 (September 3, 1990).
Banaszak, Lee Ann. *The Women's Movement Inside and Outside the State.* New York: Cambridge University Press, 2010.
Basu, Amrita, ed. *Women's Movements in the Global Era.* Boulder, CO: Westview Press, 2010.
Batinic, Jelena. "Feminism, Nationalism, and War: The 'Yugoslav Case' in Feminist Texts." *Journal of International Women's Studies* 3, no.1 (2001): 1-23.
Bayes, Abdul. "Beneath the Surface: Microcredit and Women's Empowerment." n.d., The Global Development Research Center. http://gdrc.org/icm/wind/beneath-surface.html.
Beckwith, Karen. "Mapping Strategic Engagements: Women's Movements and the State." *International Feminist Journal of Politics* 9, no. 3 (2007): 312-338.
Bendinger, Elmer. *No Time for Angels: The Tragicomic History of the League of Nations.* New York: Alfred A. Knopf, 1975.
Berkin, Carol R. and Lovett, Clara M. Lovett, eds. *Women, War and Revolution.* New York: Holmes & Meier Publishing, 1980.
Berkovitch, Nitza. *From Motherhood to Citizenship: Women's Rights and International Organizations.* Baltimore, MD: Johns Hopkins University Press, 1999.

Berkovitch, Nitza and Bradley, Karen. "The Globalization of Women's Status: Consensus/Dissensus in the World Policy." *Sociological Perspectives* 42, no. 3 (1999): 481-98.

Binder, David. "2 Republican Senators Caution Hillary Clinton on China Trip." *New York Times,* August 21, 1995.

Black, Allida. *Courage in a Dangerous World: The Political Writings of Eleanor Roosevelt.* New York: Columbia University Press, 1999.

Blumberg, Rae Lesser. "Making the Case for the Gender Variable: Women and the Wealth and Well-Being of Nations." Executive Summary, Office of Women in Development. October 1989. USAID Development Experience Clearinghouse.

Bohlen, Curtis. "US Prepares for UN Conference on Environment and Development." Assistant Secretary for Oceans, International Environment and Scientific Affairs, February 26, 1992. State Department *Dispatch* 3, no. 10 (March 9, 1992).

Bordin, Ruth. *Frances Willard: A Biography.* Chapel Hill, NC: University of North Carolina Press, 2001.

"Bosnia: 20,000 Women Raped." *off our backs* 23, no.2 (1993).

Branch, Taylor. *The Clinton Tapes: Wrestling History with the President.* New York: Simon and Schuster, 2009.

Bunch, Charlotte Papers (CB), 1967-1985. Arthur and Elizabeth Schlesinger Library on the History of Women in America. Radcliffe Institute for Advanced Study, Harvard University.

Bunch, Charlotte and Frost, Samantha. "Women's Human Rights: An Introduction." *International Encyclopedia of Women: Global Women's Issues and Knowledge* Volume 2. New York: Routledge, 2000, 1078-1083.

Bureau for Population, Refugees and Migration. "Fact Sheet: US-European Joint Information Campaign to Prevent Trafficking in Women." May 25, 1998. http://1997-2001.state.gov/www/global/prm/fs_women_052598.html.

Bush, George H. W. "America's Commitment to the Global Environment." Speech, June 1, 1992. State Department *Dispatch* 3, no. 22 (June 1, 1992).

———. "America's Role in the World." Address at West Point Military Academy, January 5, 1993. State Department *Dispatch* 4, no. 2 (January 11, 1992).

———. "Containing the Crisis in Bosnia and the Former Yugoslavia." News Conference, August 6, 1992. State Department *Dispatch* 3, no. 32 (August 10, 1992).

———. "Kuwait is Liberated." President's Address to the Nation, February 27, 1991. State Department *Dispatch* 2, no. 9 (March 4, 1991).

———. "No-Fly Zone in Southern Iraq." August 26, 1992. State Department *Dispatch* 3, no. 35 (August 31, 1992).

Calkin, Homer L. *Women in the Department of State: Their Role in American Foreign Affairs.* Washington DC: US Government Printing Office, 1978.

Cagatay, Nilufer, Gowen, Caren and Santiago, Aida. "The Nairobi Women's Conference: Toward a Global Feminism?" *Feminist Studies* 12 (Summer 1986): 401-412.

"Catherine A. MacKinnon to represent Croatian, Muslim wartime rape survivors." *off our backs* 23, no. 2 (February. 1993): 3.

Center for Reproductive Rights. "Legislation on Female Genital Mutilation in the United States." (2004). http://reproductiverights.org/sites/default/files/documents/pub_bp_fgmlawsusa.pdf .

Center for Women's Global Leadership Archives (CWGL), Special Collections and University Archives, Rutgers University. New Brunswick, New Jersey.

Christopher, Warren. "American Diplomacy and the Global Environmental Challenges of the 21st Century." Address to the alumni and faculty of Stanford University, Palo Alto, California, April 9, 1996. State Department *Dispatch* 7, no. 16 (April 15, 1996).

———. "Budget Priorities for Shaping a New Foreign Policy." Secretary of State to House Appropriations Committee, March 10, 1993. State Department *Dispatch* 4, no. 11 (March 15, 1993).

———. "Commemorating Human Rights Day." Remarks at a ceremony commemorating Human Rights Day at the State Department, December 12, 1996. State Department *Dispatch* 7, no. 51 (December 16, 1996).

———. "Democracy and Human Rights: Where America Stands." Address at the World Conference on Human Rights, Vienna, Austria, June 14, 1993. State Department *Dispatch* 4, no. 25 (June 21, 1993).

———. "Department of State Reorganization." Secretary of State to State Department Employees, February 5, 1993. State Department *Dispatch* 4, no. 6 (February 8, 1993).

———. "International Women's Day: Celebrating Remarkable Achievements." Welcoming remarks at International Women's Day ceremony, Washington, DC, March 11, 1996. State Department *Dispatch* 7, no. 12 (March 18, 1996).

———. "NATO and U.S. Foreign Policy." NATO Council, February 26, 1993. State Department *Dispatch* 4, no. 9 (March 1, 1993).

———. "New Steps Toward Conflict Resolution in the Former Yugoslavia." February 10, 1993. State Department *Dispatch* 4, no. 7 (February 15, 1993).

———. "Resumption of Mid-East Peace Negotiations." March 10, 1993. State Department *Dispatch* 4, no. 11 (March 15, 1993).

———. "The International Affairs Budget: Large Returns from a Small Investment." Statement before the Subcommittee on Commerce, Justice, State, the Judiciary, and Related Agencies of the House Appropriations Committee, Washington, DC, May 15, 1996. State Department *Dispatch* 7, no. 21 (May 20, 1996).

Christopher, Warren; Wirth, Timothy; and Shattuck, John. "Promoting Human Rights Reflects U.S. Ideals, Advances Interests." Excerpts from special briefing announcing transmittal to Congress of the 1995 Annual Country Reports on Human Rights Practices, Washington, DC, March 6, 1996. State Department *Dispatch* 7, no. 11 (March 11, 1996).

Clinton, Hillary Rodham. "Advancing the Progress of Women." Remarks to the Non-governmental Organizations Forum on Women, Huairou, China, September 6, 1995. State Department *Dispatch* 6, no. 36 (September 4, 1995).

———. "Announcement of U.S. Initiative to Expand Girls' and Women's Education in the Developing World." Department of State *Dispatch* 6, no. 13 (March 27, 1995).

———. "Combatting Human Trafficking," Organization for Security and Cooperation in Europe (OSCE), Istanbul, Turkey, November 18, 1999. http://secretary.state.gov/www/picw/trafficking/hrcosce.htm .

———. "Health Care Security for Women and Girls: An International Priority." Remarks to the World Health Organization Forum on Women and Health Security, Beijing, China, September 5, 1995. Department of State *Dispatch* 6, no. 36 (September 4, 1995).

———."Presidential Memorandum on Promoting Gender Equality and Empowering Women and Girls Globally." January 31, 2013. http://www.state.gov/secretary/rm/2013/01/203579.htm .

———. "Remarks at the [Global] Microcredit Summit," Washington DC, February 3, 1997.

———. "Remarks at special event to World Summit for Social Development in Copenhagen, Denmark." March 7, 1995. Department of State *Dispatch* 6, no.13 (March 27, 1995).

———. "Remarks to the United Nations Fourth World Conference on Women Plenary Session." September 5, 1995. http://clinton3.nara.gov/WH/EOP/First_Lady/html/China/plenary.html.

———. "Remarks at the Vital Voices Conference on Women and Democracy, Reykjavik, Iceland." October 10, 1999. http://secretary.state.gov/www/picw/trafficking/vvice.htm.

———. "The UN Women's Conference One Year Later." Washington DC, September 28, 1996. http://1997-2001.state.gov/www/picw/archives/960928.html.

———. "United Nations International Women's Day Speech on Women's Rights." New York, March 4, 1999. http://secretary.state.gov/www/picw/trafficking/hrc99.htm.

———. "Women's Economic Empowerment Zone." Remarks to the United Nations Development Fund for Women Panel, September 6, 1995. http://clinton3.nara.gov/WH/EOP/First_Lady/html/China/devfund.html.

Clinton, William Jefferson. "A New Era of Peril and Promise." President-elect before the Diplomatic Corps, Georgetown University, January 18, 1993. State Department *Dispatch* 4, no. 5 (February 1, 1993).

———. "An Historic Commitment to International Human Rights." March 11, 1998. http://1997-2001.state.gov/www/picw/archives/980311_clinton_hr_women.html.

———. "Family Planning Grants." To USAID Acting Administrator, January 22, 1993. State Department *Dispatch* 4, no. 5 (February 1, 1993).

———. "Memorandum to the Secretary of State, Attorney General, Administrator of the Agency for International Development, Director of the United States Information Agency." Press Release, March 11, 1998. http://1997-2001.state.gov/www/picw/archives/980311clinton_memo.html.

———. "Remarks by the President and First Lady on International Women's Day." Washington DC, March 11, 1998. http://1997-2001.state.gov/www/picw/archives/980311_clintons_women.html .

———. "Remarks by the President at Human Rights Day Event." December 10, 1996. http://secretary.state.gov/www/picw/archives/961210.html.

———. "Success of the NATO Air Campaign in Bosnia." Statement released by the White House, Office of the Press Secretary, Denver, Colorado, September 20, 1995. State Department *Dispatch* 6, no. 40 (October 2, 1995).

———. "The Balkan Proximity Peace Talks: A Defining Moment." Press Conference, Washington, DC, October 31, 1995. State Department *Dispatch* 6, no. 45 (November 6, 1995).

———. "The Crisis in Haiti, U.S. Interests in Haiti." Address to the Nation, Washington, DC, September 15, 1994. State Department *Dispatch* 5, no. 38 (September 19, 1994).

———. "The U.S. and Thailand: Making a Partnership Work for the Asia-Pacific." Address at Chulalongkorn University, Bangkok, Thailand, November 26, 1996. State Department *Dispatch* 7, no. 48 (November 25, 1996).

———. "U.S. Support for Implementing The Bosnian Peace Agreement." Address to the Nation, Washington, DC, November 27, 1995. State Department *Dispatch* 6, no. 48 (November 27, 1995).

Cohen, Robin and Rai, Shirin M., eds. *Global Social Movements.* London: Continuum, 2000.

Coll, Steve. *Ghost Wars: The Secret History of the CIA, Afghanistan, and Bin Laden, from the Soviet Invasion to September 10, 2001.* New York: Penguin, 2004.

Committee of Correspondence Records, 1952-1969. Sophia Smith Collection. Northampton, Massachusetts.

"Contract with Women of the USA." *off our backs* 26, no. 7 (July 1996).

Cook, Blanche Wiesen. "Bella Abzug, 1920-1998." Jewish Virtual Library. http://www.jewishvirtuallibrary.org/jsource/biography/abzug.html.

Copelon, Rhonda. "Rape and Gender Violence: From Impunity to Accountability in International Law." *Human Rights Dialogue* 2, no. 10 (2003). Carnegie Council for Ethics in International Affairs. http://www.carnegiecouncil.org/publications/archive/dialogue/2_10/articles/1052.html# .

Cowell, Alan. "Vatican Says Gore is Misrepresenting Population Talks." *New York Times,* September 1, 1994.

Crapol, Edward P., ed. *Women and Foreign Policy: Lobbyists, Critics and Insiders.* New York: Greenwood Press, 1987.

Crossette, Barbara. "Hillary Clinton Wins Praise at UN Meeting on Women." *New York Times* June 6, 2000.

Danguilan, Marilen J. *Women in Brackets: A Chronicle of Vatican Power and Control.* The Philippine Center for Investigative Journalism, 1997.

Dawkins Scully, Nan. "Micro Credit No Panacea for Poor Women." n.d., The Global Development Research Center. http://gdrc.org/icm/wind/micro.html.

Dawson, Ruth P. "When Women Gather: The NGO Forum of the Fourth World Conference on Women Beijing, 1995." *International Journal of Politics, Culture, and Society* 10, no. 1 (1996): 7-28.

Day, Shelagh. "Downstairs at the UN Human Rights Meeting." *off our backs* 23, no. 11 (December 1993).

Dispatch Magazine, 1990 – 1999. U.S. Department of State, Office of Public Communication, Bureau of Public Affairs. http://dosfan.lib.uic.edu/ERC/briefing/dispatch/index.html .

Douglas, Carol Anne. "Good Election News for a change, if you aren't a lesbian in Colorado." *off our backs* 22, no. 11 (December 1992).

———. "Eastern European, US Women Meet." *off our backs* 24, no. 3 (March 1994).

———. "Election 1994: Revenge of the White Guys." *off our backs* 24, no. 11 (December 1994).

———. "What About Bosnia?" *off our backs* 22, no. 9 (October 1992).

Dublin, Thomas; Sklar, Kathryn Kish and Henderson, Sandra. "How Did the National Women's Conference in Houston in 1977 Shape a Feminist Agenda for the Future?" *Women and Social Movements in the United States, 1600 – 2000.* Alexandria, VA: Alexander Street Press, 2004.

Duke, Robin Chandler (RCD) Papers. David M. Rubenstein Rare Books and Manuscript Library. Duke University.

Duerst-Lahti, Georgia. "The Government's Role in Building the Women's Movement." *Political Science Quarterly* 104, no. 2 (Summer 1989): 249-268.

Dworkin, Andrea. "A Feminist Looks at Saudi Arabia, 1978." *Letters from a War Zone, Writings 1976-1989.* http://www.nostatusquo.com/ACLU/dworkin/WarZoneChaptIIIA.html.

Eagleburger, Lawrence. "A Democratic Partnership for the Post Cold War Era." Deputy Secretary to Russian Republic Trade and Economic Council, May 27, 1992. State Department *Dispatch* 3, no. 23 (June 8, 1992).

———. "The Need to Respond to War Crimes in the Former Yugoslavia." Deputy Secretary to International Conference on the Former Yugoslavia, December 16, 1992. State Department *Dispatch* 3, no. 52 (December 28, 1992).

East, Catherine Papers (CE), 1941-1995. Arthur and Elizabeth Schlesinger Library on the History of Women in America. Radcliffe Institute for Advanced Study, Harvard University.

Edwards, Michael and Gaventa, John, eds. *Global Citizen Action.* Boulder, CO: Lynne Rienner Publishers, 2001.

Enloe, Cynthia H. *Bananas, Beaches, and Bases: Making Feminist Sense of International Politics.* Berkeley, CA: University of California Press, 1990.

———. *The Morning After: Sexual Politics at the End of the Cold War.* Berkeley, CA: University of California Press, 1993.

Epstein, Susan B., Nowels, Larry Q. and Hildreth, Steven A. "Foreign Policy Agency Reorganization in the 105th Congress." Congressional Research Service Report for Congress. November 6, 1998. http://congressionalresearch.com/97-538/document.php?study=FOREIGN+POLICY+AGENCY+REORGANIZATION+IN+THE+105TH+CONGRESS .

Equality Now Annual Reports, 1992-2011. http://www.equalitynow.org/about-us/annual-reports.

"Fact Sheet: The New Partnerships Initiative--Strengthening Grass-roots Political and Economic Institutions." State Department *Dispatch* 6, no. 13 (March 27, 1995).

"Fact Sheet: The United States Boosts Girls' and Women's Education Worldwide." State Department *Dispatch* 6, no. 13 (March 27, 1995).

"Fair Haven for Haitian Refugees." *New York Times,* July 31, 1992.

"Feminist Issues: Women's Right to Bodily Integrity and Autonomy." Reddit Blog Post, c. 2013. http://www.reddit.com/r/Feminism/comments/142nzm/feminist_issues_womens_right_to_bodily_integrity/ .

Ferguson, Thomas and Rogers, Joel. *Right Turn, The Decline of the Democrats and the Future of American Politics.* New York: Hill and Wang, 1987.

Ferraro, Geraldine A. "Women's Rights, Human Rights." *New York Times,* August 22, 1995.

"Fifth U.S. Report on War Crimes in the Former Yugoslavia." December 7, 1992. State Department *Dispatch* 4, no. 6 (January 1993).

"First U.S. Report on War Crimes in the Former Yugoslavia."Office of Public Communication, Bureau of Public Affairs, UN, September 22, 1992. State Department *Dispatch* 3, no. 39 (September 28, 1992).

"Five Year Review of the Implementation of the Beijing Declaration and Platform for Action (Beijing + Five) held in the General Assembly." June 5-9, 2000. UN Women. http://www.un.org/womenwatch/daw/followup/beijing+5.htm.

Fletcher, Susan R. "Earth Summit Summary: The United Nations Conference on Environment and Development, (UNCED), Brazil 1992." Washington D.C.: Congressional Research Service, 1992.

"Focus on Diplomacy: The State Department at Work, The Foreign Affairs Budget And Assistance." State Department *Dispatch* 7, no. 36 (September 2, 1996).

"Focus on Population and Development: Follow-up on Cairo Conference, USAID Programs." State Department *Dispatch* 6, no. 1 (January 2, 1995).

"Focus on Population and Development: The U.S. and the UN International Conference on Population and Development." State Department *Dispatch* 5, no. 8 (September 1994).

Foreign Relations Authorization Act, 1994, Section 137 "Women's Human Rights Protection." Congressional Record, February 2, 1994.

Fraser, Arvonne. *The UN Decade for Women: Documents and Dialogue.* Boulder, CO: Westview Press, 1987.

Fraser, Arvonne S. and Tinker, Irene, eds. *Developing Power: How Women Transformed International Development.* New York: The Feminist Press, 2004.

"Free Harry Wu." *New York Times,* July 11, 1995.

Freeman, Jo. "Feminism vs. Family Values." *off our backs* 23, no. 1 (January 1993).

Friedan, Betty Papers, 1933-1985. Arthur and Elizabeth Schlesinger Library on the History of Women in America. Radcliffe Institute for Advanced Study, Harvard University.

Friedman, Elizabeth Jay. "Gendering the Agenda: The Impact of the Transnational Women's Rights Movement at the UN Conferences of the 1990s." *Women's Studies International Forum* 26, no. 4 (2003): 313-331.

Garner, Karen. *Precious Fire: Maud Russell and the Chinese Revolution.* Amherst, MA: University of Massachusetts Press, 2003.

———. *Shaping a Global Women's Agenda, Women's NGOs and Global Governance, 1925-1985.* Manchester, UK: Manchester University Press, 2010.

Gayner, Jeffrey. "The Contract with America: Implementing New Ideas in the US." October 12, 1995. The Heritage Foundation. http://www.heritage.org/research/lecture/the-contract-with-america-implementing-new-ideas-in-the-us.

Gedda, George. "Albright Champions Women's Rights, Issue Emerges as a Priority in US Foreign Policy." *Los Angeles Daily News,* April 27, 1997.

"Gender Equality in UN Peacekeeping Operations." UN Department of Peacekeeping Operations Policy Statement, 2010. https://www.un.org/en/peacekeeping/documents/gender_directive_2010.pdf .

Ghodsee, Kristen. "Revisiting the United Nations Decade for Women: Brief Reflections on Feminism, Capitalism, and Cold War Politics in the Early Years of the International Women's Movement." *Women's Studies International Forum* 33, no. 1 (2010): 3-12.

Giddings, Paula J. *Ida, A Sword Among Lions: Ida B. Wells and the Campaign Against Lynching.* New York, NY: Amistad, 2008.

Glen, Nancy E. and Sarkees, Meredith Reid. *Women in Foreign Policy: The Insiders.* New York: Routledge, 1993.

Glendon, Mary Ann. *A World Made New: Eleanor Roosevelt and the Universal Declaration of Human Rights.* New York: Random House, 2001.

"Global Women's Rights: CEDAW." Feminist Majority Foundation, 2012. http://www.feminist.org/global/cedaw.html.

Goldstein, Joshua S. *War and Gender: How Gender Shapes the War System and Vice Versa.* New York: Cambridge University Press, 2001.

Good, Barbara J. interviewed by Charles Stuart Kennedy. May 25, 1993. The Association for Diplomatic Studies and Training Foreign Affairs Oral History Project. http://memory.loc.gov/ammem/collections/diplomacy/index.html.

Gordon, Beate Sirota. *The Only Woman in the Room: A Memoir.* New York: Kodansha International, 1970.

Gore, Albert. "Defining a Global Approach Toward Stabilizing the World Population." Statement released by the White House, Washington, DC, September 13, 1994. State Department *Dispatch* (Supplement) 5, no. 8 (September 1994).

———. "Remarks at the opening session of the UN International Conference on Population and Development." Cairo, Egypt, September 5, 1994. State Department *Dispatch* 5, no. 38 (September 19, 1994).

———. "Remarks at UN World Summit for Social Development." State Department *Dispatch* 6, no. 13 (March 27, 1995).

———. "The Cairo Conference: Defining an Agenda of Hope, Opportunity, and Progress."

Address before the National Press Club, Washington, DC, August 25, 1994. State Department *Dispatch* 5, no. 35 (August 29, 1994).

Goshko, John M. and Lippman, Thomas W. "Foreign Aid Shift by Clinton; Proposal would drop Friendly Nation Focus." *Washington Post,* November 27, 1993.

Greenhouse, Steven. "State Department Finds Widespread Abuse of Women, Stark Picture is Painted." *New York Times,* February 2, 1994.

"Gulf Crisis Update." Fact Sheet. State Department *Dispatch* 1, no. 13 (November 26, 1990).

Hamilton, Amy. "International Women's Rights Campaign: Women's Rights are Human Rights." *off our backs* 23, no. 4 (April 1993).

Harrison, Pat. *Jeane Kirkpatrick, Diplomat.* New York: Chelsea House, 1991.

Hartmann, Frederick H. and Wendzel, Robert L. *America's Foreign Policy in a Changing World.* New York: Harper Collins College Publishers, 1994.

Helms, Elissa. "Women as agents of ethnic reconciliation? Women's NGOs and international intervention in postwar Bosnia-Herzogovina." *Women's Studies International Forum* 26, no. 1 (2003): 15-33.

Hernes, Helga. *Welfare State and Woman Power: Essays in State Feminism.* Oslo: Norwegian University Press, 1987.

High Commissioner for Germany. Women's Affairs Branch Records. Sophia Smith Collection. Smith College, Northampton, Massachusetts.

"Highlights from Women 2000: Beijing Plus Five June 2000 UN Meeting, June 5-9, 2000." U.S. Department of State. http://1997-2001.state.gov/www/picw/beijing/women2000_highlights.html.

"Highlights of the State Department Activities to Promote the Advancement of Women,

Fact Sheet, May 8, 1997." U.S. Department of State. http://www.state.gov/www/global/women/factsheet.html.

Hirschmann, David. "Democracy and Gender: A Practical Guide to USAID Programs." The GENYSYS Project, The Futures Group, Washington DC, Prepared for the Office of Women in Development, Bureau for Research and Development,USAID. February 1993. USAID Development Experience Clearinghouse.

"History of the Department of State during the Clinton Presidency (1993-2001)." U.S. Department of State, Office of the Historian, Bureau of Public Affairs. http://2001-2009.state.gov/r/pa/ho/pubs/8523.htm.

Hoff Sommers, Christina. "Feminism by Treaty." *Policy Review* 167 (June 1, 2011): 37-50.

Hoganson, Kristin L. *Fighting For Manhood: How Gender Politics Provoked the Spanish-American and Philippine-American Wars.* New Haven, CT: Yale University Press, 1998.

Holzer, Henry Mark and Holzer, Erica. *Aid and Comfort: Jane Fonda in North Vietnam.* Jefferson, NC: MacFarland and Co., 2002.

Hosken, Fran P. "Toward a Definition of Women's Human Rights." *Human Rights Quarterly* 3, no. 2 (May 1981): 1-10.

———. "Win News Editorial: First Issue January 1975," *WIN News* 1, no.1 (January 1975).

Hunt, Swanee. *Half Life of a Zealot.* Durham, NC: Duke University Press, 2006.

———. "Muslim Women in the Bosnia Crucible." *Sex Roles* 51, no. 5/6 (2004): 301-17.

Inderfurth, Karl F. "The Taliban: Confrontation or Engagement?" Assistant Secretary of State Bureau of South Asian Affairs Testimony before Senate Foreign Relations Committee, July 20, 2000. U.S. Department of State. http://www.state.gov/www/policy_remarks/2000/000720_inderfurth_afgha.html.

International Women's Tribune Centre Records (IWTC) 1970-2000, Sophia Smith Collection, Smith College.

Jain, Devaki. *Women, Development and the UN: A Sixty-Year Quest for Equality and Justice.* Bloomington, IN: Indiana University Press, 2005.

Jaquette, Jane S. "Feminism and the Challenges of the 'Post-Cold War' World." *International Feminist Journal of Politics* 5, no.3 (2003): 331-354.

Jeffreys-Jones, Rhodri. Changing Differences: Women and the Shaping of American Foreign Policy, 1917-1994. New Brunswick, NJ: Rutgers University Press, 1995.

Johnson, Ralph. "U.S. Efforts to Promote a Peaceful Settlement in Yugoslavia." Principle Deputy Assistant Secretary for European and Canadian Affairs to Senate Foreign Relations Committee, October 17, 1991. State Department *Dispatch* 2, no. 42 (October 21, 1991).

Johnstone, Andrew and Laville, Hellen, eds. *The US Public and American Foreign Policy.* New York: Routledge Studies in U.S. Foreign Policy, 2010.

Karns, Margaret P. and Mingst, Karen A. International Organizations: The Politics and Processes of Global Governance. Boulder, CO: Lynne Rienner Publishers, 2004.

Kasinof, Laura and Worth, Robert F. "Among 3 Women Awarded Nobel Prize, a Nod to the Arab Spring." *New York Times.* (October 8, 2011).

Kenyon, Dorothy Papers, 1888-1972. Sophia Smith Collection. Smith College, Northampton, Massachusetts.

Kenyon, Dorothy. "Victories on the International Front." *Annals of the American Academy of Political and Social Science* 251 (1947): 17-23.

Kirk, Gwyn; Cornwell, Rachel, and Okazawa-Rey, Margo. "Women and the U.S. Military in East Asia." *Foreign Policy in Focus* 4, no. 10 (March 1999).

Knight, Louise W. *Citizen: Jane Addams and the Struggle for Democracy.* Chicago, IL: University of Chicago Press, 2005.

Kornblum, John C. "Continued Aggression in Bosnia-Herzegovina," U.S. Permanent Representative to the CSCE, May 6, 1992. State Department *Dispatch* 3, no. 19 (May 11, 1992).

Krasno, Jean E. *Interview with Jeane Kirkpatrick.* United Nations Oral History Series. New York: United Nations, November 1990.

Krieger, Joel, ed. "Kosovo War." *The Oxford Companion to the Politics of the World*, 2nd. Edition. Oxford University Press On-line, 2012.

Kristof, Nicholas and WuDunn, Sheryl. *Half the Sky: Turning Oppression into Opportunity for Women Worldwide.* New York: Vintage, 2009.

Kuehl, Warren F. and Dunne, Lynne K. *Keeping the Covenant: American Internationalists and the League of Nations, 1920-1939.* Kent, OH: Kent State University Press, 1997.

Lash, Joseph P. *Eleanor: The Years Alone.* New York: Norton, 1972.

Laville, Helen. *Cold War Women: The International Activities of American Women's Organizations.* Manchester, UK: Manchester University Press, 2002.

Lee, Lucy and Clauson-Wicker Su, eds. *Voice of Women: Moving Forward with Dignity and Wholeness*. Kalamazoo, MI: The Fetzer Institute, 1996.

Leet, Mildred Robbins Papers (MRL), 1929-2002. Arthur and Elizabeth Schlesinger Library on the History of Women in America. Radcliffe Institute for Advanced Study, Harvard University.

Levine, Suzanne Braun and Thom, Mary. Bella Abzug: How One Tough Broad from the Bronx fought Jim Crow and Joe McCarthy- An Oral History. New York: Farrar, Straus and Giroux, 2007.

Lippman, Thomas W. *Madeleine Albright and the New American Diplomacy.* Boulder, CO: Westview Press, 2000.

Lithander, Anna, ed. "Engendering the Peace Process, A Gender Approach to Dayton and Beyond," *Kvinna til Kvinna*. Stockholm: Kvinna til Kvinna Foundation, 2000.

Loar, Theresa interviewed by Charles Stuart Kennedy. August 8, 2001. The Association for Diplomatic Studies and Training Foreign Affairs Oral

History Project. http://memory.loc.gov/cgi-bin/query/S?ammem/mfdipbib:@field(AUTHOR+@od1(Loar,+Theresa)).

Loar, Theresa. "Fact Sheet: UN Trafficking Treaty: Facts/Myths." Office of International Women's Issues, January 18, 2000. http://1997-2001.state.gov/www/global/women/fs_000118_myths.html .

———. "Statement before the House Committee on International Relations, May 3, 2000." U.S. Department of State. http://www.state.gov/www/policy_remarks/2000/000503_loar_women.html.

———. "Statement on Women in Afghanistan at a mock hearing before Senator Diane Feinstein, March 2, 1998." U.S. Department of State. http://www.state.gov/www/policy_remarks/1998/980302_loar_afgh.html.

———. "Trafficking in Women: The Need for International Cooperation and a Multidisciplinary Response." International League for Human Rights, League Report "The Trafficking of NIS Women Abroad." Moscow, November 3-5, 1997. http://www.ilhr.org/ilhr/reports/traffic/report.html .

Lovenduski, Joni. *Feminizing Politics.* Cambridge, UK: Polity Press, 2005.

Lovenduski, Joni, ed. *State Feminism and Political Representation.* New York: Cambridge University Press, 2005.

Lowry, Richard. *The Gulf War Chronicles: A Military History of the First War with Iraq.* iUniverse, 2008.

Loy, Frank E. "International Trafficking of Women and Children," Testimony of Under Secretary of State for Global Affairs before the Senate Committee on Foreign Relations, Subcommittee on Near Eastern and South Asian Affairs, February 22, 2000. http://secretary.state.gov/www/picw/trafficking/loy.htm.

Lynch, Cecelia. *Beyond Appeasement: Interpreting Interwar Peace Movements in World Politics.* Ithaca, NY: Cornell University Press, 1999.

McBride, Dorothy E. and Mazur, Amy G. *The Politics of State Feminism.* Philadelphia, PA: Temple University Press, 2010.

McFeatters, Ann. "Looking Back So They Can Move Ahead." *Pittsburgh Post-Gazette,* June 4, 2000.

McKinley, James C. Jr. "UN Tribunal, in first such trail verdict, convicts Rwandan ex-Mayor of Genocide." *New York Times* (September 3, 1998).

MacKinnon, Janice R. and Stephen R. *Agnes Smedley: The Life and Times of An American Radical.* Berkeley, CA: University of California Press, 1988.

McPhedran, Marilou. "Ali Miller on Key Strategies," Refuge 17, no. 5 (November 1998): 33-40.

Malcolm, Ellen R. "The Year of the Women Voter." http://chnm.gmu.edu/courses/122/hill/hillframe.htm.

Mansbridge, Jane. "Anti-statism and Difference Feminism in International Social Movements." *International Feminist Journal of Politics* 5, no. 3 (2003): 355-360.

Mantilla, Karla. "NWSA Getting a Global Perspective: Nawal El Saadawi, Keynote Speaker." *off our backs* 24, no. 8 (August 1994).

Mantilla, Karla and Kraus, Barbara. "On the Road to Beijing." *off our backs* 25, no. 3 (March 1995).

Maran, Rita. "After the Beijing Conference: What will be done?" *Social Justice* 23, nos. 1, 2 (Spring/Summer 1996): 352-67.

Marcy, Mildred interviewed by Dorothy Robins-Mowry. February 15, 1991. The Association for Diplomatic Studies and Training Foreign Affairs Oral History Project. http://memory.loc.gov/service/mss/mssmisc/mfdip/2005%20txt%20files/2004mar01.txt.

Martin, William. "The Christian Right and American Foreign Policy." *Foreign Policy* 114 (Spring 1999): 66-80.

Mayoux, Linda. "Gender Equity, Equality, and Women's Empowerment: Principles, Definitions and Frameworks." Weman Resources: A website to promote gender justice in economic development. http://www.wemanresources.info/documents/Page1_GenderVision/GenderConcepts.pdf.

Mazur, Amy G. *Theorizing Feminist Policy.* New York: Oxford University Press, 2002.

Meijer Werthheimer, Molly, ed. *Inventing a Voice: The Rhetoric of the First Ladies of the Twentieth Century.* Lanham, MD: Rowman & Littlefield Publishers, Inc., 2004.

Mertus, Julie. *War's Offensive on Women: The Humanitarian Challenge in Bosnia, Kosovo, and Afghanistan.* West Hatford, CT: Kumarian Press, Inc., 2000.

Mertus, Julie and Hocevar Van Wely, Olja. "Women's Participation in the International Criminal Tribunal for the Former Yugoslavia." Women Waging Peace Policy Commission, 2004.

Meyer, Mary K. and Prügl, Elisabeth, eds. *Gender Politics in Global Governance.* Lanham, MD: Rowman & Littlefield Publishers, 1999.

Meyer, William H. *Security, Economics, and Morality in American Foreign Policy.* Upper Saddle River, NJ: Pearson Prentice Hall Publishers, 2004.

Miller, Alice M. "Sexuality, Violence Against Women, and Human Rights: Women Make Demands and Ladies Get Protection." *Health and Human Rights* 7, no. 2 (2004): 16-47.

Miller, Carol. "'Geneva: The Key to Equality': Inter-War Feminists and the League of Nations." *Women's History Review* 3, no. 2 (1994): 219-45.

Mirkinson, Judith. "Red Light, Green Light: The Global Trafficking of Women." Feminism and Women's Studies web site. September 13, 1994. http://feminism.eserver.org/gender/sex-work/trafficking-of-women.txt .

Moghadam, Valentine M. *Globalizing Women: Transnational Feminist Networks.* Baltimore: Johns Hopkins University Press, 2005.

Moose, Richard. "The Crisis in Rwanda: U.S. Response." Statement by Assistant Secretary before the Subcommittee on Africa of the Senate Foreign Relations Committee, Washington, DC, July 26, 1994. State Department *Dispatch* 5, no. 32 (August 8, 1994).

Morgan, Robin Papers (RM), 1940s – 2010. David M. Rubenstein Rare Books and Manuscript Library. Duke University. Durham, North Carolina.

Morrison, Ellen M. "The Clintons Go to Washington, A Healthy Move? Americans Expect Some Reforms." *British Medical Journal* 306, no. 6874 (February 6, 1993): 350.

National Commission on the Observance of International Women's Year Records (NCOIWY), 1975 (Ford Administration) 1973-78. Record Group 220.16. National Archives of the United States. College Park, Maryland.

National Organization for Women. "105th Congress Voting Record Analysis." October 1998. http://www.now.org/issues/election/analysis1998/key.html .

Noel-Baker, Philip. *The First World Disarmament Conference 1932-33, and Why It Failed.* Oxford, UK: Pergamon Press, 1979.

Oakley, Phyllis E. "Address at Ewha Woman's University, Graduate School of International Studies Seoul, Korea," May 23, 1997. U.S. Department of State. http://www.state.gov/www/global/prm/oakley059723.html.

Obama, Barak. Speech, Cairo University. June 4, 2009. The Council on Foreign Relations. http://www.cfr.org/world/obamas-speech-cairo-egypt-june-2009/p19564.

O'Connor, Karen, ed. *Gender and Women's Leadership: A Reference Handbook* Volumes I and II. Thousand Oaks, CA: Sage Publications, 2010.

Ottaway, Marina and Carothers, Thomas, eds. *Funding Virtue: Civil Society Aid and Democracy Promotion.* Washington DC: Carnegie Endowment for International Peace, 2000.

"Overview of Conference Aims, Background, International Conference on Population and Development, September 5 – 13, 1994." United Nations Population Information Network. http://www.un.org/popin/icpd/infokit/infokit.eng/1overvw.html .

Pande, Rohini and Ford, Deanna. "Gender Quotas and Female Leadership: A Review." Background Paper for the World Development Report on Gender. http://www.hks.harvard.edu/fs/rpande/papers/Gender%20Quotas%20-%20April%202011.pdf .

Paxton, Pamela and Hughes, Melanie M. *Women, Politics, and Power: A Global Perspective.* Los Angeles, CA: Pine Forge Press, 2007.

Persinger, Mildred Emory. "On Stage at Last." *Hollins College Newsletter* (May 1976).

———. "Personal Narrative." Hollins University. http://www1.hollins.edu/classes/anth220s06/lynskeyk/persinger_lynskey_transcription2.htm#_more_about_this_about_the_women%E2%80%99s_conference.

Peters, Julie and Wolper, Andrea, eds. *Women's Rights, Human Rights: International Feminist Perspectives.* New York: Routledge, 1995.

Peterson, V. Spike. *Gendered States: Feminist (Re)Visions of International Relations Theory.* Boulder, CO: Lynne Rienner Publishers, 1992.

Pishchikova, Kateryna. *Promoting Democracy in Postcommunist Ukraine: The Contradictory Outcomes of US Aid to Women's NGOs.* Boulder, CO: First Forum Press, 2011.

Pitts, David. "U.S. Condemns Human Rights Violations in Afghanistan." October 26, 1996. Relief Web. http://reliefweb.int/node/27556.

"Prep Com Highlights." *Earth Summit Bulletin* 1, no. 5 (March 5, 1992).

President's Interagency Council on Women, U.S. Department of State, "1999 Up Date: America's Commitment: Federal Programs Benefiting Women and New Initiatives as Follow Up to the UN Fourth World Conference on Women." May 1999.

Preston, Shelly. "The 1992 Rio Summit and Beyond." *Swords and Plowshares: A Chronicle of International Affairs* 3, no. 2 (Spring 1994).

"Pre-transition Council for Afghanistan." State Department *Dispatch* 3, no. 15 (April 13, 1992).

"Profile: Jean-Bertrand Aristide." BBC News Latin America and Caribbean. (updated March 3, 2011). http://www.bbc.co.uk/news/world-latin-america-12633115 .

"Propaganda - Cold War." Encyclopedia of the New American Nation. http://www.americanforeignrelations.com/O-W/Propaganda-Cold-war.html.

Ralph, Regan E. "International Trafficking of Women and Children," Testimony of Executive Director, Women's Rights Division, Human Rights Watch, before the Senate Committee on Foreign Relations, Subcommittee on Near Eastern and South Asian Affairs, February 22, 2000. http://secretary.state.gov/www/picw/trafficking/tralph.htm .

Raphel, Robin L. "U.S. Interests in and Policy toward Afghanistan." Assistant Secretary for South Asian Affairs, Statement before the Subcommittee on Near Eastern and South Asian Affairs Subcommittee of the Senate Foreign Relations Committee, June 6, 1996. State Department *Dispatch* 7, no. 25 (June 17, 1996).

Raymond, Janice G. "The New UN Trafficking Protocol." *Women's Studies International Forum* 25, no. 5 (2002): 491-502.

Rea, Samuel S. interviewed by W. Haven North. April 24, 1998. The Association for Diplomatic Studies and Training Foreign Affairs Oral History Project. http://memory.loc.gov/ammem/collections/diplomacy/index.html .

Reardon, Betty A. *Women and Peace: Feminist Visions of Global Security*. Albany, NY: State University of New York Press, 1993.

Redd, Steven B. "The Influence of Advisers and Decision Strategies on Foreign Policy Choices: President Clinton's Decision to Use Force in Kosovo." *International Studies Perspectives* 6, no. 1 (February 2005), 129-50.

"Report Card on U.S. Federal Government Action for Women and Girls' Rights and Empowerment: An Assessment of the US Implementation of the UN Platform for Action." US Women Connect website. c. June 2000, accessed 2010. http://www.uswc.org/reportcards.html .

"Report of the World Summit for Social Development." Copenhagen, March 6-12, 1995. UN Document A/CONF.166/9. http://www.un.org/documents/ga/conf166/aconf166-9.htm.

Ricciutelli, Luciana; Miles, Angela, and McFadden, Margaret H., eds. *Feminist Politics, Activism & Vision: Local and Global Challenges*. London: Zed Books, Ltd., 2004.

Riding, Alan. "Rights Forum Ends in a Call for a Greater Role by UN." *New York Times*, June 25, 1993.

Riley, Maria. "The Invisible Agenda: UN Fourth World Conference on Women Countdown to Beijing." *Center Focus: Newsletter of the Center of Concern*, no.128 (September 1995).

Roberts, Barbara. "Beijing Fourth World Conference on Women." *Canadian Journal of Sociology* 21, no. 2 (Spring 1996): 237-44.

Rowan, Hobart. "$100 Million More for Family Planning." *The Washington Post*, June 24, 1993.

Rosenzweig, Roy. "An Outline of the Anita Hill-Clarence Thomas Controversy." http://chnm.gmu.edu/courses/122/hill/hillframe.htm.

Rupp, Leila. *Mobilizing Women for War: German and American Propaganda, 1939-1945*. Princeton, NJ: Princeton University Press, 1979.

———. *Worlds of Women: The Making of an International Women's Movement*. Princeton, NJ: Princeton University Press, 1997.

"Rwandan Violence." State Department *Dispatch* 4, no. 7 (February 15, 1993).

Ryf, Kara C. "The First Modern Anti-Slavery Law: The Trafficking Victims Protection Act of 2000." *Case Western Reserve Journal of International Law* 34, no. 1 (2002), 45-74.

"Save Earth Summit" Sunshine Productions, 1992. http://www.youtube.com/watch?v=J1BUIYylmhI .

"Saving the World's Women." *New York Times Magazine,* August 23, 2009.

Sayce, Liz. "Violence, abuse and women's citizenship." *off our backs* 27, no. 1 (January 1997).

"Seventh Report on War Crimes in the Former Yugoslavia." State Department Dispatch 4, no. 16 (April 19, 1993).

Shalala, Donna. "Building a Women's Health Agenda that is Woman-Centered." Beijing Plus Five Conference at Hunter College. June 21, 2000. http://www.hhs.gov/news/speeches/000621.html.

Shattuck, John. *Freedom on Fire: Human Rights Wars and America's Response.* Cambridge, MA: Harvard University Press, 2003.

———. "Violations of Women's Human Rights."Assistant Secretary for Human Rights and Humanitarian Affairs Statement before the Subcommittee on International Security, International Organizations, and Human Rights of the House Foreign Affairs Committee, Washington, DC, September 29, 1993. State Department *Dispatch* 4, no. 41 (October 11, 1993).

Sheffer, David J. "Address on the 50th Anniversary of the UN Declaration on Human Rights." Rampoa College, September 16, 1998. State Department *Dispatch* (October 1998).

———. "Witness and Victim Protection in International Criminal Courts." January 28, 1998. U.S. Department of State. http://1997-2001.state.gov/www/policy_remarks/1998/980128_scheffer_icc.html.

Simic, Olivera. "What Remains of Srebrenica? Motherhood, Transitional Justice and Yearning for the Truth." *Journal of International Women's Studies* 10, no. 4 (2009): 220-236.

Singh, Rahul. "Hillary Clinton Issues Call." *The Earth Times* 9, no. 8 (June 2000).

Sinha, Mrinhalini, Guy, Donna, and Woollacott, Angela, eds. *Feminisms and Internationalism.* Oxford, UK: Blackwell Publishers, 1999.

Sisterhood Is Global Institute Records (SIGI), 1963-2005, David M. Rubenstein Rare Books and Manuscript Library. Duke University. Durham, North Carolina.

Skaine, Rosemarie. *Women at War: Gender Issues of Americans in Combat.* Jefferson, NC: McFarland and Co., Inc., Publishers, 1999.

Smith, Christopher H. (R-NJ) "Foreign Aid and Abortion Overseas." *New York Times*, March 16, 1998.

Sneyd, Adam. "New International Economic Order." Globalization and Autonomy. http://www.globalautonomy.ca/global1/glossary_entry.jsp?id=EV.0027.

Snyder, Christy Jo. "The Influence of Transnational Peace Groups on U.S. Foreign Policy Decision-Makers during the 1930s: Incorporating Women into the UN." *Diplomatic History* 27 (June 2003): 377-404.

Solis, Hilda L. "Remarks at International Women's Day Luncheon, Mayflower Hotel, Washington DC, March 8, 2010." United States Department of Labor. http://www.dol.gov/_sec/media/speeches/20100308_IWD.htm.

"'Stop Talking, Start Changing' That's Bias-Fighter's Goal." *Detroit Free Press,* July 18, 1976.

Strong, Anna Louise. *I Change Worlds: The Remaking of an American.* Seattle, WA: Seal Press, 1979.

"Strong Delivers Keynote Address to Plenary, Emphasizes Agenda 21 and Financial Resources." *Earth Summit Bulletin* 1, no. 2 (March 3, 1992).

Swerdlow, Amy. *Women Strike for Peace: Traditional Motherhood and Radical Politics in the 1960s.* Chicago: University of Chicago Press, 1993.

Tarr-Whelan, Linda. "Opening Statement." U.S. Representative to the UN Commission on the Status of Women, March 12, 1996. http://1997-2001.state.gov/www/picw/archives/960312.html.

———. "Statement." U.S. Representative to the UN Commission on the Status of Women, October 29, 1996. http://secretary.state.gov/www/picw/ archives/961029.html.

———. *Women Lead the Way: Your Guide to Stepping Up Leadership and Changing the World.* New York: Ingram Publishing Services, 2009.

"The Abolition of Female Genital Mutilation," Info Please website. http://www.infoplease.com/ipa/A0001524.html#ixzz1lo3xHSSF .

"The Equal Rights Amendment." Alice Paul Institute. http://www.equalrightsamendment.org/.

"The Harry Wu Opening." *New York Times,* August 25, 1995.

"The ICPD Program of Action, Chapter 8: Health, Morbidity and Mortality." http://www.iisd.ca/Cairo/program/p08000.html .

"The Iran-Contra Hearings: Abzug Bemoans Lack of Women." *Los Angeles Times,* May 15, 1987. http://articles.latimes.com/1987-05-15/news/mn-5241_1_foreign-policy.

The President's Interagency Council on Women Archives. U.S. Department of State. http://secretary.state.gov/www/picw/archives/.

"The President's Interagency Council on Women." Women's Health.Gov, A Project of the U.S. Department of Health and Human Services. http://www.womenshealth.gov/health-topics/a-z-topic/ details.cfm?oid=3328.

"The real story of Beijing." off *our backs* 26, no. 3 (March 1996).

The Spirit of Houston. The First National Women's Conference. An Official Report to the President, the Congress, and the People of the United States. Washington D.C.: Government Printing Office, 1978.

The United Nations Fourth World Conference on Women, Platform for Action. http://www.un.org/womenwatch/daw/beijing/platform/plat1.htm .

"Third U.S. Report on War Crimes in the Former Yugoslavia." November 6, 1992. State Department *Dispatch* 3, no. 46 (November 16, 1992).

Timothy, Kristen Papers (KT), 1990-2000. Mudd Manuscripts Library. Princeton University.

Tinker, Irene. "A Feminist View of Copenhagen." *Signs* 6 (Spring 1981): 531-537.

Tolchin, Susan J. "Women as Policy Makers: They Can Make a Difference." *The Earth Times* 6, no. 13 (March 7, 1994).

"Trafficking of Women and Children in the International Sex Trade: Hearing Before the Subcommittee on International Operations and Human Rights of the Committee on International Operations." 106th Congress 77 (September 14, 1999). Testimony of Theresa Loar, Director of the President's Interagency Council on Women and Senior Coordinator for

International Women's Issues, Department of State. http://secretary.state.gov/www/picw/trafficking/tloar.htm .
True, Jacqui. "Mainstreaming Gender in Global Public Policy." *International Feminist Journal of Politics* 5, no. 3 (2003): 368-396.
United Nations Environmental Program. Champions of the Earth. "2006 Laureate: Women's Environment & Development Organization." http://www.unep.org/champions/laureates/2006/Wedo.asp .
"United Nations Peacekeeping, Gender and Peacekeeping." https://www.un.org/en/peacekeeping/issues/women/ .
United States Committee for Refugees and Immigrants. "Trafficking in women and children: a contemporary manifestation of slavery." July 1, 2000. http://www.unhcr.org/refworld/docid/3c58099b8.html .
United States Information Agency. http://dosfan.lib.uic.edu/usia/usiahome/oldoview.htm#overview.
"U.S. Assistance for Victims of Violence in the Former Yugoslavia." State Department *Dispatch* 4, no.16 (April 19, 1993).
"U.S. Policy Initiatives Related to Refugee Women." March 1997, Bureau of Population, Refugees and Migration, U.S. Department of State. http://www.state.gov/www/global/prm/women_refu.html.
Van Vorhis, Jacqueline. *Carrie Chapman Catt: A Public Life.* New York, NY: Feminist Press, 1987.
Walters, F.P. *A History of the League of Nations.* New York: Oxford University Press, 1952.
Weitzer, Ronald. "The social construction of sex trafficking: Ideology and institutionalization of a moral crusade." *Politics & Society* 35, no. 3 (2007): 447-75.
Wilson, Shamillah, Sengupta, Anasuya and Evans, Kristy, eds. *Defending our Dreams: Global Feminist Voices for a New Generation.* London: Zed Books, 2005.
"Women and Girls in Afghanistan." March 10, 1998. U.S. Department of State. http://1997-2001.state.gov/www/global/women/fs_980310_women_afghan.html.
"Women Going Forward: Envisioning a Feminist Future." *off our backs* 26, no. 4 (April 1996).
"Women war resisters protest Beijing." *off our backs* 25, no. 3 (May 1995).
"We Are Listening… Report of the Vital Voices: Women in Democracy Conference, July 9-11, 1997, Vienna, Austria." Vienna: USIA Regional Program Office, 1997.
Weatherford, M. Stephen and McDonnell, Lorraine M. "Clinton and the Economy: The Paradox of Policy Success and Political Mishap." *Political Science Quarterly* 111, no. 3 (Autumn, 1996): 403-36.
"WEDO, Bella Abzug, 1920-1998." Jewish Women's Archive Women of Valor. http://jwa.org/womenofvalor/abzug/wedo .
"WEDO Fact Sheet on Women's Caucus." International Conference on Population and Development, Cairo, Egypt, September 5 – 13, 1994. http://www.iisd.ca/Cairo/wedofac2.txt.
Weigand, Kate and Horowitz, Daniel. "Dorothy Kenyon: Feminist Organizing, 1919-1963." *Journal of Women's History* 14, no. 2 (2002): 126-131.
Weiss, Thomas G. and Gordenker, Leon, eds. *NGOs, the UN, and Global Governance.* Boulder, CO: Lynne Rienner Publishers, 1996.

White, Barbara M. Papers. Arthur and Elizabeth Schlesinger Library on the History of Women in America. Radcliffe Institute for Advanced Study, Harvard University.

Willetts, Peter, ed. *'The Conscience of the World,' the Influence of Non-governmental Organizations in the UN System.* London: Hurst & Co., 1996.

Wilson, Joan Hoff. "Peace is a Woman's Job: Jeanette Rankin's Foreign Policy." *Montana: The Magazine of Western History* 20, nos. 1 and 2 (January and April 1980): 28-41 and 38-53.

Winslow, Anne, ed. *Women, Politics and the United Nations.* Westport, CT: Greenwood Press, 1995.

Wirth, Timothy. "Making the Social Summit Work: The U.S. View." Address by the Under Secretary for Global Affairs before the National Council of Churches New York City, January 10, 1995. http://dosfan.lib.uic.edu/ERC/intlorg/WS_Social_Dev/950110.html.

———. "Population and Sustainable Development: Defining an Agenda." Statement at the Third Preparatory Meeting of the UN International Conference on Population and Development, New York City, April 5, 1994. State Department *Dispatch* 5, no. 15 (April 11, 1994).

———. "Report to the President from the United States delegation to the United Nations Fourth World Conference on Women, Beijing, China, September 4-15, 1995." http://secretary.state.gov/www/picw/archives/oct95.html.

———. "Statement at Confirmation Hearings." State Department *Dispatch* 4, no. 14 (April 5, 1993).

———. "U.S. Goals at the Cairo Conference." Opening remarks at a Department of State press briefing, Washington, DC, August 31, 1994. State Department *Dispatch* 5, no. 36 (September 5, 1994).

———. "U.S. Statement on Population and Development." To UN International Conference on Population and Development, Second Preparatory Meeting, May 11, 1993. State Department *Dispatch* 4, no. 22 (May 31, 1993).

Wirth, Timothy and Shattuck, John. "Opening statements from a press briefing on the annual human rights report." Washington, DC, February 1, 1994. State Department *Dispatch* 5, no. 6 (February 7, 1994).

"Women in Congress: A Changing of the Guard. Traditionalist, Feminists, and the New Face of Women in Congress, 1955-1976." U.S. House of Representatives. http://womenincongress.house.gov/historical-essays/essay.html?intID=4.

"Women in Congress: Bella Savitsky Abzug, Representative 1971-1977, Democrat, New York." U.S. House of Representatives. http://womenincongress.house.gov/member-profiles/profile.html?intID=2.

Women in the Federal Government Oral History Project. Interviews, 1981-1983. Arthur and Elizabeth Schlesinger Library on the History of Women in America. Radcliffe Institute for Advanced Study, Harvard University.

"Women in the Newly Emerging Democracies of Eastern Europe, Phase I." Draft Report Prepared for the U.S. Agency for International Development by Ernst and Young. Project Number 940-2028.03. May 1991. USAID Development Experience Clearinghouse.

Women's Environment and Development Organization. "Mapping Progress: Assessing Implementation of the Beijing Platform." [Bound Report] March 1998.

Women's Environment and Development Organization. "US Gears Up for UN Conferences." *WEDO News & Views* 7, no. 2 (September 1994).

Women Strike for Peace Records, 1961-1996. Swarthmore College Peace Collection. Swarthmore, Pennsylvania.

Woodsmall, Ruth Frances Papers, 1863-1968. Sophia Smith Collection. Smith College, Northampton, Massachusetts.

Young, Michael. "U.S. Delegation Press Briefings," Deputy Under Secretary for Economic Affairs and alternate head of the US delegation to UNCED, June 8, 1992. State Department *Dispatch* 3, Supplement 4 (June 1992).

Zalewski, Marysia and Parpart, Jane. *The Man Question in International Relations.* Boulder, CO: Westview Press, 1997.

Zinsser, Judith. "From Mexico to Copenhagen to Nairobi: the United Nations Decade for Women, 1975-1985." *Journal of World History* 13, no. 1 (Spring 2002): 139-68.

Index

About the Book

Though recent US government attention to global women's rights and empowerment is often presented as a new phenomenon, Karen Garner argues that nearly two decades ago the Clinton administration broke barriers to challenge women's unequal status vis-à-vis men around the world and to incorporate their needs into US foreign policy and aid programs.

Garner draws on a wide range of primary sources, including interviews with government officials and feminist activists who worked with the administration, to present a persuasive account of the emergence, evolution, and legacy of US global gender policy in the 1990s.

Karen Garner is associate professor of history and women's studies at SUNY Empire State College. She is the author of *Shaping a Global Women's Agenda: Women's NGOs and Global Governance, 1925–85* and *Precious Fire: Maud Russell and the Chinese Revolution.*